Customer Service and Hotel Management

Customer Service and Hotel Management

Devesh Bhushan

Customer Service and Hotel Management

ISBN 978-93-5111-335-5

Published in 2014 in India by

Reprint 2020

RANDOM PUBLICATIONS

4376-A/4B, Gali Murari Lal, Ansari Road
New Delhi-110 002
Phone : +91-11-43580356, +91-11-23289044
e-mail: randomexports@gmail.com, sales@randompublications.com,
info@randompublications.com

Type Setting by : Keystoneprintads, Delhi-110051
Printed at : Mehra Printers, Delhi-110 092

Preface

Customer service is the provision of labour and other resources, for the purpose of increasing the value that buyers receive from their purchases and from the processes leading up to the purchase. With the rising dominance of the service sector in the global economy, customer service has grown in importance, as its impact on individuals, households, firms, and societies has become widespread.

The modern concept of customer service has its roots in the craftsman economy of the 1800s, when individuals and small groups of manufacturers competed to produce arts and crafts to meet public demand. In the 1970s, international competition increased, and producers responded by improving the quality of their products and services. The overall quality of customer service - in society and in specific industries - will continue to be determined by the relative balance of power between suppliers and consumers; it will improve as competition becomes more intense, and decline as competition decreases.

The customer service study revealed that no specific tactic, technology, or mission statement is the key to effective customer service delivery. In fact, what is clear is that effective customer service delivery is organization specific, since services are designed around the targeted customers' desires and the frontline employees delivering the services.

This book would be very useful to the management specialists and consumer activists, engaged in the task of delivering quality goods, scholars, researchers, students in the field of marketing management and as a compendium on the subject of the consumer goods industry.

I thank all associates of my group who have helped in the preparation of the book. My individual thanks go to "Random Publications" who have in print the book.

— Devesh Bhushan

Contents

1

Customer-Focused Management

INTRODUCTION

Businesses fail when the fundamental question—what business are we in?—is either ignored or misunderstood. To answer this question appropriately, businesses have to be customer focused. What does being customer focused mean? Why is it that customer-focused firms achieve a sustainable competitive advantage? What does customer-focused management involve?

A January 2001 issue of the *Wall Street Journal* featured an article titled: "Can these dot-coms be saved?" The dot-com malaise was becoming widespread. The message in the article was simple, the question straightforward, but the answers were not readily evident. A closer look reveals that the answers are implicit in the questions within the article. "Is Priceline's vaunted name-your-own-price model good for anything but plane tickets?" "If traditional catalog retailers can make money selling clothing why can't a Web site like Bluefly?" "Can Webvan's net-fueled automation turn profits delivering cornflakes?" All three of these Internet examples represent a very typical situation that most if not all dot-coms, including that mainstay, Yahoo!, had been facing. The problem was endemic to the dot-com business. The technology was powerful, but in each case, the appropriate revenue model remained elusive.

The question on everyone's mind was: Where are the profits? And, when the profits arrive, would they be sustainable? The answer is in the question. If you asked the right questions, you could find the right answers. A Francis Bacon quote comes to mind: "A prudent question is one-half of wisdom." As the dot-com frenzy reached epidemic proportions, the right questions were not being asked, and the right answers were not available. All this may (yet again) seem simplistic, but many of the dot-com failures were at least partly attributable to a lack of due diligence. The analyses about sustainable profitability must be preceded by the fundamental question of what business the firm is in. Unfortunately, the times were such that the promises of information technology overshadowed the fundamentals and good judgment on the part of many among us.

The Business You are In

To make a profit in any business, you need to be able to sell for more than it costs you to produce. This is a basic prerequisite for any business, really. A viable business must produce enough revenues to cover costs and have surplus as profit. Ironically, the dot-com phenomenon brought the term "business or revenue model" to common parlance. The business or revenue model is a model that depicts how a business will generate revenue and what it will cost to do that.

The more important question may be, is the model sustainable in the long term? Sustainable profits come from sustainable competitive advantage, which in turn comes from consistently creating and delivering superior value. The concept of that superior value is essentially the business of your business. To really understand how you are going to make a profit, you have to first examine a more fundamental question: *"What business are you in?"*

- Priceline.com started with buying unsold airline seats at a heavy discount and allowing passengers to bid for them online. This is still its core business. Priceline experimented with selling gasoline and groceries and had to give these up. So, what business is priceline.com in? General retailer or broker of airline seats? Airline seats are perishable in that, if the seats are not sold before the plane takes off, the assets in the form of unsold seats perish. Priceline.com auctioning these seats off is a win-win situation for airlines as well as for passengers who are looking for cheap tickets and are willing to make last-minute travel plans. Why is it a "win" for airlines, and why is it a "win" for which type of customer? If this is priceline's business model, does it translate to gasoline and groceries?
- Can Bluefly compete with traditional catalog clothing retailers on price? Is Bluefly really in a different business? If not, it is in direct competition with established catalog retailers such as L.L. Bean and Land's End. Can these catalog retailers not offer a Web site retail front just as easily as Bluefly? Can Bluefly provide superior value compared to these established retailers, at a sustainable profit? If Bluefly is in a different business, what is it?
- Web grocers like Webvan are out of business. Why? Most likely, their analysis of the business model was flawed. Are they in the grocery business or in the delivery business? Can they sell what they produce/provide for more than what it costs them to produce it? And can they deliver better customer value than the competition? Who or what is the competition? Ultimately, the question is: Can they provide sustainable superior customer value at sustainable profit?

With very few exceptions, such as the Internet auction firm eBay, the job-hunting site Monster.com, and the online bank NetBank, just about every dot-com firm was not profitable when they issued their IPOs in the mid to late 1990s. In 2001, Priceline.com turned its first profitable quarter. Eight months after that article in the *Wall Street Journal* about saving the dot-coms, a more direct article in the same business-oriented newspaper provided a peek at the real cause of dot-com troubles: "Latest dot-com fad is a bit old-fashioned: It's called profitability."

A handful of dot-com firms including online travel sites Expedia and Travelocity, online brokerage Ameritrade, real estate listing site Homestore.com, and online ticketing site Ticketmaster were beginning to show promise of steady profits. Most Internet firms struggled with the fundamental questions or, worse, had not even dealt with them. Many relied on advertising dollars to support profits. In the mid to late 1990s about 600 dot-coms, including such short-lived but well-known Internet brand names such as Webvan and eToys, failed. The business models at many firms appear to have been flawed.

Many of them offered free content and banked on revenues from advertising on their Web sites. Facing severe drops in advertising revenues in a slow economy, most dot-coms began charging for content in a desperate bid to attain profitability. The focus had reverted to the fundamentals of doing business: What customer value are you creating and can you make a profit doing it?

Barry Diller of USA Networks, who has been successful in lining up cash-producing Internet firms, put it bluntly: "You have to deliver a better product to your customer, not just offer an Internet retail option for the sake of dabbling in some new technology." Better product than what? Better than previously available and better than the competition. Mr. Diller was actually referring to superior customer value. The experienced business leader never loses sight of the fundamentals.

Peter Crist, vice chairman of the executive recruiting firm Korn/Ferry International, should know about management talent. He was quoted in the *Wall Street Journal* as saying, "There's a whole generation of people in their 50s and 60s, who started a business and focused on the fundamentals that we're losing." Case in point is Heartland Express CEO Russell Gerdin, who spends a lot of time on details—details of the costs and revenues of his operations, route-by-route, on a day-to-day basis. Gerdin never sways from his focus: short-haul business, where he has a competitive advantage over the "big guys."

How firms go about determining what it takes to provide superior customer value at a sustainable profit is the fundamental issue for any business. If you miss the fundamentals, you will fail in just about any endeavour, in the business world or in any other walk of life. This book is just as much about fundamentals as it is about obtaining and sustaining a competitive advantage. You cannot attain that sustainable competitive advantage unless you have mastered the fundamentals of creating and delivering superior customer value.

As discussed, the analyses confronting the fundamental question of "what business are we in?" must begin with a clear understanding of who the customer is and what customer value is being provided. Is this customer value superior to the customer's alternative? Firms must ensure that they can provide this customer value in the long term at a reasonable profit. To be able to *sustain* the profits, the firm needs to provide this customer value better than the competition. Continuously providing superior customer value leads to sustainable profits from a sustainable competitive advantage.

To make *sustainable* profits, firms must be able to continue to provide customer value at a cost lower than what the customer is willing to pay. What the customer is willing to pay is commensurate with the perceived value of the solution. If factors of production are equally accessible to all firms, what makes perceived value of one better than another?

The answer, clearly, must lie in something that is not available to all. What is unique to a firm may very well be the strength of its customer focus. When firms are focused on the customer, they understand what customer value is. A clear understanding of customer value gives the firm a clear view of its competitive status among the customer's choice of solutions.

CUSTOMER SERVICE

Customer service is the provision of labour and other resources, for the purpose of increasing the value that buyers receive from their purchases and from the processes leading up to the purchase. With the rising dominance of the service sector in the global economy, customer service has grown in importance, as its impact on individuals, households, firms, and societies has become widespread.

The modern concept of customer service has its roots in the craftsman economy of the 1800s, when individuals and small groups of manufacturers competed to produce arts and crafts to meet public demand. In the 1970s, international competition increased, and producers responded by improving the quality of their products and services.

The overall quality of customer service - in society and in specific industries - will continue to be determined by the relative balance of power between suppliers and consumers; it will improve as competition becomes more intense, and decline as competition decreases.

STRATEGIC ADVANTAGE

A company can outperform rivals only if it can establish a difference that it can preserve. Customer service can be such a difference. It is very difficult to control, and therefore difficult to imitate. It is difficult to control because of its variability. The level of service may vary greatly between two providers in the same organization. It may also vary from one moment to another, even as delivered by the same provider. The difficulty is compounded in multi-unit operations: in addition to variability within units, there is also variability among units.

That is both the challenge and the opportunity. The consistent delivery of superior service requires the careful design and execution of a whole system of activities that includes people, capital, technology, and processes. The few companies that can manage this system do stand out, and are sought out. This is the foundation of their sustainable competitive advantage.

For an organization's members to deliver superior service consistently, they must be acculturated, i.e. instilled with the values, traits, patterns, and behaviours associated with a service culture. The mechanisms of this acculturation include recruitment, training, empowerment, and accountability, within the framework of an organization's ideology of service.

An organization's ideology comprises its purpose (Why are we here?) and values (What do we stand for?). Organizations renowned for providing excellent customer service have typically defined their purpose in terms of service – to serve their customers, and to serve their members. Their values typically include integrity, trustworthiness, reliability, personal responsibility, industriousness, continuous improvement, respect, and consistency.

Training is focused on enabling personnel to deliver service in a manner that is beneficial to both the organization's customers, and to itself.

Technology has made available a wide range of very powerful customer service tools. They range from support websites and the ability to have live chats with technical staff to databases tracking individual customers' preferences, pattern of buying, payment methods etc., and tailoring products and service responses based on this advanced data. Specialist software that is designed for the tracking of service levels and for helping recognize areas for improvement are often integrated into other enterprise operational software tools such as ERP software.

Whereas outstanding service organizations allow their people to make mistakes and learn from their failures, there is little or no tolerance for violations of its core service values. People who do not fit into the culture are removed.

Delivering customer service begins with understanding what customers want. And this understanding begins with the understanding that they do not always know what they want, or why they want it. Traditional market research assumes that they do. Newer methods recognize that as much as 95% of our decision making is subconscious.

Common research methods (e.g., surveys and focus groups) reveal what customers think their motivations are, rather than what their motivations truly are. When respondents do not comprehend their true motivations, they tend to state how they think they ought to be motivated. Recent progress in neuroscience and in observational technologies have yielded more reliable, less biased results. Companies have Interaction Designers that use User

Centred Design methods, among others, to understand what customers need. They often use Personas to represent the research outcomes i.e., to describe the customer they are designing for.

In a competitive environment, however, satisfaction may not be enough. To stay in business, firms must provide at least as much satisfaction as their competitors. Moreover, firms that aim to gain profitable growth must increase the number of their customers while reducing the cost of customer acquisition. This is particularly true of companies that compete in mature industries. The objective then is not merely to satisfy customers, but to convert them into promoters (customers who recommend a company to others). Promoters serve to increase a firm's clientele, without increasing its cost of acquisition – i.e. with no additional marketing or promotional expense.

But customers do not make recommendations lightly. When they make a recommendation, they put their own reputations on the line. Firms must earn that recommendation through the consistent delivery of outstanding customer service.

Customer experience management (CEM) is "the process of strategically managing a customer's entire experience with a product or a company".

Marketing research has shown that about 70 to 80% of all products are perceived as commodities, that is, seen as being more-or-less the same as competing products. This makes marketing the product difficult. Marketers have taken various approaches to this problem including: branding, product differentiation, market segmentation, and relationship marketing.

Relationship marketing, (also called loyalty marketing) focuses on establishing and building a long term relationship between a company and a customer. There are several approaches that have been espoused including customer experience management, customer relationship management, loyalty programs, and database marketing.

The development of customer experience management originally started with a critique of three existing marketing concepts. It concluded that the following three concepts do not go far enough:

- Marketing concept—Since the 1970s there has been a gradual shift from a product-, technology-, and sales-focused orientation towards a customer- and market-oriented approach by determining the wants and needs of customers and satisfying them more efficiently or effectively as compared to competitors. However, the approach is still mostly functional, with similarities and differences between competitors being defined mostly by product features and customer benefits. In addition, the customer is perceived as being rational, which is in most cases not the case, as e.g. Kahneman and Tversky's Prospect theory has proven. Also, it is asserted that market research is mostly analytical leaving little room for qualitative assessments of customer relationships towards products, services, or brands. It is claimed (by Shultz) that traditional marketing, in practice, takes an inside-out approach (starting with internal variables like production capabilities and available capital then moving to external variables like customer needs), rather than taking an outside-in approach as marketing theory requires.

- Customer relationship management is claimed to be deficient because it primarily consists of database and software programs used in call centers and thus, focuses too much on quantitative data. By doing this, it is led by transactions rather than a desire to build lasting relationships with customers.
- Customer satisfaction is an outcome-oriented attitude deriving from customers who compare the performance or value of the product with their expectations of it. It is claimed that the customer satisfaction approach depends too heavily on outcome oriented measures like satisfaction and too superficially on direct experiential measures. A customer is said to be satisfied when a product's performance is above the customer's expectations. Thus, traditional customer satisfaction techniques are deficient if they don't help firms to understand and manage customers' experiences, experiences that lead to the following equation: good experience = satisfaction.

CEM recognizes, as does all of marketing since the early 1970s, that customers are a company's most valuable asset. What makes CEM different from traditional marketing is that it claims that marketing theory has seldom been implemented adequately.

CEM is a methodology that tries to overcome the gap between theory and practice by reformulating basic marketing principles. The result is that CEM stresses four aspects of marketing management :

- CEM focuses on all sorts of customer-related issues
- CEM combines the analytical and the creative
- CEM considers both, strategy and implementation
- CEM operates internally and externally

Although all marketing management and strategic management does all of these, CEM supporters claim that they have a methodology that will yield better results. Being convinced that the marketing concept is too product-centered, Customer relationship management too focused on quantitative data, and customer satisfaction too functional, CEM looks for another perspective on the relationship of a consumer with a product or service. And what's key? The experience linked to it is the key. This enables companies to strategically manage a customer's experience with a brand and by doing so, achieve a truly customer focused management concept.

To accomplish this, a framework is required based on clearly defined company objectives. Schmitt's book "Customer Experience Management" offers the following five step framework that should help managers understand and manage the "customer experience":

Step 1: Analyzing the Experiential world of the customer

- Analyze sociocultural context of the customer (needs/wants/lifestyle)
- Analyze business concept (requirements/solutions)

Step 2: Building the Experiential platform

- Connection between strategy and implementation
- Specifies the value that the customer can expect from the product (EVP = experiential value promise)

Whereas steps 1 (Analysis) and 2 (Strategy) form the basis for CEM, steps 3, 4, and 5 are focusing on Implementation.

Step 3: Designing the Brand experience

- Experiential features, product aesthetics, "look and feel", e.g. logos

Step 4: Structuring the Customer interface

- All sorts of dynamic exchanges and contract points with customers
- Intangible elements (i.e. value, attitude, behaviour)

Step 5: Engaging in Continuous Experiential innovation

- Anything that improves end customers' personal lives and business customers' working lives

And finally, to bring all pieces together, a holistic approach is required that provides a linkage between the different steps and connects them with the organization.

Organizing for CEM includes three tasks:

- Financial planning of CEM in terms of customers - CEM's ultimate goal is a fair and mutually beneficial long-term business relationship between a company and its customers. Customers will reward the company financially by doing business with it. The value of the customer to the firm, referred to as customer equity, will increase, and the company will grow and be profitable.
- Allocation of organizational resources - Improving the customer experience, and thus increasing customer equity, requires internal resources. The company needs to ask what financial, structural, and personnel resources it needs to engage in CEM to deliver an ongoing desirable experience to customers. Resources must be allocated to the brand experience, the customer interface, and innovation.
- Enhancement of the employee experience - The concept of experience applies also to the internal customers, the company's employees. What all employees, across all levels, get from an experience-oriented organization is a more rewarding employee experience that includes a new form of professional and personal development. Employees of such an organization live a more experiential and thus more satisfying and productive life. They are also more motivated and capable of delivering a great experience to customers.

CUSTOMER SERVICE STRATEGIES

The customer service study revealed that no specific tactic, technology, or mission statement is the key to effective customer service delivery. In fact, what is clear is that effective customer service delivery is organization specific, since services are designed around the targeted customers' desires and the frontline employees delivering the services.

The components of the process for producing effective customer service delivery include appropriately identifying and targeting the ideal customer, establishing a customer-focused vision that is consistent with the prioritized desires of the target customers, establishing the operational procedures and internal infrastructure that support customer service, continuously measuring customer and employee satisfaction, embracing change, and striving persistently to improve.

The customer service literature clearly demonstrates that both profit-seeking and public agencies that implement effective customer service strategies realise financial benefits, either through increased profits or through reduced costs associated with long-term, informed customers; customer referrals; employee retention; improved information exchange; and streamlined service delivery.

Child support enforcement, in this case, is like any other business. In order to implement effective customer service strategies and reap the benefits of good customer service, the Office of Child Support Enforcement (OCSE) agencies will need to implement the process of developing effective customer service.

In an effort to become "more results-oriented and responsive to customers," the Office of Child Support Enforcement (OCSE) contracted with Circle Solutions, Inc. to undertake a study of public and private sector practices and outcomes in customer service. The study included a review of customer service literature, a review of the annual reports and Web sites of 40 companies mentioned in the literature, telephone interviews with companies sited as leaders in customer service in the literature, and site visits to three agencies—two private and one child support agency.

Throughout the study, an advisory group of four State child support enforcement directors provided input and feedback. As a final product of the study, this report summarizes the literature on effective approaches to customer service delivery, highlights four promising practice case studies, conjectures about the transferability of these concepts to child support, and offers future research recommendations. Child support enforcement agencies can refer to this report as a guide for improving customer service, as a resource to learn the costs and benefits of effective customer service delivery, and to inspire future inquiries into effective customer service delivery.

In the 1990s, IBM conducted global research on the question, "What will keep CEOs and senior management awake at night as we begin the twenty-first century?" The study found that, regardless of the industry or geographic location, the most common response was a desire to generate a more customer-oriented culture or business vision.

Customer service is not merely customer relations or how nice frontline workers are to customers. Rather, satisfying or even delighting customers is the goal of excellent customer service. Because customers for different types of services have different needs, customer service strategies will differ and must be tailored to the target customer.

It improves trust and information exchange: In the public sector, including child support offices, good customer service generates satisfied or delighted customers. Satisfied customers lead to increased compliance, improved information exchange, improved relationships, increased trust, and, potentially, decreased workloads or costs. For instance, police departments across the Nation have embraced the concept of community policing. Through community policing, police departments incorporate a customer focus as well as an attitude of partnership with customers, to increase satisfaction and trust and even reduce fear of crime in the community. Customers actually participate in addressing crime and disorder problems, thus reducing the workload on patrol officers.

It saves money and increases profit: In the private sector, good customer service leads to satisfied or delighted customers, which generates customer loyalty, which produces increased revenues and reduced costs. For example, during the early 1990s, IBM transformed itself into a customer-driven organization. From 1994–1999, customer satisfaction increased by 5.5 per cent, revenue increased from $63 billion to over $80 billion, cost and expense savings equalled $7 billion, and stock prices improved over 1,000 per cent.

Upon becoming CEO of Greater Southeast Hospital, a private, nonprofit community hospital, Tom Chapman refocused customer service strategy to save the faltering hospital. Instead of trying to attract more clientele outside the community or turning away the uninsured in the community it served, under Chapman's leadership, Greater Southeast sought to provide better customer service—improving the quality of life and creating community-specific services. The emphasis shifted to treating people when it was cheapest—not in the emergency room but rather when their problems were minor—and to instituting preventative care.

He opened a clinic in the high school to address minor health issues and provide health education resources to teach students about prevention. Additionally, Mr. Chapman improved coordination with the local health clinic and obtained the specific technology from which patients served by the hospital would benefit. Before his arrival, Greater Southeast spent only $20,000–$30,000 a year on a blood pressure programme, although a single stroke victim could cost $30,000 to treat.

The public and private sector customer service literature concurs on the process for delivering great customer service, even if outcomes differ. The current literature supports an outside-in strategy of customer service, rather than the traditional inside-out model for providing services. In the private sector, profit and growth are the *outcomes*, not goals.

Profit and growth are generated by customer loyalty. Loyalty is generated by customer satisfaction. Customer satisfaction is the *goal* that companies should seek and focus on, because high customer satisfaction, as a matter of course, produces customer loyalty and subsequently profit and growth. At this point, the public and private sectors converge—customer satisfaction is the *goal.*

Customer satisfaction is achieved by providing valued services and products, where value is the positive difference between customers' actual experiences and their service delivery expectations. Productive employees also create value.

Employee productivity stems from employee loyalty, and loyalty is a product of employee satisfaction. Satisfaction is generated by high-quality support services (people, information, and technology) and by being empowered to provide value and resolve customer complaints.

This customer service culture must be supported by leadership that emphasizes the importance of each customer and employee. These leaders must be creative and energetic (not lofty or conservative), participatory and caring (not removed or elitist), that is, one who can be a coach, teacher, or listener (not just a supervisor or manager).

Such a leader demonstrates company values (rather than simply institutionalizing policies) and motivates by mission (rather than by fear).

Some components of this model are cyclical. A 1991 study of property and casualty insurance companies found that employees who felt that they were meeting customer needs had twice the job satisfaction level of employees who did not believe they were meeting customer needs. In that study, when a frontline service worker left the company, customer satisfaction levels dropped from 75 to 55 per cent.

In the customer service literature, five guiding principles are adopted by public as well as private agencies delivering excellent customer service:

- Embrace change and persistently strive to improve (be a learning organization).
- Continually ask the target customers what they want and then give it to them.
- Empower, support, and reward frontline personnel.
- Harness the power of information.
- Establish an enabling infrastructure.
- Identify the Target Customer.
  - Begin by identifying the target customers and by considering the point of purchase, point of service delivery or receipt, and point of consumption.
  - Cluster or segment target customers based on their common behaviours, knowing that targeting the wrong customers can have adverse effects on the organization.

- Determine the priorities of various clusters of customers, knowing that the capabilities of the organization are crucial in addressing these priorities.
- When possible, focus on customers with high current or future value. (Perhaps in child support this is a custodial parent with many children in the system.) This does not mean that other customers will not receive service, but it may mean that they will receive a different level of service. Consider the frequent flier programmes that airlines and hotels offer to their customers with high current and future value. This does not mean that other passengers will not receive services, but services may not be at the same level.
- Discourage non-target customers, those who are not likely to be satisfied by the services, and those to whom it is expensive to provide services, which is a necessary part of a customer focus. A simple example is offered as an illustration. A fire department could discourage residents from contacting the department to remove cats from trees by charging a $20 fee for performing the service and by advertising their busy emergency call load. The equipment and time investment of sending a ladder truck and several firefighters may reduce the effectiveness of the department at responding to an emergency and may not be the most prompt means of accomplishing the task for the customer.

• Determine What Customers Want..

- Determine what target customers want (not just what they need right now) by asking them in person or as part of a mail or telephone survey or by using other mechanisms (e.g., electronic tracking and researching marketing trends) to determine what they want. Be aware that advertising, word of mouth, and public relations influence customers' expectations. Meeting customers' basic needs or expectations does not always bring high levels of satisfaction. Exceeding expectations produces high satisfaction-therefore, determine customers' ideal desires.
- Determine how the target customers prioritize their "wants." Generally, customers want convenience, quality products and services, variety or selection, low prices, and protection or security. However, each organization must identify what is most important to its customers.
- Weigh how important the customer-identified "wants" are to the organization. Are the services something that the organization does, is capable of doing, or wants to pursue?
- Determine how well the organization can meet the customers' "wants" in comparison with competitors. The success of other

companies at meeting and exceeding customer expectations changes a customer's frame of reference and increases a customer's expectations.
  - Determine which "wants," if performance delivery were to be improved, would most impact the organization's bottom line (profit, cost, loyalty, trust, or compliance).
- Establish an Organizational Culture Supportive of Customer Service.
  - Utilizing the information gathered, establish the company's customer-focused vision. The vision statement should be simple and may also identify what the company does not want to be. Some examples of simple vision statements include "Absolutely, Positively Overnight" by Federal Express and L.L. Bean's promise "Guaranteed. Period."
  - Live up to what is promised by concurrently developing and applying externally and internally oriented strategic service concepts that reflect the vision. If the organization does not implement both internally and externally oriented service strategies consistent with the vision, the organization will have good intentions but poor customer service (Thompson).
  - Continually reflect on the vision and goals and the way services are delivered to customers. Be creative about the mechanisms used to create and deliver new services. Be willing to change existing practices to integrate improvements.
- Implement an Externally Oriented Strategic Service Concept. The externally oriented strategic service concept establishes how the organization's service is designed, marketed, and delivered to target customers.
  - Take into account the costs of providing services and ways to minimize those costs while implementing quality control. The service concept must be developed with the frontline worker at its centre. Determine the necessary financial, human, and technological resources necessary, as well as how the organizational structure and flow can enable the frontline worker to delight the customer and deliver the promised vision.
  - Use advertising/educational strategies to set appropriate customer expectations.
  - When planning, realise that control of information can take the place of assets. For instance, the Rural/Metro Fire Department in Scottsdale (AZ) has reduced the size of its crew and trucks because of technology that allows crews to view microfiche floor plans on the way to a fire. The added knowledge of the building layout allows fewer fire fighters to accomplish the same task that requires more firefighters when they do not have this advance knowledge.

- Provide a feedback loop for incorporating customer comments and complaints into the planning processes. Customer complaints are an invaluable resource and source of information without which organizations cannot be successful. Complaints brought to the organization are one of the most efficient and least expensive ways to obtain information about customer expectations of products and services. Complaints are a more direct means of obtaining information than conducting research studies of customer expectations, conducting transaction studies, or reviewing customer expectations in parallel industries. Another means of soliciting customer feedback that has been implemented by a number of service leaders is to interview lost customers-those who have switched service providers. (Perhaps in child support these customers were custodial parents who had been making timely payments but who stopped doing so.) Still other options are holding customer meetings, hosting social events, and attending seminars or conferences where customers are present.

  Ensure that the complaint resolution strategy supports the customer-focused vision. Most research shows, "...if customers believe their complaints are welcomed and responded to, they will more likely repurchase." British Airways found that 67 per cent of its complaining passengers fly again if their complaints are handled well. British Airways even implemented a creative and convenient way to allow customers to complain by installing video booths at Heathrow Airport so that customers could immediately go into a booth and state a complaint, even during non-business hours. The videotapes are reviewed and addressed during business hours.
- One final element of an externally oriented service strategy is to regularly measure customer satisfaction or delight in the products and services.

• Implement an Internally Oriented Strategic Service Concept.

The internally oriented strategic service concept establishes how the organization's internal processes will support the customer-focused vision. The premise behind the internally oriented strategic service concept is "...capable workers who are well trained and fairly compensated provide better service, need less supervision, and are much more likely to stay on the job. As a result, their customers are likely to be more satisfied...". A study by Sears in 1989 found that "employee turnover and customer satisfaction are directly correlated." Stores with high customer service ratings had a 54 per cent sales force turnover versus 83 per cent in stores with low customer service ratings. This is supported by examples throughout the literature. Taco Bell found that the 20 per cent of stores with the lowest employee turnover rates have 55 per cent higher profits (an outcome of customer satisfaction) than the 20 per cent of stores with the highest turnover rates.

A number of other studies provide convincing evidence as to why companies should avoid employee turnover. Merck and Co. found in 1990 that turnover costs were 1.5 times an employee's annual salary. Clearly this varies based on a number of cost factors (e.g., workers compensation claims, hiring process costs, training costs, and lost business), but it is commonly noted that employee turnover is an expensive problem. Abt Associates studied an automobile dealer's sales and determined that it cost $36,000 to replace a salesperson with 5–8 years of experience with a salesperson with less than 1 year of experience. The economic costs of excessive employee turnover in one trucking company were analysed, and it was determined that the company could increase profits by 50 per cent by cutting driver turnover in half.

- Ensure that leaders of the learning organization exhibit the company values. Leaders must foster the creation and testing of new ideas and be unabashedly willing to change existing practices to integrate improvements.
- Identify employee groups important to implementing the externally oriented service concept. Frontline workers are of central importance.
  - Identify the characteristics and needs of the employee group(s) and how well those needs are met. This may include resources needed to successfully perform the job or needs can refer to compensation, work environmental factors, or personal needs. Understanding employee needs helps an organization to develop successful processes as well as employee retention policies. Learn how targeted employees perceive the proposed customer services. An organization cannot change without the participation of its employees.
- Focus on recruiting employees who support the customer service vision. The costs of employing people who do not support the customer service vision are considerable. Forum Corporation research in the service industry showed, "...only 14% [per cent] of customers who stop patronizing service businesses do so because they are dissatisfied with what they bought. More than two-thirds defect because they find service people indifferent or unhelpful." Oftentimes, the right employees are those that fit in with the corporate culture's customer service vision, not necessarily those with the most experience in the industry. Additionally, develop career paths that allow successful customer-oriented employees to remain on the frontline.
- Focus on training and employee development throughout employment. A study by Ryder Truck from 1988 through 1989 found that increased training meant lower employee turnover.

- Empower frontline employees to do what it takes to satisfy the customer. Management must support employee empowerment by clearly defining the parametres of the empowerment, while remaining flexible within the parametres. This will encourage creativity. Rules should be simple and few—Continental Airlines actually had an employee handbook burning party to signify the change from a procedural environment to one of empowered customer service. Also, in support of internal customers, the Department of Defence reduced its 230 pages of travel regulations to 17 pages.
- Ensure that management supports employee decisions and judgment calls, even if this means that the cost of satisfying customers initially increases. In positions of high customer contact, quality control is not met by increased supervision, but by the use of incentives to emphasize quality, making service providers highly visible to customers, and by building a peer group to instill a sense of pride and teamwork.
- In addition to skills and empowerment, equip frontline personnel with the technology, information, and internal resources to do what it takes to satisfy the customer. The literature is replete with examples of how incorporating the latest information technology can improve employee productivity. For example, Charles Schwab developed IWIN, a system that allows an agent to identify and view electronically Charles Schwab literature to respond to customer questions received by telephone. Before this system was implemented, agents who were unfamiliar with the literature in question could not provide immediate and succinct answers to customer questions.
- Ensure that divisions and individuals within the organization communicate. Frontline employees and other employees need information and a support network. A customer should never have to tell one employee what another employee already knows.
- Develop cross-functional teams for operations and improvement tasks. First ask those who are doing the work for suggestions to improve productivity. The Social Security Administration nearly doubled its telephone-answering capacity by implementing automated features, utilizing additional technology to change the way employers' reports of wages are recorded, and cross training its employees to work outside their normal areas of responsibility during peak periods.
- Link all employees' compensation to (and offer rewards for) good customer service performance. Rewards can be money, status, praise, acknowledgement, or perks such as trips or special events. While Charles Schwab does provide monetary incentives based on the amount of money a broker team brings into the company, if the

customer service survey for the quarter does not show strong customer service by the team, the reward is reduced or even eliminated for the quarter. This policy in a profit-seeking environment leaves no doubt that customer satisfaction is the primary goal.

- Finally, measure employee satisfaction regularly. Leaders in the service industry have employed such methods as toll-free numbers, periodic roundtable meetings, and surveys to collect employee satisfaction information.

THE CUSTOMER-FOCUSED ANALYSIS

The analytical frame to understand customer value consists first of identifying the customer and understanding the customer's problem and solution needs. This leads to an understanding of what the solution does for the customer and everything associated with it. The next issue is to focus on the options that the customer would consider appropriate in meeting the need and how the options compare with each other. Are there other options provided by other firms whose value-creating assets have a sustainable competitive advantage? This would dictate whether the firm should be in this business at all; if so, is there the potential for a sustainable competitive advantage? The kinds of questions that need to be asked by the customer-focused firm as it examines its business and how it can provide superior customer value for a sustainable competitive advantage.

The Key to a Sustainable Competitive Advantage

The core of any product is essentially a commodity. Competitive advantage comes from services as product enhancements made to the core. To compete on service, firms need to understand the opportunities and challenges presented by the special nature of services. Sustainable competitive advantage comes from an ability of the firm to compete through service.

A common misconception is to view services as being synonymous with customer service. "Services" are not limited to customer service. Customer service is only one of the services that enhance products. Managers who are product focused and not customer focused usually see services as meaning customer service. They see service as something that is done when a product fails or invoked to prevent it from failing. Others who see service as "freebies" that you toss in with the product are probably sales focused.

Firms with such a product or sales orientation actually do a disservice to the customer in the name of service. Their tendency is to offer a refund or return policy, which is often enough structured to favour the firm rather than the customer. These firms may offer a customer service toll-free telephone number, which is usually set up to be a frustrating encounter for the customer service personnel as well as the customer who may have been calling in for retribution. Such is often the unfortunate consequence in firms that are not customer focused. In customer-focused firms, customer service is not just an add-on, a little something extra to keep the customer happy. Customer service is an integral part of the total product.

Service is not what you *do to the product,* it is what you *do for the customer.* The customer-focused firm looks at the core product as an incomplete solution for customers. These firms supplement the core product with services that help customize or otherwise enhance solutions for customers. Such product enhancements add value for the customer. The Aramark employee being on location at Sears adds value to the core product of catering for Sears. It allows Aramark to be more customer focused by obtaining first-hand customer information and being able to deliver on it. By being on hand, Aramark can be immediately aware and responsive to the customers' needs. Service-based product enhancements are an imperative for the customer-focused firm.

This establishes the frame of mind required for the customer-focused firm to be service oriented. You will see what the inherent characteristics of services are, and thus the challenges and opportunities you need to recognize when you incorporate services into the value you create and deliver to the customer.

The Service Orientation Imperative

The traditional view of services is to treat products dichotomously, in two categories—*either* services *or* (physical) goods. Sometimes the term *product* is even used interchangeably with packaged goods but not with service. Not only has this usage caused unnecessary confusion, but it has also encouraged the flawed approach that services and packaged goods are separate and mutually exclusive entities. Scholars have gone as far as to suggest that "most product manufacturers and service providers alike are largely service operations."

They asserted that the role of services is critical for any organization in providing value in the form of "technological improvements, styling features, product image, and other attributes that only services can create." The fact is that all products come with some services. As a matter of degree some products have more services than others and are therefore more intangible than others.

Picture a continuum ranging from products that are most tangible (and least intangible in proportion) at one extreme to products that are most intangible (and least tangible in proportion) at the other extreme. At one end of the continuum, services such as education, consulting, and financial services have very few physical goods that customers take title to. At the other end, packaged goods such as a bar of soap or table salt come with no apparent service unless, for example, the customer initiates a customer service phone call.

In the middle of the continuum are products such as fast food restaurants and custom-made clothing that have an almost equal proportion, with no real predominance of tangibles or intangibles. In products that are predominantly intangible, where the customers don't take title to anything physical, such as in banking services, the service provider might use tangibles such as documentation, statements, and billing. The value for the customer is in the information contained in them.

As a proportion of what the customer is getting in the total product, the predominant source of customer value is from the intangibles in the total product. For physical goods, services enhance the core product and provide opportunities for competitive advantage. Thus, any product has some proportion of services attached to it, and this part of the product has a special nature that needs to be handled differently. If all firms provide some proportion of service components as part of the total product, it behooves them to have an understanding of the nature of services.

Only with such an understanding can we truly get into the service-orientation frame of mind. Take for example, the table salt manufacturer, Morton's. For this firm to look at itself as a packaged goods firm and therefore not concerned with services is a mistake. The fact that Morton's makes the product available at the retail store through the appropriate distribution channels is a service to the customer.

Morton's has essentially outsourced its distribution and retailing to channel intermediaries. To be truly customer focused, Morton's needs to view all the value-added it provides the customer, over and above the product of the production process—the salt—as services it provides to the customer. Morton's cannot manage its service components in the same way that it manages the production of its table salt. Most B2B manufacturing firms intuitively recognize the importance of the service component in enhancing its product. Caterpillar, the earth-moving equipment manufacturer, recognizes that prompt and reliable service is critical to its success and organizes the whole firm around customer locations. You need a service orientation to see such product enhancements as service dimensions that add value to the core product. Service orientation is

- A philosophy or frame of mind reflected in the firm's culture
- An attitude to serve the customer reflected in the firm's treatment of its customers, and
- A view of services as necessary enhancements to any core product to make a complete solution.

To provide complete and competitive solutions to the customer, one needs to understand and adopt the service orientation. The service-oriented frame of mind requires a grasp of the fundamental nature of services (whether as the product or a component of a product). Once the inherent characteristics of services are clear, it becomes apparent that their implications for the customer and the provider offer a number of opportunities and pose a variety of challenges.

As a preface to a discussion of these issues, it would be useful to note the evolution of interest in the concept of service. Prompted by the frustrations of practitioners in the service sector who were finding that marketing practices from the packaged goods world did not make sense for services, scholars began to get interested in the problem. In the late 1970s and early 1980s, for a number of reasons, the academic research community in business disciplines, particularly in marketing, operations, and human resources, began a serious intellectual debate as to whether products that were services, compared to products that were packaged goods, needed to be studied differently.

For example, could you study the marketing of hospitality services the same way as you would the marketing of toothpaste? Some scholars maintained that marketing is marketing regardless of *what* you are marketing. Either way, they argued, one had to go through the tasks of segmenting the market, positioning a product, and making product, pricing, distribution, or promotion decisions. Others argued that although that might be true, one would need to approach these tasks very differently; and they proceeded to offer the rationale for this argument. There was a great deal of interest in this effort, especially among those who recognized the tremendous growth of the services sector.

Around the same time there were environmental changes in the economy and in the competitive landscape. Services sectors such as airlines, telecommunications, and, later, banking and insurance were going through deregulation in the United States. Manufacturing was moving to cheaper labour markets in the Far East and in Latin America. Meanwhile, by the late 1980s in the United States, even professional services such as health care and legal services began to recognize the need to employ marketing practices.

Not surprisingly, even manufacturing firms were being forced to add service components to their product offerings. As these changes occurred and services were being established as an integral aspect of doing business, the United States had become a service economy. Ultimately, the debate over whether services were really different from physical products produced the rationale that the skeptics demanded. The evidence and essence of this argument epitomizes the service orientation.

Characteristics of all Services

There are certain fundamental characteristics that are inherent in all service products and in the service components of any product. Let us begin by defining service as *a deed, performance, or action.* Thus, by definition, services are intangible. The product that is a service or that component of the product that is a service cannot be seen, touched, or felt. As a deed, performance or action, a service is consumed as it is produced, such that the acts of production and consumption are inseparable. Thus, services are also perishable, in that they cannot be inventoried or produced and stored for later use. Nor can they be produced without some level of customer interaction.

Since services are produced and consumed in real time, they are inherently variable—from customer to customer, from provider to provider, and from time to time for the same customer and/or the same provider. These statements describe features that are fundamental and are inherent in products or components of products that are deeds, performances, or actions, and may sound very simplistic until you delve into the meanings and consequences of these inherent characteristics to the customer and to the provider.

It is generally accepted that services are different from physical goods along four fundamental characteristics labeled as intangibility, simultaneity or inseparability, perishability, and variability. These characteristics are conceptually inherent in all services or in the service component of any product. Although this framework is more useful as a pedagogical vehicle rather than a framework for research or practice, it is powerful in fully capturing the concept of service orientation and accomplishes the objective of placing the reader in the necessary frame of mind.

This mindset is grounded in the appreciation of the fundamental nature of services necessitating appropriate managerial decisions and actions. The fundamental character of services and the associated consequences may play out for the manager. A service orientation requires a thorough understanding of how these inherent characteristics of services are manifested for the customer and the manager.

Intangibility—Services

Services are performances. Services cannot be seen but they can be experienced. The product is a process. As a service provider, you cannot show your product as you could if you were the marketer of a packaged good. Yes, services are the result of value-creating activities, just as physical products are, and may employ tangibles or physical products in producing the service. However, the product being purchased is an experience and not a physical good. Customers cannot take ownership or title to a service. For example, hotels provide the service of overnight stay as their core product. The customer does not take title to the room that is being rented. The hotel provides the use of the room for the duration of the time that the customer has paid for. Similarly, customers don't take title to anything in air travel or in entertainment. When office copiers come with service, there is no ownership involved with the service component unlike with the copier itself. When your automobile comes with free service under warranty, unlike the automobile itself there is no real ownership of the service component.

Now, as a manager, you might say: "All this is well and good, but if it doesn't change the way I manage the product, its production, or its marketing, whether it is a packaged good or service, why should I care? Services are intangible and service components in products are intangible—yes! But so what?" Let us examine this question from the customer's point of view. For customers, one immediate consequence of the intangibility is increased perceived risk. When you cannot see the product or what you are going to get before the purchase, customers have to acknowledge a certain amount of risk they are taking. While there is perceived risk in the purchase of a packaged or physical good, you cannot return a vacation as you can a defective lawn mower.

Thus, you accept a certain amount of risk as unavoidable in the case of a service. When you book your vacation, do you really see the product? If you have previously been to the locations, you may have seen the facility, but your product was the experience. Complicating the perceived risk is the fact that the evaluation of services or the service component of the product is inherently subjective. Compared to packaged goods, customers find it harder to evaluate services before the purchase. In some cases, services are harder to evaluate even during and after their performances.

In the case of health care, for instance, you use several proxy elements, such as the cleanliness of the facility, the medical professional's "bedside manner, " and the process you had to go through. What you are evaluating is a lot more than the core product, the medical treatment itself. Being intangible, services cannot be produced until you have purchased (whether you pay before, during, or after) the service.

Simultaneity—Services

The acts of production and consumption occur simultaneously in services. This is primarily because services are produced and consumed in real time. There is a great deal of interaction before, during, and/or after the service between provider and customer. Some sort of customer interaction is necessary even if customer physical presence is not. At the very least, customers have to specify their needs and their need situations. In most if not all cases, it can be argued that production and consumption cannot be temporally separated. (Thus, this characteristic is also termed "inseparability.") A related complication for services is that in services, the provider is part of the product.

As a customer, the frontline personnel you interact with are a part of the product. In professional services, for instance, the lawyer is part of the (legal service) product, the doctor is part of the (medical care) product, the professor is part of the (education) product.

Comparing this to packaged goods: Do you have to interact with Procter & Gamble and the shop floor employee who made your particular tube of Crest toothpaste? You do interact with the retailer of the toothpaste, but remember that the retail store that makes the toothpaste available to you is a service. What you are consuming from the retailer as it is produced by the retailer is a service. In fact, you interact with the provider of the service component of the packaged good. If you interacted with P&G, it was with customer service.

Once again, let us confront the question: "So what?" To understand what difference it makes for the manager, the customer-focused firm must examine the consequences to the customer from the customer's perspective.

The customer has to interact with the provider at some stage or at all stages of the production process. The customer is in the service factory in the case of an amusement park. Sometimes the service factory comes to the customer, as in the case of the landscape contractor. Sometimes the interaction is at arm's length, such as in the case of an online travel agent like Expedia.com. In each case, there is some interaction that the customer usually initiates. Thus, there is some effort on the part of the customer for the product to be produced.

The customer takes on a role in the production process. To perform the expected role, customers have to be educated and sometimes socialized into the process. For example, at a fast food restaurant, the customer needs to get familiar with the process of ordering and picking up the food. When you call your long distance phone company for a question on your bill, you need to have some information ready for the service to be performed. These days you have to be familiar with complex automated voice menus before you can get anything done over the telephone. Since consumption and production are simultaneous, the customer is consuming as the product is being produced. The product cannot be produced ahead of time and then consumed. This means that the product cannot be inventoried.

Perishability—Services

Since services cannot be produced and stored for later use, as physical products can, services are said to be perishable products. What actually perishes? In fact, what perishes is the productive capacity of the service, or more precisely, the opportunity to produce a product. A hairdresser's time is wasted or unproductive when he or she is not serving a customer. The customer service personnel ready to handle customer enquiries is not producing a service unless there is a customer to serve. An empty airline seat perishes without a passenger in it on takeoff. The factors of production such as labour, facilities, equipment, and billable time are the value-creating assets for the service provider.

The opportunity to produce the product from these assets perishes without the adequate number of customers for which the capacity is designed. And the service provider needs to maintain a certain level of capacity that is not easily adjustable. Some services are more capacity-constrained than others. A hotel cannot reduce the number of rooms in its facility when there are not enough guests. A management consulting firm with fulltime employees would be hard pressed to release its staff when there are not enough clients to fill the capacity.

For the customer, service products need to be available and accessible when and where they are needed. When the productive capacity is sometimes not able to meet the demand, customers are likely to have to wait in queues or find another provider. Whether it is on the phone for customer service, at the doctor's office, or in line for a ride in an amusement park, customers will have to get used to waiting. In some services, customers need to plan ahead of time and place reservations. That is how managers instinctively manage the utilization of capacity in the operation.

Conversely, when there is more productive capacity than there are customers to be served, service providers have to look for other customer segment opportunities for their value-creating assets. Service providers have to manage that balance between capacity and demand. They employ methods to anticipate and manage the pattern of demand and to manage the capacity accordingly.

Variability—Services

Service products as experiences vary from one experience to the next, from customer to customer, as well as for the same customer from one occasion to the next. In fact, this variability is compounded with differences among frontline personnel. When there are several steps in the service process where the customer interacts with several different personnel of the service provider, there could be variation from one interaction to another. In some cases, customers will prefer specific frontline personnel with whom they have become familiar and comfortable. Since services are produced and consumed in real time, it is clear that customers will likely see a great degree of variation in product quality.

Customers can receive a different experience each time, even at a standardized operation like McDonald's. Service managers attempt to deliver consistently high quality with frontline training and technology and to customize where possible and standardize where necessary. Customers expect customization even when it is not feasible. Managers have to balance the economics of standardization with the quality issues around customization.

Thus, the fundamental characteristics of services force their implications on the customer. The manager of services and products that involve a significant degree of tangibles are forced to orient themselves to these implications. The complexity of managerial situations as a consequence of these characteristics is manifested as opportunities and challenges. Consequently, the services manager must analyze these consequences, and be prepared to take some actions to address them.

CUSTOMER FOCUS AND SERVICE ORIENTATION

A customer focus necessitates a deep understanding of customers and their activities, interests, and opinions around the particular value or solution that the firm is providing. It should be an attitude that is pervasive and that permeates throughout the firm such that it becomes ingrained as a culture. Once this focus becomes a given, then the firm will find itself in the mode of serving the customer while ensuring a reasonable profit. The realization is that you cannot achieve a sustainable competitive advantage to command sustainable profits unless you are customer focused.

Serving the customer contrasts with the notion of marketing a product. It is more than providing a solution for the customer. It is about *serving* the customer. The firm looks at the customer's need in the broadest possible context, going beyond the scope of the core product that satisfies the core need in a particular consumption activity. The product is redefined to include all value-added components in a total solution. By definition, the product is extended to include several dimensions that would include as part of the total product the value added in any and all customer interactions. The service-oriented firm is one that focuses on serving the customer, regardless of whether its core product is a physical good or an intangible.

Such firms are better positioned to deliver that customer value in its products. When all competing firms provide the same core product, the competitiveness of a firm or its superiority has to come from enhancements to the core product. The key to competitiveness is in these enhancements, which are invariably provided by service dimensions. These service dimensions contribute to providing superior customer value. To successfully provide these service dimensions firms have to be service oriented. When you look around, you will find that successful firms exhibit a frame of mind that is service oriented and focused on the customer.

The service-oriented firm owns responsibilities over and above just providing a product. Such a firm is proactive in anticipating customer needs and situations in customer interactions. For example, customer education is seen as a significant responsibility of the firm. The customer-focused firm views the customer's role in consumption activities as an integral part of its solution. A customer-focused firm truly cares for the customer. Such a firm's behaviour demonstrates that it feels privileged to have the customer. When its product fails the customer, the service-oriented firm will evoke built-in customer recovery procedures implemented by customer-focused employees.

The total customer experience at such firms goes beyond the core product and is superior to other firms. The quality of the total experience includes a whole host of components or experiences other than that of the core product. The value that the customer seeks includes all of these components and not just the core product. When Lexus, Toyota's luxury division, found that its customers in the United States were having to drive hundreds of miles to buy a Lexus, the carmaker converted trucks into mobile service stations so that customers didn't have to drive that far to have the car serviced. Singapore Airlines provides its fliers a wide range of choices from what and when they eat to how and when they are entertained. The costs are worth the value the flexibility adds to the customer experience. Customers choose firms that provide this customer value in a total solution. Such firms are service oriented.

Firms add a number of dimensions typically encompassed in "services" to augment the product. Customer service is a common term used to denote these dimensions. But it is important to understand that customer service is a specific type of customer interaction and as such, it performs a narrow but necessary function. While customer service is typically involved with nonroutine customer situations such as recovering from a service failure, being "service oriented" can include, for example, anticipating that service failure and proactively initiating a service recovery. EMC, the storage devices provider, builds its products with redundant systems.

When the primary system fails and the redundant system takes over, the design and service team assigned to the client looks into the causes and alerts the client if necessary. EMC's diagnostics cover competitor products that are part of the storage and retrieval system. In service-oriented firms such as EMC, service recovery processes are built into the design of the total product offering. EMC's service orientation is reflected in the design of its products and in its concern for the customer's experience with the product performance. EMC claims a 99 percent customer retention rate. The total product offering includes serving the customer during all stages of consumption of a solution.

In service-oriented firms, services complete the product as a total solution. These services are also the primary key to a sustainable competitive advantage within that total value bundle. Providing these services requires a completely different mind-set with an understanding of the complex characteristics of services. This is true even in products where the core benefit is delivered by a physical good that the customer takes title to. The services that go along with the physical good are a significant component of the total product. As illustrated in the EMC example, this perspective is readily apparent in the business-to-business (B2B) situation, where firms are naturally inclined to focus on service to the customer. Their perspective includes service elements to augment the product and to establish and maintain customer relationships.

For manufacturing firms, the physical good is only part of the total solution toward customer needs. Indeed, the physical components of any product are easily matched by competitors, thus reducing what might have been a competitive advantage to a commodity. Firms really compete on the noncommoditized part of the total product. When these aspects of the product are meaningful to the customer and the firm can provide customer value better than the competition, the firm has a sustainable competitive advantage. Firms compete with each other on the total solution comprised of commodities and noncommodities—a complex set of benefits or value bundle.

For a number of firms, especially in the information technology industry, the product has become the service more than the physical technology itself. By the year 2000, for example, 40 percent of sales and 40 percent of profits at IBM came from its Global Services division. At Unisys, 69 percent of sales came from services. Sun's $3.3 billion services business was closely tied to its server business. Compaq purchased DEC in 1998 for its service business. Hewlett-Packard later purchased Compaq for the same reason.

A number of articles in the popular press have lamented the sorry state of service in the United States. When packaged-goods firms are included in the list of examples, it is in the service component of the total product that the failures are apparent. Why it that firms are unable to provide the desired levels of service to satisfy customers?

Beginning in the late 1980s, there has been a great deal of research on what exactly customer orientation or "customer focuses" means and on what exactly a firm should be doing to implement such an orientation. Peppers and Rogers, known for their one-on-one marketing concept, consider customer-focused management as synonymous with relationship marketing or customer-relationship management. Information technology offered firms a way to obtain, process, and use individual customer information so that firms would be able to personalize customer experiences. Some scholars have called it "market orientation."

One set of researchers suggested that customer orientation is a subset of market orientation. Their definition for *market orientation* is "the set of cross-functional processes and activities directed at creating and satisfying customers through continuous needs-assessment." Following their lead, market orientation has been treated as being composed of three components: customer orientation, competitor orientation, and interfunctional coordination.

Can the terms *customer orientation* and *market orientation* be used interchangeably? If we accept the definition of a "market" as being a set of potential customers and treat the terms *market* and *customer* as synonymous except for the level of aggregation in numbers, then we can use the terms interchangeably. Such an argument does not necessarily negate the three-component structure of the concept of customer focus. To be truly customer focused, the firm has to be driven by the goal of providing the customer with the highest level of satisfaction. This implies that the firm concentrates on how the customer is better served (by the firm) compared to the competitive offerings and that all processes and activities in the entire firm are integrated and coordinated to accomplish this goal. The customer-focused firm has all aspects of the firm directed at providing the superior product to the customer.

Thus, we can define *customer focus* as:

A form of culture in a firm that directs all processes and activities of the firm toward providing superior value to the customer so as to sustain long-term profits.

It is now generally accepted that market orientation or a customer focus is a type of culture and is exhibited by a firm that is committed to providing superior customer value. When compared with different types of business cultures, the customer-focused culture has been found to be superior in delivering the best business performance. Such a customer focus was strongly correlated with the use of customer information in a study involving about 5,000 salespeople and sales managers. This study also found a strong correlation between market orientation, job satisfaction, and trust in management.

Another study of 278 salespeople and sales managers found that market orientation significantly influenced job attitudes and the customer orientation of the salespeople. A firm was seen as clearly supporting the salespeople when the salespeople perceived that the firm was being attentive to customer needs and satisfaction, aware of competitor strategies to deliver superior value, and coordinated through the entire firm. There are proven bottom-line benefits from a customer orientation. In another study using a sample of 127 strategic business units in firms listed in the Fortune 500, customer-focused firms achieved higher profitability, sales growth, and new product success.

With such evidence of strong correlations between customer-focused cultures and successful business performance, it behooves us to learn what these firms are doing to be customer focused and what it takes to be a customer-focused firm. It is clear that there are firms that have been successful in developing and implementing the customer-focused culture. Scandinavian Air Systems, Walt Disney, and British Airways are firms that pay attention to establishing the appropriate culture and climate that fosters customer orientation. The list of issues that have to be addressed runs the gamut from organizational structure and behaviour, operations, and value delivery mechanisms to internal and external metrics such as in balanced scorecards and customer loyalty measurement. This book will cover many of these issues in a comprehensive yet concise manner.

Based on the critical links in the logic espousing the merits of a customer-focused management, we first look at the elaboration of the fundamental premise of customer value and service orientation. Following this we begin to examine the specific issues in developing a customer-focused and service-oriented firm—managing customer information, creating and delivering customer value, managing customer relationships, and ensuring a customer-oriented culture. Thus, the rest of the book is organized into the following five parts.

DELIVERING SUPERIOR VALUE REQUIRES A CUSTOMER FOCUS

Every firm provides a bundle of values as a product. The firm that provides the superior value bundle wins the customer. *Superior* is a key word here. Why? Consider this. Research by Jones and Sasser has shown that even satisfied customers defect. These Harvard researchers were studying the link between customer satisfaction and customer loyalty. Their findings suggest that customers are satisfied at different levels. Different levels of satisfaction result in different levels of loyalty, which in turn result in varying levels of behavioural disposition to patronage with a provider.

This logic implies that there is a range of customer satisfaction levels. Satisfied customers may not necessarily translate to loyal customers. Other researchers have introduced the notion of delighting the customer. A customer may defect to a competitor even if satisfied with the current provider because the competitor may be offering a value bundle with the perceived potential for a *higher degree* of satisfaction for that customer. Therefore, firms have to strive to achieve higher levels of satisfaction than their competition by providing superior customer value. This is the essence of achieving a sustainable competitive advantage. If you are unable to provide superior customer value, even your satisfied customers could leave you!

What can a firm do that its competitors cannot match? To answer this question, one must clearly understand the context of competition—the landscape or playing field, as it was. Pine and Gilmore might call such a competitive landscape the "experience economy, " where products are quickly commoditized and firms compete on other aspects of the total offering. People, processes, and technology combine to create products. Technology is easy to copy, but customer-oriented employees and corporate culture are much harder to copy. In fact, technology is eventually commonly available to any firm that has the necessary capital and resources. Commenting on the recovery prospects of information technology firms after the recent recession, Marc Andreassen of Netscape says that a lot of innovation is going on now. However, most innovations are quickly becoming commoditized. One reason may be that processes and systems can be designed appropriately to deliver customer satisfaction, but they can be relatively easily replicated. Employee attitudes, however, are less easily replicable.

Customers look for convenience, cost, and quality of the total experience. The service-oriented firm concentrates on the capabilities of employees and not just on the technology or the tangible features of the product. The realization that the "clicks" store is not going to replace the "bricks" store has demonstrated that technology is not the solution. Rather, it is a means to enhance the solution. In this case, technology has simply provided a different solution.

Almost all bricks-and-mortar firms now have an Internet presence; it is an inexpensive service enhancement for them compared to what the dot-com firms have to do to establish a brick-and-mortar presence. Those dot-coms that have conducted the appropriate analysis of what customer value they were creating and delivering and how they were going to be superior to existing alternatives have had a good start. Subsequently, those that figured out how to sustain it while realizing the profit potential are still around.

It is not a stretch to say that many of the dot-com failures may have occurred because they were focused on the technology and not on the customer. Meanwhile, specialty retailers who are experienced at serving the customer have combined technology with their reputed customer service to make a winning combination. With the established catalog retailers, shoppers get an audio connection in real time over the Internet with customer service personnel who help customers with any questions they may have.

Experience the L.L. Bean or Land's End service at their Web sites to understand how well these specialty catalog retailers have adopted the technology of the Internet. Customer experience with these firms with or without the technology sets them apart from the rest of the players. Technology alone will not provide a competitive advantage. The combination of superior technology and superior employees with a service orientation will contribute to achieving sustainable competitive advantage.

You need a customer-focused and service-oriented culture within the firm. It also quickly becomes evident that you need suppliers as well as distributors and agents who have a similar and compatible culture. Thus, there are two strong themes in any discussion of "creating superior customer value at a sustainable profit": a customer-focus imperative and a service orientation. If all aspects of the firm and how the firm creates and delivers value to the customer are focused on the customer, the firm can provide a superior level of customer value. Such a firm is well positioned for a sustainable competitive advantage. Now, what does it take to be a customer-focused firm? What does customer focus really mean? And, what exactly is a service orientation?

THE IMPORTANCE OF SERVICE IN MODERN SOCIETY

The growth of services is nothing new. More early as 1900, both America and Britain had more jobs in services than in industry. By 1950, services employed half of all American workers. And in 1993, America had the biggest service sector, accounting for 72 percent of its Gross Domestic Product (GDP). Services are also the fastest growing part of international trade, accounting for 20 percent of total world trade and 30 percent of American exports.

Tourism is one of these services. By the year 2000, it is likely to be the world's most important economic activity. According to a report of the World Travel and Tourism Council, there were 255 million jobs in tourism in 1996. This amounts to 10.2 percent of all world employment.

The Special Nature of Work in the Service Sector. Work in the service sector is quite different from that in agriculture or manufacturing. A service has been described as a "deed, act, or performance. Two functional issues are: at whom (or what) is the act directed, and is this act tangible or intangible in nature?

These two questions result in Lovelock's four-way classification scheme involving: (1) tangible actions to people's bodies, such as hair cutting and surgery; (2) tangible actions to goods and other physical possessions, such as air freight, lawn mowing and janitorial services; (3) tangible actions directed at people's minds, such as broadcasting and education; and (4) intangible actions directed at people's intangible assets, such as insurance, investment banking and consulting (13).

This categorization scheme is useful in answering questions like the following, having to do with analyzing and marketing services. Does the customer need to be physically present: throughout service delivery? Only to initiate or terminate the service transaction? or not at all? Does the customer need to be mentally present during the service delivery? Can mental presence be maintained across physical distances through mail or electronic communications? In what ways is the target of the service act "modified" by the receipt of the service? And how does the customer benefit from these modifications?

Work in the Hospitality Industry. Especially in the tourism sector—where services are created as they are consumed and the customer is often involved in the production process—there are many different ways to tailor the service to meet the needs of individual customers. Customization can proceed along at least two dimensions. First of all, you have to consider whether the characteristics of the service and its delivery system lend themselves to customization. Second, you have to determine how much judgment customer contact personnel can exercise in defining the nature of the service received by individual customers. Some service concepts are quite standardized, while other services offer customers a wide range of options.

There is a class of services that not only involves a high degree of customization, but also requires customer contact personnel to exercise judgment about the characteristics of the service and how it is delivered to each customer. This type of service is called "prescriptive" and the focus of control shifts from the user to the supplier. Professional services such as law, medicine, accounting, architecture and tour guiding fall within this category. They are all white-collar, "knowledge industries," requiring extensive training to develop the requisite skills and judgment needed for satisfactory service delivery. As a result, much of the literature on the service industry refers to the encounter between the customer and the service contact personnel as "the moment of truth," because it determines the level of customer satisfaction. This is especially true in the hospitality industry.

Alienation in Marxist Understanding of Work. Karl Marx was undoubtedly the harshest and most influential critic of the inequalities that private property institutions and free markets are accused of creating. In his writings, he detailed the suffering and misery capitalism placed upon its workers. The living conditions that capitalism imposed on the lower working classes contrasted sharply with Marx's view of how human beings should live. According to Marx, human beings should be enabled to realize their human nature by freely developing their potential for self-expression and by satisfying their real human needs. People should develop their productive potential and have control over what they produce. They know what their real needs are, and are able to form satisfying social relationships. Capitalism "alienated" the lower working classes by neither allowing them to develop their productive potential nor satisfy their real human needs. The service sector is one area where this alienation can be overcome if w orkers are truly empowered in their work situations.

Spirituality of Work

Today people are less and less sure about what "work" really means. Their expectations of work, especially getting it and enjoying it, are now matters of both deep anxiety and mundane reality. There are several reasons for this. First, there are high unemployment rates in industrialized societies. For many people in modern society, work is no longer something that happens in a fixed place during a fixed unit of time, producing a fixed output and reward (5). Come points out how societies frequently define human beings in terms of the work they perform (7). The question "what do you do?" is a central one in many people's lives.

Religion teaches that work is its own reward, and that it will lead a person toward the virtuous life, if not salvation. Work is the natural course of action a human follows to find his or her role, niche, position, and the shape of his or her soul. Therefore, steady employment, a life in which one's lot continually improves, sits as the cornerstone of rational and calculable human action. It may well be the cornerstone of physical and mental health as well. How can it not shape the nature of spirituality?

It is in the work and working that a person's consciousness takes shape and life reveals its meaning. For it is in working that a person believes he or she has made sense of life's mystery and has found reasonable ways to avoid vexing metaphysical questions. For the content and structure of a person's consciousness, story and spirit remain his or her work, or lack of it.

Faith and the World of Work

Wright points out that many contemporary Christians experience some discomfort when they seek to relate their faith to the world of work, especially the work of wealth creation in industry, commerce and other services (27). The workplace is perceived as a Godless and even immoral part of their human condition. As a result, many people feel the need to find consistency between their work and the rest of their life.

Christians should be affirmed in their work as a central part of the human condition for the very reasons that it involves wealth creation and the provision of services. The problem is that written materials do not offer enough concrete guidance regarding a comprehensive theology and spirituality of the modern world of work. a few notable exceptions include the core teaching of the series of Papal Encyclicals that have followed Rerum Novarem in 1891, Laborem Exercens in 1981, as well as Centesimus Annus in 1991, all of which contain much profound thinking about human work.

In any case, there is a fundamental question here. Why should one be concerned with the relationship between faith, work, and the world of wealth creation and provision of services? First of all, work is where most people spend a great deal of their time. Second, the creation of wealth and provision of services are the processes whereby all people survive on this earth, since they serve to satisfy their needs and wants.

Finally, and most important, there is a unique Christian truth and revelation: the Incarnation. Christians believe that, in Jesus, God became human at a particular moment of time and lived on this same earth that we inhabit. Jesus was very much involved in the world of work of his day. Many of his stories came from everyday life and the workplace. The world of work and wealth creation is very clearly part of God's creation, and God took part in these very activities. Hence, there is a need to relate them to our Christian beliefs and to face up to any discomfort we perceive and feel in doing so.

Difficulties Relating Faith and Work

According to Wright, there are four main reasons Christians find it difficult to relate their faith to their work in today's industry, commerce and other service sectors:

1. The experimental and scientific method has transformed our understanding of the world in which we live. This growth in understanding has been most uncomfortable for the Church. Many have the false impression that advances in the fields of science and business are made at the expense of God and religion.
2. The world of work may lie in what is popularly referred to as the "Protestant work ethic." Hard work and the accumulation of wealth were the routes of salvation. The problem here is that there are harsh realities in today's work world, such as indifferent supervision, employee turnover, caste system attitudes and long working weeks. In the hotel industry, these concepts are sometimes considered justified in order to attract better-qualified employees and to remedy the alarming shortage of labour.
3. The reconciliation of the contemplative life and the life of every day action has been difficult. There has been a tendency for Christians to regard the active life as in some way inferior to the passive or spiritual one. Teilbard de Chardin looked for a general sanctification of human endeavors in all aspects. He rejected the notion that the active life is inherently inferior to the passive. Hence, Christians engaged in business are in fact contributing as positively to God's work as when they engage in prayer.
4. The dominical and Church teaching present difficulties here. Jesus had some very hard things to say about the dangers of material goods and excessive attachments to riches. Nevertheless, nowhere does one find in the Gospels or the teachings of the Church any suggestion that the process of wealth creation and provision of services is in itself reprehensible or to be condemned. The encyclical Centesimus Annus (1981) identifies the tension between the role of the individual in the wealth creation and service provision process and the needs of the community. The system itself must not overwhelm the individual. People must in fact recognize the limits of private wealth (27).

Panmunin concluded that to improve public perceptions and enhance employees' experiences, industry must create a working climate that is challenging, secure, trusting, caring and promising (17). Unfortunately, employees' eroding working conditions have eroded the traditional Thai spirit of hospitality. Ensuring the return of Thai hospitality will take some doing, in areas like: nurturing a pride in serving, wearing a service uniform, providing the opportunity for learning and advancement, and demonstrating employer appreciation both in words and pay.

The Nature of Spirituality

The Historical Background and Methodology of Spirituality Studies. Before World War II, spirituality, as it refers to a person's life experiences, was an almost exclusively Roman Catholic term. But now it has taken on new meaning with the Second Vatican Council's invitation to a new awareness of, dialogue with and appreciation of other denominations and non-Christian religions (25). For example, there is now growing interest in the spirituality of various Protestant traditions as well as the traditions of Judaism, Hinduism, Islam and Buddhism. The Second Vatican Council has also called Catholics to a new dialogue with the human sciences—especially in the fields of psychology, sociology and anthropology—in which spirituality refers to the human spirit apart from religion. Some even speak of the spirituality of inter-religious movements, such as secular feminism and atheistic Marxism.

In short, spirituality has become a broad, inclusive term that is no longer confined to, or defined by, religion. It names a human reality difficult to define but whose patterns can be verified in quite different religions and movements. Spirituality now focuses on the human spirit of believers and non-believers in their lives as a whole; that is, on the physical and emotional, the intellectual and social, the political and cultural, and the secular and religious dimensions of their lives. According to Kinerk, the study of spirituality needs: (1) a definition of itself, (2) some tools for analyzing a particular spirituality, (3) some guidelines of relating a spirituality to other spiritualities, and (4) some criteria for evaluation.

The features of a workable definition of spirituality should: (1) limit the material to what is expressed, and (2) contain the idea of personal growth. Thus, spirituality is the expression of a dialectical personal growth from the inauthentic to the authentic. There are, in fact, three ingredients in this definition: expression, dialectical personal growth, and movement from inauthentic to authentic. According to Thompson, a person's spirituality is individual and collective, and reflects how a person responds to God's initiative while facing the challenges of everyday life within his or her specific historical and cultural environment.

Just how does God's Spirit work in some one's life? First, it works in the subjective element. Second, it works in the objective dimension of one's real-life experiences and situations—encompassing all creations and all other people you encounter in your life. Put simply, God works in the people you meet and acts through your real life. He is present in human events and their history. His presence gives a necessary meaning to how you relate to other people and the world.

According to Kinerk, the questions or tools for analyzing a spirituality must serve two purposes. They must: (1) provide a means of organizing the material of a spirituality so it can be more easily assimilated, and (2) provide for comparison and contrast such that they can be asked more or less equally of any spirituality. Here are two questions that can help focus and organize the material: What are the expressions of the authentic and inauthentic? What is the organizational form that could give the expressions depth and a relationship to one another? All spiritual life is a type of growth, but in many well-developed spiritualities there are specific stages, and the key to detecting these stages lies with the expressions of both the authentic and the inauthentic forms.

Hope Replace Obedience

According to Regan, personal development of healthy human qualities occupies a more central position in one's personal outlook toward spirituality today. Accepting what is authentically human leads people to use their native talents, creative expressions and heightened personal initiatives. On the other hand, anything that dehumanizes a service provider or "receiver" in the hospitality industry is viewed as unchristian. This approach allows more emphasis on an individual's personal response of his or her religious and inner values, both human and Christian. Empowerment, decentralization, co-responsibility and subsidiarity become the new hallmarks of what was once viewed as religious "obedience."

Many post-Second Vatican Council authors now present the Christian life based on a central theme of God's call and a person's response. This "call-response" morality and spirituality replaces the former stress on law and self-perfection. In the basic meaning of grace—God's self-gift—God gives Himself to a person and acts in them, enabling them to respond. Furthermore, New Testament teachings hold that the virtue of charity directed toward God and neighbour takes precedence over all other virtues. The law-centred approach has thus given way to a more love-centred approach: life is seen in its entirety as a loving response to a personal and loving God. A morality of relationships conceived along these lines sees each person in dialogue with God and meeting God in the events, people and prayer experiences of daily living.

Spirituality has important consequences for the overall tone or mood Christian professionals adopt in their lives. These professionals represent an intense cell of vibrant Christian life. They witness to Heavenly values, which imply that they should show what faith in God can mean based on the way they live their lives. Specifically, it means: hope, confidence, optimism in ultimate destinies; faith and charity in everyday concerns. By moving away from an excessively "obedience-centred" approach, they instead experience a Christian life and spirituality centre on faith, love, hope in God and in ultimate realities, manifested in the love and service of humankind. These constitute

Gospel values that should characterize a renewed professional life and genuine Christian spirituality.

Kinerk has emphasized that, ultimately, evaluating a Catholic spirituality is the responsibility of the Catholic Church (11) and over the centuries she has generally given a wide latitude to the expressions claiming to be of the Spirit As long as a spirituality refrained from making its charisma normative for all Christians, maintained a balanced view of theology and human nature, and did not habitually defy the directions of the hierarchy, the Church has been at least tolerant, if not actively supportive.

What Makes a Good Spirituality? There are three indicators of a good spirituality: good theology, good sense and good results. Good spirituality must flow out of the Christian community's understanding of the Gospel and hence must exhibit good theology. Spirituality is a human movement, and so good spirituality should reflect a keen sensitivity to the human condition—good sense. Finally, a good spirituality will produce good results because it will be the work of the Holy Spirit.

To develop models of spirituality it is necessary to select criteria for differentiation. This selection is always arbitrary, however. It simply establishes the parameters by which the models are distinguished. Here the criteria will be "attitudes" toward two potential environments for expressions: the world (including human history and institution) and history (especially change and conversion).

We can determine the models by asking the question: Does a spirituality view the world and/or history as a positive locus for expressions of the authentic? If a spirituality is not positive toward both, we call it apopathic; if it is positive toward both, we call it apostolic; if it is positive toward the world but not toward history, we call it city-of-God; and if it is positive toward history but not toward the world, we call it prophetic. Most spiritualities are mixtures of all four, with perhaps one or more predominating. However, it is clear that a spirituality for hospitality professionals must be apostolic.

Regan has pointed out that it is no longer possible to hold a monolithic conception of spirituality due to the pluralism in modern Church life and theology today (19). With the obedience-centred approach, the traditional stress on a person's spiritual life focused on the rules, authority and the virtue of obedience. This is similar to the law-centred approach of moral theology. A person's individual acts received more emphasis than his or her overall stance or attitude. Obedience to law in all exactness comes through in traditional moral theology as the centre of Christian life.

With today's personal response-to-inner values approach, there's a greater emphasis placed on personal responsibility and individuality. In this approach to the spiritual life, a person is viewed as entering a profession or a community to develop oneself fully in the service of Christ and neighbour, to put one's full talents at the disposal of people, and to take part in and share responsibility for the Church and for the community itself. Rather than obedience, selfless charity becomes the primary Christian virtue. Life itself is seen as a response of love to God and in the neighbour in accordance with Jesus' teaching. This approach seems particularly appropriate for hospitality professionals, whose training now emphasizes their empowerment to make decisions by themselves.

Spirituality of Work

Cassin points out that in the Christian scheme, work has always been understood as a human sharing in the creative activity of God (5). This means believing in the inherent dignity of work itself and the ultimate worth of any of the products of work. According to another, different Christian view, work has been seen as a penalty, a consequence of original sin or the Fall, rather than something intrinsic to God's creative purpose. This pessimistic view is certainly present in the thought of many influential figures in the history of theology, especially in the Western Church.

However, our Catholic and Protestant tradition does, thankfully, allow for a more positive theology of work. For example, there are the two creation accounts in the Book of Genesis; Paul's exhortation on the new creation in the Letter to the Romans; the unification prayer and work found in the Benedictine Rule; the impetus given to lay spirituality by Protestant and Catholic reforms; the Papal Encyclicals, especially Laborem Exercens by Pope John Paul II; and, attempts in the middle decades of the 20th century to affirm human dignity in the face of industrial blight and oppression.

In spite of all this, it is not easy to affirm the dignity of work and the worker when the characteristic form of work in an industrial society is symbolized by the assembly line. Repetitively carrying out a mechanical task gives faint image of the worker as a sharer in God's creative activity. It was much easier to promote the Christian vision of labour in a pre-industrial society when the dominant form of work was a craft, with the worker involved in the entire production process. The same is true of work in the service sector, including the hospitality industry.

New work structures, therefore, pose challenges, but also offer opportunities. To be efficient, the new workplace requires employees to take pride in their work and each other, and promoting such feelings can provide multiple benefits for any manager. It fosters loyalty toward the firm and one's fellow workers. At the same time, the experience of building solidarity vindicates a traditional Christian understanding of the dignity of the human person. For Wright, the starting point for a Christian perspective on the world of work is Teilbard's divinization of human activity (27). The Incarnation substantially strengthens that perception, showing that the tension and paradox in the human condition are part of our working lives.

According to the analysis of Svoboda, the book of Genesis tell us three important things about work (24). First, God works. Second, God works not because He has to, but because He wants to work. His work is not for His own sake but for others' sake, mankind's sake and our sake. God chooses to work because He chooses to share something of Himself with someone else.

Therefore, work is seen as being intimately associated with the act of self-giving — a self-giving for the benefit of others. Third, God seems to enjoy His work. God takes delight in the work process, pronouncing creation, the product of His labours, as "good" at the end of each day. In other words, work is good — even God works. Work is an act of self-giving directed toward the good of others. Work consists primarily of cultivating and care, in bringing forth new life. Work should basically be a joyful activity, even though it often entails fatigue and pain. Don't forget, though, that rest and leisure are good, too, and are, in their own way, integral to the work process.

Spirituality of Work for Hospitality Professionals

There are many qualities of life rooted in the example of Jesus, with three basic qualities specifically reflecting Jesus' life of hospitable service to others: responsiveness, competence and respect. Underlying Jesus' desire to serve those in needs were sensitivity, adaptability and willingness that are today basic building blocks for an apostolic spirituality of hospitality. Sensitivity to the situation at hand is essential if a hospitality professional's response is to be effective. Adaptability to the situation as it changes is also essential if their response is to be appropriate.

Willingness to be involved is essential if their response is to be consistent ultimately, the driving force behind this responsiveness is compassion, which is not the same as pity. The true core of compassion is the urgency to act. Compassion never merely observes; it initiates and interacts. In Jesus' work, compassion is second only to love.

On the other hand, when personal benefit becomes the primary goal of service in the hospitality industry, this compassion gives way to conceit. Competence shapes the overall effectiveness of our response. However sensitive, adaptable and willing that response maybe, its lasting effect must reflect competence. Service industries require a level of competence quite different from that in agricultural or manufacturing work.

The hospitality industry revolves around two separate realities: material variables and personal variables. Material variables differ among the various areas of the hospitality industry, but they generally include some common elements. First, there is a body of living knowledge, with new information replacing old on a regular basis. (I use the word "living" in the sense of growing and changing.) Second, there are natural or acquired skills that enable hospitality professionals to use their knowledge.

Third, there are the willingness, capacity and commitment to acquire new and refined skills to match developments within the field of knowledge now called hospitality, leisure or tourism studies. Finally, there are resources necessary for hospitality professionals to use skills with knowledge. Personal variables for hospitality professionals include the personalities, preferences and predicaments of those they serve.

Respect is characterized by a hospitality professional's recognition of each person's uniqueness. It is their affirmation of the dignity of each person, a dignity based on their creation as God's image and likeness, as well as their efforts to listen, communicate and interact through ways and means consistent with that uniqueness and dignity. Work in the hospitality industry brings professionals to encounters and interactions with many people. Respect reminds them that, regardless of what they have to do in the work of hospitality, the value of a human being can never be compromised.

The driving force behind respect is love. Christian spirituality should acknowledge the goodness of all that is human. Emotions, sexuality, temperament, personality and the prayer life should all enter into the Christian response of the whole person. Development and fulfillment of these truly human aspects should be incorporated into any authentic approach to the Christian spirituality of work in the hospitality industry.

Job Satisfaction in the Hospitality Industries

The "rational" parts of any organization put a high value on efficiency. All jobs and tasks should be designed to achieve the organization's goals as efficiently as possible. Jobs are specialized along two dimensions: horizontally (restricting the range of different tasks) and vertically (restricting the range of control and decision-making over job activities).

Job specialization is most obvious at the operating levels of organizations. However, highly specialized work can injure the well-being of workers and thus poses an important problem of justice for employers (for example, unskilled workers without freedom of choice). Such injustice can actually lead to decreased productivity.

On the other hand, there is a significant link between worker productivity and programmes that improve the quality of the work life of workers by giving greater involvement in, and control over, a variety of work tasks. Velasquez [26] points out that there are two determinants of job satisfaction:

1. Experienced Meaningfulness. The individual must perceive his or her work as worthwhile or important by some system of values he or she accepts.
2. Knowledge of Results. The worker must be able to determine, on some regular basis, whether or not the outcomes of his or her work are satisfactory.

To influence these determinants, jobs must be expanded along five dimensions:

1. Skill Variety. The degree to which a job requires the worker to perform activities that challenge his or her skills and abilities.

2. Task Identity. The degree to which the job requires completing a whole and identifiable piece of work – doing a job from beginning to end with a visible outcome.
3. Task Significance. The degree to which a job has a substantial and perceivable impact on the lives of other people, whether in the immediate organization or the world at large.
4. Autonomy. The degree to which the job gives the worker freedom, independence and discretion in scheduling work and determining how he or she will carry it out
5. Feedback. The degree to which a worker, in carrying out the work activities required by the job, gets information about the effectiveness of his or her efforts.

Traditionally, employees have relied on their supervisors for task guidance and good feelings—especially consideration and being treated like adults in order to perform their jobs both well and happily. Schneider and Bowen point out that when employees do not get this from their supervisors, they may turn to customers as "substitutes for leadership"

(20). Customers may be given a say in designing the organization that produces the goods and services. With services, it's often possible—and desirable—for customers to actually participate in production.

But the problem is that customers are not subject to the same kinds of fears, commitments and structures as employees, so they are very difficult to manage. To best capitalize on customer competencies, management must be able to:

1. Explicitly determine exactly what role/job they want their customer to perform.
2. Ensure that customers have what it takes to perform their jobs well through role clarity, ability and motivation.
3. Regularly appraise customer performance.

Service customers also often play the roles of directors, guides and even "order-givers" for employees. Customers play a dual leadership role by providing employees with guidance and providing them with positive feelings. There are two reasons. First, the employees' supervisors tend not to provide the guidance and good feelings they should. Second, customers of service firms feel they have a right to give orders. Employees like the positive feelings they receive from customers but do not like customers telling them what to do.

The lesson here is fairly simple but too often overlooked: Feedback is a critical part of job enrichment. Service firms need to think creatively about how to respond to these opposite reactions to customers' leadership behaviours. Customers can be trained to be a source of good feelings for employees and, at the same time, socialized to limit task direction over employees. Although management may have great "legitimate influence" over its employees, service work puts employees closer to their customers and, therefore, more involved with the kinds of rewards they receive and the distribution of those rewards. When a hospitality enterprise meets the various needs of employees through rewards—dispersed equitably and fairly—customers will experience superior service quality as well.

Mainardi has pointed out that hospitality professionals are dependent on contact with, and reception of, the public. Therefore, they presuppose some degree of availability toward the client, a considerable margin of initiative and a generally strong sense of personal responsibility. In fact, employees in the tourist transaction play an intermediary role between the industry's structure and its clientele. This role is particularly decisive in achieving the results desired by both sides.

All these situations are undoubtedly favourable to bearing witness to the spirit and practice of the Gospel before others. The hospitality professional's conduct is not only circumscribed by the material manifestations of the tourist industry. It must also be determined by psychological and ethical factors aimed at completely satisfying the tourist's wishes. Tourists want to be treated differently—better—than they are normally treated in their daily routines (e.g., with tradesmen, fellow workers, etc.). Furthermore, there is substantial evidence that customers like to interact directly with people in the tourism trade, not machines. This is also unavoidable, since providing tourist services without human assistance remains inconceivable.

This contact with the hurried or solitary traveller enables tourist professionals to reveal their own personalities—both as expert and human being—responding to each client's unique wishes via their own mental attitude, manner, initiative and creativity. The human person is truly the central and fundamental point of the tourism industry, with the economic aspect clearly secondary. Simon used the concept of satisficing behaviour to accommodate the balancing act of achieving multiple objectives in human behaviour.

Normative economics fails to include some of the central problems of conflict and dynamics. Simon attacks the hypothesis that firms strive to maximize profits for three key reasons: (1) The theory leaves ambiguous whether it is short-run or long-run profit that is to be maximized, (2) The entrepreneur may obtain all kinds of "psychic income" from the firm apart from monetary rewards; and (3) the entrepreneur may simply want to earn a satisfactory return, not looking to maximize gains. Simon points out that "economic man" is a satisfying animal whose problem-solving is based on his or her search to meet certain aspiration levels, rather than a "maximizing animal" whose problem-solving involves finding the best alternatives in terms of specified criteria This is certainly true in the case of the hospitality professional who seeks job satisfaction rather than merely looking to maximize salary.

The true mark of hospitality professionalism is excellence on the technical level and fellowship toward the client on the moral level. Such a global commitment involves a wide range of material services and mental attitudes in welcoming, guiding and assisting the tourist It also opens up more far-reaching horizons to practice Christian witness in so many privileged circumstances—in the form of personal contacts, conversations, exchanges of view, good conduct, etc. Nevertheless, this world also brings a lot of "baggage" with it for most people in the tourist and similar industries. Such difficulties include stress, high anxiety, burn out, low social status, feeling like a "hired host," low pay, tensions between career and one's personal and family life, as well as high turnover and mobility.

In professional activity, a concrete and unmistakable sign of integrity is to observe professional ethics. In other words, professionals should conduct their business honestly—giving clients the right amount of service and goods proportionate to their requested price. Whether you're talking about a travel agency or a tour company, a hotel or a restaurant, personal service must focus on the needs of the beneficiary of hospitality—i.e., the client Specifically, the 10 dimensions of service quality are: reliability, responsiveness, competence, access, courtesy, communication, credibility, security, understanding/knowing the customer, and tangibles that include the physical evidence of the service.

Generally speaking, hospitality clients are not equipped with the controls and consumer protections many other customers enjoy when they purchase industrial products. With the exception of large-scale fraud, it is, in fact, very difficult for clients to contest the quality of tourist goods or services purchased. In the majority of cases, the tourist client is thus put in an inferior position. That's why it's all too easy for hospitality professionals to "swindle" and behave in unjust and dishonest ways. This is a recurrent risk faced even by the well-intentioned, and one that can only be dispelled if the will to bear witness is cultivated systematically in the depths of the individual conscience.

Regard toward the client's "person" can—and should—be demonstrated by imbuing him or her with a sense of psychological and physical well-being, and by being willing to serve. Customers should also benefit from: material protection of their person and possessions, the constant good functioning of the tourism facilities, professional correctness and an effort by service providers to achieve maximum standards of hygiene (in food and environment). Modern managerial conduct should also aim to overcome the "coldness" and lack of intimacy typical of bureaucratic organizations. What's more, the influence exerted by hospitality managers and their staff may play a significant role in "educating" clients in the use of tourism, whether aimed at recreation or any creative endeavor. In the words of Paul VI, we should strive to "humanize and spiritualize tourism."

The spirituality of work for hospitality professionals needs to be considered in relation to the general concept of job satisfaction. Using Simon's concept of satisfying behaviour, hospitality work needs to be seen simultaneously in all its dimensions: economic, human, professional, moral, cultural and spiritual. Because of the interpersonal nature of their work, hospitality workers need to consider the guests they serve. In other words, hospitality is a single phenomenon that simultaneously involves three components—employers, employees and guests—in different and interacting ways.

Welcoming strangers as our brothers and sisters, understanding that they need us, and always regarding them as worthy of our help are concepts that should fascinate and encourage those in the hospitality field. This approach to service lightens the cares and overcomes the thousand difficulties that can intervene when you're coming into constant contact with strangers. It also adds greatly to job satisfaction. Unfortunately, strangers can often be hostile to the host's principles of contact, even when they're at their best. In these cases, the inspiration of the Gospel will help overcome any embarrassing situation and even educate the guest.

The hospitality professional's response to the Gospel call enhances, uplifts and augments the act of being hospitable and of receiving tourists as guests. It is no longer a job, but a vocation from God. Furthermore, the search for spiritual peace and authenticity comes in the reciprocal interplay of influences, intentions and actions between the hospitality professional and the guest. It emphasizes the privileged position given to those who are professionally engaged in providing hospitality. The Christian hospitality professionals are called to perform their duties scrupulously and promptly in each circumstance and in each relation. In this way, others may derive satisfaction from them, and receive the beneficial influences wished for by the Christian call to be a loving person.

All work understood in this fashion is worthy of the reward promised by Christ at the final judgment, when the just will receive their eternal job satisfaction based on how they served those in need.

2

Customer Value and Service Orientation

INTRODUCTION

Understanding the business begins with a clear understanding of customer value. Providing a superior customer value requires an understanding of service orientation. Against this backdrop, the rest proceeds to follow the logic that sound decisions and actions cannot be made and performed without a solid understanding of the customer.

You cannot claim to be customer focused if you don't have the appropriate information on the customer. What kinds of customer data are important and why? How do we collect, interpret, and use this data? Where are the opportunities for gathering customer information? Information on all customer preferences, attitudes, and activities associated with the acquisition and use of the product provides a deeper understanding of the customer. This part develops the various methods and approaches to ensuring that the firm is adequately prepared to make customer-focused decisions.

Customer information should drive the design and delivery of customer value. What is involved in conceiving and designing a customer-focused product offering or service delivery? How would a firm go about tracking whether it is maximizing the returns from its value-creating assets? In this part are about effective and efficient value creation and delivery.

Who are the right customers and how can the firm ensure their loyalty to the firm and its products? This part covers topics such as service quality and guaranteeing quality service. When the product fails the customer, what does the firm need to do to recover from that failure in the context of customer service? What must firms do to proactively manage customer defections?

How does the firm create and maintain a customer-focused culture—a culture that is so focused on the customer that all decisions and actions of all personnel and systems in place create superior value for the customer at a reasonable profit? This final part provides the framework to analyze and manage the firm's value systems to be customer focused.

The principal concepts can be stated as a truism: Businesses cannot succeed in the long term unless they are focused on its customers so as to provide them with superior service. This is how firms attain and maintain a competitive advantage and therefore provide superior customer value at sustainable profits. Thus, the two fundamental and closely related concepts evident here are "customer focus" and "service orientation." After reading this book, you will be able to engage yourself and the firm in a service-oriented mode of designing and delivering customer-focused value to maintain profitable relationships with the right customers. You will appreciate what is required to sustain a competitive advantage for sustainable profits by:

- Adopting a customer-focused and service-oriented frame of mind
- Understanding the business by understanding customer value
- Capitalizing on the opportunities and use of customer information
- Designing and delivering profitable customer value
- Focusing on the right customer and managing that relationship
- Establishing a customer-focused and service-oriented culture in the firm

Customer-focused firms are the product of customer-focused employees and processes. Customer-focused employees are the responsibility of the executives of the firm. As an executive, you will find that when you stop and think of the ideas and concepts, you will have begun to engage in the intellectual exercise leading to a customer-focused and service-oriented frame of mind. You will be able to specify what the firm should actually be doing to be customer focused.

CUSTOMER VALUE

Many firms focus on the product rather than on the customer. When the focus is on the customer, the business is defined in terms of customer value, not in terms of product. The product is viewed as a customer solution and experience. That is, for any firm, the most fundamental definition of its business.

Try this one. What business is Amazon in? That you can buy just about anything on Amazon may not be too much of an exaggeration. The company abandoned or at least cut back on its strategy of buying up companies, as it did with Drugstore.com in 1999. It now handles retail for such established brands as Toys 'R' Us, Target, and Circuit City. Amazon shocked everyone in early 2002, when they announced their first operations profit of $59 million and a net profit of $5 million in the previous quarter. What value does Amazon provide its customer?

Customers don't buy products. They buy solutions. If firms are focused on the customer, they ought to see themselves in the role of providing solutions, not products. The information technology sector has popularized the term "solutions providers, " with labels such as application service providers (ASPs, as they are called) or technology solutions providers. These labels may be appropriate at the very general level and allow people to gloss over and take for granted the real meaning of the term *solutions*. The label has no real meaning as a concept unless it can be translated into customer value terms. Customers buy value in the solutions. Thus, customer value defines the primary purpose of any business.

This presents an approach to conducting a critical analysis of this fundamental question of "defining the business of a firm." In doing so, it defines "customer value" and redefines "products" in the customer-focused perspective. Finally, this briefly indicates the fruits of a customer-focused organization providing superior customer value.

Management guru Peter Drucker said in his 1954 book, *The Practice of Management*, "to know what a business is we have to start with its purpose." He goes on to say: "There is only one valid definition of business purpose: *to create a customer*." Drucker reiterates this concept in a number of different ways, always emphasizing that "it is the customer who determines what a business is." It is not important what the business thinks it is producing.

The customer determines the value of what the business produces based on what the customer thinks he or she is buying. Such a perspective places the final result in focus—what the product *does* for the customer. Thus, the purpose of a business is what it creates for the customer. The first and foremost question for any firm to ask is, what business are we in? How many firms diligently confront this question? And, when they do encounter this question, whose perspective do they take?

Taking the customer's perspective to answer this fundamental question forces a number of thought processes that benefit the firm in different ways. In fact, businesses will find that approaching the question of *what business are we in?* in so fundamental a manner not only allows the firm to understand its existing customers, but will also help open up new market potential. It forces the analysis of value-creating assets, including the firm's skills and knowledge sets. The question also opens up the analysis of who the competition is. When firms strive to beat rivals, they typically end up competing within the confines of existing business.

Firms sometimes do not realize that they compete with firms in other industries. They are able to see this if they articulate their business from the customer's perspective. When customers consider their options in meeting a need, they don't limit themselves to one industry. Without realizing it as such, their solutions may involve different industries. Firms are forced to redefine their competitive landscape when they take the customer's perspective because they will find themselves competing outside their well-defined spaces. Kim and Mauborgne call it competing in a "market space.

They urge firms to expand their view of their business by looking "across substitute industries, across strategic groups, across buyer groups, across complementary product and service offerings, across the functional-emotional orientation of an industry and even across time." They argue this point with examples of how Home Depot cultivated the do-it-yourself market from homeowners using contractors, how Intuit saw that people managing personal finances using a pencil and paper calculation actually competed with their software, how overnight package delivery firms FedEx and UPS competed with telephones and fax machines, and how Southwest Airlines competed with driving. This argument illustrates the definition of a business from the perspective of the customer. Not only does it underscore the value that the customer places on what the firm delivers, but it also reveals that the customer's perspective redefines the business.

Well-known Harvard scholar Ted Levitt expanded on Drucker's thesis of defining a business from a customer's perspective when he popularized the concept "marketing myopia, " where firms and entire industries (such as buggy-whip makers) could perish when inwardly focused. He used the example of railroads as an industry that suffered from marketing myopia because it did not see itself in the business of transportation, but rather in the railroad business. Contrast this with a firm like the Williams Companies, one of the world's largest pipeline builders. Until a few years ago, it built steel pipes to move oil and natural gas. Today, it also builds fiber-optic pipes for the big cable companies. Clearly, Williams did not see itself as being in the oil and gas business, but as being in the business of serving big companies that needed to move material (or data) through pipes. Would Williams have seen this opportunity if it had been focused on competing within the oil and gas industry?

To expand your opportunities, you need to look beyond the product horizon and into the customer's space. For example, if a family was looking for something to do on a Saturday, consider their options: have some friends over for dinner, go out for dinner, go to a nearby mall, go to the movies, go to a play or a show, go bowling, go to a miniature golf course, go for a drive to the lake or the beach—and many other options. Now, look at these options in terms of all of the different industries that are competing with each other. If you were a firm in any one of these industries, you could be defining your business the same way as any of the other industries, depending on who your typical customer is. The customer's perspective broadens your own view of your product.

Taking the customer's perspective helps firms identity what they are about—their mission and their values. They are better able to understand their strengths and sources of competitive advantage. Firms are better positioned and more effective in allocating resources and efforts, both strategically and operationally. They are better situated to understand what would be considered superior customer value.

Products as Solutions

Where do you even begin when you want to define your business? Let us consider the basics. What *do* businesses sell, at the most general level? In what terms will your response be made? Do you see services and goods as solutions to a customer problem—a need to be met? Customer needs are problems searching for solutions and firms are providers of solutions to customer problems. When seen this way, firms draw focus away from products and orient themselves to the customer with the sole purpose of delivering solutions to problems. The business is defined in terms of customer solutions. Firms suffering from a product focus define their product by its capabilities in terms of product features and promptly lose sight of the customer. The solutions-to-problems approach emphasizes the customer rather than the product. It emphasizes product benefits rather than product features.

Firms must align processes, people, and their entire culture to serving the customer rather than on making and selling products. In customer-focused firms, processes are designed with customers in mind. The output of the processes, the product, is defined by the customer need it serves. In serving the customer, firms offer a combination of benefits or values. Are all products, therefore, a service to the customer? In a sense, yes! The solution represents the value that the firm is providing customers by serving their needs.

Firms' activities produce solutions as value bundles that we call products. All products involve a mix of value producing components—tangibles and intangibles—in value bundles. The proportion of tangibles and intangibles in the entity that the customer takes title to prompts the artificial distinction between services and products. This unfortunate dichotomy detracts from the necessary customer focus in the conception of the product. Regardless of whether the total product is predominantly a packaged good or a service, in a business-to-business (B2B) or business-to-consumers (B2C) context, all solutions to customer problems can be seen as bundles of benefits or value bundles designed to deliver value by meeting customer problems or needs. This book adopts the approach that all products are a mix of physical goods and services in some proportion.

Some solutions employ more tangibles (physical goods) than intangibles (services) in meeting customer needs, while others may provide an intangible (service) involving physical objects. The important question is, what is that total solution from the customer's perspective? It is more important to understand what the value bundle *does* for the customer than what the bundle *is*. To identify the value bundle, one needs to identify and understand the customer.

THE VALUE CREATION AND DELIVERY PROCESS

As, the execution of the product concept as the delivery of the product involves a process, a sequence of activities. Therefore, designing the product must necessarily include a design of the delivery process. Lynn Shostack proposed a technique called "blueprinting" to detail the process design in the delivery of services. The service blueprint is a map or flowchart as a visual representation of the process of service delivery.

Essentially, the blueprint design is diagramed in three steps. In the first step, all types of customer interactions with the firm are listed. Next, these interactions are arranged in sequence of occurrence. In the final step, processes within the firm that are required to create and provide each customer interaction are mapped. How and what information, materials, facilities and equipment, and people are processed must be included in the service blueprint.

The customer-focused blueprint is one that is designed with the customer in mind. With the activities in the customer's consumption cycle in mind, processes within the firm need to be designed in such a way that the desired value added in the solution is reflected at each and every encounter with the customer. Commerce Bancorp, for example, encourages its employees to make suggestions in streamlining the service delivery process. Commerce Bancorp employees receive a fifty-dollar reward for finding something about a process that does not contribute to customer value and instead is an impediment to serving the customer; the bank immediately adjusts its operations.

Even as a simple representation of the value creation and delivery process, the service blueprint has a variety of important strategic, analytical, and diagnostic uses. In designing the delivery of the product, it can be used to determine the uniqueness of the service process. When compared with competitive blueprints, where and at which points in the process the firm derives its competitive advantage and superiority in customer value become evident.

Thus, the service blueprint can be used in a strategic analysis of the differentiating features and benefits of the service delivered by the firm. Only with such comparative analysis of the service blueprint is it possible to ensure that the value creation and delivery processes are commensurate with the superior customer value planned in the product concept and operations design.

The service blueprint has two major dimensions that characterize the nature and scope of the service delivery process: complexity and divergence. The complexity dimension reflects the number of steps or activities in the process. A highly complex service process has a great variety of activities during the series of customer interactions. Some of these activities occur in the front stage and some in the back stage, away from the customer's view.

A so-called line of visibility determines what the customer sees or does not see. The customer-focused firm will need to examine everything that the customer sees and experiences to determine whether the service delivery at the service encounter is contributing to or detracting from customer value.

The divergence dimension reflects the degree of flexibility at each customer interaction. The greater the divergence, the greater the customization built into the service—the greater the number of options the customer is given to choose from at each interaction. Therefore, supplementary product benefits such as customization must be mapped into the service delivery process.

Complexity and divergence decisions will determine the position of the firm's offering compared to competitive offerings. Competitive blueprints can be compared to determine how competitive value bundles differ from each other. It becomes clear that the positioning of each competitive offering is reflected in the service blueprints.

The patient experience is very carefully orchestrated to support the entire concept of the "Shouldice Method." The surgical procedure itself is probably the least sophisticated element of the whole process. The recovery process is more important than the surgery. Every step in the blueprint is designed for a speedy recovery and an overall "enjoyable" experience—despite the anxiety and pain of the surgery. The method is known for a very low recurrence rate and high customer satisfaction. The hospital even has patient reunion parties each year that are sometimes attended by as many as a thousand former patients.

For this service, its critical steps are not in the surgical procedure but in in the recovery process and the total customer experience. All customer interactions depicted in the blueprint are not of equal importance in terms of criticality toward customer value—some are more important to the customer than others. It is imperative that the firm employ its knowledge of customer expectations so that the critical interactions are highlighted for priority when allocating resources of the firm.

This is the primary application of the blueprint technique. Jan Carlson, CEO of the SAS airline, popularized the notion of the "moment of truth" in services.

While each customer interaction is a moment of truth, those product features and customer encounters with the firm that are considered critical to the satisfaction of the customer are considered *critical incidents.* The critical incident technique has been applied in the managing of services to understand what can make or break the customer's experience. The method was initially developed for the U.S. Air Force in simulations to help in cockpit design and pilot training.

A simple question to the customer soliciting a verbal description ofmct is stocked and well displayed and that the floor salespeople are presenting the product to the customer in the way Handspring had instructed them to do. Microsoft hands out a free Casio pocketPC to every sales rep who completes its training. These examples show an awareness that customer interactions at these intermediaries are failpoints and need to be monitored.

Critical incidents help in assigning the appropriate level of resources within the firm. Thus, the service blueprint is useful from a quality control perspective. Customer evaluations of a firm's service can be linked to specific customer encounters in the blueprints and all processes directly affecting or affected by the critical incidents must be monitored for quality. Customer-focused quality control efforts can be focused on critical variables that can be controlled. Service recovery procedures must be designed into the process at these points.

Interactive technologies provided by the information age revolution are now an integral part of the design of the value creation and delivery process. These technologies work through the three primary productive components of customer value—the people, the infrastructure in facilities and equipment, and processes and systems of value creation and delivery. Consider all the ways in which the customer can interact with a firm. Each touch-point can be made by the converging technologies of today. For example, in some interactions the location of either buyer or seller becomes irrelevant.

Customers can interact by wireless or wired means, which can be by voice, video, or text, initiated by either party; they are constantly getting cheaper and better in features and functionality. The basic difficulty with any of this newer interactive technology is that the objective and role of the technology can be lost sight of and the technology itself become the focus. The final measure is whether the technology is contributing toward sustainable profits for the firm by improving customer value.

The benefits of interactive technology come in the form of efficiency and efficacy. Efficiency is reflected in increasing productivity and efficacy is reflected in improved customer value. Both of these outcomes contribute to the bottom line of the firm. For a firm competing on service, interactive technology is critical to sustain profits because of what it can do to customer value.

Maximize the return from interactive technologies by deploying it at the critical points; prioritized by its customer value-creating power. For example, a common source of dissatisfaction and irritation to the customer is the length of waiting time before being served. Any point in the process where there is likely to be a wait is a potential critical incident requiring the firm's express attention. If there are interactive technologies that can be used to effectively manage the customer in these situations, customer value is not threatened.

The Problem of Waiting Time

All the service components in the total product, being susceptible to the inherent characteristic of being produced and consumed in real time, force customers to the experience of "wait." As, demand and supply need to be matched as closely as possible. To avoid idle capacity, services adopt the queuing (and scheduling) approach to processing customers, resulting in a certain amount of wait before the process begins. In multi-stage processes, which many services are, in-process waits are common as well. The problem of course is that no one wants to wait.

Customers will wait for a certain amount of time that is reasonable to them as per their expectations. What is reasonable is a very subjective judgment, of course—one that requires analysis of the factors that determine the perception of waits.

Maister's work on the psychological cause and effects of wait suggests a way to reduce the negative consequences where wait is a given.

- Preprocess waits feel longer than in-process waits. Allow the customer to begin the process by completing the first step in the value delivery process.
- Unoccupied waits feel longer. Keep the customer in wait occupied with activities, preferably related to the product or service.

- Uncertain waits feel longer. Keep the customer informed about how long the expected wait is to likely to be.
- Unexplained waits feel longer. Keep the customer informed about why they are having to wait.
- Inequitable waits feel longer. Serve customer based on priority, determined by what is considered just in the ambient society.
- Value of the service. Ensure that the customer value you are providing is clearly superior to any alternative.

The most important common thread through all of these suggestions is that they all have to do with managing the customer perceptions. The firm is better placed if the customer perceptions can be influenced favourably by managing customer role and expectations in the value creation and delivery.

The Customer-focused Firm

To varying degrees, customers play a role in the production of products and not just in the consumption. Firms that realize this have paid serious attention to how the customer fits in the organization. In services, the role of the customer is abundantly evident. Customers engage in a coproduction role. In services or in the service component of the product, customers are coproducers in self-service configurations.

All services as we saw earlier involve some kind of customer participation, as in the case of providing required information to the tax preparer, for example. Even when placing the order with the provider, the customer is essentially contributing to the production of the product by providing input into product specifications.

When the customer is interacting with the firm and this interaction has some relevance to the production of the product, by definition we have the customer engaging in coproducing the product. Service firms instinctively manage the role of the customers in their participation in the service.

Restaurants have menus, professors have syllabi, airlines have their method of emplaning passengers according to a certain priority, etc. Sometimes managing customer roles may be in the form of a complementary service. For example, Universal is experimenting with a calming zone adjunct to its roller-coaster rides, for people who need help with coaster-phobia before they get on the ride.

UPS and other package delivery firms instinctively accommodate special customer requests as to where their packages should be deposited if the customer is not at the location of delivery. It is a matter of perspective. If we take the notion of value creation a step further, we could argue that even in the case of packaged goods, the value hasn't really been created to the customer until the customer actually begins to use the product.

Value creation and value consumption are both inextricably interwoven into a continuous and overlapping set of activities. This is an important issue in a service orientation. In the case of services, customer interaction is a given. And the firm must include the customer in the design of its operations.

The customer-focused firm by always keeping the customer in central view manages the role of the customer in the value creation and the value consumption activities. For example, providing excellent product assembly instructions improves the value created for the customer in an "easy to assemble yourself" product.

Conversely, even with a well-engineered product, poor instructions reduce customer value. Recent product innovation studies have shown that some firms are equipping customers with the tools to design and develop their own products, ranging from minor modifications to major new innovations. PTC (formerly Parametric Technology) is a world leader in computer-assisted-design (CAD) technology, whose software solutions bring suppliers and customers together so that a client can use the software during product development to virtually interface with upstream and downstream players.

Ultimately, anything that the firm can do to manage the customer's role in the value creation as well as value consumption process is an imperative for the customer-focused firm. As mentioned earlier, Procter & Gamble is recruiting families to allow a team of their ethnographer-filmmakers to observe their daily routines to get a better sense for how their customers use household products.

The actual use situation says a lot about how a product should be designed. It would also be a way to learn how the customers should be instructed in the appropriate use of the product. How does a firm take a systematic approach to managing the customer? First, the firm identifies all the activities that the customer enacts in the value creation as well as value consumption blueprint.

Next, the firm scripts the role for the customer at each activity. Firms then have to determine how best to communicate and educate the customer in playing the appropriate role. Customers' performance of their roles will depend on their ability and inclination to perform those roles. The consumer's ability will depend on consumption skills that the customer's past experience may have provided.

The customer's inclination will depend on the personal characteristics of the customer. Familiarity with the service and service provider could affect the ability and the inclination of the customer in the role performance. In the case of services and the service components of a product, customer role is managed by the service provider. The service provider's production skills and motivation could affect the way in which the service provider manages the customer's role.

The service provider's familiarity with the segment and the specific customer will influence the service provider's skills and motivation in managing the customer's role performance. The service provider's production skills are reflected in its operations and customer interaction skills. The personal characteristics of the service provider can affect the service provider's motivation. When designing the service delivery process, it is important that the firm incorporate these factors on the customer's role performance.

Staging the Customer Interaction

The essence of customer-focused design of the value delivery process is in the design of the customer interactions that make up the blueprint. Customer interactions have gone by various names in research on services—service encounters and moments of truth, for example. Designing the customer interaction requires analysis and decisions regarding three of the structural dimensions of the value delivery process: the process itself, the participants, and the physical facilities and equipment. Customer roles have to be defined so that customer participation can be designed into the delivery process as appropriate.

One useful framework that has utility in managing customer interactions is to view service encounters metaphorically as "drama." When firms and customers interact, firms try to put on the best performance—like theater. The firm's *actors* perform their roles for the *audience,* the customer. In any service, there are actors and audiences involved in producing *performances* in a *setting*.

For example, restaurant customers are audiences with hosts and waitstaff as actors in the physical setting of the restaurant. Just as in theatrical production, there is a stage (the dining area) and a backstage (the kitchen); there are acts (welcome and seating, appetizers, main course, and dessert), scripts (menu and specials), props (menu card and table setting), and costumes.

Each element is carefully choreographed to produce the intended impression on the audience. Any service provider can examine each of these elements and determine the exact impression that would be appropriate for each customer segment. The "drive-thru" or take-out type of fast-food restaurant confronts different impression management challenges compared to the sit-down type of restaurant.

Different types of services would require a different combination of these theatrical elements for the desired impression. Services rendered at arm's length over the telephone or by mail, such as in investment brokerage services or credit card services, would see these elements differently from the face-to-face setting of hotels or airlines.

Internet "clicks" retailers would find a different set of issues compared to the "bricks" retailers. Hybrid retailers have to approach the issues differently for the two different settings. In some cases, the performance is shared by a number of customers, as in a restaurant or a hotel or airline where customers share many aspects of the firm's productive factors—employees, facilities, and equipment.

The setting dictates a shared product, and some aspects of the setting are visible (onstage) to the customer and some are invisible (backstage).

Performers or actors (frontline employees) utilize scripts, costumes, and props in their performances. Every feature or theatrical element is carefully choreographed for the intended impression.

Therefore, just as in theater, managers can focus on impression management for customer-focused business activities. World-class service firms like Disney employ a service orientation profile (personality and skills) in their hiring; they call their employees the cast and carefully train them in both operations and customer interaction skills. Disney's "guests" are treated in a customer-focused manner evident in the culture, in the way the cast is empowered and motivated to provide customer-focused performances.

What is the type of setting where the customer value is delivered? There could be no interaction necessary with the value provider at certain phases in the consumption cycle, and there could be phases of physical, face-to-face interaction, or electronics-mediated interactions. At each interaction, the value provider must determine the line of visibility between onstage and backstage, what is or should be visible to the customer.

What is the process and duration of the various steps in the interaction, and what kinds of orientation must there be for the participants? What is the customer role in each setting, and are there other customers in shared experience?

Ultimately, all of the theatrical elements need to be carefully directed and choreographed to provide the appropriate impression. *Servicescape* is a term that refers to the immediate physical and social environments containing a service experience, transaction, or event.

The servicescape plays a number of different roles such as packaging the value bundle, facilitating the value delivery activities, socializing the employee and the customer, and differentiating the product. Managers must understand which servicescape elements can be controlled for the desired behaviours from both employees and customers.

The process of delivering the product must be analyzed, using techniques such as blueprinting and choreographing impressions on the customer. What is the role of each process in the value creation and delivery as seen by a firm with a customer focus? What should the structure and content of the process include by way of design?

What are the critical points in the process for its meeting customer needs and preferences? The firm should have in place metrics and customer-determined benchmarks that will trigger recovery procedures, anticipating that the firm will sometimes fail the customer. A boutique hotel set in the heart of downtown will win the race for new and repeat business with the help of customer-relationship management. Beating the competition is not an easy task in the highly competitive world. The Hotel Customer service always has been king at the room property known for unique amenities.

Using the theatrical metaphor, any impression that the actor, the audience, the setting, or the performance imparts must be examined and managed by the firm. The focus is on the effect each customer interaction or service encounter has on customer value from the customer's point of view. Customer-focused firms design the value creation and delivery process with the customer in mind.

GUARANTEEING CUSTOMER VALUE

Maximizing customer equity requires maximizing customer satisfaction by providing superior customer value. Ensuring product quality as the key driver of customer satisfaction requires checking the links between the firm's assessment of customer expectations and its ability to translate that assessment into product concept, operations design, and execution.

The doorman greeted the guest as the taxi pulled up to the Windsor Court Hotel, a 324-room hotel in downtown New Orleans, one of 120 independent luxury hotels of Preferred Hotels and Resorts Worldwide. Later, the waiter at the restaurant in the hotel accommodated off-the-menu orders—but the waiters did not make eye-contact with the diners. The guest room did not have the current edition of the Yellow Pages. This guest was one of Richey International's hotel spies, who had just conducted the Preferred test for the hotel. He has determined based on his experience as a customer that this hotel had met 88.5 percent of the Preferred standards, passing the 80 percent minimum. Firms such as Preferred want an unbiased assessment of the quality of their product and hire independent quality assessment firms such as Richey International to do the benchmarking of its hotels.

Firms also want to hear from you directly if you are a heavy user of their product. For instance, if you have over 1 million miles on your Sky Miles frequent flier account, or you fly 100,000 miles, or 100 trip segments, or 20 transoceanic segments in a year, you are a most-valued "platinum member" of Delta Air Lines and may be called to dinner in a private dining room in a luxurious setting. Delta wants to know what you think about the quality of their service.

Customers, especially the most profitable and valuable ones, are being called on for their perceptions of quality of the product received. Deliver a quality product and you are likely to have satisfied and loyal customers. The logic is pretty straightforward, and yet most firms struggle with at least some of the links in the chain: What is quality from the customer's perspective and how can the firm ensure the design and delivery of that quality?

Beginning in the late 1980s and continuing into the early 1990s, there was a groundswell of attention and interest in quality, primarily as a result of falling competitiveness of U.S. firms in the wake of Japan's advances. Quality gurus like Deming, Juran, and Crosby preached the gospel of quality. The Total Quality Management (TQM) movement's cornerstone, the prestigious Baldrige award programme administered by the National Institute of Standards and Technology, was a coveted prize for a great deal of effort by companies large and small. *Business Week* ran a number of articles profiling such winners as L.L. Bean, FedEx, Xerox, Motorola, Disney, and others.

As established and emphasized throughout this book, an understanding of customer value is a fundamental element of customer focus and service orientation. This provides a model for delivering customer value by focusing on the quality of the product, as judged according to how it meets customer expectations. To maximize profitability, the firm must maximize the lifetime value of the customer.

A key driver of this goal is customer loyalty, which is dependent on customer satisfaction. To achieve customer loyalty, it is imperative that firms create and deliver a quality product—as defined by the customer. What does the customer evaluate in determining the quality of a product? And, what actions of the firm can be linked to that customer perception of quality?

Perhaps the most significant research on perceived quality in services was conducted by Parasuraman, Zeithaml, and Berry and sponsored by the Marketing Science Institute in Cambridge, Massachusetts. Their contribution was timely and thorough, and revealed a number of important facets of customer perceptions of service quality. These researchers defined service quality as the difference or gap between customer expectations and customer perceptions of service. Their systematic study of customer evaluations across a variety of services revealed that customers evaluate services along certain key dimensions grouped under the acronym RATER: the R eliability of the firm's products, the A ssurance customers feel that their needs and expectations will be met, the T angibles associated with the service, the E mpathy displayed by the firm, and the R esponsiveness of the firm to their specific and individual needs.

Further, they found that there were four principal factors that contributed to the difference between what customers expect and what the firm delivers:

- How accurate is the firm's understanding and interpretation of customer expectations?
- Is this understanding of customer expectations effectively translated into product design?
- What is the gap between what is envisioned and what is delivered?
- How good is the match between what is delivered and what is advertised?

Quality translates customer experience with the product to customer value. Quality of customer experience is framed with the costs of access to and use of the product. Customer value is what customers ultimately evaluate in making the decision on future patronage. Their loyalty to a solutions provider depends on their comparison of actual customer value with expected customer value. What determines how well a firm meets a customer's expected value?

THE PERCEIVED VALUE OF A SERVICE IN HOSPITALITY

Most Hospitality Operators use the term "Quality" somewhere in their advertising and promotion. What exactly does that mean? One would compile multiple responses, as Management tried to define "Quality". The same would be said for their Staff, and, just as importantly, the Guest. We all have different perspectives. Hospitality invites a Quality Experience, but, if expectations are not met, you have a disappointed Guest, reduced Revenue, unhappy employees and a deteriorating reputation.

So, what is the Value of Quality: the Concept, the Experience and Reward, and how does this relate to your Hospitality Business?Recent research has revealed that few leisure providers integrate marketing techniques into programming efforts and that "leisure service agencies have long attempted to serve diverse and, at times, non-responsive populations". A marketing perspective would suggest leisure and tourism providers analyze the needs and desires of their participants, in order to develop the most appropriate delivery methods. In doing so, leisure/tourism programmers may benefit by attracting more responsive and possibly more loyal participants.

Quality is a Process. There are Performance Standards created, communicated and implemented. The Standards are reviewed constantly to stress Continual Improvement. Success Stories are heralded. Problem Areas are immediately addressed. Steady "feed back" is required. This is not a one day exercise. Quality must become integral to your Business Performance.

Does your definition of Quality translate to the Guest's expectations? Hospitality Operations are boldly diverse. We present to the Consumer various locations, architecture, ambiance, price, amenity, and activity. When they make a reservation – book a room, a table, or a ticket – the Guest has an Expectation. Now, we must deliver and not create a disconnect, because we may be at cross purposes with our Guest and their concept of Quality.

How do we create a "common ground" to meet these expectations and avoid the false steps in fully serving our Guest? The Quality Process begins with recognized, reasonable Hospitality Performance Standards. All parties understand cleanliness. The environment you represent must be clean and not assault the five senses. We need to feel safe and secure. We require certain "creature comforts".

We look for our needs to be attended with some courtesy, accuracy, speed and pleasant attitude. Finally, we expect the facility to present an acceptable appearance / condition. These elements are how you will be judged by your Guest. They represent the Benchmarks for a memorable Quality experience or not. These Performance Standards are the foundation, and the Guest needs to know you are serious and sincere. Particularly for those Destinations which are Family oriented, recognize that the greatest influence on where the Family will stay, dine and recreate is the Mother, and she holds Quality Standards dearly.

The success of a Process needs to be measured – a Performance Evaluation. Where do you rate with these Hospitality Standards? Do you deliver, and, just as importantly, does your Staff? Your Quality message must be communicated daily. Your Staff must abide by your Message. Clear guidelines, need to be in place, practiced and assessed.

Attention to detail and meeting the Guest's needs are the Mantra. There are many means to evaluate your Performance: the personal relationship you have with your Guests; in-house mechanisms, like Comment Cards; Mystery Shop Services; Assessment Companies; and formal Guest Satisfaction Systems. They are all meaningful. Further, many leisure and tourism providers would benefit by obtaining a more consistent participant base as it has been shown that it is six times less expensive to plan marketing strategies for retaining consumers, than it is to attract new consumers.

In the field of marketing, the construct of perceived value has been identified as one of the most important measures for gaining competitive edge, and has been argued to be the most important indicator of repurchase intentions.

Yet, in regards to leisure and tourism services, repurchase intentions and consumer loyalty are often predicted solely by measures of consumer satisfaction, and/or service quality. Woodruff (1997) states, "if consumer satisfaction measurement is not backed up with in-depth learning about customer value and related problems that underlie their evaluations, it may not provide enough of the customer's voice to guide managers where to respond".

Further, just because a consumer is "satisfied" with a product/service, does not necessarily mean the product/service is a good value. It is quite possible a consumer who is very satisfied with a product or service, may consider it a poor value if the costs for obtaining it a re perceived to be too high. On the contrary, a moderately satisfied consumer may find a service to have good value, if they believe they receive good utility for the price paid.

Since perceived value has been found to be an important indicator of repurchase intentions it is believed leisure/tourism providers could benefit from refined measures of the construct. Valid and reliable measures of perceived value would allow for comparison of value between leisure/tourism programmes, and would allow individual leisure/tourism providers the ability to identify the dimensions of perceived value in which they perform well or poor.

While recent multidimensional scales have been created for measuring the perceived value of tangible products, a multi-dimensional scale for the measurement of perceived value of intangible products (services) does not exist. Thus, the purpose of the current study is to develop a multidimensional scale for the measurement of perceived value of a service.

Perceived value has been defined as "the consumer's overall assessment of the utility of a product based on perceptions of what is received and what is given". Within this definition, Zeithaml (1988) identified four diverse meanings of value:

(1) Value is low price,
(2) Value is whatever one wants in a product,
(3) Value is the quality that the consumer receives for the price paid, and
(4) Value is what the consumer gets for what they give. The majority of past research on perceived value has focused on the fourth definition.

A fundamental base for the conceptualization of perceived value of a service was developed by Zeithaml. Her research utilized focus groups and in-depth consumer interviews to explore the relationships between consumers' perceptions of price, quality and value. The focus groups were utilized to determine the salient attributes and variables related to perceived value, while the interviews were utilized to reveal the causal links among product attributes, quality and value. Open ended questions were then used to examine the information needed to make judgments about quality and value (i.e., advertising and packaging).

Results of her study showed that perceived quality leads to perceived value, which leads to purchase intentions. Both intrinsic (i.e., how the purchase makes you feel) and extrinsic attributes (i.e., reputation of the product/service), as well as price, were found to be positively related to perceived quality. Moderating variables of perceived value included perceived sacrifice (non-monetary price), extrinsic attributes and intrinsic attributes. Overall, Zeithaml reported quality, price (monetary and non-monetary), reputation of the product/service and how the product/service makes one feel (emotional response) were dimensions related to perceived value.

Similarly, the Profit of Impact Marketing Strategies (PIMS) study conceptualized value as the relationship between quality and price. They ascertained competitive success is obtained through "perceived relative value" of the total package of products and services that influence customer behaviour. Relative value, is the value received from one product/service, in comparison to similar offerings.

According to Bojanic: "the notion of relative perceived value results in three possible value positions: (1) offering comparable quality at a comparable price, (2) offering superior quality at a premium price, or (3) offering inferior quality at a discounted price." Perceived value may thus be altered if management changes what they are doing, a competitor changes what they are doing, or if consumer's desires or needs change.

More recently, Parasuraman and Grewal (2000) conceptualized perceived value as a dynamic construct consisting of four value types: acquisition value, transaction value, in-use value and redemption value. They define acquisition value as the benefits received for the monetary price given, and transaction value as the pleasure the consumer receives for getting a good deal. In-use value is the utility derived from utilization of the product/service, while redemption value is the residual benefit received at the time of trade-in or end of life (products) or termination (for services). Utilizing these definitions, the relevance of each of the four dimensions are different during varying times of the product/services life (i.e., acquisition and transaction value are most salient during purchase, while in-use value and redemption value are more pertinent after purchase).

While all of these theorized frameworks aid in the understanding of perceived value, they do not offer measures for collecting perceived value data. Perceived value is most commonly measured by using a self-reported, unidimensional measure asking respondents to rate the value they received for their purchase. The problem with a one-dimensional measures is that it assumes that consumers have a shared meaning of value. Zeithaml states, "quality and value are not well differentiated from each other and from similar constructs such as perceived worth and utility."

Thus, it has been argued that one-dimensional measures of perceived value lack validity. Another inherent problem is unidimensional measures result in the knowledge of how well one is rated for value, but give no specific direction on how to improve value.

It is believed that a formal measurement tool for the perceived value of a service, would allow comparisons similar to comparisons of service quality that are now available due to Parasuraman, Zeithaml and Berry's (1988) SERVQUAL scale and Cronin and Taylor's SERVPERF scale. With the use of reliable and valid multi-dimensional measures, leisure and tourism providers should be able to identify the dimensions in which they are succeeding and/ or failing in regards to both their own past measures and those of their competition.

Current efforts to measure perceived value have shown it is difficult to quantify perceived value. Kantamneni and Coulson focused on the development of a multi-dimensional measure of perceived value of a product. They utilized undergraduate business students to identify potential measurable dimensions of a product's perceived value. Results identified the distinct factors of societal value, experiential value, functional value and market value.

Societal value was termed to be the product's benefit/value to society. Experiential value was related to the senses: if the product feels, smells and looks good, while functional value was related to whether or not the product is reliable and safe. The final factor, market value, was the product's worth regarding price for value. Another multi-dimensional scale for the measurement of perceived value of a product was presented by Sweeney, Soutar and Johnson.

Utilizing exploratory factor analysis of 29 items generated from a literature review, the factors of quality, emotional response, price and social emerged as dimensions of perceived value of a product. Quality referred to how well the product was made, and emotional response to how a product made the consumer feel. Price was operationalized as whether or not the money paid for the product was reasonable, and social as the impression that the purchase of the product had on others.

While the aforementioned studies show promise for the measurement of perceived value of tangible products, there is need for a different scale to be developed for measuring the perceived value of a service. Past research has shown that scales developed for measuring a product's perceived value are difficult to use when measuring perceived value of a service. Further, the dimensions inherent in a service differ from those of a product. Lovelock argued that services differ from products in that they are intangible, perishable, variable and inseparable. Thus, multi-dimensional measures of a service must consider these properties.

Following the theoretical model conceptualized by Zeithaml, current conceptual frameworks, and the properties of a service, multiple dimensions of perceived value of a service can be identified. Most researchers agree that perceived value is a comparison of what a consumer "receives," with what the consumer "gives" for the attainment of a product or service. Perceived price is what a consumer gives up or sacrifices in order to obtain a product.

While some consumers may know the exact price of the service purchased, others may only remember (encode) that their purchase was expensive or inexpensive in relation to past purchases. Still others may not encode a price at all. Consumers also evaluate non-monetary costs in their determination of quality received for price paid. Non-monetary costs include such things as time, search costs, brand image and convenience. It is therefore a combination of both perceived monetary and non-monetary costs that equate to consumers' overall perceived sacrifice which, in turn, affects their perception of product or service value.

In regards to what a consumer "receives" past research has identified emotional response, or the joy received from purchase, and quality as dimensions of perceived value of a product/service. Further, the product/services reputation has been identified as an influence on consumer's perceived quality, and perceived value. Thus it could be argued that dimensions of what a consumer receives from the purchase of a service include: the emotional response to the service, quality received from the service, and the reputation of the service rendered. While the dimensions related to what is given, consist of monetary and non-monetary (behavioural) price.

Utilizing these dimensions, a hypothetical model of one of the roles that perceived value plays in the assessment of a service. It is suggested that the perceptions of service quality leads to the purchase and experience rendered by the service. This experience results in the perception of the value received from the service. It is further postulated that perceived value influences intention to reinvest in the service experience, and how positively or negatively individuals talk to others about their service experience.

This process then effects future assessments of the quality of a service. While it has been postulated that perceived value changes during different stages of a purchase, the proposed scale will only measure perceived value after completing a purchase. Thus the role that perceived value plays in the decision-making processes of the current conceptualization can only occur after service has been rendered.

Instrument Development

The operational definition of the construct of perceived value that was used to guide development of the scale was "the consumer's overall assessment of utility of a product based on perceptions of what is received and what is given. Further, perceived value was a priori conceptualized as a multi-dimensional construct, including the dimensions of quality, emotional response, monetary price, behavioural price, and reputation. Since reliability has consistently been found to be the most important dimension of quality for recreation and tourism managers, quality was defined as a consumer's judgment about a product or service's overall excellence or superiority.

Emotional response was defined as a descriptive judgment regarding the pleasure that a product or service gives the purchaser. The definition utilized for monetary price was the price of a service as encoded by the consumer. Behavioural price was defined as the price (non-monetary) of obtaining a service, which included the time and effort, used to search for the service. Finally, reputation was defined as the prestige or status of a product or service, as perceived by the purchaser, based on the image of the supplier.

The initial pool of items was accumulated from various scales developed by others relating to the construct of perceived value. Fifty-two items were acquired from a review of both scientific and popular literature.

In order to examine the scale's external validity and generalizeability it was administered to samples on two different seven-day Caribbean cruises, on board the same vessel. To ensure that cruise passengers taking back-to-back cruises were not sampled twice, the two samples were taken three weeks apart. One questionnaire was distributed to each cabin on board the vessel that was accommodated by a paying cruiser on the second to the last evening of the cruise. A letter was included with the questionnaire explaining that only one member in the room was to complete it, and that it was to be returned to their cabin steward.

The scale was operationalized by asking participants to rate each item on a scale from 1, definitely false, to 5 definitely true for their cruise on board the vessel. The survey also included single-item measures of overall perceived value and overall satisfaction. Overall perceived value was measured by asking respondents to rate the value received for their money when purchasing their cruise. The single item, 10-point scale, was anchored by extremely poor value and extremely good value.

A total of 591 questionnaires were distributed during the first cruise, and 592 during the second. Of these 394 (66.7%) and 398 (67.2%) completed questionnaires were returned from the first and second sample respectively.

Among passengers who participated, the average age was 51.6, the median household income was $75,000 to $99,999, 58.7% were female and, on average, respondents had taken 8.1 cruises in their lifetime.

Eight expert judges, from four different universities (all faculty members with Ph.D.'s and expertise in service marketing), were selected to refine and edit the initial 52 items for content validity. The judges were given the following operational definition of perceived value: the consumer's overall assessment of a product, or service's utility based on the perceptions of what is received and what is given. They were also given operational definitions for the proposed dimensions of quality, emotional response, perceived monetary price, behavioural price and reputation.

Consistent with Zaichowsky and Lee and Crompton (1992), each of the judges were first asked to rate each of the 52 items as either clearly representative, somewhat representative or not representative of the perceived value construct. The judges were also asked to assign each of the items as either "clearly representative" or "somewhat representative" to one of the five proposed dimensions of perceived value. They were further asked to identify if any items were representative of more than one dimension.

Following the same criteria utilized by Lee and Crompton, a series of rules were established in order to determine whether or not each item was to be discarded. An item was also discarded if less than five of the eight-member panel assigned it to the same dimension. This process resulted in 25 of the 52 items being eliminated.

The judges were further asked to: a) edit and improve the items to improve their clarity, readability and content, b) identify any items which they believed may be objectionable to respondents and c) offer any suggestions they felt might improve the study. This process resulted in the slight rewording of one item, and the removal of two others. The items removed were due to the judges' belief that the items were too similar to others in the scale. In both cases, the item with the weakest rating by the panel of judges was removed.

The resultant scale consisted of 25 items. Of these items, four were assigned to the dimension of "quality", six to "perceived monetary price", and five each to "emotional response", "behavioural price" and "reputation".

To examine dimensionality and internal reliability of the scale items, a convenience sample of 344 undergraduate students was used. Students were selected from two undergraduate tourism classes, and three undergraduate marketing classes. All students who attended the class periods on the date the questionnaire was administered were asked to complete a questionnaire. To enable a majority of the students to be familiar with the service context, respondents were asked to rate each of the 25 items as they related to lunch at a well-known fast food restaurant.

Respondents were further asked the last time that they had experienced a lunch at the restaurant. Only respondents who had been to the restaurant within the last month were included in the study. Of the respondents included in the study (n 278), approximately one half (51%) were female. Respondents had visited the restaurant 3.6 times on average in the last month.

In order to validate the a-priori assignment of the 25 items to their respective dimensions (as assigned by the expert panel), confirmatory factor analysis (CFA) was employed. The analyses were conducted with the use of the SAS System's proc calis procedures and followed guidelines suggested by Hatcher. Fit indices were chosen following recommendations by Hu and Bender. Fit indices included in the current investigation are the Bender comparative fit index, or CFI, Bender and Bonett, normed fit index, or NFI, and Joreskog and Sorbum root-meansquare residual, or RMSR.

Both the CFI and NFI may range in value from 1.0 to 0.0. According to Bender (1989), a fit index of 0.0 is associated with a "null" model (one specifying that all items are uncorrelated), while a fit index of 1.0 represents a "saturated" model (a model with zero degrees of freedom that perfectly reproduces the original covariance matrix). Values greater than 0.9 indicate a good fit of the data, while values higher than 0.95 indicate an excellent fit of the data. Conversely, An RMSR of less than .10 suggests a good fit of the data.

Since both the CFI and NFI are greater than 0.90, and the RMSR is less than .10, results suggest that the model is a good fit of the data. This finding further suggests, that each item is uniquely related to the factor to which it was assigned. A review of the resultant Wald and Lagrange tests did not suggest any conceptually sound changes to the model. Therefore, the proposed model was tentatively accepted, pending further tests to examine its reliability and validity.

The resultant standardized path coefficients are displayed. The t-tests investigating the null hypothesis that each of the coefficients are equal to zero were all significant, suggesting that all paths were assisting in the prediction of their assigned factors. These results provided evidence supporting the convergent validity of the indicators.

Composite reliability is analogous to coefficient alpha, and reflects the internal consistency of the indicators measuring each CFA factor. Results show that all five factors have composite reliability scores greater than 0.70. Utilizing the criteria set for the current analysis, this suggests that each of the factors are reliably measuring their respective constructs.

Combined, these findings support the reliability and internal validity of the hypothesized model. Since the model was found to be a good fit of the data and all paths were found to be significant, it is suggested that the proposed scale effectively measured the pretest subjects' perceived value. Thus, the scale was tentatively accepted, pending further examination and given the name SERV-PERVAL scale.

In order to further test the reliability of the 25 item SERV-PERVAL scale, separate confirmatory factor analyses (CFA) were conducted on the two samples of cruisers. The analyses were conducted utilizing the procedures described previously. Since the CFI and NFI fit indices for both samples are greater than 0.90 and the RMSR scores are less than .10, results suggest that both models are good fits of the data.

This finding also suggests, that each item is uniquely related to the factor to which it was assigned. Further, review of the resultant Wald and Lagrange tests did not suggest any conceptually sound changes. Therefore, the models were tentatively accepted, pending further tests to examine their reliability and validity.

The resultant standardized path coefficients are displayed. The t-tests investigating the null hypothesis that each of the coefficients were equal to zero were all significant, suggesting that all paths are assisting in the prediction of their assigned factors. These results provide evidence supporting the convergent validity of the indicators.

Results show that all five factors from both samples have reliability scores greater than 0.90. Utilizing the criteria set for the current analysis, this suggests that all of the factors are reliably measuring their respective constructs for both data sets. Combined, these findings support the reliability and validity of the hypothesized models.

Since the model was found to be a good fit of the data and all paths were found to be significant, it is suggested that the proposed scale effectively measured the proposed factors of perceived value for both samples. To further validate the scale, the perceived value factors were tested for criterion validity (sometimes called predictive validity).

According to Babbie, criterion validity is demonstrated if scores from the developed scale show expected relationships with one or more external variables that provide direct measure of the construct measured. It would be expected that each of the five factors would be positively related to an overall measure of perceived value. Thus, Pearson's correlations were employed to examine the relationships between each of the factors of perceived value, and overall perceived value. All five factors correlated positively and significantly to overall perceived value for both samples.

To further examine criterion validity, multiple regression with overall perceived value as the dependent variable, and the factors of perceived value as independent variables was employed. It would be expected that the five factors would explain a majority of the variance in perceived value. The regression analysis predicting perceived value was significant and explained 63.5% of the variance in the model.

Therefore results suggest that the proposed five factors of perceived value are related to the construct of perceived value (have criterion validity). Further validation of the scale was completed by testing the factors of perceived value for discriminant validity. Discriminant validity can be examined by comparing the inter-correlations of the constructs to the square root of the average variance extracted. The square root of the average variance for each of the factors is greater than any of the inter-correlations of the constructs. This finding suggests that the factors of perceived value have discriminant validity.

Results demonstrated a valid and reliable five dimensional scale for measuring perceived value. With the use of a panel of experts, the scale was judged to have content validity. The scale consisted of five interrelated, but unique dimensions: quality, emotional response, monetary price, behavioural price and reputation.

Utilizing CFA on the data from a pretest, and two separate samples, the generated items were found to saliently load uniquely on their predicted factors. Further, all of the resultant standardized path coefficients were found to significantly assist in the prediction of their assigned factors. This finding provided evidence of the convergent validity of the proposed indicators.

In order to confirm the reliability of the five factors, composite reliability scores for each of the factors were computed. All reliability scores for the three samples were deemed acceptable, suggesting that each of the factors were reliably measuring their respective constructs. Criterion validity was investigated by examining the correlations between perceived value and each of the factors. It was found that perceived value was positively and significantly related to each of the five factors. Finally, discriminant validity was investigated by comparing the inter-correlations of the constructs to the square root of the average variance for each of the factors. It was revealed that discriminant validity was found for each of the factors of perceived value.

While the current methods were thorough, the study was limited to a specific context. More research is necessary to determine how generalizeable the scale is across service sectors. Also, the future research should examine interrelationships between each of the factors. While the identified dimensions are unique, the causal paths between each dimension would assist in theoretical development of the construct of perceived value. It is believed that this knowledge would assist leisure and/or tourism management in better understanding the role each of the dimensions play in consumers' decision making processes. It is also recommended that future research examine the redundancy of items in the scale.

Redundant items could thus be removed to make the scale more succinct, and less taxing on respondents. Further, it is possible that potential dimensions of perceived value were not identified in the final instrument and the items included were not exhaustive of the five dimensions identified. Thus, it is suggested that future research examine the potential addition of both different factors and different items.

As suggested by Havitz, marketing literature, while seldom utilized in leisure research, is consistent with many of the important "perspectives within the leisure literature". It is thus postulated that the adaptation of tools in the field of marketing, for the fields of recreation and tourism may have far reaching benefits for leisure and tourism providers.

Since there are currently no multidimensional measures of perceived value of a service, and evaluations of perceived value of a service have been found to differ from evaluations of products, it is believed that the current conceptualization is important to leisure and tourism providers. Further, it has been suggested that current perceived value measures are difficult to quantify, though perceived value has been recognized as one of the most salient determinants of purchase intentions and repeat visitation. Thus it is hoped that, similar to the Paraṣuraman et al., the scale offered here will facilitate comparison of value within, and across services.

Since the seminal work of Chandler, the notion of a linkage between strategy and structure has become widely accepted-that is, if an organization is to implement its strategy most effectively, it needs the appropriate structure and support systems. At the same time, it needs the flexibility to exploit strategic options that arise from environmental changes. However, at least in the short run, a firm cannot easily change its organizational structure, and this may be a major impediment to its ability to change its strategy.

In an increasingly globally integrated world, firms attempting to become major players in their industry need to cope with and exploit environmental changes and adjust their organizational structure to create what Bartlett and Ghoshal (1989) termed "transnational" organizations. In other words, firms need to be able simultaneously to achieve local responsiveness, global efficiency. and the creation of knowledge (learning).

Chandler based his conclusions on a study of four of the largest corporations in the United States — General Motors, Dupont, Standard Oil, and Sears Roebuck — of which only Sears Roebuck was a service organization. Indeed, much of the literature on both the strategy of multinational firms and organizational structure has emanated from studies of large and powerful manufacturing firms, notwithstanding the ever-increasing importance of large multinational firms in service industries.

While some of these service industries have more in common with MNEs producing goods, others are quite different. The purpose of this chapter is to explore the effects of globalization on the organizational structures and systems of service firms in general, and professional service firms in particular. The paper postulates certain relationships between key success factors in multinational professional service firms and the structure and systems of these firms. The resulting propositions help provide the basis for a contingency theory of organizational structure and systems.

In the first section, some of the contributions to organization design theory and to organizational taxonomies are briefly surveyed. In the second section, some of the relevant theories on the organizational structure of multinational enterprises are reviewed. The third section discusses the globalization of services, while the fourth proposes a taxonomy of multinational service firms by the key factors contributing to their success, and it hypothesizes on the implications for organizational design.

This analysis is offered as preliminary to devising a contingency theory of organizations for service multinationals' particularly professional service multinationals. Organization theory is a positive theory focused on understanding organizations. On the basis of its findings, the organization focuses its design on normative solutions, that is, on the optimal means of creating an organization to achieve given goals and missions. Organization theory has moved a long way from the belief prevailing at the beginning of the century in immutable general laws of organization design or in the classical depiction of a "machine" organization.

March and Simon summarized the state of the art as follows: "Much of what we know or believe about organizations is distilled from common sense and from the practical experience of executives. The great bulk of this wisdom and lore has never been subjected to the rigorous scrutiny of scientific methods". Many assertions have since been tested to check whether or not they are supported by the facts. In addition, the importance of such factors as information, motivation, power, conflict. and innovation have been subjected to much scrutiny.

Moreover, different theses have also been tested in a variety of national and cultural contents. The organizational structure of the firm has been shown to be a reflection of its operating environment. Lawrence and Lorsch examined the firm's differentiation and integration characteristics in three industries. By differentiation, they meant orientations toward goals, time, and interpersonal relationships, as well as toward the degree of formality of the structure; by integration, they meant the degree of collaboration among departments working on common projects.

They demonstrated that these characteristics depend on the degree of turbulence in the environment: in a highly stable environment, organizations tend to be much more integrated, whereas in a turbulent environment, differentiation becomes more necessary. In Lawrence and Lorsch's model, complex tasks are performed through increased task specialization and subsequent coordination.

The different needs in different stages tn an organizational evolution have also been recognized. Child called attention to the ımportance of growth as a means of meeting the aspirations of the participating members of the organization. Kimberly argued for a dynamic perspective — researching the different stages in the life cycle of organizations — from creation to transformation to maturity and then decline. Pfeffer and Salancik distinguished between internally generated growth, to achieve individual or organizational goals, and growth based on biological systems limited by constraints and resources. They saw growth as a purposeful response to external constraints.

Mintzberg developed a taxonomy of organizational structures in different categories of organizations — the entrepreneurial, bureaucratic (machine and professional), divisional, adhocracy, and matrix. He suggested that, as organizations grow. they undergo structural changes – from the entrepreneurial to bureaucratic. divisional, and finally matrix structures. An organization can be bureaucratic without being centralized. This happens when professionals are needed because of the complexity of tasks, but the tasks themselves can be perfected through standardized operating programmes. The result is the professional bureaucracy structure.

Structural changes, therefore, correspond to both internal requirements and environmental demands. They arc contingent on quite a large number of factors. Organizations must change and adapt to internal political conditions, to external changes in the environment, and to technological changes and the opportunities they create. Integration mechanisms are needed to achieve coordination and these needs also depend on situational variables such as the competitive market structure or the stage of the life cycle. Although empirical research has failed to lend unequivocal support to the hypothesis that strategy follows structure, the implementation of any strategy must be based on a certain structure and on systems, including rewards.

Organizations are basically information-processing entities, and must match the demand for information processing with the capacity of the firm to do it. The information required depends on the environment, on technology, and on other variables such as size and complexity. Nowadays, firms can create significant competitive advantage on the basis of sophisticated use of information systems.

New information technologies are facilitating new forms of organizations and different structures, allowing greater integration across national borders. The increased power of personal computers, for example, is profoundly affecting both structures and systems. Computers have also allowed service firms to achieve both low-cost positions and customized services. All these new developments arc allowing new types of structures, such as the "infinitely flat" organization.

New telecommunications capabilities have eroded the boundaries between firms and their suppliers, as well as between geographic territories; and organizations can run borderless networks connected by electronic data interchange (EDI) and electronic mail with very little formal hierarchy. Moreover, in a knowledge-based society, the ability to tap all possible knowledge to achieve the task is crucial.

Much of the needed knowledge cannot be maintained in books on standard operating procedures, but is tapped by professionals communicating with each other. Professional workers must be willing to cooperate across tasks, professions, and geography to implement the strategy of the firm. This kind of cooperation has been achieved by professionals such as engineers and consultants. However, when a firm needs to trim its staff, self-preservation, fear, and frustration may lead individuals to be much less cooperative.

The organization of the future is sometimes portrayed in terms of project management and flat structures. This type of structure is perhaps more appropriate to expert organizations such as consulting firms or CNN (Cable News Network), with their prima-donna "star" performers, than to organizations that can standardize their operation to allow a machine bureaucracy as the optimal mode.

Indeed, companies such as CNN, EDL, and McKinsey & Co. are organized around many small teams carrying out shifting project assignments. They employ mainly bright, aggressive, though not arrogant, individuals who are unwilling to abide by too many arbitrary rules and standard operating procedures, but are happy to do all it takes to get the job done. These organizations focus on solutions to customers' problems, which they achieve at a much greater speed than the older, hierarchical bureaucracy.

Much in the way of theoretical contributions and empirical evidence is available on the relationships between structure and contextual factors. A survey of the organization theory literature certainly shows a diverse and sometimes inconsistent set of rules related to the organizational structure of firms.

In many cases, the number of variables to be taken into account is quite large. Duncan, for example, suggested a decision tree for structures based on three possible dimensions of the environment: complexity, change, and segmentation. Robbins discusses environmental hostility, positing that greater hostility necessitates greater centralization. Perrow discussed the impact of technology, while considered the impact of size.

If one combines all these variables with Mintzberg's (1979) basic configurations (simple, functional, divisional, matrix, machine bureaucracy, professional bureaucracy, ad hoc), a very large number of possible combinations emerge. Organization theory guides managers in choosing those configurations that allow fit between the organization and various parameters, such as environment, strategy, size, technology, and management style.

These variables may or may not be different in an international context. Bartlett and Ghoshal in particular stressed the role of overseas operations (as well as the development and diffusion of knowledge) in creating unique configurations for international operations.

According to these authors, firms operating in many countries can be based on self-sufficient national units and a decentralized system ("multinational"), on a globally scaled centralized system ("global"), on a hybrid design in which only sources of core competence are centralized and the rest of the operations are decentralized ("international"), or in the transnational mode, in which functions are dispersed across the globe but integrated to achieve competitive advantage, with knowledge being developed in different parts of the system and shared by all of its parts. The transnational design, according to Bartlett and Ghoshal, goes beyond the matrix configuration (for somewhat similar configurations. Integration can be achieved by several means, to be discussed later.

The Organizational Structure of the Multinational Enterprise

The increasing importance of various forms of multinational enterprises spreading their activities across national boundaries has not escaped the attention of academics. A large number of treatises have been written, attempting to explain, inter alia:

1. The reasons for internationalization;
2. The reasons for the various forms of internationalization, such as licensing, joint ventures, strategic alliances, or wholly owned subsidiaries;
3. Factors explaining the competitive advantage of a multinational firm vis-a-vis its domestic rivals;
4. The ways multinational enterprises compete with other similar enterprises on a global basis;
5. The organizational structure of the multinational enterprises;
6. The relationships between the multinational enterprise and home and host countries.

Almost all of these works have aimed at explaining the extracting and/or manufacturing multinational enterprises. Until the beginning of the 1980s, it was assumed that services were nontradable.

Thus, internationalization has been studied mainly by the Uppsala school and has been viewed as a process in which the enterprise gradually increases its international involvement. Three decades of research on multinational firms since the seminal work of Hymer (1976) have led to the conclusion that a multinational firm must have some advantage to offset the additional costs of running its operation, compared with domestic rivals.

Different authors have proposed different types of advantages, most of which are assumed to be intangible and firm-specific. In a producing enterprise, most of these advantages are based on scale, specific knowledge, or brand names. John Dunning attempted to combine many of the explanations in his eclectic theory, while Ozawa (1979) proposed some differences between U.S.- and Japanese-based multinationals. With time, research evolved from a total reliance on economic factors to a focus on internal issues of firms' operations. It was only toward the end of the 1980s that researchers began to relate to management issues.

Again, much of this research is not always applicable in attempting to explain why some service-providing firms have become multinational and others have not. Thus, if reputation and brand names are important firm-specific advantages, why was the Harvard Business School unable to exploit these advantages when it tried to build an executive development programme in Mt. Pelerin, Switzerland?

In the past decade or two, most studies have stressed the globalization of operations. Within multinational firms, globalization means the increased integration of resources and capabilities, and it can be operationalized by the extent of transfer of these resources within the multinational enterprise. The resources crossing borders can be capital, products, or knowledge. In a "transnational" firm, the flows are two-way — from subsidiaries to headquarters and from headquarters to subsidiaries — and they are associated with increasing information flows.

Managing international interdependencies is inherently more complex than managing activities within a single nation. Firms must organize to derive, combine, and transfer resources. Thus, international management theory can benefit from the knowledge to be derived not only from economic theory or strategic management analysis but from organization theory too.

Yet very little research has been done on organizational structure. A notable exception is the work of Stopford and Wells, who were the first to show that firms adopt different strategies in different stages of their internationalization; while Egelhoff (1988) stressed information processing. Organizational structure is no longer considered a sufficient explanation of multinational operations, and an understanding of managerial systems and control mechanisms is perceived to be a necessary additional line of inquiry.

Organizational structure is nevertheless a major constraint on the strategic flexibility of the MNE. Once a certain structure has been adopted and functions, authority, and operations have been distributed among different units in different countries, any reorganization is both time-consuming and costly. It also often works against a firm's "administrative heritage". Thus, a firm that has enjoyed a long tradition of a multidomestic strategy will have to contend with serious challenges if it is to move swiftly to a global strategy, as the history of firms such as Procter and Gamble or Philips amply demonstrates.

In a multinational enterprise, the key decisions relate to the means of coordination, degree of integration of activities from the home centre, and the degree to which authority is dispersed across countries. The giant European (and a few American) multinationals of the pre-World War II era developed a very decentralized structure in which each subsidiary was allowed a great deal of autonomy and maintained its own production, markcting, and even development facilities.

Headquarters appointed key personnel, approved major capital expenditures, and received dividends. Each subsidiary was allowed a high degree of differentiation as well as local adaptation. Given the state of the managerial arts and the relatively high costs of transportation and communications, this structure seems to have been the most appropriate for its time.

The U.S. multinationals in the period after World War II were generally much more integrated and centralized, and all new technology and products stemmed from the home country. The greatest strength of these firms was their ability to internalize the transfer of technology and of management skills across national boundaries. The subsidiaries did enjoy a high level of autonomy, but their competitive advantage derived mainly from transfers of technology, know-how, and brand equity from the centre.

Many of these firms, which Bartlett called "coordinated federations," lost ground in the 1970s and the 1980s to Japanese competitors that used "centralized hubs" — a very efficient domestic hub and a global, integrated system based on economies of scale in manufacturing at the centre, with subsidiaries supplying mainly distribution and service functions, at least initially.

When scale is a key factor of success, global integration turns out to be very effective. Yet, local responsiveness — to the domestic conditions as well as to the different governments — is often required too. Many MNEs advocate both global integration and local responsiveness — what Bartlett termed "the transnational solution." Bartlett believes that, during the 1990s. firms will be forced to achieve both efficiency, through scale and integration, and local responsiveness, through catering to differentiated demands from customers and to pressures from governments for local content as well as other regulations. The simultaneous pursuit of these two requirements (global integration and local responsiveness) is also important in maintaining a high level of innovativeness.

This objective may be achieved by using different structures for different parts of the value chain, and often by outsourcing certain activities. Scale economies call for integration, but innovations are best encouraged by decentralization. The centre ceases to be the only source of ideas or new products. In contrast, each national unit is a source of ideas that are shared throughout the whole network, and each may achieve global scale by being the world source of a certain product for the whole system, with different subsidiaries having different roles. The centre, for its part, should foster "supportive organizational norms and values".

The experience of manufacturing MNEs shows that increasing internationalization may threaten their stability because domestic markets are no longer sheltered from the onslaught of intensified global competition. They are also broadening their global scope in many service industries. The new demands on multinationals have come about because of globalization and because of the enormous advances in information technology.

Many firms have achieved advantage by the use of proprietary software. Some were able to achieve "mass customization"; others created global networks that made it easier to share information with suppliers as well as customers and across geographical areas. Computers not only allow speed but enable the firm to install intangible assets and to trade in ideas. Only ten years ago, centralized mainframes comprised about three-quarters of all computing power, whereas today the figure is between 1 and 5 percent.

Sales of the personal-computer (PC) industry (both hardware and software), by contrast, grew from $2 billion in 1981 to $82 billion in 1990. In the new age of modern information technology firms can build and sustain a competitive advantage based on information systems. This is particularly apparent in services such as reservations systems and frequent flyer (or user) programmes of airlines and hotels.

Another anticipated change is a reduction in the importance of scale. The giant diversified firm of two or three decades ago is now trying to shape itself up and reduce its size. In 1954, the first year for which Fortune magazine published its "500" ranking, these firms represented 37 percent of U.S. GNP. By 1979, the share was 58 percent. Since then, they have been losing ground in the market. Their share was 42 percent in 1989 and 40 percent in 1991, which is equal to the 1959 figure.

It is argued that the only way giant firms can survive is by becoming less hierarchical, more decentralized, and organized on the basis of teams carrying out ever-changing projects. In short, manufacturing MNEs will have to learn from service firms. An idea of the corporation of the future that will operate in the borderless world may be seen in the professional business services and the many strategic alliances that already exist today.

Information technologies and other changes have allowed many new forms of organization.

The common denominator of all these entities is the form of the organization's various boundaries. The legal boundaries remain the same, as in strategic alliances, so that coordination has to be achieved among legally separate organizations. This active coordination means extensive expansion of the information boundaries and often of management boundaries. Thus. suppliers may be allowed to get into the computer of a firm and supply goods without a specific order.

In a network type of activity, the organization must be defined to include all the separate legal entities that comprise the network. The management boundaries are extended to the whole network to ensure coordination. Coordination itself can be achieved through different forms that may or may not be centralized. The process of coordination and integration may be formal-developing systems, policies, and standards; it may be effected through central processes — by the direct intervention and actions of an elite group based in a unit designed as headquarters in the management of each separate division; or it may be achieved through socialization.

The latter prevails when the task is unique, integrated, or ambiguous. Bartlett and Ghoshal (1993) argue that, in new organizations, each subsidiary is a self-contained unit that is part of a whole. These and other new forms of organization are more prevalent in service firms, particularly in professional service firms.

Globalization of Services

In recent decades, growth in the service sector in most countries has been very impressive, particularly in the operations of global service MNEs, which may or may not have become not only multinational but also global for the same reasons as the manufacturing firms. The accelerating trend of corporate internationalization has put a premium on the ability of service firms to serve their clients uniformly worldwide.

Financial institutions, accounting firms, law firms, and management consultants have all followed their manufacturing clients abroad. In addition, some leading firms have expanded internationally to create challenging work opportunities. Thus, McKinsey & Co. created its London office in 1959, and by 1990, 63 percent of its income was generated outside the United States. By the 1980s, the belief among service firms that they must follow their clients to other parts of the globe had become pervasive.

Moreover, the United States has gone further than any other country in deregulating its airlines, trucking, and telecommunications, compelling these industries to restructure and reengineer to meet competition by undergoing a wrenching overhaul of management systems. U.S. firms also recognized earlier that advantage lay in a lead in brainpower and innovation, and accordingly spent large amounts of money on R&D. Today, of course, the U.S. lead in brainpower is eroding with the increasing level of technological sophistication of firms from other countries.

All service organizations operate in several distinct markets and must satisfy at least three sets of goals: economic goals (profitability, growth). satisfaction goals (of staff, often desiring professional challenges and variety), and client goals. To achieve all or a subset of these goals, some firms opt to become global players, as part of a network of independent entities sharing common services or by managing a single global firm. Of course, the firm must organize its value-creating activities in a way that will help it achieve the greatest degree of success.

Studies of national accounting firms in North America indicate governance structure and primary task as important characteristics. Governance structure is based on partnership, with local offices as the principal place of business. Managers return to these offices after a temporary assignment in the top office. Local offices are independent, inter alia, because of professional norms of independence. Tasks are carried out by principal partners helped by associates, in proximity to the client. Greenwood et al. (1990) point out that these task characteristics are not amenable to central control. Control is achieved mainly through certain shared norms, agreed standards, and peer review.

Yip identified certain "globalization drivers" and global "strategy levers" that explain why certain firms (or certain industries) have become global. One group of globalization drivers are those based on market. A second group stems from cost. A third are government globalization drivers, and the fourth are what Yip terms "competitive globalization drivers." Johansson and Yip found that market and cost drivers were more significant than government or competitive drivers in their sample of manufacturing businesses. This finding may or may not hold for service industries, where government globalization drivers might be more relevant.

Yip also identified five global strategy levers, to measure international strategy on a scale of pure multi domestic to pure global. The global ends are as follows:

- Global market participation: countries are chosen according to their potential contribution to globalization benefits, not only on the basis of their stand-alone attractiveness.
- Global products/services: a standardized core product or service with a minimum of local adaptation or none at all.
- Global location of value-adding activities: the value chain is broken up so that each activity may be conducted in a different country.
- Global marketing: a standard marketing approach is applied around the world, even though not all elements of the marketing mix need be identical.
- Global competitive moves: these are integrated across countries. The same type of move is made in different countries at the same time or in some systematic sequence, or a competitor is attacked in one country in order to drain its resources for another country, or a competitive attack in one country is countered in a different country.

The same levers may be conceptually identified in service industries, though their importance may not be significantly different. In some cases, the levers relate to industries. In others, they relate to firms.

In services, Heskett, Sasser, and Hart used the concept of the "strategic service vision" (SSV) to analyze the alignment between target market segments, the service concept, the operating strategy, and the service delivery system. When target market segments are in different countries, the service delivery system is often guided by standard firm practices across countries, as in the case of American Express travellers' checks or McDonald's. Service firms must be able to guarantee standardized quality services across many countries.

Clearly, one advantage of a multinational hotel system is that it can promise "no surprises." By contrast, however, some global service firms, notably professional service firms that sell expertise, focus on diagnosis, and the projects they handle are customized and specialized. To address each local market with customized service, some firms find that they have to be much less integrative and to differentiate across market segments. The problem with such a choice is the greatly increased complexity.

The decision to serve vastly different customers in different geographic locations fosters a need to develop entirely different strategic service visions with all the added complexity this entails. In the extreme, if the firm is totally differentiated, it may find that it has no communality and therefore no competitive advantage over a domestic firm.

It may find it better to use a loose, ephemeral network of professionals who do not share all standard operating procedures or profits worldwide.

Even within professional business services, however, there are cases where firms offer less creativity and more standard procedures. Thus, in auditing and information-systems consulting, the firm offers more standardized service. The blend of standardized procedures and customized solutions is different in different professions.

The more standardized the elements, the easier the integration, the less complex the structure needed, and the greater the probability of global operations.

Clearly, both the globalization drivers and levers and the key factors of success are different in different types of firms. Some sell expertise. others efficiency, and still others experience. In some types of business, the uncertainty in the mind of the client is very high — sometimes even after the service has been rendered (as in the medical profession). In others, it is not. Some are people-intensive, while others need scale and/or capital. All of these factors may have an impact on the organizational structure. The next section proposes a fuller taxonomy and advances some contingent factors in terms of organization structure.

Professional service firms are different from manufacturing multinationals in several important respects. First, they are people-intensive and demand minimal investment in fixed assets. In addition, key persons capable of creating value added do not have to work for a particular firm. They can move easily and can also work on their own — in other words, the firm becomes a "voluntary" organization. A corollary of the above is that, in some firms, the most critical assets walk out the door every night and a crucial success factor is the ability to recruit and retain the best and most imaginative talents.

These persons have to be carefully nurtured, motivated, and allowed to grow. They have to be trained and retrained and their values reinforced through indoctrination. Incentive systems need to encourage teamwork and cooperation. These factors, though important, are not crucial to success in travel-related business, for example. In some professional service firms, economies of location are important. That is, it is important to have a branch wherever the multinational clients have branches. Failure to participate in a certain strategic market can undermine global competitiveness.

For example, the fact that some European firms were unable to establish a strong base in Japan limited their ability to use economies of scale and reduced their exposure to new innovations; more importantly, it prevented them from creating a hostage for good behaviour on the part of their major Japanese rivals. It is hypothesized that this participation is less crucial in some service industries such as auditing than in others such as travellers' checks or airlines.

Professional service firms are marked by a "think versus grind" mentality. Professional business services that offer mainly expertise can leverage the time of senior professionals much less than even other professional service firms, not to mention hotels or restaurants. Their staffing requirements call for getting the best persons or top-percentile graduates from the best schools. Others that deal with familiar, often standard types of problems depend for their success on efficient performance.

The "think" expertise type is much more difficult to globalize, and it attracts clients by the reputations of its employees rather than by the firm's name. The more standardized the solution, the greater the importance of integration and of centralization, and the smaller the need for differentiation, the easier it is to offer global services and to enhance the ability of each location to serve clients by drawing on the firm's systems, its accumulated knowledge in databases, and the experience of the whole network.

A related factor is the degree of customization. The success of certain service firms (such as McDonald's) has been largely based on the ability to create standard performance based on routine and repetitious work. It is important to distinguish between routines and standardization. Audit work, for example, is based on routine and repetitious work, but there is a great deal of variability in the different audits performed for firms from different industries.

The degree of importance of information systems (e.g., reservations in hotels or airlines, databases of firms on systems' experience, or skills available within the firm) is another critical factor. The more important and developed the information systems. the easier it is integrate activities, even across national borders.

Another factor is the degree of the client's uncertainty before or even after the service has been rendered. Service firms need to be client-centreed. Clients may or may not appreciate the intellectual challenge of a solution or may even be unable to distinguish between competent and outstanding technical work. Often, a large number of contingencies cloud the ability of a client to assess the work (e.g., is a lawyer good even though he or she did not win the case?).

One result is that clients focus more on what they perceive as the quality of delivery than on the quality of the work itself. Clients are often shopping for peace of mind, reassurance, trust, or confidence. Maister says that, in the medical profession, people look for availability, affability, and ability-in that order. Because of all these considerations, clients often use proxies for quality, one of which is size.

Finally, the higher the uncertainty, the greater the willingness to pay for reputation and brand, and therefore the greater the competitive advantage of those firms that succeed in creating a major integrated global organization. These variables may be a vector in a matrix that explains firms' decisions to use different structures and systems.

In addition, an interim variable that will affect the choice is the form of entry: A firm may opt for a very weak form of a global network such as using correspondents (as in financial institutions), or it may refer the work to a trusted domestic firm; it may decide to create or to join a network of independent firms, as accountants often do; it may choose strategic alliances or joint ventures, or it may acquire or create a wholly owned subsidiary.

Another critical factor in the internationalization success of professional service firms is governance structure. Firms registered as corporations such as consulting firms — are often organized hierarchically.

Many other professional firms are partnerships, with ad hoc committee structures and therefore very weak central headquarters. In other words, the legal boundaries of service multinationals tend to be different from their management and information boundaries. In a strategic alliance or a network overall strategic direction is limited to certain functions agreed upon by all participants through a process of negotiation and consensus building. Successful implementation of the strategy depends on acceptance of the ideas by the different legally autonomous entities. No hierarchical relations exist, at least not formal ones.

In this type of firm, different sets of management skills are needed. The first relates to recruitment — or the way subcontractors, partners, or vendors are chosen. The right choices are crucial to the operational success of the network as a whole. Second, top management has to manage an array of independent persons who are not cogs in the wheels of a corporate hierarchy but a part of an autonomous organization. Since added value comes from knowledge, those with more knowledge will enjoy more power.

Third, the network must be flexible and flat: flexibility is important because very often changes cannot be anticipated; flatness is important because, if communications have to go up and down hierarchies, much time is lost. To achieve responsiveness to markets, communications must be unimpeded, and horizontal consultation has to be encouraged. In addition, initiative has to be encouraged or even mandated through a socialization process. Managing such a network is a rather delicate affair, since the system may run out of control.

From the conceptual discussion up to this point, particularly that relating to the very useful differentiation/integration framework, the following rules for organization design in service multinationals appear to emerge.

First, the higher the degree of homogeneity among clients in different countries, the greater is the need for formal standard systems. Therefore, the more a firm serves global clients, the greater the pressures for common standards and centralized coordination and control. Global clients demand service of consistent quality and quick access to the best experts available. These demands increase the need for linkages across different entities, better integration, and more formal processes of coordination.

Second, the more complex and/or diversified the work performed for clients, the greater is the need for experts from across the network and formal integration.

Third, the greater the importance of scale, the greater is the tendency of the firm toward integration. Integration is also important when the economics of location are salient or when capital-intensive services are being provided. It is easier when the tasks being performed are repetitive. By contrast, the more expertise and thinking that are needed, and the greater the need for innovation or brain work, the more difficult it becomes to formally enforce standards and the greater the need for differentiation.

In the extreme, when the key factors of success are the expertise and superior minds of individuals who tend to resent formal processes, integration is almost impossible. The organization will be extremely flat and based on project management. The contradictory pressures for more central control and more independence are the major challenge of the global service firm, in particular, the professional service firm.

These firms are also constrained by their administrative heritage, based on an organization of independent partners. Enforcement may be achieved by moral suasion, by appeals to collegial loyalty, by socialization processes, by training, and even by indoctrination, to get what Maister termed "the one-firm firm," or by a constant flow of information and horizontal transfer of knowledge.

Fourth, coordination and integration among units are based less on traditional forms of organizational structure such as divisional or formal bureaucracy than on committees designed to achieve coordination in the flow of resources among the different units. These resources are capital. technology, persons, and information.

Fifth, while manufacturing multinationals allocate capital for investment and repatriate dividends, professional service firms hardly move capital across borders. The resources transferred are mainly persons and information, and, to a lesser extent, technology.

Sixth, some professional service firms will increasingly be organized as centralized bureaucracies if they are able significantly to increase the part of their work that is based on experience, with the availability of databases-of both past experience and available skills — a key factor of success. The greater the need for a network of scholars and professionals, the more individualistic they become, and the less central control the firm has over them. To be sure, advances in information technologies allow much more differentiation while, at the same time, tapping into centralized resources. However, old-fashioned centralization is detrimental to the work of the organization.

Seventh, information flows are difficult to manage because of their volume, complexity, and diversity. However, professional norms, as well as rules, roles, and responsibilities, may allow more effective horizontal transfer of knowledge. As one example, university professors devote a significant amount of time learning about the work of others through a word-of-mouth web of relationships.

Senior professors spend an inordinate amount of time refereeing papers or writing letters of recommendation for tenure or promotion at other, often remote' universities. This work is not remunerated financially, but is still meticulously carried out because of the commitment to professionalism and excellence. Academics know one another and socialize at conferences, where they receive instant feedback. Thus, the individual reputation stakes are very high.

Eighth, a major difficulty is the means of enforcing priorities for work done by an entity in one country for one in another country. Thus, the audit of a subsidiary of a multinational in a certain country can be of great importance for the auditors in the country where this multinational's headquarters reside.

Finally, bargaining and consensus building among committee members as well as ad hoc task forces and individual partners with high status provide alternatives to hierarchical structure.

Although the list of possible propositions connecting the contingency variables and organizational structure is much larger, the major lesson of this chapter is that there is a need for much more research on alternatives to structure as a means of achieving coordination and integration.

A firm operating globally must manage the flow of people. information, services, and money across national borders. It must nurture and cultivate distinct competence that will allow it to offer better or more efficient services than the domestic firm, as well as the executive reward system and the systems of coordination and control that will nurture its strategy. Even more than in extractive and manufacturing firms, the success of the global service MNE depends on its ability to gain and to maintain clients. In addition, firms must make sure they are able to recruit and maintain the human and other resources needed to operate in the market of their choice.

A major constraint on the globalization of services is the ability to integrate all activities, particularly as most service firms need to have a high degree of local autonomy and flexibility. An important question is what kind of value-adding support does each subsidiary receive from headquarters?

Because of the speed of change in the marketplace, on the one hand, and better information processing on the other, globally operated firms can learn a lot from the way organizations are designed in the investment-banking business, or in the professional business services or in networks such as CNN or EDL.

The new knowledge-based organization in a brain-based economy will have to be organized more like professional service firms or institutions of higher learning, which have traditionally faced a more fickle environment of shifting temporary assignments. This chapter proposes some variables that impinge on a contingency theory of organizational design of global service firms.

MUTUAL VALUE OF CUSTOMER AND FIRM

Just as the customer value analysis requires an examination of the benefits versus the costs, the firm makes a similar analysis to determine its profit potential. In providing the customer value, what does the firm get in return? How do the monetary and nonmonetary benefits from the customer compare with what it cost the firm to provide that solution to that customer? Can we sustain these profits in the long term? A firm creates value for itself by creating value for the customer. In many ways, the value of a firm is reflected in the profits it provides its investors and the value of the customer to the firm is reflected in the profits that the customer provides the firm. The greater the values of the customer to the firm, the greater are the profits.

This means that the surplus from the revenues after costs is greater if you can attract and retain profitable customers in the long run. Part IV in this book covers the valuation of the customer by the firm. Firms can attract and retain customers if they can provide superior value. It could boil down to, can we command a premium on our solution? If you can, it turns out that the margins are not in the commoditized part of the product, it is in the services provided by the firm. The margins increase when you are able to extend your role in the customer's space. This may come in the form of "cross-selling" or "up-selling." It may be the case that the total solution provides such value to the customer that the customer is better off with you than with the competition.

As the firm gets more valuable to the customer, the customer gets more valuable to the firm. The value from a customer is derived not only from purchases. Customers can become advocates for the firm, the benefits of which are frequently less understood. The value of the customer in terms of purchases and referrals over the lifetime of the customer should be an imperative calculation for firms who are focused on the customer. It appears that in the final analysis, it is the customer-focused firm that can provide a complete solution through a service orientation that succeeds in providing superior customer value and in return enjoys sustainable profits. So, how is it that a firm is able to provide superior customer value? What gives them a sustainable competitive advantage, such that the firm has sustainable profits?

Delivering Superior Customer Value

What characterizes firms that can provide *superior* customer value? To answer this question, we have ample evidence from research on such firms. Every firm in any industry provides some customer value. The firm that provides superior customer value is the one that has a sustainable competitive advantage. Firms compete with each other on differentiable aspects of the total solution. If we can conceptualize that every product has parts that are commodities and parts that differentiate it from others, superior value is in the augmented product, not in the conceptual core.

For example, all airlines provide transportation from point A to point B. But the total solution includes aspects other than the physical transportation of the person itself, such as amenities on the airplane. A firm must seek opportunities to differentiate itself from the competition in ways that are meaningful and relevant to the customer. How do firms find opportunities to differentiate themselves in a way that it is sustainable?

Consider how CDW creates superior customer value. CDW is the leading B2B e-commerce firm selling technology equipment to small and medium-sized firms. Wall Street analysts claim that the firm uses a "clicks and people" strategy. Supposedly, their competitive advantage is superior customer service and lower customer acquisition costs. The firm's Web site is tailored to each specific customer as a "custom extranet." How are they able to sustain this competitive advantage? Their own chief financial officer, Harry Harczak, notes that retaining people is key. In his experience, the productivity difference between an employee who has been at the firm six months versus one there three years is a factor of six. CDW values employee commitment.

What are the generalizable characteristics of firms that create superior customer value? A team of Harvard Business School researchers set out to discover exactly this and concluded that successful firms such as BancOne, Intuit, Southwest Airlines, ServiceMaster, USAA, Taco Bell, and MCI made employees and customers paramount. These researchers modeled the findings from their case studies into a framework they called "the service profit chain." Their cases provided data to establish powerful relationships between profitability, customer loyalty, and employee satisfaction, loyalty, and productivity. Evident in the whole model is the focus on the customer and the service orientation of satisfied employees, and the implications on investors and other stakeholders of the firm.

As firms focus on customer needs and become service oriented to deliver satisfaction, there are favourable ripple effects throughout the firm. Consistent delivery of customer satisfaction persuades customers to be loyal because perceived risk in buying a product from that firm is substantially reduced. When providers of solutions to customer needs are able to consistently deliver expected value, customers are more likely to be consistently satisfied. By way of their continued patronage, they become more valuable to the firm. When customers are loyal to the provider by choice, it is also in their best interest to support the provider because the prosperity and longevity of the provider is beneficial to the customer. Similarly, with regard to employees, research has shown that when employee satisfaction is high employees are more likely to be loyal to the company. When employee loyalty is high, employees are likely to be more productive and to be providing quality products and service.

Neither employees nor customers are likely to be loyal unless their expectations are met and they are satisfied. Therefore, customer satisfaction and employee satisfaction are inherently tied to each other, in that, when employees are loyal to the firm, they provide superior performances driving customer loyalty. When employees are productive and customer loyalty is high, the firm is successful and can command a premium.

With increased profitability and growth prospects, investors are attracted to the firm, which in turn makes more resources available to the firm. With more resources available to the firm, capital is available to continuously improve value-creating assets (people and processes) and to produce consistently superior customer value in its products and service. This sequence of events, presented as the "loyalty circle", contributes to profitability and growth and requires that people and processes are aligned to deliver superior customer value. Delivering superior value should be a relentless endeavor for the firm.

CUSTOMER VALUE OPPORTUNITIES

An understanding of the role that the firm's product plays in the customer's value chain could open up value-creating opportunities. A customer-focused firm has a detailed picture of the customer's consumption domain. When a firm views value consumption activities, it can see if there are other value creating opportunities that it can leverage from its assets. The watchmaker Swatch, for example, offers wrist watches with the technology that allows them to function as electronic passes at ski resorts in Switzerland or for public transportation in Finland.

Wrist gadgets can now serve not only the function of telling time, but also making phone calls, playing music and videos, browsing the Internet, or sending email. This example defies categorization of product. What is the product? It is a wallet or a pocketbook, as well as a telephone, a personal stereo, a personal VCR, and an Internet communications device! The exercise of determining what revenue opportunities Swatch's value-creating assets would offer forces a complete redefinition of the product.

The (product) solution is conceived to take advantage of opportunities to meet the needs in the customer's life with the assets that the firm has. Swatch has found a way to provide value to a recreational activity—skiing—and a functional activity—public transportation. It is contributing to the "customer access" components of the ski resort's and public transportation's product. By enabling customer access, information technology provides a whole range of supplementary benefits to a variety of products.

Contrast this with the example of a firm that does not understand the value of complementary product components and the customer's value chain. A customer came out of a movie theater in Kendall Square, Cambridge, and experienced a 40-minute ordeal trying to leave the theater's parking lot. She spent 30 minutes standing in line in frigid weather to pay the $2.50 parking fee and a further 15 minutes to exit the parking lot. When complaining to the management of the movie theater, she asked if she could pay the parking fee as she bought the movie ticket. She was told that the parking lot was owned by a different company and the theater would not take responsibility for the customer's bad experience at the parking lot.

In contrast, the airline SAS has been known to provide an annual dinner to taxicab drivers in Stockholm because the SAS management wants the drivers to treat passengers on the way to and from the airport with professional courtesy and respect. Clearly, firms that are customer-focused conceive their product differently from other firms, because of their intimate knowledge of the customer's consumption activities.

Information about the customer's consumption cycle, therefore, is a key prerequisite to exploring the opportunities that might be tapped. An understanding of how the customer actually benefits from the solution and the information of how, when, where, and with whom the customer consumes the product should provide some interesting revelations of what the firm is doing and can be doing in the composition of the total product solution for customers.

Thus, Procter & Gamble sends its researchers to homes to observe how people actually use laundry detergent. When Samsung was trying to break into the microwave business in the late 1970s and early 1980s, their design engineers observed homemakers shopping for microwaves at the retail store. You can stay ahead of the curve by offering value through supplementary product that your customer information tells you customers will be willing to pay for.

Even if the value-producing feature or activity cannot be priced separately, you may be able to command a premium for your superior customer value. Being customer-focused is critical in identifying opportunities for establishing superiority in customer value.

Conceiving and Designing

All decisions about the product and, therefore, the value-creating activities of the firm are based on an understanding of the value-consumption activities of its customers. What are the decisions and what are the issues to be considered in determining the total product by a firm? The three major decisions constituting the product strategy are: the product concept, the operations design, and the value creation and delivery process. The *product concept* defines the customer to be served and what value is to be provided. The *operations design* defines the productive assets of the firm required to create and deliver that value for that customer.

Together, the product concept and the operations design define the scope and configuration of the productive assets that can be leveraged to produce the specific customer value that maximizes profits to the firm. The *value creation and delivery process* executes the product concept with the operations design. In developing the product strategy, the firm makes a fundamental decision in answering the question of how the product will be positioned among all potential solutions to the customer's need.

This positioning question poses an asset- and market-based decision that comprises two perspectives.

- The *market-based perspective* looks outward at the market and asks what customer needs can be most profitably served by the firm.

- The *asset-based perspective* looks inward, at the firm's assets, and asks what assets of the firm can be most profitably leveraged by the firm.

The market-based perspective drives the product concept and the asset-based perspective drives the operations design. Thus, the initial step in developing product strategy involves two critical analyses. The product concept requires analyses of the various segments in the marketspace, while the operations design requires analyses of the firm's productive factors. These two sets of analyses are essential to determining what value-creating activities the firm should engage in to generate the maximum revenue from its assets.

The Market-Based Perspective

A market analysis to determine what would be the most profitable segment mix for a configuration of the productive assets of the firm is the foundation for product strategy. First you need to identify the segments and the solutions that are currently available to the segments. The target market selection or the selected market segments to be served can be based on the profitability and size of each segment that the firm's assets are best positioned to serve.

Here, a formal comparison of all the current solutions from the customer's perspective is necessary. Based on this analysis, the firm is able to determine what it can provide better than the alternative available to the appropriate target market, thus framing the firm's competitive advantage. Only after such customer needs analysis is it possible to specify what would be the desired customer value in the product offering.

The intended customer value in the product offering can now be translated into a detailed picture of the product concept—what the core and supplementary product ought to be.

Remember that the customer value also reflects the customer's implicit assessment of the firm's solution compared to competitive offerings and, indeed, all solutions that are available to customers in the segment. To ensure that the product concept can effectively be superior customer value, the core product should combine the imperatives that have become commodities in the product category with the appropriate features in the supplementary product to reflect superiority in customer value. Thus, the product concept embodies the product differentiation and the superiority in customer value.

The Asset-Based Perspective

The operations design decision rests on how best the assets of the firm can be most profitably leveraged and follows a sequence of questions that pertain to the productive assets and capabilities of the firm and how they should be deployed: What people, facilities, equipment assets are needed to create and deliver the product? Which employees' skills and knowledge would be needed? When and where would specific human capital be needed and for how much time? Similar questions are asked about the facilities and equipment of the firm. Of course, when the asset or resource is not available within the firm, it seeks suppliers or outsources that part of the value creation. Ultimately, the question is what competitive advantage the firm is capable of and how the assets needed should be configured.

Value Creation and Delivery Process

The process decisions are about determining the specific activities of the value creation and delivery. The process of making the product and delivering it to the customer must be detailed. The value creation and delivery activities required are set in a specific sequence. The firm must deliberate on the structure, content, and process of creating and delivering the product to the customer.

No product differentiation from supplementary product can be seen in isolation. If the total benefits from the product are not worth the costs that the customer incurs in acquiring and using the product, the product is likely to fail. The more carefully the firm designs the process with the customer in mind, the more likely the process ensures ease, convenience and quality for the customer. Thus, the customer-focused firm designs the creation and delivery process with the customer's perception of benefits and costs in the value consumption process.

Ensuring Customer-focused Value Creation

Firms must also recognize that since customer value is dynamic, they need to continually monitor and improve this customer value. Ignorance of the need to innovate to sustain competitive advantage is a common mistake committed by the complacent firm. The argument is sometimes made that the firm's priority of customer focus minimizes the attention to innovation. Customer focus and innovation are not contradictory, an either/or strategic decision. Indeed, to be customer-focused would mean that the firm is continually looking for new ways and solutions to meet customer needs—and to be aware that customer needs evolve as well.

Visualize what the firm needs to do to ensure that it is creating and delivering customer-focused value that can be sustained. To sustain superiority in customer value the firm must ensure that management continually assess its market and its assets to ensure that the choice of customer and the value being created and delivered by the firm maximizes the profit goals of the firm.

How well is the customer value in the product concept translated to the operations design and the value creation and delivery process? Is the superiority in customer value being executed. The answer lies in the customer's judgment. Customer-focused firms will let the customer decide whether the firm's value creation and delivery is customer-focused.

Continual customer satisfaction assessment information needs to be available for the customer-focused firm to improve by changing the product concept, the operations design, and the value creation and delivery process, or to continually reassess whether its assets and capabilities are being leveraged to realize the maximum profit potential. To ensure customer-focused value creation and delivery, firms must assess customers' perceptions of the benefits they receive as well as the costs incurred by them.

As an ongoing assessment of customer value, firms must continually assess customer needs and customer satisfaction. As customer needs change, the value bundle needs to be reviewed in terms of its product concept, operations design and delivery. An assessment of customer satisfaction presents an opportunity to improve customer value. The smart firm will continually monitor customer satisfaction to understand what customers perceive as the benefits they are getting from product compared to the costs that they incur.

Based on customer satisfaction, does the value bundle need to be modified and redesigned? Are the assets and capabilities of the firm being leveraged for maximum sustainable profits? If the expected customer value cannot be delivered with the existing value-creating assets, then the firm has two choices. Either it acquires or outsources the required value-creating assets and capabilities, or it determines that the target market decision needs revisiting. These questions are posed as a frame for a customer-focused analysis of the value creation and delivery of the firm.

Managing Customer Interactions

The process of delivering value is a tricky and detail-rich exercise; it requires careful planning, using techniques such as blueprinting to visualize the entire customer experience. From the customer perspective, some service encounters are critical incidents requiring more attention than others. All service encounters must be staged for a customer-focused experience just as in the production of theater.

Why does Kimberly-Clark manage the discount retailer Costco's inventory of its diapers? The firm has a salesperson live near the Costco headquarters, and a data analyst responsible for overseeing stock at 155 Costco stores in the western United States. Similarly, Procter & Gamble stations 250 people near Wal-mart's headquarters in Bentonville, Arkansas. Large retailers are asking suppliers to more actively manage the movement of products from factory to retail store shelves. P&G estimates that stock-outs amount to 11 percent of an average retailer's annual sales.

When firms like Kimberly-Clark pay more attention to how its immediate customers—the retailers—create value to their customers, they demonstrate that they are being customer focused. In fact, the Kimberly-Clark salesperson passed on information on how customers place packages in their shopping cart that played into package design for diapers. Wayne Sanders, chairman and CEO of Kimberly-Clark, attributes this change to the information age.

Prior to the industrial revolution, a service orientation and the individual-to-individual interaction was the predominant mode of competitiveness. Assembly-line production distanced the firm from the customer due to the sheer number of customers and the physical distance between the customers and the firm brought about by the wonders of modern transportation. Manufacturing goods became the engine of individual and collective (national) economic growth.

Mechanization far outpaced services and replaced producer-customer interaction, relying instead on intermediary institutions to provide a specialized set of competencies that the producing firm lacked. Businesses lost sight of the customer. Now, information technology has brought this full circle, back to the customer.

We call it the information age because what has changed in our time is that new technology has revolutionized the way information is handled. Another equally significant revolution is the change in the customer's domain. Customers not only have access to more information on products and service offerings, they also have the ability to interact with the providers of products and services in ways not previously possible. Providers can also present enhancements to customer experiences from the functionalities presented by technology. Service providers must, however, also manage customer participation when they utilize technology.

When firms take advantage of online marketplaces, it might be necessary to make changes in organizational structure so that value creation and delivery processes are adjusted to the addition of the online delivery. Two key technologies underlie this information age technology phenomenon: the Internet and wireless communications. What customer access to these technologies has done is to bring customer interactions to a new level and to the front and centre in how a firm deals with the customer. These interactions are essentially service encounters with the customer.

Much has been said about the service encounter—customer interactions with the firm. In a way, all customer relationship management (CRM) solutions are basically technology support to ensure that the firm maximizes returns from customers by enabling customer-focused interactions. The service encounter is truly "where the rubber hits the road"—where the prospects of customer loyalty are materialized or lost. It is where promises made in advertising are honored or reneged on, and where expectations of customers are disappointed or met. It is where all the assets of the firm need to be brought to bear.

Service encounters with the customers are also laden with the challenges of a product that is produced and consumed in real time, where failures are bound to happen. When the firm designs the value creation process with the customer in mind, it will be prepared for all predictable eventualities. When the service fails, smart firms have smart processes, that recover and learn from the failure. They have service recovery and knowledge management processes in place.

As firms compete more and more on services, the management of the customer interaction becomes critical to ensure superiority in customer value. As the core product is a commodity, and most facilitating services approach the commodity state, the competitiveness comes from how the customer is treated by the firm at each and every encounter.

This discusses a method for designing the value delivery process with special attention paid to the service encounter and the critical incidents in the value creation and delivery process. A framework for designing the service encounter based on the theatrical metaphor is offered as a way to examine the customer focus of value creation and delivery.

The Ingredients of Customer Interactions

Analyzing customer interactions can be very rewarding. Amazon constantly tracks the reasons for every customer contact. It has made numerous changes to its value creation and delivery process based on customer input. The customer service function at Amazon is considered a research lab for ways to improve the Amazon customer experience. We can turn to the unique characteristics of services to obtain a clear understanding of what is involved in a customer interaction. Something intangible is always exchanged in the interaction (intangibility). Without a customer, there is no interaction and the separation of production and consumption is irrelevant (inseparability).

To conduct the interaction, the firm has the resources and infrastructure in place that "perish" when not utilized (perishability). Each interaction is unique (variability). From these characteristics, emerge situations that are challenges and opportunities typical to the service firm. We need to keep these in mind as we design the process of creating and delivering customer value. At the most general level, all customer interactions occur in a certain place (or space), at a certain time, for a certain duration, between certain entities, in a certain manner for a certain purpose.

Consider these as ingredients in a customer interaction and categorize them into elements of structure, content, and process. When the customer interaction is mapped onto the consumption activity cycle, the objective of the interaction becomes the driving force behind the design of the interaction in terms of its structure, content, and process.

- *Structure* relates to who or what entities are involved in the interaction.
- *Content* relates to the subject, the task, and its significance in the interaction.
- *Process* relates to the sequence of steps in the interaction.

The primary decisions that would configure the structure of the interaction involve the nature of the interaction—what entity should represent the firm, should the interaction be face-to-face or not, what technology can be utilized, where should it occur, and so forth. As a complementary question about the customer: What entities from the customer's domain are involved in the interaction? Similarly, decisions determining the content of the interaction should centre around the task and include what information should be required in the interaction, what should transpire between the parties, and what value should be created and consumed in the interaction.

Decisions about process would include a script of the interaction and the roles of both parties in the interaction. Any of these decisions must be based on the information that the firm has about the customer's consumption cycle and on preferences regarding these dimensions of the interaction. For example, technology may provide the firm with scale economies, but the customer may want to disengage from the script and interact with a person instead. Ultimately, the important question is what value is being created in the interaction.

CUSTOMER VALUE AND SERVICE ORIENTATION

Customers buy solutions, not products. Every firm needs to understand what it is providing the customer in terms of customer value, not by focusing on the product but by focusing on the customer. In doing so, the firm is able to assess whether it is providing superior customer value and whether it has a sustainable competitive advantage. Competitive advantage cannot be sustained unless it can be protected from competitor matching. Any aspect of the product can be matched by the competition. What is most difficult for the competition to match is how the firm approaches and treats the customer. The firm *serves* the customer by providing product enhancements in the form of service. When other firms can provide the same service, the differentiator is in the service orientation of the firm.

IDENTIFYING THE CUSTOMER

To understand the customer is to understand your business. To understand the customer's perspective is basic to defining a business. The first obvious question is, who is the customer? If the firm defines the customer too narrowly or without context, any subsequent analysis is flawed. Firms either focus on their end users as packaged-goods firms tend to do, or as in the case of industrial firms, the focus is on the immediate customer. Both cases reflect a narrow view and a lack of understanding of the context. To determine who the customer is, the question to ask is, how does what we produce or provide add value to the client's value creating process?

Most important, what do customers see as the value we are providing to their value creation process? This point is central to what we know as the "value chain" concept. An understanding of customers requires an understanding of the customers' value chain that includes the set of their value consumption activities. If the value created by the immediate customer creates value for a subsequent customer, that customer is also an indirect customer of the firm. We really need to identify the customer as a first step to determine whose perspective we should take and to understand the customer value that we are providing.

Performing the analysis of the customer sometimes forces the redefining of the customer. For Bright Horizons, a workplace child care and early education service company, it made a huge difference in how they went about their business when they viewed employers, and not parents, as their primary customers. The company could now tap into the financial and other resources of corporations and gain access to a much wider pool of parents. The value they were providing to the employer became the focus of the company. Chase Manhattan, for example, figured that its child care centre was yielding 110 percent return on investment through reduced absenteeism. Similarly, Merck found that its employee retention rate among those who were young parents went up dramatically.

The customer-focused perspective blurs the boundaries between entities in the value chain. Take the case of Aramark Corp., a firm that caters special events and runs cafeterias for big corporate clients. Nancy Naatz, resident district manager for business services for Aramark, has an office in the premises of her customer, Sears, in Chicago. Since Ms. Naatz is on location at her client's company, she is able to observe and interact with the local vendors Aramark has contracted to supply and serve Sears. Ms. Naatz is able to understand Sears executives' and employees' nutritional needs and interact with the vendors to ensure that the appropriate choices are made available. In this case, Aramark matches the food vendors' solution with the needs of the Sears employees who are the real customers.

So, who is the customer? The perspective of *which* customer I inspect and analyze, so as to help determine the business of my business, is the question. This question also raises the fundamental marketing decision of what or who our target market should be. It is a logical place to start before making any marketing or operations decision. Of all the potential customers that make up the market, which particular type of customer is most appropriate for our solution? The analysis involves segmentation, and the decision involved is one of targeting.

We are able then to determine which particular type of customer from the universe of all customers for this product would find most value in what our value-creating assets can produce. We thus segment the market and target those segments for whom our value-creating assets can provide differentiation and a cost advantage. To know who the customer is necessitates an understanding of the typical customer in that segment at a general or aggregate level.

Traditionally, customer profiles have come out of the segmentation exercise. Segmentation variables in the B2C context have included demographic, psychographic, and behavioural variables. For customer-focused management we need information on all of the characteristics of the need or problem or use-situation that the customer is involved in, encompassing all of the activities of the customer that the product is a part of. Consequently, the question, who is the customer? You want to know how the customer purchases and uses the product.

Similarly, the profile of the customer in a B2B context involves understanding the business of the organizational customer. For either the B2C or the B2B context, an understanding of the customers requires analysis of their use-situations, and the contexts within which a product helps them in what they do. Of what value are you to them? Now we begin to hint at the notion of what customer value really is. The answers lie in the *consumption* of the product, not in its production.

Customer Value

Customer value is what the customer thinks he or she is getting in return for what the customer has to part with, reflecting an implicit comparison akin to "give and receive." It has been described as the quotient of quality over price. Understanding the customer is about understanding customer value. Customer value is a complex concept and measuring it is complicated. But in the exercise of trying to understand customer value, the manager benefits from a better understanding of the customer and of the opportunities for a superior solution. Here are some characteristics of customer value that any manager should examine in an analysis of the firm and its activities: Customer value

- Is what the customer believes that a product or service provides in a certain use situation.
- Is an implicit comparison between what the customer receives from the provider and what the customer provides in time, effort, and money. The frame of reference is not just the price tag on the product, but also the ease and convenience in the acquisition and use of the product and the whole interactive experience the customer has with the firm.
- Is the customer's rather than the provider's perspective. It has to do with customer perceptions of the product and the firm, and not the provider's perspective of what the firm is delivering.
- Is dynamic, in that it can change over time before, during, and after the purchase, use, over repeated use of the product, and during all the various stages in the relationship with the providing firm.
- Can vary over different use situations. Your automobile may provide less or more value in transporting a group of kids to the ballpark compared to taking the spouse to the boss's house for a party.
- Can be shaped by attitudes, opinions, and behaviours of others, such as friends, family, media, the providing firm, and other competitors in the industry as well as in substitute industries.
- Determines customer satisfaction and the likelihood of brand or firm loyalty. This cause-effect relationship could be affected by comparisons with competitors and other substitutes.

- Is hard to measure and keep track of. Customers may find it hard to articulate all the different dimensions of customer value and firms may find it a rather onerous task to keep track of all the manifestations of customer value.

Your Value to the Customer

In order to determine what business a firm is in, therefore, the fundamental and imperative exercise is to understand customer value. Let us begin the analysis with the question, what exactly does customer value consist of? It is not easy to determine what the customer is getting as value from a product or service. To understand customer value, you really need to get into the customer's way of thinking about products. In a recent *Harvard Business Review* article, Chase and Dasu urge the use of behavioural science to get into the head of the customer, to understand their total experience with the product or service. Only then can you grasp all the components of customer value.

Examining the components and determinants of customer value is a critical step in the analysis. It requires analysis of the benefits as well as costs to the customer. The benefits seen are evident in the perceptions of the product performance. Perceptions of product performance are framed in the context of customer expectations. The expectations are shaped by past experience with the product and by messages about the product received from a variety of sources such as friends and family as well as from the marketer.

From an analytical perspective, product performance comes from functional (core) benefits and supplemental benefits. Functional benefits arise from the core attributes of the product. For instance, you buy a set of golf clubs. How the golf clubs affect your game is a core and functional benefit, as in the primary benefit from the product. The prestige of the brand image, the product return policy, and other customer service features would translate into supplemental benefits. Every customer value analysis requires that we identify and examine core and supplemental benefits.

Similarly, we need to identify the costs to the customer—both monetary and non-monetary costs. Monetary costs include costs incurred in the acquisition, use, and disposition of the solution. Non-monetary costs could include the time and effort in acquiring and benefiting from the solution and the opportunity costs where the product failed. Tom Wright, Buy.com's vice president of operations called his company's old way of handling returns "almost embarrassing." To return a product that a customer bought from Buy.com, the customer had to telephone Buy.com to generate a return authorization, which led to a shipping label from the package delivery firm (UPS) to be mailed to the customer, who then used that label to send the product back to Buy.com. It was weeks before the customer got credit for the product return! Imagine the non-monetary cost of aggravation to that customer.

Many firms that focus on acquiring customers do not retain customers because of their shallow understanding of customer value. Customer value includes interactions with the firm before, during, and after the consumption of the product. Smart firms are focusing on the whole customer and defining their business in terms of market spaces. The market space is the actual set of customer solutions defined by the consumption activities to which the firm caters.

In recognizing that customer value is dynamic, we need to place this analysis in the context of different use situations and how they are changed over time by various influences. Customers' concepts of what to expect from a provider change with each consumption experience. They learn from their own experiences with the product as well as vicariously from others. Competitor offerings and marketing messages continually shape their expectations. Therefore, implicit in the assessments made by the customer is a comparison with expectations based on the alternative—that is, the competition. Customer value analyses can be performed at a qualitative level and with some difficulty can be quantified as well.

Data-driven representations of monetary worth of what a firm does for a customer are what Anderson and Narus called "customer value models." Such models are useful in assessing the customer value of your product and comparing it with the competition to determine whether you are providing superior customer value or not. The next fundamental question is, Can you provide this superior customer value at a sustainable profit by commanding revenues to cover costs and profits?

3

Selecting and Attracting the Right Customers in Hospitality

INTRODUCTION

The task of creating and delivering superior customer value must be complemented with the selection of the appropriate customers and the effective management of relationships with those customers. The hospitality industry is a fascinating one from a CRM perspective, because of the quality and quantity of customer touchpoints. In the world of servicing guests, there are as many challenges as there are, well... challenging customers, but in the current age of "branding" one of the biggest ones is ensuring a consistent customer service experience. Today's hotels offer a multitude of lucrative services, all of which need to be recorded immediately against the right customer's bill.

Zonal can integrate any third party billing program to ensure that all room-charged items can be cross-checked quickly and easily at the point-of-sale for matching name against a stated room number. Commonly, hotels have a number of different sales areas for patrons to drink, eat and enjoy services.

Hotel management has the ability to define different products and prices for each of these sales areas, allowing them to apply premium price bands for exclusive areas. This challenge is three-pronged: First, managers must be able to manage consistency in the face of interchanging slow and busy times and seasons. Second, consistency needs to be ensured across job titles, roles, and pay ranges.

Third (or perhaps First, if you'd like), the marketing message must be in tune with a plan to set guest expectations according to the season and customer tier considerations. Customer retention leading to more custom and bigger profit is easier if you can keep your customers happy. This can be achieved in your restaurants with minimal wait times for food orders and accurate service delivery - every time.

The fully integrated kitchen management system communicates all food orders, with special instructions if necessary, automatically from the PoS in your sales areas directly to the kitchen to minimise customer wait times. Real-time awareness of current stock holding and usage gives you the power to manage supply and monitor profit margins more effectively. The stock control system is one of the most powerful in the industry and gives you the flexibility to monitor movements of products of all divisions between the different zones in your site. Emergency transfers of champagne cases from the cocktail bar to the function room can now be recorded easily.

As with any strategy, the goal is to help meet the corporate objectives, which often begin with defining the customer segments that can help move the enterprise in the right direction, and then approach them with the right marketing message, via the right marketing channels. On the subject of job roles, while some job roles had specific training on interacting with customers, others did not, or worse, were trained in an inconsistent way.

So the first order of things in this area is to establish a clear procedure for greeting, servicing, and addressing guest issues across various situations. All employees which come in direct contact with guests need to be in tune with this common standard. A set of behaviour and service standards also provides clear guidelines which can empower employees to provide special, or "magical" moments to their guests. The guest servicing standards themselves should focus on not just consistent responses, but also should prevent consecutive negative experiences.

In other words, if a guest has experienced a negative event (i.e. complained that the room wasn't clean upon check in), this fact needs to be captured and made available to customer-facing employees so that they can put an extra effort into making sure that the remainder of the hotel stay or restaurant experience is as positive as possible. A further back-end benefit to capturing the negative event information is that it will enable analysis of customer experience shortcomings. This in turn allows for active methods for managing, monitoring, and predicting customer satisfaction, which can then lead to fine-tuning the marketing message, interaction standards, and employee training.

Predictive analytics can be used to understand latent pain or dissatisfaction before it percolates and impacts customer loyalty.Managing customer relationships should be guided by an understanding of what the customer's equity is to the firm. Customer equity, the value of customer to the firm, improves as superiority in customer value improves. Since customer equity is perhaps the firm's most valuable asset, the firm must continually seek to improve customer value for it best customers. A firm's potential return on customer equity should determine the investment it makes in customers. For its most valuable customers, the firm must guarantee superior service quality and customer service, with special attention to recovering from inevitable product failures when they occur.

Maximizing long-term profitability comes from maximizing customer equity—firms must maximize the lifetime value of the customer, including revenues, referrals as well as costs of serving the customer. Customer acquisition and retention efforts must be guided by the worth of the customer to the firm.

Maytag provides premium service to its premium customers—those who purchase the Neptune line of laundry machines. Neptune customers get a dedicated staff, a separate toll-free number and fast response on service calls. This is an example of the common business practice where firms allocate resources by the profitability and value of the customer. They utilize the opportunity in directly interacting with individual customers to determine customer profitability and allocate assets accordingly. And what are the benefits of the practice of differentiating among your customers?

Broadly referring to the practice as CRM can sometimes defeat its purpose by losing sight of the basic meaning of the term: managing customer relationships. Managing customer relationships would mean actively planning, organizing, directing, and controlling a firm's business relationships with its customers. The term might be "new" in its current usage, but the business practice of managing relationships with customers is certainly not new.

What has prompted the increased attention to CRM is new technology: how well firms can practice CRM has been advanced by information technology in the new economy. Technology brings with it the risk of missing the benefits of huge investment costs if used inappropriately, however. The benefits can seem so attractive that the costs are rationalized until the technology fails to deliver.

The American Customer Satisfaction Index, a measure of customer attitudes toward about 200 companies from over 30 different industries, has actually shown a decline, while at the same time CRM technology investments had grown about five times. When used with a fundamental understanding of CRM's purpose, the benefits of CRM technology enabling the business practice of managing customer relationships are clearly powerful. Siebel, Peoplesoft, Oracle, and other CRM technologies are really customer information management or customer knowledge management systems. These systems gather data and convert it to knowledge that will help firms in their customer relationship management activities.

The most significant contribution of CRM technology to the practice of business is not the technology itself, of course. It is in what the technology does to the practice of managing customer relationships. Because technology has now made it easy to do all the tasks of gathering and analyzing customer information, firms have been able to discover and realize the incredible benefits in proactively managing customer relationships. For example, Continental Airlines' customer information system allows its staff to mine data on passenger profitability and is also able to suggest remedies and perks for special requests or complaining customers.

Customer benefits from relationships with firms have been conceptualized under three categories: social, psychological, and customization benefits, in a two-part study using interviews and surveys. Financial services such as brokerage and banking are heavy users of CRM technology. Deregulation and information technology have effectively blurred the boundaries between those two once-different financial institutions.

They have had a heavy reliance on information because these are primarily knowledge businesses. "Signature"-level customers at Charles Schwab wait no longer than fifteen seconds to reach a customer service person, whereas other customers can wait ten minutes or more. Some banks have coded their customers so that customer service reps can decide on rates and fees depending on the customer's profitability code. Centura Banks rates its customers on a profitability scale of 1 to 5.

The most profitable customers get service calls from staff and an annual call from the CEO. Attrition rate at the bank is down 50 percent in four years, and—more interesting—the percentage of unprofitable customers has gone down from 27 percent to 21 percent. The hospitality industry was able to slash 50 percent of its promotion programmes and increase response rates by 20 percent with a good database of response behaviour from its mailing list. CRM systems have provided firms with the data they need to determine the revenues and costs to serve at the individual customer level, allowing firms to prioritize their allocations of value-creating assets and resources to the more profitable customers.

According to AMR research, the CRM market grew from $200 milllion to $1.1 billion between 1994 and 1997, and is expected to reach as much as $16 billion—an indication of how much firms want this technology to manage customer relationships. A firm's knowledge about its customers has allowed it to adjust customer value based on the profitability of the individual customer.

Just as with power, information technology has to be used judiciously. Discriminating against less profitable customers can seem unreasonable to all paying customers and could backfire with publicity. AT&T withdrew its minimum usage charges for its basic-plan customers who were unprofitable. GE Capital tried to charge credit-card users who were not accruing a minimum level of interest charges and ended up having to sell its credit card business. When used appropriately at the individual level, information technology can be very rewarding. Capital One's senior vice-president for domestic card operations, Marge Connelly, says, "We look at every single customer contact as an opportunity to make an unprofitable customer more profitable."

CRM systems are not just about profiling customers and loyalty programmes. To derive maximum benefits, one must broaden the thinking about CRM technology. The technology should be viewed as knowledge-based systems that seek to prioritize commitment of a firm's assets and resources to the more profitable customers while enhancing the relationships with ALL (right) customers. Pricing may not be the appropriate means to deal with the unprofitable customer. CRM systems give the firm access to information that may reveal other ways to manage the unprofitable customer. *Enabling* the managing of customer relationships is the goal of the CRM system.

Managing customer relationships is about selecting, acquiring, retaining, and enhancing relationships with customers by using an intimate knowledge of the customer's consumption domain to maximize the return on the firm's assets. With CRM systems, firms have the knowledge and the technological capability to identify, retain and enhance more desirable customer relationships.

This covers issues regarding which customers to acquire and retain for maximum sustainable profits. How do you assign value to customers and what is involved in that evaluation? Who is the right customer? Who should be in your customer portfolio? Firms look at customers as investments. How do you value these investments? Or, What is the equity of your customers?

WHO IS THE RIGHT CUSTOMER?

The concept of brand loyalty is a well-researched topic. The notion of a customer having a lifetime value and the prominence of database systems in managing customers have spawned a renewed interest in relationship marketing. Just making repurchases doesn't make a customer brand loyal. There must be some commitment by the customer to the firm for relational continuity reflecting a positive patronage bias. Not all brand-loyal customers have a positive disposition to the provider—some relationships may be forced because of a lack of choice.

Brand loyalty reflects a financial, social, or structural bonding with the customer. Relationship marketing seeks to enhance the mutual benefits from the relationship with the right customer—seeking brand loyalty from the right customer. To determine who the right customer is, we need to understand what benefits the firm expects from an ideal customer. Management system is designed with you in mind. Knowing the needs of modern hotels, simplifies the communication between the waiting and kitchen staff.

Customer's orders are communicated automatically to the kitchen for display on a kitchen management system or for printing on a kitchen printer. This minimises wait times and eradicates ordering mistakes that can irritate customers and cost your restaurant unearned revenue. When combined with handheld terminals, orders can be taken directly from tables, speeding up the ordering experience further.

At the outset, it is clear that the stream of purchases from the brandloyal customer is the primary benefit. In truth, the value of a brand-loyal customer to the firm must go beyond the purchases made over the lifetime of the relationship with that customer. As shown, revenues can be direct and indirect. Direct revenues are all of the customer's purchases, and indirect revenues are the cash value of all of the other benefits the customer accrues to the firm, in the form of direct revenues from referred customers. Costs to serve are drastically reduced, as brand-loyal customers are generally easier to serve. The argument is that as customers get familiar with the firm, its processes and products, customers will require less costly assistance from the firm in purchasing and using the product.

Loyal customers may even be able to open up ways in which to reduce the costs of serving the customer. Other benefits of brand loyalty would include product improvement contributions, new product opportunities, ideal sources for market information, and favourable word of mouth. At an overall level, all these benefits add up to a degree of stability and potential growth for the firms. Those brand-loyal customers who are committed in their patronage recognize their benefits from the firm and show commitment in the provider firm.

To select the right customer, the firm must be able to measure the value of the loyal customer from all these benefits as well as the costs of acquiring and retaining that customer. It is not easy to quantify all of these benefits. But it is possible to calculate the direct and indirect revenues from each customer. It is also possible to calculate the acquisition costs and relationship maintenance costs. Information technology has allowed us to obtain that data and made it easy to calculate the lifetime value of a customer.

The Calculus of Lifetime Value

A commonly used practice inherited from the direct marketing industry experience is called RFM (referring to "recency, frequency, and monetary data")—a method to determine whom to send promotions from among your customers. It takes into account the value of a customer's purchases, how recent they were, and how often they were purchased. As with the danger of any one approach, RFM has been used without much consideration for other important dimensions of the most valuable customer, such as how profitable the customer really is. RFM is therefore not a proxy measure for the lifetime value of a customer.

Indeed, if the costs of serving different customers show a variance, then the RFM method could attract the wrong customer. As, there are three main factors in calculating the lifetime value of a customer. It is not just a simple product of the value of each purchase and the number of times the customer will purchase the product over that customer's lifetime. The lifetime value of a customer should also include referral value. And, it should include the lifetime costs as well. CRM technology has made it possible to do this, but, how many firms actually use this understanding in how they design and implement their CRM solutions?

Lifetime Revenues

Lifetime revenues are the sum of all purchases that the customer will make. An assessment of the progression of purchases over the lifecycle of the customer is a key point to be made here. For instance, consider what a college student's financial lifecycle would mean to a bank. First, it is a savings or checking account with a debit card and perhaps even a credit card. The college student may also be a good candidate for an education loan. Once graduated, this ex-student is now in the market for a car loan, and quite soon a home mortgage.

Once other life events such as marriage and children occur, there are more car loans, mortgages, home equity loans, trusts, custody accounts, education loans for children, and associated financial products that a typical family would need. USAA, the life insurance and financial services company, follows marriages, births, and other life events so that it can advise customers on changing needs.

Every firm should attempt to develop such a long-term consumption profile for the typical customer in each segment, charting their potential purchases over a lifetime to take into account the life events of the customer—a customer lifecycle analysis. A similar case may be made for business customers based on an assessment of growth potential, so that any B2B firm has to project the growth of its customers and factor that into a lifetime value calculation.

Not all customers become brand loyal. We have seen that superior customer value is a prerequisite for brand loyalty. What percentages of new customers find the firm's customer value to be superior? The lifetime value of a customer must also factor the probability of the acquired customer becoming brand loyal. Thus, the lifetime value of a customer is the first purchase, plus the probability of repeat purchases for the duration of the relationship with the firm. The probability consideration takes into account that a customer may not be a good fit, that a competitor may have been able to provide a better fit, or that the need situation changed for the customer, such as in the case of relocation of the consuming unit.

Lifetime Costs

An activity-based costing approach allows a firm to account for direct costs that the firm incurs in the relationship with a specific customer. Once again, with information technology it is possible, where it makes sense, to attribute marketing and operating costs to individual customers. To obtain the full benefit from CRM investments, it is important to track costs at the individual customer level as well. Costs include acquiring and remarketing to the customer over the lifetime of the customer.

Costs also include value creation and delivery costs of serving the customer. Thus, the costs after acquisition include not only the costs of serving the customer, but also relationship maintenance and development costs such as the costs of cross-selling or upselling, called remarketing costs. Once again, the costs related to the first purchase are separated from that of lifetime purchases so that the probability of repeat purchase is taken into account when calculating lifetime costs.

Referral Value

The indirect revenue of referrals from a loyal customer is an often overlooked aspect of customer equity. The typical CRM solution and database marketing approaches ignore the referral power of a customer in calculating the lifetime value of a customer. Most firms do not even capture this data, partly because it is difficult to obtain information when knowledge systems in a firm are not configured to obtain it. The other reason may be that firms are not proactively looking for referrals from their loyal customers in any systematic way.

How is the value of referrals from a customer calculated? To answer this question requires looking at the process and mechanics of how referrals work. Who provides a referral? Customers who are satisfied and who have a certain degree of loyalty are the ones who are likely to convey favourable messages about a firm and its products and services. A key piece of information needed here is what level of satisfaction a brand-loyal customer needs to have before being likely to refer a customer. The next obvious question is, who receives the referral? Customers are likely to convey this information to family, friends, and colleagues.

However, not all who receive the referrals are appropriate customers for the firm. What proportion of the customers who received the referral are good candidates for the firm? Out of the ones that are appropriate for the firm, not all are likely to be suitably influenced by the referral to make the first purchase. Finally, if a purchase is actually made, what proportion of referred customers makes repeat purchases? Those that are moved to try the product may not all turn into loyal customers, but if they do, then their lifetime purchases add to the value of the customer making the initial referral.

ATTRACTING AND RETAINING THE CUSTOMER-FOCUSED EMPLOYEE

Turnover at Dallas-based The Container Store is 20 percent compared to the industry average in retail operations, which generally ranges from 80 percent to 120 percent. Full-time employees at the company get 235 hours of training in their first year and are constantly asked what they need to do their job well. The company won *Fortune* magazine's "America's best workplace" honor in 2000. Similarly, at the 60-employee sports apparel company, Athleta Corp., employees set their own schedules and handle personal matters during the workday, backed by a CEO who believes that they will make up the time. To break the cycle of failure, firms have to value their employees. They ought to rethink the way they hire and groom their employees and managers. To do this, firms should be asking, what kind of employee do we need to attract and retain so that we can create and deliver a customer-focused solution? Managers from the functional areas of human resources, operations, and marketing management should jointly help determine the ideal employee for any position that is directly involved in creating and delivering value to the customer. Human resource decisions centre on hiring and training and are critical to acquiring the appropriate human capital in the firm. Study firms such as Disney, Nordstrom, Southwest Airlines, Ritz-Carlton, and American Express, which are known for their customer-focused culture, and you will see that all of them are very careful in how they select and hire their employees. They have in mind specific profiles that characterize the desired skills and personality traits that are necessary for the customer-focused employee in their business. Some of them use quite sophisticated ways of assessing the service orientation of the recruit. With the training and education these companies have in place, new employees are socialized into the corporate culture, whatever that culture might be. In a study within a large firm of five strategic business units (SBUs), 3,500 managers responding to a survey confirmed that the degree of market orientation in the processes of recruiting, training, and reward/compensation were found to strongly correlate with job satisfaction and trust in management.

A very revealing and useful exercise would be to investigate the hiring practices of the firm and check for how well the requirements for a customer-focused employee are reflected in the hiring and training practices. Does the firm have customer-focused criteria in their employee selection process? Do the job requirements and ideal candidate description reflect a customer focus? If the firm is well coordinated and integrated, customer knowledge is likely to be well utilized by the human resources department as well as the operations functions. Knowledge of the consumption activities of the customer should guide the practice of attracting and retaining human capital. If this is in place then the training and education is also likely to be designed to develop the employee for operational excellence contributing to creating and delivering the desired customer value. The operational excellence assumes the appropriate knowledge and attitude of the value creating and delivering role of the employee. Many firms now complement operations skills training with training on customer interaction skills or other customer-focused skills for the frontline employee.

Previously, for example, banks would provide operations training for tellers but not customer skills training. Once hired and trained, the operations and marketing functions take over the direct allocation, motivation, and supervision of the employee. Employees must be able to enjoy their work and find it rewarding not just financially but emotionally as well. How well these functions value the employee will have a major effect on the efforts of the firm to create and deliver the desired customer value. The customer-focused firm ought to be very interested in the welfare of its employees. Otherwise, employees tend to disconnect from the firm and are not committed to their jobs. For example, Dupont began a programme to "re-engage" with employees by helping employees design their career paths in an attempt to win back employee loyalty.

Northeast Delta Dental is one of the major dental care insurance providers in New England. CEO Tom Raffio expresses his main challenge as "how to retain the customer-focused culture that has given us success as we continue to grow." He succeeds by being very close to his employees. He goes to the extent of meeting the families of his employees so that he has an intimate knowledge of his employees' lives. His office is in the middle of the busiest floor of the corporate office. He likes being accessible and close to his employees. Tom brings customer feedback directly to his employees and asks them what they thought the firm ought to be doing. He is genuinely interested in the growth and development of the employee. The employee is empowered with the operational skills and with customer knowledge.

The customer-focused firm is proactive in rewarding employees for being customer focused. As we saw earlier, Commerce Bancorp of New Jersey gives its employees $50 to come up with any practice of the bank's that is not customer-focused. The company almost instantly rewards an employee for specific customer-focused actions in a customer experience or incident. Whoever has wowed the customer gets a "Wow" award hand-delivered the next day from head office. The customer-focused firm ensures that the workplace is a place where people can grow, where they are comfortable at what they are doing.

Several firms have begun to include a measure of customer satisfaction in the compensation and bonus criteria for employees. Here is an interesting example of a culture spillover from a merger that benefits the bigger company. PTC, formerly Parametric Technology, which acquired Computervision, found that their own salespeople were not concerned with managing the customer relationship after the sale while those who came from Computervision emphasized customer service. Today, all salespeople in the company are evaluated on customer satisfaction scores as well, and PTC is focusing on solutions rather than the software product. More than a decade ago, GE began a customer education programme at its Management Development Institute, where customers and employees are educated on the firms' goals and processes. The idea was to get the customers and employees together and explain the goals and strategies of the firm.

In this new economy, knowledge-based employees are very mobile with their expertise. Firms would be well advised to assess each employee's worth, including replacement cost, similar to the analysis in managing customer relationships, to determine the firm's need to retain the individual. Retention efforts should be prioritized according to that worth of the employee. When firms reluctantly started laying off workers during the recent recession, employers were also offering enticements with bonuses so that they would return to the firm when it was ready to rehire workers. Charles Schwab was offering bonuses and $20,000 worth of college tuition money, hoping that these workers would come back to Schwab when the company started to hire again.

Treacy and Wiersema argued that a firm has to have at least one of the three value disciplines they organize their thesis around—operational excellence, customer intimacy, and product leadership. Either firms have to be very good at the customer value that they create and deliver, their values should be built around intimate customer knowledge, or they should be at the forefront of product innovation. The argument that these are separate value disciplines is often commonly accepted. However, in a discussion of the customer-focused firm, the distinction appears to be irrelevant. The customer-focused firm assumes that it has to be good at all these three value disciplines simply because they are interrelated. A customer-focused firm derives its competitive advantage from its service orientation. With its intimate knowledge of the customer (customer intimacy), the firm excels in creating and providing superior customer value (operational excellence), and by anticipating and responding to evolving customer needs it continues to improve its customer value (product leadership).

In the new economy, a firm with a customer-focused culture leverages its people and its information technology to be close to the customer so that it can create and deliver superior customer value. Its people and information technology, as the primary productive factors, have to be employed in such a way as to ensure the firm's ability to understand the customer and to use that knowledge in its value creation and delivery. Thus, the importance of customer intimacy and operations excellence is taken as a guiding element in corporate strategy and performance. This approach requires a culture that is customer focused as a prerequisite to derive a sustainable competitive advantage.

Ensuring that the firm is staying customer focused should be a constant endeavor. It requires assessing the level of customer intimacy that the firm can claim. It requires the continuous assessment of the operational excellence that the firm is able to achieve. Key questions to ask would concern customer knowledge management.

MARKETS CONSIST OF THE RIGHT CUSTOMER

Markets consist of customers with diverse needs and differences in customer profitability. When serving multiple groups of customers, the goal must be to maximize the profitability of the combination of segments. When different segments are targeted, the firm essentially has a portfolio of customer segments—just as investors have an investment portfolio that maximizes returns at a certain level of risk, firms manage customer portfolios for maximum profits. As standard, hotels are fitted with an integral magnetic stripe reader for credit and debit cards and our EFT system is approved by all the major banks and clearing houses.

However, in an age when credit card fraud is on the increase, hotels can protect you and your customers from fraud with the addition of Chip and PIN devices. Chip and PIN solution can be integrated to operate with your Hotel billing system's configurable client credit limit.

In other words, this is the selection of customers at any point in time, compared to other segments, from which the firm can generate maximum profits. Firms must attract these most profitable customers and then must establish systems and procedures to retain them.

Most firms serve different segments depending on how the definition of segment is aggregated. The "segment-of-one" used in common business parlance to refer to customization at the individual level is really a maximum disaggregation of a market segment. As we saw, most firms facing fluctuating demand and experiencing peak, shoulder and low periods of demand find it inevitable that, at different times, different segments must be served.

Of course, each of these segments must have a compatible fit with the overall corporate image as well as a compatible fit with the products, services, employees and other customers. The question is, are they selected based on their combined long term value to the firm?

Most firms forecast the volume and revenues from various segments at certain price points at different times in the purchase cycle. In the typical firm, sales and communications efforts follow these underlying assumptions in pricing and in messages targeting sales prospects. The typical firm then attempts to formalize advertising campaigns to reach as many people as possible in the case of packaged goods. In the case of business-to-business services, the salespeople focus on making a sale.

Most firms then struggle to orchestrate all these messages for acquisition of the customer in a coordinated fashion. Much less attention is paid to the retention of the customer. Barring the well-run operation, common business practice for many firms is short-term oriented. On the contrary, a customer-focused firm begins by approaching sales as acquiring the right customer. The customer-focused firm also approaches the acquisition of customers as only the first step in managing the relationships with its customers. Once acquired, the customer must be retained. But, not always retained at any cost—a necessary condition is that the benefits outweigh the costs of acquiring *and* retaining that customer.

Customer-focused firms align all their activities and processes in acquiring and retaining the right customer. They see their value-creating assets as most profitably leveraged by focusing on the most valuable customers. In principle, the value of the customer is determined by contribution to the firm's objectives over the lifetime of the customer. The right customer is that customer whose inclusion in the firm's target market helps maximize returns on the firm's assets.

Customer Equity

Ask a manager, "What is your firm's most valuable asset?" Chances are that you will not get the response, "my customers." You will find even fewer firms that actually make an assessment of this value in any real sense. The valuation of the customer is implicit in sales figures—essentially, the revenues generated by customers of the firm. What is the flaw in using sales as a proxy in valuing a firm's customers? Consider this.

Two customers with the same cash value of purchases may not be of the same value to the firm. There may be differences in the cost of serving these two customers. The true value of the customer to the firm, or the equity that the firm has in that customer, must include all revenues and also all costs related to that customer, as in financial investments. A recent framework by a team of researchers defines customer equity as the "total of the discounted lifetime value of all the firm's customers."

They articulate three drivers of customer equity: value equity, brand equity, and relationship equity. They define value equity as the objective assessment of the utility of the brand, and value equity is driven by quality, price, and convenience; brand equity as the subjective assessment of the brand above and beyond the perceived value, and brand equity is driven by brand awareness, attitude toward the brand, and corporate ethics; and relationship equity as the tendency of the customer to stick with the brand, and relationship equity is driven by loyalty programmes, special recognition and treatment, affinity programmes, community-building programmes, and knowledge-building programmes.

Their framework—the customer equity diagnostic—is offered as a way to determine which customers to acquire as well as what will enable their retention. If we define customer value as the value of the firm or a product as perceived by the customer, customer equity is the converse and refers to the value of the customer to the firm. If the objective is to maximize the returns from your investments—the customer portfolio—you must maximize customer equity. This makes sense because you can maximize sustainable return on assets by maximizing customer equity for the long term.

To maximize customer equity, we must be able to measure it. If customer equity is simply the value of a customer to the firm, we can articulate that value in the same way that customers articulate our value to them. Just as customer value is the difference between benefits and costs to the customer, conversely, customer equity is the difference between the benefits and costs to the firm in serving a customer.

One team of researchers describes their method of measuring customer equity as follows: "[we] first measure each customer's expected contributions toward offsetting the company's fixed costs over the expected life of that customer. Then we discount the expected contributions to a net present value at the company's target rate of return for marketing investments. Finally, we add together the discounted expected contributions of all current customers." Evident in their metric are the following important points about customer equity:

- It is the sum of the equity of all of a firm's customers.
- It summates the gross contribution of each customer, taking into account benefits as well as costs of serving a customer.

- It includes consideration of future revenues and variable costs from each customer.
- It is a time-discounted present value of future benefits to the firm.

It becomes evident that the customer equity concept when disaggregated to the individual customer level allows us to look at the revenues and costs of serving an individual customer. It helps answer the question, which customer should we serve? The ideal customer to the firm is the one that gives it the maximum long-term customer equity, which theoretically you want as a brand-loyal customer. However, the converse is not true, because not all brandloyal customers provide maximum customer equity.

MANAGING CUSTOMER INFORMATION

Firms cannot claim a customer focus or attempt to satisfy customers unless they have customer knowledge—that is, a deep understanding of the needs of the customer. Customer-focused firms really understand their customers by proactively acquiring information on the entire consumption process, especially the consumption activities of the customer. Such information must be processed and used to guide each and every interaction with that customer. This information can be used not only to make changes and improvements in the value-creation and delivery processes of a firm but also in managing relationships with the right customers.

Managerial decisions and actions cannot be customer oriented when customer data is lacking. Do we know enough about the customer's consumption activities to enable us to create and deliver customer-focused value and manage relationships with the customer?

As Lew Platt, former CEO of Hewlett Packard, is widely quoted as saying: "If HP knew what HP knows, we would be three times as profitable" With the increasing ubiquity of information technology, there is an increasing focus on information—in a way, simply because it is there. Most managers understand the crucial role that good information plays in decision making. And here is a seemingly radical proposition: most data is underutilized in business. If you don't know what data is important, you may not recognize it when you see it. When there is an opportunity to obtain what may be valuable data, you will not access or gather, process, or utilize it.

Careful observation would reveal that as a norm, firms don't capitalize on opportunities to gather critical customer data. One reason may be that firms focus on the sort of data that is needed for a specific decision, such as in the development of a new product or an advertising campaign, especially in the B2C context, where there are no direct interactions with the customer. In the B2B context, where there is direct interaction with the customer, there is a greater amount of customer information being utilized for decision making. This is partly because formalized systems are in place to document customer information. The customer being a business is very likely to have formalized purchasing procedures. Information-age technology has very naturally developed in the B2B case earlier and faster than in the B2C case. In the B2C business, where there is direct interaction with the customer, this technology is opening new thinking about customer data. A basic question is, what information is needed and for what purpose?

The convergence of numerous information technologies in the gathering, storing, processing, disseminating, accessing, and using data has revolutionized the most generic of all business tasks—making informed business decisions. Communication, storage, and computational technologies have made this possible. Firms have found ways to deploy these technologies toward of increasing productivity. When the promise of technology is not delivered, as in many CRM and ERP projects, the focus has turned to how and why this data is useful for a business to support the investment in information technology. One of the primary information systems of a firm is the customer information system. Customer-focused firms have used their information technology to develop smart customer information systems and broaden the scope of this business function. The role of the Chief Knowledge Officer, a title that was unheard of just a few years ago, is to manage the creation, discovery, and dissemination of knowledge in firms. In the context of managing the knowledge resident with the firm about its business, customer information is one of the key pieces of the knowledge this person manages. The status given to this function is reflected in the seniority of the position and indicates the commitment of the firm to managing customer information that can be used to improve the value created and delivered by the firm.

The key issues discussed in this chapter are: what kinds of customer information are needed to perform as a customer-focused firm, what information is required to usefully profile a customer, and how such a customer profile helps a firm understand the customer.

We saw that delivering superior customer value is a prerequisite for sustainable competitive advantage and that to be able to deliver superior customer value, a firm requires a good understanding of what customers value. A good understanding of customer value presupposes good customer information. You cannot claim a customer focus, or seriously attempt to satisfy your customers, unless you understand their needs. An effective customer information system ensures that the appropriate knowledge of the customer is available for customer-focused decisions and actions. Without customer information, for example, it would be impossible to customize customer experiences, let alone manage customer relationships.

Knowledge of the customer is about being intimate with the customer. Customer intimacy is not just a cliché. Customer intimacy is a value discipline for firms that value and use an intimate knowledge of their customers to determine precisely which types of customers to serve and then align all their value-creation processes to create and deliver solutions to their specific type of customer. In a competitive landscape where competing products with little defensible product differentiation are becoming commodities, customization is one very powerful way to de-commoditize a product and build customer relationships. *Customization,* as a term, is used broadly here to denote making changes in value creation and delivery such that the customer value is adjusted to each customer when and where appropriate. To know when and where customization is appropriate, you need to know your customer. Customer-focused firms pay attention to their customers. They listen to their customers. They really know their customers. The more knowledge the firm has about its customers, the more poised and able the firm is to deliver superior customer value.

Ritz-Carlton is known for its ability to personalize its service encounters with its frequent guests by maintaining a detailed preference profile at the individual customer level. With smart customer information systems, Ritz-Carlton's frontline employees are empowered to address guests by their first names and with knowledge of the guest's specific preferences. CLASS (Customer Loyalty Anticipation and Satisfaction) is an example of the information technology backbone to the Ritz-Carlton's guest relationships management programme. Nadia Kyzer knows that having a database system is not enough, saying: "If our employees didn't put the information to real concrete use, the system would be worthless" Many firms use their knowledge of the customer to tailor their products and messages, or to promote new services to their customers. For example, on the Internet, firms use knowledge gained from cookies to model patterns of customer behaviour on their Web sites so as to target promotions deemed appropriate for that customer. But good customer information management goes beyond targeting messages and promotions. QVC, the television-based retailer, uses a "daily activity report" to capture, monitor, and respond to customer perceptions of quality. Indeed, customer information should drive all business processes of the firm, including anticipating and meeting customer needs, creating and delivering services, and anticipating and recovering from service failure. Customer-focused firms must have good customer information to support the decisions and activities of the firm.

Customer-focused decisions affecting customer value require information on customers' needs, their product preference criteria leading to brand choice or loyalty and their perceptions and behaviour with regard to the product. This is true not only in the acquisition and use, but also in the disposition of products. Since service firms interact with the customer during consumption of the product there is ample opportunity to obtain and respond to customer information. For example, New England's largest bank, FleetBoston, recently instituted the "customer experience crusade."The firm hired new staff to be stationed in the lobbies of its large-volume banks to serve as "meeter-greeters" assisting customers with their banking problems. Ostensibly, the attempt was to reverse the lousy service reputation FleetBoston had acquired due to its preoccupation with challenges following its merger with BankBoston. With the knowledge gained from the activities of these customer service agents, the bank could be learning a lot about customer experiences and about how its customers actually use a number of the bank's services. This knowledge could then be used to drive all decisions about structuring and delivering the bank's services.

Good customer information is an asset of the firm. Logically, anything that contributes to sustainable competitive advantage is an asset to the firm. Since information on customers is useful in better matching a firm's products as solutions to customer needs, customer information is an asset that contributes to sustainable competitive advantage. For example, retailing has become so fiercely competitive that customer information assets are now seen as a competitive advantage. Customer loyalty programs in retailing are an attempt to link customer information to transaction data. Customer databases with purchase histories showing shopping preferences can be used in customercentric business decisions. Customer information is so valuable that firms who share customer information have to be careful about ownership of the database. At the end of a joint project, for example, Wells Fargo bank and Microsoft went to court to determine who owned a customer database that was created as part of that joint venture.

A good example of the power of customer information is on the Internet. Personalized Web pages use customer information "on-thefly" to customize the online customer experience. It is common knowledge now that firms have data that tells them who is visiting, how long they are staying on the site, and where on the site visitors are spending their time. Firms have knowledge of customer behaviour on their Web site with information on where visitors were entering the Web site (beyond the home page) and leaving the Web site, what keywords or links brought them to the site, and so on. All this is possible with data-warehousing and data-mining techniques. In the Internet age, entire new services, such as online investment brokerage firms, have sprung up with value propositions enabled by technology-powered databases of customer information. In the brave new investment world, such new business models have forced traditional investment brokerage houses to incorporate these added value propositions to their existing businesses. Other new financial service models have emerged. For example, a number of online firms offer instant mortgage or credit application and approval. Much of this is possible because rules-based algorithms created from studying databases allow firms first to offer conditional approval then then to be able to verify the credit risk because financial institutions have well-developed databases of an individual's financial history with them.

While the technology is available to do more with information, it is unfortunate that the kinds of information that most firms obtain on a regular basis are usually limited to transactional data—such as what was purchased, when, and for how much. With this information, firms are able to use recency, frequency, and monetary data and conduct what is called RFM analysis. Patterns of relationships between the variables are used to determine the best prospects among the customers in the database—those that might be high-propensity targets for a promotion. Transactional data is important, but not adequate to make customer-focused decisions. In addition to being able to individualize interactions with the customer, with customer information that goes beyond transactional data a firm can derive knowledge to guide anything from cost-saving measures in operations to new product decisions. To really understand the customer, firms need information on a multitude of dimensions other than just transactions around their other actual consumption activities.

Customer-focused decisions and actions require customer information at two levels. At the aggregate level, customer information is about the market—or more specifically, about the typical customer in the segment(s)—and at the individual level, it is about a specific customer. When the number of customers for a firm is large and there is no opportunity to directly interact with the customer, it does not make economic sense to get down to the level of individual customer-specific profiles. For example, Procter & Gamble may not be able to interact with each and every Crest toothpaste user. In such a situation, the customer profile is aggregated and constructed at the market segment level. On the other hand, for firms that directly interact with the customer, it makes sense to profile specific individual customers. For example, General Electric interacts with individual customers of kitchen appliances who contract customer service agreements. GE can use their knowledge of each individual customer to target service contract renewal offers or offers for replacement products when the normal life of the appliance has passed. In general, it should become apparent that the more the aggregation, the less specific and accurate the information on individual customers. As seen the level of aggregation of the information will also determine whether that information is useful for individualized or segment-level decisions, processes, and activities. As the level of aggregation of customer information increases, the level of aggregation of the customer solution increases and the firm is working at the segment level. With lower levels of aggregation, the firm is working at the individual customer level.

Customer information, whether at the market segment level and/or at the individual level, provides a profile of the customer that guides a customer-focused firm's decisions and actions. A customer profile should be based on two broad categories of information: *Background profile* is general customer information not directly related to the product and is not product-specific; and *consumption profile* is directly related to the product and is product-specific, in that it is about behaviour related to the consumption of the specific product.

REMARKETING TO THE RIGHT CUSTOMERS

To maximize the total lifetime value of their customers, firms must proactively manage customer relationships. As, proactive customer relationship management should seek customer appreciation from the heavy user and attract more interest from light users with better value bundles if they can contribute more in their lifetime value to the firm. This is in contrast to the firm that may have good customer service, for example, but in its reactive mode will leave the light user relatively indifferent to the firm and the heavy user susceptible to a competitor.

Most loyalty programmes involve some kind of reward for the continued patronage of their customers. Referred to as frequency marketing, continuity programmes, awards or points programmes, or simply loyalty a programme, the goal of these programmes is to market and manage relationships with customers. First instituted by American Airlines in the 1970s to get around government regulation that prevented price competition, now many firms' programmes attempt to solidify their relationships with its customers. The rewards or awards, as they are called, may come in the form of free products and services at the firm, or sometimes even free products from other firms.

The smart firms impose restrictions on the use of these rewards, so that they are used to increase demand when and where needed. For example, the hospitality industry blocks out certain dates so that the promotions are targeted at different segments to entice customer utilization at low demand periods. The problem is that many of these programmes are misguided in design and implementation. One obvious omission is evident when the lifetime calculus is compared to the criteria for the rewards. The rewards focus on revenues for the most part. That costs are taken into account is not clear at all.

A recent *Harvard Business Review* article offers data that would be a surprise for managers who have not considered costs of serving the customer. Brand-loyal customers are not necessarily profitable customers. In their knowledge of their own value and indispensability to the firm, the brand-loyal customer could make costly demands of the firm.

The firm, in doling out the goodies along with the product and other business favours, may actually be spending more than it recognizes as costs of serving that customer. The only criterion for these (brand) loyalty programmes should be that they should maximize the customer equity for each customer, based on the calculus of lifetime value that we have discussed. To be meaningful and powerful in managing relationships with the right customers, these customer acquisition and loyalty programmes must specify the following:

- Objectives of the programme
- Market and customer scope of the programme
- Value for customer scope of the programme
- Impact scope (costs, timing, impact on people, process, physical assets, other customers, publicity opportunities, etc.)

The objectives of the programme need to be stated in the context of customer relationship management. What is the expected value of the programme to the firm? What specifically must the programme accomplish?

Perhaps it is to shift demand from peak to low periods, to attract new segments, to get light users to become heavy users, to promote a new product offering, or some other specific objective. Without a known objective, no programme can be assessed on merit.

The next specific decision for customer relationship programmes is to specify the customer that the programme is intended for. Often, frequency programmes are so loosely formulated that the rewards are earned by the wrong customer. Consider this example of the unfortunate consequence of a poorly guided programme. One Mr. Phillips logged 1.25 million frequent flier miles—about $25,000 worth of airline travel—with an investment of 50 hours of his time and $3,140. Mr. Phillips took advantage of an offer he found on the package of a Healthy Choice frozen entrée: 500 American Airlines miles for every 10 UPCs, with early birds receiving a double count of miles! A Mr. Fisher participated in the same programme and got 12,000 Northwest Airlines Miles.

Even if the airlines got an awfully good financial deal with Healthy Choice, one must ask who the loyalty programme attracts—whether the airlines are in the grocery business or in the airline business. How do their returns from this investment compare with the returns that they would have achieved with programmes that targeted the frequent flier instead of the frequent grocery shopper? The objectives of the programme should determine the appropriate segment or customer for the programme.

The problem with most programmes is that they don't take into account the profitability of the customer. Who should be the target of the programme? Not every customer is right for the firm, as we have seen, nor is every customer right for every programme. The best programme is one that tailors the award to the target customer. Thus, giant supermarket retailer UK-based Tesco mails 100,000 variations of promotions to its loyal customers.

Further, some customers may be more costly to retain, while others may be increasing their profitability to the firm. As, it is evident that firms need to look at the acquisition costs and retention costs of its customer base when determining the focus of their retention efforts. The calculus of the lifetime value of a customer is clear in its indication of what needs to be factored into deciding to which customer to target the promotion. Low acquisition costs and low retention costs are realized from your most profitable customers.

At the other end are your customers who were costly to acquire and cost you a lot to serve. Given the acquisition costs, the firm must keep a close eye on the customer's cost of retention. If the firm misjudged a customer's lifetime value or committed more resources to the acquisition of the customer than the revenue stream would justify, the firm has to either reduce retention costs or stop serving the customer if possible.

For the chosen customers, the firm needs to decide what they would do to motivate the customer to act. Customer knowledge should indicate what the customer is sensitive to, so that the value of the promotion can be appropriate for the specific customer or segment. The value of the promotion may be in the form of additional product, a complementary service, a straightforward price-break, or a discount for future purchases or a gift, among other things. Software firms are able to use lead customers in beta-tests and other benefits about new and innovative offerings before the rest of the market will find out, giving these B2B customers early mover advantage in their value chains in their industry.

Of course, a projected cost/benefit analysis is a must—what additional revenues have been realized and at what cost? For service firms, and where the programme is about service components, it is imperative that the promotion take into account what it would do to the demand patterns of customers. The last thing you want is for customers to strain your operation if your programme ends up drawing more customers during peak times when you are already at optimum levels of served customers. Any programme must consider the impact on other customers, on the staff, physical assets, and the delivery system or process.

For example, a shortage of airline seats infuriates frequent fliers who, as brand-loyal customers, having diligently set aside miles for use on family vacations, find they are not able to use the miles because use of awards is limited to a certain proportion of the volume on each flight and are restricted to certain times and dates. Estimates are that about 10 percent of all miles flown on a carrier can be from people cashing in on these rewards.

Does it make sense for frequent flier awards to range from personal digital assistants to designer watches? Are the costs and impact of these awards assessed? Another less obvious criterion is the potential for publicity in a promotion. A promotion that is newsworthy could attract the attention of a large number of potential customers and other stakeholders.

Firms must prioritize the management of customer relationships as a firm-wide imperative. Dell Computer, for example, has a "customer experience council" consisting of senior executives from each division or business line and major function that reports to a corporate vice chairman, no less. The council oversees measurement of several aspects of customer behaviour, including the effectiveness of its loyalty programmes. Dell even measures all the costs its customers incur in purchasing and using their products, including such things as shopping, ordering, installing, operating, servicing, and disposing of products.

The real value of tracking these revenues and costs over the lifetime value of the customer is that it allows firms to understand their brandloyal customers and anticipate their future needs. Such management practices will be able to deliver benefits to the heavy user to maximize their lifetime value. The lifetime value of the customer must be calculated for each customer—an assessment of revenues and costs over the lifetime of the customer's relationship with the firm. The investment in acquiring and retaining a customer must be made based on the customer's lifetime value to the firm.

A continuous monitoring of up-sell and cross-sell opportunities could increase the lifetime value of the customer. The potential customer equity from each segment or customer should determine the extent of value-creating adjustments to be made in terms of delivery process or product outcome customization in terms of value or other benefits to the customer or in terms of adjusting the price and other costs to the customer.

These changes in promotion offerings to acquire a new customer or remarket to a current or inactive customer will impact both costs and revenues and their effect on the lifetime value of the customer will determine subsequent investments in acquiring and retaining customers.

RECRUITMENT AND SELECTION

The philosophy is if you create spaces where people like to spend time, they will spend money. So it's very much a design-driven experience. And although the restaurants were designed for the local market, hotel guests must be treated as "preferred local customers, if they come in without a reservation. Hotel guests must be offered reservations upon check in. Also, as the hotel itself has ample meeting and ballroom space, the restaurants were designed with significant private dining components to capture the dollars of group guests, as well.

High levels of recruitment activity can be attributed to specific conflicting pressures. On the one hand the HI worldwide reports skill shortages and fails to fill current vacancies, inferring a quality problem. Employers may not be targeting appropriate groups of people or national training frameworks may be inadequately geared to the industry's needs. Considering only locals as a source of labour may be outdated in a global economy.

Technological advances facilitate the finding of required labour by targeting recruitment in developing countries, where there are high rates of unemployment among skilled workers, e.g. in Bangladesh 40 per cent of people with a Master's degree are unemployed or under-employed. The increasing presence of MNCs in tourism, in countries such as India, may not necessarily be met by an adequate supply of skilled workers. Skills shortages in Florida are overcome by recruiting from Puerto Rico.

On the other hand the consequences of employment flows, which management may seek to perpetuate, and cost-minimization policies encourage recruitment systems that are highly responsive, flexible and ad hoc. Given high leaver rates noted, it is not surprising to find a high rate of recruitment in Britain.

HI workplaces are significantly more likely to have workforces with 50 per cent or more new employees, and this is three times greater than in AIS. Large workplaces have the lowest rates of recruitment activity.

In the twelve months prior to WERS HI workplaces were most likely to have vacancies for unskilled and sales staff. HI workplaces were significantly more likely to have vacancies for personal service, sales staff and routine unskilled manual workers, and significantly less likely to have vacancies for professional, technical and scientific, clerical and secretarial and operative and assembly workers.

Half the workplaces in AIS, PSS and the HI had no difficulty filling vacancies, while skilled and unskilled job were most problematic in a small minority of HI workplaces. Considerable variations within sub-sectors reflect the different skill bases within them.

A different set of pressures is observed in post-Communist Russia, where bringing in new staff to respond to new demands is difficult to achieve. Overstaffing is rife because of low pay, problems making people redundant and the social responsibility to keep staff in jobs. Consequently staff becomes bored and lazy.

Table. Recruitment in Last 12 Months in Context and by Size of Workplace

	AIS	PSS	HI	<25	25-49	50-99	100+
Total recruits							
Mean number	13	14	20	10	25	42	53
As % of total employees 1 year ago	27	34	63*	62	72	64	33
New permanent							
Yes (%)	91	93	93	93	89	100	100

Notes:

All weighted cases where there have been recruits (AIS, N = 2,142, PSS, N = 1,331 and HI, N = 154). Means are rounded. *Significantly different at the 5% level from AIS and PSS.

Table. Recruitment in Last 12 Months by Sub-sector

	Hotels	Campsites	Restaurants	Bars	Canteens
Total recruits					
Mean number	29	2	21	15	10
As % of total employees 1 year ago	59	5	66	71	24
New permanent					
Yes (%)	97	100	97	88	100

Notes:

All weighted cases where there have been recruits. Means are rounded.

Approaches to Recruitment

Recruitment and selection are an important part of managerial work and workplace life. To proponents of the quality-enhancing employment approach 'employee selection is an important issue. Investing in techniques and skills which improve the selection decision is essential for organisational success'. Good recruitment and selection is based on an assessment of work values, personality, interpersonal skills and problem-solving ability. Testing potential employees can be used to control 'type' and help mould organizational culture.

On the other hand those pursuing a cost-minimization approach may have little incentive or will to deploy other than the most basic of methods, and may respond in an ad hoc way. Using casual staff as ports of entry not only maintains control over staffing levels but also over behaviour and discipline, as casuals can be more easily dismissed. Ease of dismissal may act as a barrier to the adoption of more systematic recruitment and selection, especially where there is a plentiful supply of labour. Lack of job security is likely to undermine the achievement of SQ, and may also reflect the low status of the personnel function or its absence.

The 'employment decision', when the vacancy is filled by an appropriate candidate, is a mutual and voluntary decision, based on employers' and candidates' freedom to withdraw from the process at any time. The process involves chance and risk. Managers have considerable discretion but are never in complete control. Managers' own ways of maximizing cost-effectiveness have different meanings within firms' own employment standards and different labour market conditions.

Studies consistently report high levels of informality, including 'word of mouth' recruitment. Most British students gain employment by initiating contact themselves or through friends and family, which is even more common in Bulgaria, Hungary and Slovakia. Greater formality may be found in larger hotel firms, but is by no means comprehensive. Larger hotel companies looking overseas for staff are providing more accommodation as a first temporary step in the first two months of employment.

A large majority of British HI workplaces in WERS are significantly more likely to treat internal and external candidates equally than in AIS and PSS. Consequently they are also less likely to give preference to internal candidates over external candidates except in medium and large workplaces (one-third favour internal candidates). This is mirrored in slightly lower levels of internal recruitment in the HI. Goss-Turner (1999) notes that multi-unit managers are normally recruited internally on the basis of perceived task and people orientation, without any systematic selection procedures.

Recruitment Criteria

We noted how in customer-service work recruitment is more likely to be based on people's personal and aesthetic skills than technical skills, while the preceding discussion suggests availability is also important. Dickens argues that attitudes, behaviour and personality tend to interact with gender and racial stereotypes, which may lead to discrimination in recruitment. Managers' preference for recruitment is made on the basis of personality. Aesthetically employers can signal the type of labour required by using terms such as 'smart young person' in an advertisement, or requiring the enclosure of a photograph with applications. By presenting themselves in person young people enable employers to screen for aesthetic skills. Hence recruitment (and training) is on the basis of customer focus, interpersonal skills, emotional control and empathy. Training in grooming and deportment may follow.

The 'personality' criterion is to an extent confirmed by WERS, which shows that the four most important recruitment criteria in the HI are motivation, references, skills and availability; each is used in three-quarters or more workplaces. The three most important criteria in AIS of experience, skills and motivation apply in 86 per cent or more workplaces. Availability, experience and personal recommendation are significantly more important in the HI than in AIS and PSS. Qualifications are more important in AIS and PSS. Availability is of major importance to restaurants, while age is more important in bars than in any other sub-sector.

We know that a combination of volatile demand, age-related factors, and worker attributes makes young workers, particularly students, a valuable commodity within the HI. Yet firms have not fallen to the temptation of employing more young workers on officially sanctioned lower rates of pay under the NMW. This fits with their pay structures, policies on employing particular age groups for particular jobs or periods of time, or legal restrictions on the serving of alcohol and the operation of dangerous machinery.

Selection Methods and Tests

The interview remains popular with managers and candidates alike, as it is simple, quick and cheap, in spite of reliability and validity concerns. It fulfils a social function, enabling social and aesthetic aspects that are so integral to customer-service work to be addressed, however inadequately. Behavioural interviewing, where standard questions address how the candidate dealt with past situations that are likely to arise in their new job, provides better quality information and encourages a more reciprocal approach to employment decision-making. Like other simulated group exercises its limitations are assumptions that actual behaviour will be in line with intentions, and that a snapshot view is representative of general behaviour. Competency-based interviewing has produced exceptional performers and reduced turnover levels at the Buckhead Beef Company.

Paraskevas suggests that HI managerial selection techniques should be aimed at the application of skills, rather than their possession. Personality is an important consideration, and HI selectors are as likely to accept the validity and usefulness of sophisticated selection techniques as their counterparts in other sectors. Hotels do not use them because of cost and reliability concerns.

According to WERS personality and attitude tests have limited use in general, more so in the HI than in AIS and PSS. They are more likely to be used in HI firms employing 25 or more employees. While performance or competency tests are used by half of AIS firms significantly fewer HI workplaces (one-quarter) use them. They are most likely to be used in the largest HI workplaces but are rarely used in bars. One view is that tests are best suited to jobs involving special knowledge and abilities. Hence such tests have limited application among a largely unskilled workforce.

Appointment

Terms and conditions of employment (pay, hours, sick leave, grievance procedures, training opportunities and holiday) are made available in writing in most HI workplaces. However 13 per cent do not convey any of these details in writing, over twice the proportion in AIS and PSS. Restaurants are the worst offenders (one-quarter). Three-quarters of AIS, PSS and HI workplaces have standard employment contracts for their largest occupational group (LOG), although one-fifth of bars do not give their LOG contracts.

Retention

The recruitment and retention of managers and skilled workers is a global HCT sector problem. While Redman and Mathews (1998) contend that effective retention programmes will achieve higher levels of SQ, there is a view that the most talented people leave the sector, while the less competent stay for fear of becoming unemployed. In spite of the increase in hospitality management programmes and more hospitality graduates, there are poor graduate transfer rates and demand outstrips supply.

Part of the problem may lie in unsystematic graduate recruitment and selection that relies upon impressions and subjective judgements of character, and pays little regard to academic achievement and performance and supporting evidence from tutors. Poor impressions created by work placements may prompt hospitality graduates to seek careers elsewhere.

A number of the larger hotel companies have adopted training initiatives to improve retention in a tight UK labour market. The Thistle Tower Hotel introduced Modern Apprenticeships in-house, while employees at Harrington Hall were given the chance to study National Vocational Qualifications. The London Heathrow Marriott offers a wide range of courses including Modern Apprenticeships, graduate training schemes, NVQ programmes and English lessons for non-English speaking staff, while Accor also offers NVQs and Modern Apprenticeships. Rowley and Purcell (2001) note how leading edge employers' retention policies include anything, short of raising pay.

Training and Development

The state has a vested interest in VET in seeking to develop a more highly skilled labour force to improve economic performance and competitiveness. National systems vary considerably in general and in their specificity towards hospitality and tourism, with many developing countries not yet providing sufficient state support. In India the framework of tourism education is inadequate to a growing tourism sector where increasing professionalism, particularly at managerial levels, is required. Russia may have a highly literate and well-educated workforce, but this presents challenges to bringing managerial staff to the requisite level of skills and competencies where cultural attitudes are non-western.

The training culture of the US can be described as voluntarist and largely uncoordinated, and places emphasis on individual effort and individual payment - a 'protean' career. Germany, France and Sweden have directed and more centralized systems. In Spain many employees (43 per cent) have no school-leaving certificate. A state-funded scheme entitles employers to financial aid on presentation of an annual training plan.

Employees are eligible to up to 150 hours training on full pay. In Australia McDonald's offers employees access to an approved fast food accredited traineeship of 12 months' duration in return for a government subsidy. These arrangements have been incorporated into sectoral agreements. The British system is voluntarist, and not particularly industry-oriented since the demise of the industry training boards in the 1980s.

Hospitality and tourism management education is provided in many countries, but not in Denmark, Sweden or Japan. The corpus of knowledge for hospitality management is the preserve of the HCIMA, which represents 24,000 managers in 106 countries. Baum and Nickson press the case for a stronger pedagogical base in the learning experience of HRM in higher education, arguing that responding to industry demands may perpetuate existing (poor) HRM practice and make little or no contribution to change. Even major chains do not have any involvement with leading UK and US Business Schools.

In response to the 1997 National Targets for Education and Training for the UK, the HI's target for 2000 for the proportion of employers offering NVQs and SVQs was 50 per cent from a base of less than 1 per cent in the mid-1990s. The target for employees to have job-related qualifications increased to 60 per cent from 30 per cent. Such highly ambitious targets, even if met, would still leave major gaps in training provision.

MANAGING THE CUSTOMER

Since the customer is part of the process and some degree of interaction with the customer is necessary and inevitable, managers of services must find ways to educate customers on their roles. If the customer fails in playing the appropriate coproducer role, it could ruin the process and the outcome quality. A clear understanding of the steps in the process and how, where, and when customers interact with the process is a must. Doctors, nurses, and pharmacists provide directions and instructions for patient roles. Banks and other financial institutions have specific protocols for various financial transactions. A key question to ask is how the customer should participate in the process and whether you have the appropriate instructions for your customer. Differences in customer willingness and ability to participate in the production of the process force the issue of segmentation on the service delivery process. Thus, restaurants have self-service, take-out, or drive-through options. Automatic teller machines are an early example of self-service in banking services. Hotels have express check-in and check-out facilities. Airlines have electronic ticketing options. Self-service checkout facilities have become a standard option at grocery stores in the United States and elsewhere.

It is clear as we think about these issues that not all services are alike. While all services face all these challenges to some degree, the challenges manifest themselves differently in different services. In fact, the management solutions presented are more applicable in some and inappropriate or impossible in others. There is a systematic way of addressing these differences among services by examining characteristics that differentiate services from one another. A service that shares characteristics with another service exhibits similar challenges and opportunities.

In employing the service orientation, every manager needs to understand that there are different types of services in every product, each with its own manifestations of the fundamental characteristics of services. The nature of these manifestations in different services implies different situations for the customer and the manager. While all services are fundamentally intangible, inseparable, perishable, and variable, services differ from each other along dimensions peculiar to their category. These category characteristics provide the manager with an insight into the specific situations that they have to deal with in their particular service category.

Christopher Lovelock demonstrated that this sort of categorizing is necessary and powerful as a means of understanding the managerial situations specific to each type of service. Service managers should look toward other services that share similar characteristics and expect to find similar challenges and transferable solutions to those challenges. Consider for example that hospitals provide executive-style rooms for the businessperson who is a patient. They learned this from hotels that have executive-style suites for the businessperson. Now consider the service characteristics that are shared between hospitals and hotels. In both cases, the customer comes to the factory and frequently requires an overnight stay. In both situations, the executive is likely to be away from an office with all its business support for an extended period of time. Both services are similar in the type of customer interactions, even though they are in two completely different service sectors. An analysis as depicted earlier represents the benefits of learning from the successes of services that share certain specific service characteristics.

Managers of services can understand the specific challenges and opportunities presented by the characteristics of their product and corresponding situations by examining a number of characteristics that profile a service category. Here are a few characteristics to examine:

- Tangible or intangible act
- Person or thing as recipient of the act
- Type of interaction between provider and customer
- Service delivered by people or equipment
- Extent of customization or standardization

What are the tangible and intangible acts involved in the services that you are providing? Is the service act delivered on a person or a thing? For example, if you are an entertainment electronics repair and service provider, you perform tangible acts on a DVD player and intangible acts with the customer as you obtain information on what problems the customer has experienced with the DVD player. Now, examine the nature of the acts and the impact on the customer. When you are working on the DVD player, the customer needs not be present and the process that you employ need not be visible to the customer. However, you do interact with the customer at a number of points, from the initial customer call to the final interaction at delivery or pickup of the DVD player.

Similarly, you might analyze your service about the nature of interaction of with the customer. Is it face-to-face or arm's length, via telephone or the Internet? Do you visit the customer or does the customer visit your premises? How much technology is involved in the interface with the customer? Sometimes the customer does not even interact with a person. How much standardization is built into the service? Are there options provided to customers who require a customized interaction? What benefits does this analysis provide the manager?

The challenges and opportunities discussed earlier as fundamental are common to all service managers. By understanding the characteristics of their specific category of services, the manager can find ways to take advantage of the opportunities and address the challenges of their specific situation. Additionally, in understanding how the fundamental characteristic of intangibility manifests itself in their particular situation, managers can understand customers' perceived risk and use the tangibles in the customer experience to reduce the risk that customers perceive. By understanding the nature of the interaction, managers are in a better place to manage the roles of customers and recognize opportunities for customization and standardization to improve the customer experience and, therefore, customer value. What is most interesting is that you may find that service businesses in a different industry sharing certain characteristics may offer you innovative ideas to meet these challenges and capitalize on opportunities to better serve customers in your business.

In order to understand how the required service-oriented frame of mind needs to be handled in the customer-focused firm, the firm analyzes the various services with which it augments the product. Each service is analyzed from a fundamental and category perspective. The fundamental nature of services requires an analysis of the implications of the intangible, inseparable, perishable, and variable nature of services for managerial action. The analysis of category characteristics specific to each type of service should deal with how these consequences of these characteristics manifest themselves in that situation.

A TYPOLOGY OF SERVICE ORGANIZATIONAL MISMATCHES

One may assume that for any given range of actions provided to customer contact personnel, protocols exist that prohibit, obligate, and permit selections of alternatives that depend on the encounter circumstances. Within this normative framework, the exercise and use of judgment and discretion can be extensive or limited to the point of being virtually nonexistent.

Where their use and exercise are extensive, it is to presumably match and conform the job to the needs and expectations of specific customers. Where their use and exercise are virtually nonexistent, the job as it is designed and its supporting organizational infrastructure are presumably adequate to also match and conform the job to the needs and expectations of specific customers.

Organizational mismatches, therefore, arise between the job design and its supporting organizational infrastructure when customer contact personnel are confronted with a service demand that cannot be met without their being at odds with how they are to do their job and/or with the goals and objectives of the organization.

This section provides a typology of such mismatches based on job design and IT as the significant infrastructural component of interest providing the contexts in which judgement and discretion are used and exercised. Violations of the job design can occur in a number of ways. First of all, do customer contact personnel follow courses of action that fall outside what the technology circumscribes for them? Examples of such behaviour are abundant.

One can imagine an employee breaking open a cash register to make change for a customer because there is no sale with which to ring it open or no access to a key with which to unlock it. One can also imagine a situation where a hotel guest is permitted to take a free muffin from the breakfast line because the cash register is not programmed with a "muffin" key.

As job violations go, breaking open a cash register to make change is certainly more extreme than giving away muffins. Both cases, however, suggest that the customer contact job as it is technologically circumscribed may be inadequately designed to satisfactorily address every encounter for providing service that might come its way.

Such design inadequacies typify mismatches. Such mismatches could lead to service failures that in some cases only the extraordinary use and exercise of judgment and discretion can repair. Thus, the exercise of extraordinary judgment is a legitimate topic to examine.

The job design/service package is totally circumscribed, consisting of other organizational inputs including customer encounter personnel who have no leeway whatsoever using or exercising judgement and discretion in their conduct of the service encounter. As long as these encounters are routine, i.e., match the job's design, encounters are successful and customers are satisfied. Non-routine encounters, on the other hand, do not match the job design.

From the viewpoint of the organization, such an encounter is a non-event. It is certainly not a success but neither is it a failure, for the organization has not defined the customer's need as something the job was designed to satisfy. From the viewpoint of the customer seeking satisfaction, however, it is hard to argue that the encounter can be anything but a failure. The customer encounter personnel may, however, be able to satisfy a non-routine need and achieve a service encounter success attended by a mix of other results, but they must do so by abandoning altogether the use of the technology that is a fundamental functional part of their job's design.

Violations can occur within the job as designed and technologically circumscribed. These violations involve judgments that disregard organizational protocols and lead to particular technologically-doable ends that the technology installed is not intended to support. Such judgments may be conflicted or perverse.

The exercise of judgments that are conflicted may result in a service encounter success in the view of the customer and probably the customer encounter service person as well. Take for example, a customer who wishes to make a last minute change to his/her discount fare airline ticket at an airport airline ticket-counter. Penalties for making such changes are part of the terms to which the customer agrees when he/she purchases such a ticket.

Yet, the customer encounter service personnel at airline counters in airports rarely assess such penalties. Not only will they change flights for discounted tickets, they will even change airlines. They are perfectly capable of assessing such penalties, taking money, even making change. They have the IT available to do it, but they rarely do despite the fact that airline management directs them to the contrary.

Apparently, such personnel are empowered to exercise a great deal of individual judgment and discretion in such matters as they weigh such issues as customer flow, acceptable aircraft load factors, and customer goodwill. The authors regard conflicted judgments as being made in situations where the customers can be better served even though providing such service could prove detrimental to the service organization.

The job design/service package consists of a partially circumscribing IT and other organizational inputs including customer encounter personnel who have substantial leeway in terms of the judgement and discretion they can use and exercise in their conduct of the service encounter. Given that non-routine/custom service encounters are within the realm of possibility, success certainly occurs when customer contact personnel use and exercise judgement and discretion only insofar as they choose to strictly adhere to organizational guidelines and policies.

Thus an airline customer contact person could change a customer's discount ticket and assess the prescribed penalty and neither party would have any reason to regard such an encounter as anything but successful, for the desired change was made and the customer was assessed only the agreed-upon change fee. Such customer contact personnel can, however, use and exercise their judgement and discretion and not adhere to policies by choosing not to assess a customer a penalty for changing a discount ticket.

This also results in a successful service encounter from the point of view of the customer. It is, however, one that is lavish compared to assessing the customer a penalty for making the change. Furthermore, such a choice on the part of the customer contact person does not involve abandoning: the technology that is a part of his/her job design but putting it to use. The exercise of perverse judgments and the behaviours that ensue are often motivated by a perceived need on the part of various employees to "beat the system" and almost invariably jeopardize the success of the service encounter and well being of the service organization as well.

A study the authors did of a well-known fast-food service franchise, referred to as Flex-Mex, serves as an example. Flex-Mex's market qualifiers were a number of competitive priorities, "mass customization" of its product and speed of service. Its employment of IT contributed to a great extent in making this possible.

Flex-Mex's cash register(s) transmitted orders through a computer to display screens located in its back room where ingredients were assembled into menu items and orders filled. The assembly employee who completes the last step in filling the order removes it from the display screen. The screen then displays the next order in the queue.

Screens may hold many orders at a time and rarely do they become overloaded. This is due in part to screen capacity and in part due to the fact that an order can be "bumped" (erased from the screen) at anytime. Assembly personnel, therefore, do not necessarily need to wait until a customer physically receives his/her order to remove that order from the screen.

IT, however, performed more than an order communication function for Flex-Mex. It was used to monitor order delivery speed performance and foodstuffs wastage. Crews were rewarded for above-standard performance with half-price menu items for their meals and were denied half-price menu items for their meals and/or penalized individually with demotions or dismissal for sub-standard performance. As a result of this additional set of functions IT performed, assembly personnel would often "bump" an order before it was filled because that would stop the timer on that particular order.

Thus, assembly personnel were able to insure that no one order ever took an excessive amount of time quite independent of whether a customer had to wait an excessive amount of time for his/her order. Such a practice also resulted in misfilled orders since employees often carried as many as five different orders in their short-term memory. Several other downside phenomena accompanied these service failures. First, the correct order had to be refilled.

This took additional time but IT was not timing this activity. Second, the shelf life of these menu items is very short once prepared, less than five minutes in most cases. Thus, a certain amount of foodstuffs had to be scrapped if no new customer came along shortly ordering the same item. The assembly crew could only compensate for this waste by shorting other orders by small amounts of the ingredients.

The job design/service package consists of a partially circumscribing IT and other organizational inputs including customer encounter-personnel who have no leeway whatsoever in terms of the judgement and discretion they can use or exercise in the conduct of the service encounter. What is noteworthy is that it is not an encounter with a customer that elicits a perverse use of the technology of which the job design is in part constituted, but the encounter with limited measures of employee performance upon which a system of rewards and punishments is based. The encounter with the customer is irrelevant.

Analysis of these cases can establish the utility of a conceptual framework to explain the use of judgment by customer contact service personnel when acting within the technology paired to their jobs. Thus, what would otherwise be anecdotal information can be processed into knowledge about the management of operations, technology, and human resources. Such knowledge will permit decisions to be made as to the extent to which customer contact service personnel should use judgment and exercise discretion to the benefit of both the customer and the servicing organization.

The first case involves two examples in the use of extraordinary judgment. One is the example of breaking open the cash register to give a customer change. The other is the hostess who gives away breakfast muffins. Both examples suggest that the involved customer contact personnel are committed to effectively serving the customer. Both, however, constitute organizational mismatches that derail the organization's pursuit of its goals.

The circumscribing technology has not adequately comprehended all the different kinds of service encounters involving customer needs. Given that service operations management does not recognize needing change or wanting only a muffin as legitimate customer needs, the protocols in place are not adequately conceived. The ends of the organization and the ends of its customer contact personnel are at odds because the technology as employed by the organization is divisive.

Given the conceptual framework the authors have constructed several alternative courses of action that can be proposed. There may be very good reasons why customer contact service personnel are not allowed to make change. If management wishes to continue that restriction, the protocols must be very clear that customer contact service personnel are not so empowered.

If the failure to make change results in needless loss of goodwill, the most obvious alternative course of action would be to give the operator the cash register access key. Such a change in policy would invariably require additional protocols as to whom change can be given and when it can be given, thus empowering the register operator to use his/her judgment and exercise discretion in applying those protocols.

Concerning the muffin give-away example, the most obvious failure is that the technology inadequately captured the range of service encounters.

This failure should be easy to rectify by merely programming the register with alternatives to selling just the buffet. This would further circumscribe the register operator's job and remove the need for extraordinary judgments from time to time. Given that part of the hotel's breakfast line consists so often of a breakfast buffet, there may be little incentive to go to that kind of trouble since little control would be exercised over breakfast buffet customers as to how many muffins they might take in the first place.

Be that as it may, over time, the practice of muffin give-away could prove costly and, while the cost of operating a breakfast buffet line is partially subsidized by hotel registrations, there is little reason to carelessly add to its cost.

Despite upper management level directives urging airline ticket counter personnel to assess penalties more frequently, they continue to use and exercise their judgment and discretion in this matter and assess them much less frequently than upper management would prefer. They do this without fear of sanctions. This is a case of conflicted judgments and could of course be resolved by technologically circumscribing the process by which those changes are made.

It would be an easy matter to programme for such changes so that the change could not be finalized until the penalty was assessed for the change. This would take the control of assessing such penalties out of the hands of the airline ticket counter personnel. Such programming has not however, been done. The reasons for not doing such programming could be several, the most likely one being that airline ticket counter personnel have as a primary task facilitating the movement of traffic through the terminal.

Anything contributing to impeding that movement must be regarded as undesirable and costly. Airline ticket counter personnel are, therefore, left to use judgment and exercise discretion in such matters since assessing penalties could prove time consuming. On the other hand, changing discounted tickets disrupts the yield management schemes designed to optimize flight revenues.

Changing discount tickets involves a cost for which airlines can make a compelling argument. Penalties are assessed to offset this loss. This conflict between what is practiced and the protocols in place suggests that from the standpoint of the conceptual framework the airline ticket counter personnel have not been sufficiently empowered.

They certainly have been sufficiently empowered in terms of their use and exercise of judgment and discretion. They have not, however, been sufficiently empowered to have a say in how the protocols are devised and applied. The higher levels of airline management would do well to so empower them. Working together on equal footing, both parties might be able to agree on protocols that would garner more revenue through penalties that would offset the organization's yield management shortfalls while keeping the traffic moving at an acceptable rate.

The case of Flex-Mex provides a true-life example of the judgments service personnel (in the case, back room personnel) make that are perverse. Unlike extraordinary and conflicted judgments that work for the most part to the benefit of the customer but are potentially debilitating to the service organization, perverse judgments are debilitating to the service organization including the quality of the customer service it provides. The conceptual framework the authors have constructed provides a basis for identifying the factors that contributed to the Flex-Mex mismatch and proposing alternative courses of action to remedy it.

First, the extent to which technology circumscribed the jobs of the Flex-Mex employees, particularly those in the back room, was not extensive enough. This resulted in Flex-Mex's reward/punishment system and its performance measurement method that were intended to motivate high performance actually leading to the contrary.

In addition, Flex-Mex's employees were not sufficiently empowered for management to be receptive to their observations concerning their dysfunctional work setting or suggestions they might submit as to how that work setting could be made more functional. Thus alienated, they acted in a way to protect their individual interest that put them at odds with some of the organization's goals and objectives.

The conceptual framework constructed suggests several alternative courses of action Flex-Mex could pursue to remedy this mismatch. First, it could extend the application of its IT to more completely circumscribe the tasks of its employees. This could include timing an order from when it is placed with the order taker to when it is placed on the customer pick-up portion of the front counter and not electronically permit back room employees to "bump" orders from their screens.

The IT system could also be reengineered to account for redoing misfilled orders. Such changes in IT's application would certainly restrict the extent to which employees could make perverse judgments. It would also, however, undoubtedly further intensify the hostility of the work environment and could lead to other undesirable results.

Flex-Mex could also consider empowering its employees in ways that could possibly even dispense with any need to reengineer its IT system.

Revising the incentive and performance measurement systems would be a start. Tying their rewards to the success of both their local operation and the organization at large might do better at gaining the loyalty and dedication of Flex-Mex's customer service personnel than providing them half-price menu items.

This would be especially so if these personnel had some say as to what those rewards would be and how their performance should be measured. This does not necessarily mean that the use of judgment and the exercise of discretion in doing their jobs would be increased. These jobs require the use and exercise of little judgment and discretion. Rather, it would mean that Flex-Mex's customer contact service personnel had a stake in how well Flex-Mex does.

This chapter has provided a conceptual framework for exploring the dynamics that arise in managing the integration of operations, technology (primarily IT), and human resources. It has focused on how mismatched combinations of operations, technology, and human resources impact the use and exercise of judgment and discretion by customer contact service personnel and how these organizational anomalies can be eliminated.

The few examples presented in this chapter hardly provide sufficient data to empirically validate this framework and the kinds of organizational mismatches it identifies. Furthermore, the off-diagonal categories have not been addressed.

Therefore, further work empirically validating and perfecting this framework or developing one to more accurately categorize types of service organizations in order to better isolate types of intra-organizational mismatches is in order.

Beyond that is the issue of determining from among a set of alternative courses of action the framework specifies which alternative is the most appropriate to pursue in eliminating organizational mismatches.

Thus, it will be necessary to identify, select, and develop measures as well as techniques to process these measures to rigorously determine the appropriate alternative course of action.

This programme of applied research is both fruitful and valuable inasmuch as it addresses potential service operations ineffectiveness and inefficiency resulting from failures integrating technology and human resources and could contribute to sorting out the factors that have resulted in the "information technology paradox."

1. This empirical observation, the Clark-Fisher hypothesis, explains employment shifts toward sectors of lower productivity.
2. According to Cook, Gho, and Chung (1988), researchers have developed different typologies to answer specific questions w a pragmatic consideration. Therefore, the authors believe that they have sufficient warrant to employ one of Lovelock's typologies because of its implicit usefulness to the question at hand.

3. A competitive advantage can be achieved by providing a low-cost speedy standardized service to a large market segment with similar needs or by providing customized service to a segment whose needs are dissimilar. In the first case customizing services would be inefficient, strategically contradictory, and possibly annoy customers delayed by the preferential treatment they perceive others receiving. In the latter case, such customization would be strategically necessary because it would be what was expected.
4. A totally circumscribed job design is one in which every organizationally sanctioned course of action customer encounter personnel can take as a part of their job is executed through the IT system.
5. The extent to which a particular service is technologically circumscribed, if at all, depends of course on factors other than the mere fact that it can be done. Certainly the benefits gained and the costs incurred to so circumscribe a set of tasks are major considerations.
6. From conversations with Delta, USAir, and TWA airport ticket/check-in counter personnel.

4

Customer Knowledge Management in Hospitality

INTRODUCTION

Among other reasons firms have a low return on their information technology investments is that they only poorly understand what the technology makes possible. The objectives and role of information in customer-focused management must be understood. Customer-intelligent firms use their customer knowledge to drive all of the firm's activities and decisions.

When firms have so much opportunity to interact with their customers, why is it that they treat their customers like strangers? The reason is not lack of information on their customers, but a lack in a firm's managing of that information. Firms may have the ability to capture that information, but may not process and utilize the knowledge to manage relationships with their customers. Information technology has only placed this realization in sharp focus.

On the other hand, the power of information technology has also raised the ugly specter of abuse of privacy when firms have access to a vast amount of customer information. Network Solutions, the first company that registered addresses on the .com, .org, and .net domains for the Internet, now a unit of VeriSign, raised eyebrows when it planned to sell names, street addresses, and other information gathered from businesses and individuals who signed up for an Internet address. There are several examples of Internet companies that have been reined in for their use of customer information. DoubleClick Inc., decided against combining Web-tracking data with offline databases. Toysmart was not allowed to sell its customer database when it shut down.

Hagel and Rayport suggest that customers will become savvy about their personal information and be reluctant to divulge it unless they receive some value for it. They predict that customers will win the battle over their information and firms they call "infomediaries" will "become custodians, agents and brokers of customer information, marketing it to businesses on consumers' behalf while protecting their privacy at the same time."

Nevertheless, customer information is crucial for a customer focus because of the need to make and execute customer-focused decisions in all aspects of the business. Firms will continue to require customer information to do business. Information technology will continue to challenge a firm's judgment in obtaining and using customer information.

Traditionally, research on the customer has been at the aggregate level, most utilized during the new product development process, to test new product ideas, in test marketing, and to test new campaign concepts in the realm of advertising. Marketing research has been standard practice preceding the launch of new products or advertising campaigns. Most firms conduct regular market research activities to direct segmentation decisions such as targeting and to determine how to reach segments.

Scholars have implored managers to "spend a day in the life of your customer" and to "get inside the lives of your customers, " so as to obtain a deeper understanding of customers. The quality of the knowledge on the customer is much greater because of direct observation. Obtaining that knowledge is only the first step. The basic skill of listening involves competence in sensing, evaluating *and* responding. A study of 500 new car buyers found customer perceptions of these three dimensions of listening to be strongly linked to trust in the salesperson.

There are also benefits within the firm when the practice of listening to customers is emphasized by senior managers. Senior managers at First Chicago discovered that in emphasizing listening to the customer they found a cultural change within the organization. Customer knowledge gained from firsthand customer contact is very persuasive. Smart CEOs at firms like IBM, Cisco, and EMC intuitively realize this, and their senior managers contact their major customers on a regular basis. These firms also act on that information to improve relationships with those important customers.

The benefits of customer knowledge management have concentrated at the individual level. For example, Dreyfus, like other mutual fund firms, keeps track of client activity, claiming that they can predict when a client is going to shift money out of their mutual funds. Clients receive a call from a Dreyfus representative, who wants to know how the client feels about the investment and if his or her goals are being met. If Dreyfus is able to track clients at all stages of the consumption process, then the firm has a better chance of retaining the customer.

A number of CRM- and ERP-type software programmes allow companies to track processes in the life of a specific sales order from order entry all the way to delivery to customer. Of course, FedEx introducing package tracking is a well-known example from years ago. There are a number of benefits of information technology for firms of any size.

Siebel software allows Honeywell to spot problems and opportunities by tracking and analyzing all customer interactions; and at Marriott, Siebel empowers sales reps to respond more quickly to customer needs by integrating customer information from different departments. Lexmark International used Microstrategy software to help build what they call a data warehousing solution that accomplished a reduction in product delivery time by 70 percent, a threefold improvement in being able to deliver a customer's order on the desired date, and a 60 percent reduction in the information costs.

Package delivery firm UPS's selfservice tracking system, built by IBM, saved the company $450,000 a day in customer service expenses; and, the Clarify call centre software helped payroll-processing firm ADP improve customer retention rate by 5 percent and increase revenues by $100 million in 1999 simply by providing its customer service reps with customer information on its 8000 clients. There are numerous such examples of technology-based customer information management systems having a profound impact on a firm's productivity and in customer retention. Both outcomes are the basis for achieving and sustaining profits.

The marketing research practice has undergone a major transformation in recent years. A primary function of marketing research activities is to collect and analyze customer information. Technology has enabled all phases of the marketing research process ranging from sampling and data collection to analysis and reporting. With newer technologies and faster cycle times, firms conduct research at all stages of the product life cycle and not just at the product development stage or the test marketing stage.

This is at the aggregate level, whereas there is another change in research on the customer at the individual level, where technology is enabling customers to interact with the firm in a multitude of different ways not previously possible. These interactions can now occur during all stages of consumption. At every interaction with the customer, a firm has the opportunity to acquire valuable customer information, as well as to process and utilize the information for creating and delivering superior customer value.

Once the data is available, the challenge is to provide the user of the information and decision maker with targeted information. Enter rulesbased approaches, which are simply programmes that make sense of data using preconceived models. Sadly, the majority of CRM and ERP packages fail the firm not for lack of data, but simply because the firm does not have the appropriate understanding and appreciation of the fundamentals of customer-focused management. The rules for decision-making should be founded on customer-focused management principles.

The better the understanding of the customer and the utilization of that knowledge, the more customer focused the rules are. The best technology is only as good as what you tell it to do. CRM and ERP packages are really knowledge management software, tools to manage knowledge of the customer and enable the processes within the firm that are working to meet specific customer needs. To be more effective with these tools, firms need to gather the information, analyze and process it to obtain a good understanding of the customer, and utilize it at every opportunity in the value-creation and delivery process. Therefore, for a thorough understanding on how to manage customer information, it is important to understand the principles of knowledge management, in general.

Organizational Learning

What is knowledge management? To answer this question, we have first to deal with a more fundamental question: what is the difference between data, information, and knowledge? Are these terms just synonyms that are interchangeable? No, they are not! The simplest way to understand the differences among these terms is to picture a continuum. As we add value to data, it becomes information; and as we add value to information, information becomes knowledge. When we interpret data in a context, we convert that data into information that has some meaning. When we categorize and elaborate on that information with explanations, then we have added more value and the information can now be considered knowledge.

Thus, *knowledge management* is the management of data and information so that a firm can optimally capture, process, and utilize its knowledge for effective decision-making and operation. *Customer knowledge management* is the management of the acquisition, processing, and utilization of customer information for effective customer-focused decision making. Knowledge management practice has been studied in the context of how organizations learn. Before we discuss the methods of managing customer knowledge, it would be useful to understand knowledge management and, specifically, information processing from the perspective of organizational learning. Organizational learning can be broadly depicted as a three-stage process:

- Information acquisition or generation
- Information transmission or dissemination
- Information analysis or interpretation

Studies have demonstrated that a customer-focused firm has a formal and systematic method for gathering, interpreting and using customer information. To be customer-focused, therefore, firms need to be committed to the importance and value of customer information and to the use of customer information in guiding the creation and delivery of customer value. Thus, recognizing information's value to the firm and realizing when and where it is accessible is a prerequisite for knowledge management.

Richard Schulze, CEO of Bestbuy, the runaway success in electronics retailing, says: The best way to find out whether a store is running smoothly is by asking the cashier. "The cashier really understands where the problems lie. They're the last people to see the customer." To consider all of the sources of customer information we also need to first identify the natural state of the information. Customer information is available as tacit and as explicit knowledge.

The explicit knowledge is present in the databases of the firm or as documented information. Customer information files in databases are usually quantitative data. More and more firms are also using qualitative data when the technology is used to accommodate that type of data. Otherwise, most of this rich information remains as hidden knowledge. This information that is not recorded is the tacit knowledge that is usually resident with the employees and managers of the firm. For example, records of customer service interactions capture the actual transaction, complaint, or feedback from the customer. At the same time, employees, based on their prior experience, will unconsciously record and bring to bear their judgments of the situation, which are not necessarily documented. The knowledge that employees have that is not recorded anywhere is deemed the tacit knowledge of the firm.

While at the individual level information is available from customer information files in the firm's databases, other types of information at the aggregate level may be gathered during the course of product development activities and other specific projects and reside in research reports. There is information on the customer at several locations within the firm, from sales to customer service, to name the most obvious areas.

Besides this explicit knowledge, there is a wealth of information at both the aggregate and the individual levels. Wherever the firm has interfaced with the customer, the "touch-points, " there is information on the customer. It immediately becomes apparent that several product and service delivery contact points within the firm have access to customer information, but not all are part of the customer information management system.

CRM software packages enable the firm to capture all of the information gathered at each touch-point into a central database and make it available at any touch point. To determine all of the opportunities for gathering information on the customer, firms can develop a blueprint of the order delivery or customer service processes depicting all of the touch-points from the consumption cycle when the customer interacts with the firm.

Knowledge gained on the customer from each and every customer interaction when recorded and made available can be valuable in improving the customer focus of any of the firm's decisions or actions. The major sources for customer knowledge are discussed below.

Customer Information Files are typically transaction-related and purchase-related individual-level customer data found in sales records, customer interaction records, and customer service incident records. What is perhaps not in these files, which needs to be considered as a necessary component of individual customer profiles where available, is information related to the activities of preconsumption, consumption, and postconsumption.

Research Reports have segment-level aggregate data that are found in product development reports, advertising research reports, sales and marketing reports, and customer service reports. What needs to be seen is whether research on market segments is an ongoing pursuit of the firm—to indicate that the firm is proactively assessing customer value being delivered by the firm.

Knowledge held by employees and managers—Tacit knowledge of the customers—is by definition not completely identified and its utility not realized. If there is no formal process to regularly capture and utilize this information, a wealth of knowledge resident in the firm is being ignored.

Upstream and downstream sources: When suppliers and intermediaries are regularly included in discussions of value-creation and delivery decisions, there is an opportunity to discover information on market trends, technology, ideas for product improvement, and so on that are useful at the aggregate level. At the individual level, where there are (downstream) intermediaries, if it is possible, it would be highly valuable to obtain individual customer level information.

Now let us look at opportunities that may be missed by firms that are not proactive in looking for customer information. For example, how many firms capture and utilize data on referrals? If it is appropriately captured and analyzed, firms can use this information to proactively stimulate referrals. Firms can identify customers who could be bringing in new customers. Firms can determine what incentives would be effective in stimulating referrals. From the referring and referred customers, firms can learn what messages are being conveyed about the firm and which messages are most effective in stimulating product trial from new customers.

Firms can learn what types of customers are most liable to switch from their current patronage based on word of mouth. Firms can track and follow the patronage behaviour of these new customers and nurture their loyalty and referral behaviour. Firms can also find out from these new customers valuable information on the competition as well. Similarly, what about prospective customer queries? How well is this information captured and utilized? What would such information contain?

They are a good source of what customers look for in a product, a reflection of their choice criteria. How many firms systematically record information on complaints and praises? This type of information would be very helpful in understanding how the firm is faring on creating and delivering customer value. It could highlight failpoints in the value-creating processes and provide input into frontline evaluation and motivation activities.

Many firms have loyalty programmes to reward the frequent user. What sort of frequent-user data do these firms maintain? How many firms really use the frequent-purchase data? Some firms who know their customers well recognize the importance of sorting out the most profitable customers from their customer base and treating them differently. Some customers are indeed more equal than others! Most firms use frequent-purchaser data for targeting specials and promotions. However, this data can also provide invaluable information on customer value and customer profile information to align the firm's value-creation and delivery processes.

Traditionally, firms have gathered routine customer information only at purchase and when a customer returns a product for a refund or invokes a guarantee. Firms have also attempted to obtain customer reactions through customer feedback mechanisms. Feedback forms and customer surveys are administered on a regular basis in some firms. However, most often the information gathered from these efforts is worthless because of faulty designs and worse, sometimes even result in misdirected decisions because of flawed survey methodology. More often than not, the surveys are neither reliable nor valid.

While reliability and validity as statistical measures of the psychometric stability of a scale are important for a scientific, unbiased study, management can improve the utility of customer surveys with a rather simple analysis. Examine the design, administration, and use of any survey along the dimensions of structure, content, and process. Structural features such as length and the time it would take the respondent to fill out the survey, the layout of the various questions in the survey, and the response format for the questions affect the effectiveness of the survey.

Content decisions, such as the categories of information sought from the respondent and information identifying the type of respondent filling out the survey, affect the utility of the survey, which will only be as good as the effectiveness of its administration and its usability. Thus, the process of survey delivery, customer response delivery mechanisms, and the customization of the reports to the decision maker and user of the information in their value-creating and delivery roles is critical to the success of the customer feedback exercise.

There are other sources of customer information that the firm has access to and may not fully utilize. The systematic way of determining what these sources might be is to list all the possible touch-points where customers interact with the firm and placing them in sequence in the three phases of consumption. In the preconsumption phase, customers may interact with salespeople or customer service or other frontline personnel.

Recognizing what these touch-points are and what kinds of information is shared between the firm and the customer is an important step. Firms must decide what data needs to be captured at the touch-points and how it is to be used in guiding decisions and activities.

How many firms systematically utilize frontline operations personnel for gathering customer information? Frontline operations personnel are in an ideal position to gather customer information. They can be trained on when, what, and how to observe or elicit information from customers. They need to be motivated and recognized for their ability to obtain, process, and disseminate such information.

Similarly, there are also the intermediaries or resellers of the firm's products and services that represent the firm in different ways. These intermediaries might perform functions of delivery and distribution, promotion, or customer service on behalf of the firm. Walmart recognized and wielded the power it held with such customer information in negotiating terms with powerful packaged goods manufacturers, including Procter & Gamble.

In the consumption phase, customers may call for assistance in using the product or on some aspect of how the solution works. This information needs to be captured and incorporated into customer education activities such as product directions-for-use instructions, or used in product development and improvement efforts. There is also a wealth of information within the firm available from customer complaints and suggestions.

Service failures and recovery situations provide valuable information on customers and their experiences with the firm and its solutions. If these are recorded and maintained on a systematic basis, they can be "mined" for patterns that yield insights not otherwise available. For example, recurrent complaints about customer service response time might suggest that the customer service process needs redesigning.

Often when the data is not available on which to base a decision, the firm has to collect that information. For example, say the firm has received several complaints about customer service access and wants to determine what changes need to be made to the customer service operation. In this case, the firm may want to conduct some research in order to determine the customer needs and preferences with regard to customer service.

For each decision that directly relates to a customer, the firm has first to determine what kind of information is needed to make the most effective customer-focused decision. Some of this information is available in existing databases, while some may have to be gathered. To gather information, the firm needs to set up a method of determining what information needs to be gathered, how it can be obtained, and in what form it will be available.

MANAGEMENT STYLE OF CUSTOMER IN THE HOSPITALITY INDUSTRY

It is widely accepted that managers' approach to employment relations, often referred to as management style, is the result of choices that are influenced by certain constraints. The nature of the product and labour markets, organizational status and structure, including size of workplace, and culture are chief among the factors thought to place constraints on managers. Managers, as much as workers and customers, are never truly free agents. We have already noted how economic, technical, social, legal and political factors external to the workplace provide boundaries that may constrain managers' behaviour and actions. We also discussed how managers' personal frame of reference will inform the choices they make about the strategies, policies and practices they pursue, and why power relationships are integral to this process. Of particular note here is the virtual absence of trade unions to act as a countervailing force to counteract managerial power. The HI sustains a mere 2 per cent trade union density.

Managers must be able to exercise choice otherwise we would not be able to account for variations in management style among similar types of firm. In seeking to control events managers may be constrained by their own rational thinking of what is good and bad, failing to recognize that opposites are often very closely related and may even coexist simultaneously. The right to manage is so deeply ingrained into behaviour and thinking that it may dominate over their tacit acceptance of a more pluralist ethos. Hence 'a constant underlying pressure within management both to resist any extension of joint regulation and to restore unilateral regulation wherever and whenever circumstances allow'. HRM is often seen as unitarist and a reassertion of managerial prerogative, especially the 'hard' version, even though the 'soft' variant contains some positive attributes.

While we can debate the extent to which particular constraints affect the choices that particular managers make in particular circumstances, this approach still implies a rationality that does not account for pragmatism, opportunism and reacting to events. This approach is beginning to emerge as an alternative. That said, we take as a universal truth that all HI employers place high priority on seeking to control labour costs. As we shall argue this is achieved predominantly through 'low road' practices that may be both intentional and/or the result of pragmatism or opportunism. This approach is so successful that managers have no incentive to take the 'high road'. Organizations that focus on quality in the service encounter exceptionally approach the management of employment by the 'high road' using more sophisticated and developmental HRM practices, but not necessarily in respect of the workforce as a whole.

Constraints and choices

To cope with market uncertainties managers can opt for the external regulation of employment matters, choose to develop their own internal responses, or use a combination of both. Grimshaw et al. (2001) argue that internal and external market pressures mutually interact to shape employment strategy, generating a wide range of possibilities for different workforce groups. The weakening of national regulatory and collective bodies in the UK, and the accompanying widening of scope for managerial prerogative, has made managing an even more uncertain process.

Marchington and Parker (1990) suggest that stable product markets will encourage the development of 'high road' practices based on partnership, job security, systematic recruitment, selection, training and development, two-way communications and formal procedures. Turbulent market conditions, which affect large parts of the HI, militate against long-term policies, even in larger companies. They will drive 'low road' practices based on hire and fire, ad hoc recruitment, selection, training and development, low pay, one-way communication, if any, from management, and lack of procedures, reinforcing a culture of macho management.

If the economic climate deteriorates firms may be forced to change route towards 'low road' practices, graphically illustrated by the case of British Airways (BA). Keenoy (1997) identifies a wide-ranging programme of 'soft' measures, including improvements to communications and leadership, while maintaining a 'hard' approach to headcount. In respect of cabin crew, Boyd (2001) argues that 'soft' HRM in the form of a sanctimonious mission and policy statement may have provided a smoke screen for short-term, costrational HRM leading to work intensification.

Case study research has identified a more complex pattern of highly firm specific policy solutions in response to a variety of different internal and external pressures. Contradictory outcomes emerge as new policies capitalize on changing external conditions at the expense of organizational demands. New policies may be unsustainable where on aggregate they fail to develop workforce skills or fulfill career expectations. Considerable emphasis on recruitment and training in hotels, which is symptomatic of labour flux, militates against uptake of new HRM initiatives of a longer-term nature.

Organization status and structure, including size of workplace will also serve to constrain the extent to which managers can exercise choice. Not all managers own and control their own business, and in larger hotel companies, restaurant and public house chains, and contract catering firms, managers are themselves also workers reporting to a more senior manager. Managers' choices are constrained by organizational policies, as well as by the actions of other managers and subordinates. Management is necessarily a messy business. Achieving organizational goals through people is a complex and political process, political in the sense that it involves choosing how to reconcile differences among colleagues of different status and power who may be senior managers, peers or subordinate workers. Some large HI organizations comprise many small workplaces, so we cannot necessarily generalize their management style to singlesite workplaces.

Owner managers of small firms have more freedom to make rules on the 'hoof', as there are no precedents or constraints from any higher authority. Surplus labour supply of amply skilled labour, and the simple division of labour are conducive to an ad hoc management style within the economic determinism approach of externalization. As Riley et al. (2000) note, productivity is largely a matter of matching supply to demand in the short term, because of the almost instantaneous impact of customer trends on labour supply. This dynamic instability based on stochastic demand creates and continually reinforces a short-term perspective where small unit structure creates a style of management that is good at improvising. Reliance on a plentiful supply of unskilled labour from the labour market and hire and fire serve to enhance managerial power. The manager may be aware of the constraint of unfair dismissal legislation. By making a simple risk assessment, the manager will calculate that a fired worker will probably not bother to make a claim, if eligible, because alternative work is easily secured (and a replacement easily obtained). If the worker does proceed to employment tribunal, at worst there will be a cheap out-of-court settlement, because of the worker's low pay and short service.

Culture can be considered on three levels - organizational, national and occupational - with some crossover between the first two in the case of MNCs. Two American Case study 3.1 Workplace structure in the Australian hotel industry

Hotels may appear to be structured bureaucracies under the control of a general manager, but are essentially organic structures within which departmental managers have considerable autonomy and responsibility. Each department is a unique entity controlled by a manager skilled in that work who hires and fires, and determines the categories of labour to be used, the tasks to be performed and the timing of work.

The autonomy and responsibility invested in departmental managers encourages an informal management style and a system of rule-making that shapes the pattern of labour use (initial engagements tend to be casual), and encourages the growth of informal work practices between manager and worker designed to engender loyalty and commitment. Departmentalization and labour flexibility forms part of the hierarchy of control, shifting transaction costs (of uncertainty) to the worker, protecting the hotel from unfair dismissal litigation, and using behaviour and discipline to determine permanent employment status.

Weak and low-status HRM within hotels militates against participation in new HRM practices, such as multi-skilling, because managers fear other departments may poach good staff. This acts as a barrier to strong internal labour markets, so the external market becomes a significant mechanism for the allocation of skill.

MNCs, McDonald's and Disney, have been hailed as 'influential models of excellence in the development of particular organisational cultures or systems of production and job design with their respective implications for management and the conduct of employee relations'. International chains display more sophisticated HRM, e.g. in Greece. Larger units and those owned by foreign chains appear to veer towards the 'best practice' models of HRM.

Organizational culture encapsulates 'the way we do things around here'. Culture and values underpin the organization's identity and core purpose and new initiatives in employment relations and HRM may entail programmes of culture change, especially where there is a conscious shift towards a service quality (SQ) culture. Redman and Mathews (1998) argue that the traditional dichotomy between the 'high road' and the 'low road' has been increasingly challenged by effective quality management systems resulting in both improved quality and reduced costs. This reflects a new approach to corporate management. 'Organisational culture is rooted in the future and change' whereas work-based culture is rooted in the here and now. Occupational culture may be more readily identifiable within skilled occupations such as chefs, and may create adversity in the employment relationship where professional values conflict with commercial values. Employment relations systems reflect the society in which they operate.

Case study : Effects of Institutional Change on Large Hotels in New Zealand

A major change in the law in 1991 was designed to shift employment relations from a highly regulated environment to a minimalist and market led regime. In spite of the opportunity presented for firms to innovate on the basis of high commitment work practices, there was neither any evidence of a complete displacement of the traditional pattern of collective relations nor any indication of HRM practices designed to secure workforce commitment. Rather, any changes made to improve communications did not diminish the level of managerial control typical of the industry.

People in different countries approach work in different ways. Interestingly many of the countries discussed in this book (Australia, Canada, Britain, New Zealand and the US) display 'Anglo' characteristics - a belief in equality, acceptance of uncertainty, emphasis on personal initiative and achievement, and the right to a private life. Money and material standards are important. By contrast European countries, largely in relation to geographical location, fall into four groups and are more diverse. Approaches that may work well in one country do not necessarily transplant well to other countries. Local managers may resist the incursion of expatriate managers who are socialized in a different culture. The application of western practices to transitional economies such as Bulgaria, and Russia may be difficult to achieve, particularly in Slovakia where there are few MNCs. Differences in national institutional arrangements and the extent to which employment systems rely on detailed regulation and labour codes contribute to national cultural differences. Changes to national institutions have not necessarily impacted upon employment relations practices.

Models and Maps

Models and maps of employment relations have developed from the constraints and choices approach in an attempt to depict variations in the management style of employment relations. A useful start point is Purcell and Sisson's (1983) five ideal types of industrial relations management:

- Traditionalists are hostile to trade unions, exploit their workforce and believe in management's right to manage.
- Sophisticated paternalist/human relations embodies strong management, but with concern for employees' welfare. Unions are kept at bay by giving employees good pay and terms of employment.
- Sophisticated moderns accept trade unions as a positive force, and there is strong emphasis on developing and maintaining informal and formal procedures for resolving disputes. There are two types of sophisticated moderns. 'Consulters' accept unions but also deploy

techniques designed to enhance individual commitment. 'Constitutionalists' place more emphasis on collective agreements.
- Standard moderns take a pragmatic approach to industrial relations with recognized trade unions, with line managers taking the lead.

In reviewing management styles we have discounted any model that embraces trade unions and a collective approach because, to all intents and purposes, these are not relevant to the HI in Britain. Indeed Streeck's (1987) system of industrial governance without trade unions bears a remarkable resemblance to the way in which many HI managers have traditionally 'done business'. The managerial line of command and authority is the only institution necessary to maintain control in highly uncertain market conditions, hence the perceived legitimacy of a unitarist form of employment relations. While we do not include the McDonaldization model here, we can note that managers often display a management style derived from an individualist and unitarist approach. HRM is dealt with separately. Of course models and maps are not absolute constructs, as Kessler and Purcell note:

- Style is a preferred way of managing employees that may be amended in practice.
- Firms may have no real style, being essentially opportunistic in reaction to events, and cannot be depicted.
- Styles may differ in relation to different groups, notably managers, highly skilled workers and peripheral workers.

We can add a fourth point - management styles may be gendered. Rutherford's (2001) study of male and female managers in an airline confirms differences in their approach to management. Men tend to follow a more command and control style with a distancing of personal self, while women are more communicative and caring, with more emphasis on people skills such as listening rather than mere performance of the task. That said the business function is the most important determinant of management style.

The locus of management style for employment relations in the HI is best identified as falling somewhere within the models and maps of non-union relations. All authors, with the exception of Scase (1995), attribute directly or implicitly their particular approach as applicable to the HI. We should note that Lucas's (1996a) and Sisson's (1993) approaches were based on WIRS3.

Approaches to non-union employment relations

'Traditional' cost-minimization/no collectivism (Kessler and Purcell, 1995)

- Labour is a cost and factor of production
- Employee subordination part of the natural order
- Fear of union interference '! opposition or kept at arm's length
- Low pay and no job security
- Little or no training

'Fraternal autocracy'

- High financial rewards to obtain short-term commitment from skilled workers
- Owner-managers work alongside employees
- Managerial prerogative conditioned by weak market position of most employees who are unskilled
- Low pay, poor working conditions
- Non-union

'Bleak house'

- Unorganized conflict (high labour turnover and accidents)
- No grievance and health and safety procedures
- No communications and employee involvement
- No consultative committees
- Lack of employment security, including temporary contracts
- High rate of dismissals

'Black hole'

- No HRM or industrial relations
- Small privately owned organizations
- Pragmatic and authoritarian cost-cutting approachs
- Low-skill, short-service marginal workers
- Low pay and insecure conditions of employment
- Little employee involvement

'Unbridled individualism'

- High degree of managerial prerogative in the absence of organized labour
- Employers regard workers as a commodity to be controlled and constrained
- Low pay
- High employee quit rates, sickness, absence, injury, and use of grievance procedure
- High use of disciplinary sanctions and dismissal
- More limited opportunity for employees to challenge management
- Little consultation, especially on health and safety, or employee involvement

'Determined opportunism'

- High degree of managerial prerogative in the absence of organized labour
- Workforce structuring includes high reliance on so-called casuals with no contract
- Majority of workforce ('peripheral' unskilled) are subject to more 'hard' form of HRM
- Not constrained in dismissing workers, failing to comply with many minimum legal requirements, or observing the law in spirit
- Extreme instance of 'retaining control/cost-control' management

Doherty (2002) argues that the way in which the state of employment management in the HI is perceived depends on how it is benchmarked, either as industrial relations/personnel management or HRM. She suggests that the measure of HRM may invite more positive conclusions, especially in larger organizations and workplaces.

There may be some truth in this where the issue of service quality has been embraced, predicated on a redefinition of organizational purpose and a programme of culture change that embraces a clear strategy for long-term success and competitive advantage. Here there is some considerable interest in HRM within hotel and restaurant chains cite the case of a luxury hotel in New Zealand where a distinct set of HRM practices introduced in support of the strategic decision towards quality enhancement demonstrated very positive outcomes against key performance indicators, especially overall guest satisfaction and financial performance. Indeed Hoque (1999a) asserts that hotels are more interested in HRM than manufacturing firms. Conversely do not find a clear relationship between business strategy and the approach to HRM in designer restaurants.

However, there are two problems with Doherty's argument. All been developed explicitly as an alternative to the trade union/collective industrial relations paradigm. Second, her conclusion that HRM is about managerial control gained through indirect and direct methods is not necessarily a good deal for the workers. Indeed one major piece of evidence she cites in support of this comes from research about management development, which suggests that managers may be the beneficiaries of 'soft' HRM, but not the workers, reaffirming that this variation of HRM is directed only at managers. Rather it infers a cost-minimization route for the majority, and is symptomatic of McDonaldization where labour flexibility and work standardization militate against the development of strategic HRM systems and internal labour markets.

In discussing the role of HRM in the management of employment, we begin with an overview of key issues that encapsulate the way in which HRM has emerged and become established in mainstream thinking. Not everybody subscribes to a new HRM model and orthodoxy of 'people management', notably those maintaining the broadly personnel management tradition. Even then among both camps there is a considerable divergence of view as to what HRM (or personnel management) is and means, how it can be operationalized and its effects measured, and its relationship with corporate performance. As Woods (1999) suggests HR(M) is a paradox that has never really been mastered. We then turn in more detail to issues that have most relevance to the management of hospitality employment, notably to account for a psychological contract and service work.

Key Issues in HRM Discourse

HRM is a phenomenon of the 1980s when, according to Streeck (1987), the key issue for management was to find ways of managing in an unprecedented degree of economic uncertainty, which derived from a need for continuous rapid adjustment to an increasingly turbulent market. Hence the imperatives that HRM issues should be integrated with business strategy, and that HRM should be able to demonstrate its contribution to business performance (from the expectancy model, see high performance practices below). Issues such as commitment, quality, flexibility and adaptability became important. And so HRM was born. HRM also stresses the importance of the devolving the ownership and delivery of HR initiatives from specialist HR managers to line managers.

Others deny that HRM represents anything different or new. Armstrong claims HRM is a 'construct largely invented by academics and popularised by consultants', yet Grant and Oswick (1998) found a majority of practitioners agreed that HRM was different from personnel management. Gennard and Kelly (1995) and Torrington et al. (2002) are among those who regard HRM as the next stage in the evolution of personnel management. Equally there has been a growth in the proportion of specialists using HR in their title. These specialists are better qualified, more involved in strategic planning, more likely to use HRM practices than their counterparts using the title 'personnel', and most likely to be found in foreign-owned firms.

One outcome has been a realignment of the personnel/line manager relationship, with more personnel work being devolved down the line. Yet in the more cost-conscious and value-added environment line managers are making more, not less, use of their specialist personnel advisers. The personnel function does contribute to corporate objectives by being delivered in many different but flexible forms. It is not necessarily the case that an organization not acting strategically will mean that the workforce is not managed in a strategic way. Hence strategic management of people is not purely within the domain of the HR department, and can be diffused throughout the organization and owned and directed by the line.

The emphasis within HRM discourse has remained largely managerialist because of the emphasis on management's cost and performance concerns, hence a management practice research agenda. The management of employment also tends to be discussed in terms of bipolar opposites in and around the metaphors of 'hard' and 'soft'. Key instances include high and low trust work practices, direct control vs. responsible autonomy, control vs. commitment and 'high road' vs. 'low road'. Here managers may exercise strategic contingency choice in terms of which approach best fits their organization. In some respects these divergences are symptomatic of some of the differences between personnel management and HRM. Within personnel management people are more likely to be recognized and treated as human beings, whereas in HRM they are treated as people in the 'soft' variant and resources in the 'hard' variant.

A further criticism of HRM is that it is not gender neutral, with Townley (1994) being an exception in making gender more visible within her analysis.

Dickens (1998) argues HRM policies and practices perpetuate rather than challenge gender inequality. In terms of securing employee commitment assumptions about women being less committed than men will affect the shape of the core-periphery, and determine which jobs are full-time or part-time. Cost-cutting 'hard' HRM has underpinned existing sex segregation. Wajcman (2000) echoes these observations, pointing out that men are most likely to be found in occupations where management is convinced of a high quality strategy, whereas women are most likely to be found in low-skill jobs where management feels competition on costs is the most viable option.

High Road' or 'low road' HRM

There are two broad approaches to HRM, both of which have been found wanting. The first, a 'high road' version, is generally agreed to comprise a list of tangible practices, with 'best practice' HRM or 'bundles' of practices having the greatest impact on performance. Two groups of practices can be identified:

Some practices may be core requirements, e.g. selection, training, communications and reward. Others are more marginal because they do not necessarily have general application, e.g. family-friendly policies, profit-related pay and share ownership. An alternative approach stresses that HRM may be contingent, with 'best fit' HRM differing according to the stage in the business life cycle, the strategy-structure configuration and the business strategy being pursued. Schuler and Jackson (1987) identify three alternative 'best fit' strategies - innovation, quality enhancement and cost-reduction - but acknowledge that organizations may pursue two or more competitive strategies simultaneously. Hence 'best fit' may embrace both 'high road' and 'low road' approaches. Espousal of the 'best practice' approach suggests that the 'sophisticated paternalist' and 'consultative' models of industrial relations management (Purcell and Sisson, 1983) triumph over 'bleak houses' and 'black holes', in effect denying them legitimacy when they undoubtedly exist. Legge (1995b) proceeds from the basis that HRM has never been anything but 'hard'. 'Some managements have always preferred a unitarist approach and have exploited their workers - HRM may have provided a language to justify that approach but was not responsible for it'. Marchington and Grugulis (2000) point out that the rhetoric of HRM disguises the way in which it reinforces managerial control, sometimes against workers' interests or wishes. Indeed the rhetoric of 'best practice' HRM can be turned on its head to depict 'low road' HRM as the following examples show:

- The practice of teamworking can be regarded as a means to replace over the shoulder managerial control by peer surveillance.
- Empowerment is about getting workers to take more responsibility with no commensurate increase in reward.
- Using the management chain to cascade information simply denies employees any voice in what is going on around them.

In support of the contingency approach Cappelli and Crocker-Hefter (1996) caution against 'best practice' and benchmarking, suggesting each organization should develop its own set of core competencies to reflect its own distinctiveness. Conversely others have observed that international pressures have driven countries and companies to adopt similar HRM concepts, regulations and practices.

Purcell (1999) considers that a 'best practice' prescription is a cul-de-sac, while contingency and 'best fit' HRM are a chimera. Both are predicated upon the logic of rational choice and neglect other organizational processes at work.

Importantly they fail to identify circumstances in which particular HRM practices are successful. Others share Purcell's scepticism, denying that HRM can exist in the diametrically opposite forms of 'soft' and 'hard'. Policies are always both 'hard' and 'soft', e.g. McDonald's provides all the support that employees need to perform to the required level, yet it deploys a 'no excuses' policy if they do not conform. Legge (1995b) sees the implementation of Walton's soft model of mutuality being restricted to knowledge-based industries seeking value added. Even though the majority of employees may fall within this larger than normal privileged core, there may still be a minority for whom harder conditions exist.

Keenoy's (1999) metaphor of HRM as a hologram, or virtual image, usefully encapsulates why the HRM debate has become somewhat sterile. As a hologram HRM changes its appearance as we move around its image, and appears different each time we look at it. It is akin to quality, something that is always in the process of becoming (a continuous and never-ending process).

The paradox remains why so few American (Milkman, 1998) and British workplaces take the 'high road' to employment management. While the UK historical tradition does not favour this approach, it is also likely to have been undermined by the devolution of HR activities and associated budgets, which are necessary to measure the contribution of HRM. Thus line managers' HR actions will be driven by adherence to short-term financial targets, and working to budgets will drive a short-term employment relations agenda, encouraging a deterioration towards 'low road' practices.

Ultimately people are always expendable. Labour costs may be a significant proportion of operating costs, and are always far easier to trim than other fixed costs. BA cannot cut the cost of fuel or new aircraft, so it is cheaper to sack and re-employ sizeable numbers of workers because re-employment costs are lower than exit costs. It is hardly surprising, then, that the overall conclusion from WERS was that the broad approach to employment relations management in Britain was 'one of retaining control and doing what they could to control costs'.

As the HI product is highly diverse and ever-changing, there is no reason why 'high road' HRM should be effective, and there will be circumstances in which other HRM strategies, including cost-control will be effective. Indeed support for this comes from contingency models of HRM. In new businesses the personal influence of the founder and an entrepreneurial spirit will predominate over a clearly defined organization or HRM structure. As organizations mature and become more complex quality assurances, standardization, systems, structures controlling costs and increasing efficiency begin to emerge. These are heightened where there are plans to expand a chain under franchises. Concurrently more attention is given towards systematic 'people management', including motivating managers, spreading values and developing a service culture, in order to sustain the business. In short there is a mix of 'hard' and 'soft' measures that conforms to Lashley's 'promise of control and commitment'.

A Psychological Contract

A further problem with the 'best practice' approach is that it does not take account of employees' view of HRM within the psychological contract. Renewed interest in the psychological contract and taking account of employees' expectations has become an increasingly important dimension of HRM. The concept of the psychological contract, where employees' needs are necessarily satisfied to ensure commitment to organizational objectives that will translate into business success, has remained the keystone of Torrington's philosophy of HRM as an emergent version of personnel management. Grant (1999) identifies two approaches. The first derives from Argyris (1960) and Schein (1978) who focus on employer-employee perceptions to the exchange implied by the employment relationship within the broader context of social processes. Alternatively perceptions are shaped in the mind of the employee. All approaches draw from expectancy theory, where the state of the psychological contract is influenced by our desired goals and outcomes, while the experience we have of these goals and outcomes determines our motivation to work and our behaviour at work. Two types of contract can be identified:

- Transactional - characterized by short-term security with most emphasis on financial reward.
- Relational - where long-term employment security is based on a mixture of loyalty, commitment and financial reward.

The nature of the contract following recruitment appears to be linked with new recruits' career motivations and intentions to stay. In transactional contracts workers may perceive regular job change as a prerequisite to career development, a point frequently noted in respect of hospitality workers. Consequently they may expect less from their employer in terms of consultation, appraisal and job security in the knowledge that they will be moving on. While in one sense 'soft' HRM is implied in a relational contract, and 'hard' HRM is implied in a transactional contract, Grant (1999) questions the extent to which HRM policies and practices viewed across these dichotomies have led to a change in the nature of the psychological contract. Indeed employees may experience both types of psychological contract simultaneously, as noted in the case of part-time students, but it is important to emphasize that their financial reward is relatively poor.

Employees draw on past and current employment experience in order to rationalize and create their own sense of reality in relation to work. A satisfied employee will adopt and believe the prevailing HRM rhetoric. Gibb (2001) also argues that bringing employees into the equation will help to shed light on whether HRM leads to real benefits or exploitation and injustice. Fears that employees are more likely to display a preponderance of negative work attitudes have not been borne out by the WERS findings of general employee satisfaction at work. Employees are generally appreciative and positive about HRM systems, while unhappy employees may still experience effective HRM.

HRM and Service Work

The growth in importance of service work has pointed to the need to develop new theories of alternative forms of work organization and HRM. This is particularly challenging in transitional countries in Central and Eastern Europe in the post-Communist era. Clearly, front-line service work is heterogeneous. Some forms of service work, e.g. call-centres, have been transformed by advances in digital technology. Technology cannot necessarily substitute for the personalized nature of service work that is integral to many hospitality and tourism activities. However, intensified international competition, with its attendant concentration on marketing and operational strategy, has prompted businesses to focus greater attention on managing the service encounter. The behaviour and performance of indirect service workers are also important, as poor quality food or rooms cannot be compensated by a high standard of direct service delivery. The character of service work and the HRM practices deemed necessary to support a 'best practice'.

We have already noted that the extent to which management is able to achieve its organizational goals through people will depend on the extent to which workers' or customers' aims and aspirations are met. The need to draw the employee- customer relationship into the analysis of HRM derives from the critical role of employee in determining SQ, as Redman and Mathews note: to a very real extent the employee is the service, given the absence of any tangible artefact. They carry the responsibility of projecting the image of the organisation and it is in their hands that the ultimate satisfaction of the consumer rests.

'Delighting the customer' may be marketing objective to ensure repeat business, but it is also highly dependent upon management's ability to 'manage' employees so that they display the right attitude and behaviour, an issue discussed in the previous. The simple point is, if managers are not meeting employees' or customers' expectations, this has negative implications for organizational performance, reinforcing need to consider a three-way psychological contract.

Branded hotels in particular are inevitably very concerned about customer service and quality standards. Hoque's work indicates that larger hotels do attach a large degree of importance to strategic HRM issues, although the findings should not be extrapolated to smaller hotels where 'poor' practice may be commonplace. McGunnigle and Jameson's (2000) study of high commitment in the top 50 hotel groups challenges conclusion that the hotel industry has undergone change, including finding new ways of managing staff.

Service quality and Human Resource Management

The character of service

- Intangibility of services - cannot be evaluated until consumed.
- Inseparability of service producer from consumer - immediacy and importance of encounter.
- Heterogeneity and variability - every service encounter is different.
- Perishability - the service disappears if not consumed.

Eight key HRM practices

- Recruitment and selection - based on identification of personality and skills needs, and uses a range of methods.
- Retention - effective programme.
- Teamworking - semi-autonomous, cross-process and multi-functional teams.
- Training and development - quality-related including teamworking process and interpersonal skills.
- Performance appraisal - goals focus on quality goals and effective behaviour, utilizing customer-driven data.
- Reward - payment systems linked to achievement of quality goals.
- Job security - high security, including support where redundancies necessary.
- Employee involvement - fosters open, supportive and participatory employment relations climate.

Case study : HRM and performance in hotels

The relationship between HRM and performance is dependent upon:

- A hotel's business strategy;
- Hotels having a quality focus within that strategy;
- HRM being introduced as an integrated and coherent 'bundle' of packages.

While it is not claimed or shown that a quality-enhancing approach leads to high performance, this study is claimed as unique in demonstrating strong contingency effects, possibly because it is a single industry study. In short high commitment HRM is practised only when there is a 'fit' with product and service strategy.

They take Peccei and Rosenthal's (1997) lead that recruitment and selection, and training and development, including performance appraisal, are all important in developing individual commitment to customer service and culture change. A clear desire for commitment, recruitment and selection is not found to be commensurate with this aim, where there is little development for line managers or strategic integration of training. In designer restaurants:

the lack of coherency both in terms of internal consistency across policy areas and the ways in which different staff groups were managed, suggest that the relationship between approaches to HRM and business strategy is a more complicated one than that suggested by the models based on notions of fit.

Lashley (1998) argues that the amount of employee discretion required to fulfil a particular customer-service need is crucial to understanding 'best fit' between the service offer and the management of employees. His model of four ideal types of HRM relates to the amount of employee involvement and participation in shaping the service encounter, hence the kind of empowerment employees are afforded.

The variations on the vertical plane reflect the fact that service work is a mix of tangibles and intangibles, with the latter being regarded as the defining feature of services. Their relationship is an influential factor in determining employment strategy and the form that HRM takes.

Although within food and beverage service vending machines are wholly tangible, fast food is high in tangibles (high technology, standard products), and the intangibles of the service encounter are standardized by use of scripts. Highly personalized service in a gentleman's club might incorporate a high element of intangibles where 'delighting the customer' and considerable discretion are exercised in the conduct of work. The extent to which work needs to be standardized or customized is the most important influence on HRM strategy.

Horizontally the parameters of 'external control' and 'internal control' are broadly in keeping with the 'hard' and 'soft' approaches to the management of employment noted earlier, including direct control vs. responsible autonomy and control vs. commitment. Lashley argues these approaches are misleading in service work because employment strategy is concerned with both control and commitment, and because they fail to recognize the importance of employee discretion as an element of job design, which is crucial to an understanding of the service delivery.

While Lashley's model is a helpful start point to understanding employee management in hospitality and tourism, in practice there are likely to be many variations that reflect the fact that professional, participative, command and control and involvement are not four discrete alternatives. Further he overlooks how employee attitudes to customer service and individual and group behaviour may affect HRM practices and organizational performance in services. As many firms continually seek to reposition themselves the market place to achieve competitive advantage, these approaches are not static.

Case study : Quality Enhancement in a Luxury New Zealand Hotel

A luxury hotel pursued a strategy of quality enhancement over a six-year period to be at the top of the market. Bundles of HRM practices, including changes to work design and organization structure, achieved measurable positive effects on the key indicators of service used. The approach changed from traditional hotel management incorporating elements of command and control to an involvement style.

Mayer (2002) claims that strong HR practices in hiring, development, providing appropriate support systems and retention have led to the delivery of superior guest services in a Florida Theme Park. Nankervis and Debrah (1995) observe differences in the way HRM practices are implemented within SQ in hotels in Singapore and Australia, attributing these to national, cultural, social and labour market phenomena, a finding also applicable in the US.

Halim's (2001) comparative case study research of six SQ hotels and six non-SQ hotels evaluated the degree of effectiveness of the SQ philosophy in achieving better HR practices in the Room Service Division of five-star hotels in Egypt. Differences in the implementation of approaches to the philosophy within SQ hotels were revealed, as well as some significant differences between SQ and non-SQ hotels. Factors were also identified that affect the implementation of the SQ philosophy to achieve better HR practices. A model modifying the HR aspects of the Malcolm Baldrige National Quality Award has also been developed to provide simplified guidelines on effective implementation.

Largely in support of Lashley (1998), Nickson et al. (2002) conclude that HRM in hospitality is more 'best fit' than 'best practice'. A 'best fit' approach to designing HRM contingent upon the particular notion of 'good service' seems apposite. Hence practices will differ across market segments, and between tangible and intangible aspects of service production. Although good practice has been identified by Hoque (1999a) and Kelliher and Perrett (2001) in upmarket organizations, it may also be found in small firms. For many firms high pay, extensive training and job security are unlikely to be cost effective. Poor practice may reflect a number of reasons but is not immutable, and the 'high road' is not the only route to competitive advantage. Case study illustrates an example of Lashley's (1998) command and control style at Pret à Manger.

While moving towards greater customer responsiveness and an SQ philosophy may be a longer-term objective in post-Communist countries such as Slovakia, hotels have found it difficult to move away from the traditional rigid 'socialist' type of personnel management. They have yet to reach a point in terms of current practice that is fully adequate to the new economic environment, and remain a long way from achieving a 'western' model of HRM.

Case Study : Service quality and Effective HR Practices in Five-star Hotels in Cairo

The SQ philosophy gives management the opportunity to create a better quality culture, select the most qualified staff, set an efficient job design, design effective job training plans, and establish an appropriate base that can sustain the achievement of quality objectives, provided that hotels use the proper approaches to implement the philosophy.

Factors that affect the effective implementation of SQ to achieve better HR practices are lack of sufficient knowledge about the philosophy, lack of expertise among some senior managers, bureaucratic management, centralized management and the heavy involvement of hotel owners in operations. Insufficient allocation of financial resources, too much emphasis on achieving profit rather than on improving quality and absence of detailed guidance to aid implementation militate against effectiveness. Behavioural norms of employees embedded in their ways of performing duties and high turnover also contributed. Quality approaches need to be integrated into all elements of a hotel's operations. The unstable political climate in the Middle East and some Egyptian labour laws are perceived as inhibitors to reaching the desired quality standards.

Total involvement and employee empowerment, and employee evaluation of their own performance, are difficult to implement due to the low level of education in some departments.

Residues of the Communist ideology and practices are still apparent and handicap the wish to compete for increasingly demanding global tourism clients in Bulgaria. Deeply entrenched custom and practice present formidable obstacles to change. While a growing number of foreign hospitality companies are willing to invest in Russia, a production-oriented viewpoint is challenging in terms of developing an SQ-focused ethos.

CUSTOMER SATISFACTION

Most firms understand the importance of customer satisfaction and will provide basic training to their employees. The more sophisticated firms actually have instruments that they use to measure customer satisfaction and establish benchmarks for future comparisons. Benchmarking is a process whereby a firm establishes a level of performance by comparing current performance against past performance, or by comparing current performance against the performance of other companies or an entire industry.

Data are used to create benchmarks, which then become the standard against which current and customer satisfaction future performance is evaluated. Unfortunately, many firms still only pay lip service to customer satisfaction and the complaints received from customers.

The following information was collected through the efforts of the Technical Assistance Research Programme in the 1980s, but it remains accurate today:

- The average business does not hear from 96 percent of its unhappy customers.
- For every complaint received, 26 other customers have the same problem.
- The average person with a problem tells 9 or 10 people, and 13 percent will tell more than 20.
- Customers who have their complaints resolved to their satisfaction tell an average of 5 people about the experience.
- Complainers are more likely to do business with you again than non complainers who have a problem: 54–70 percent if resolved, and 95 percent if resolved quickly. These statistics support the contention that a dissatisfied customer tells people about a bad experience more often than a satisfied customer tells people about a good experience. However, firms should take note that it is beneficial to have customers voice their complaints so that they can be resolved and increase the likelihood that the customers will return.

Improving Customer Service and Customer Satisfaction

Improving customer service should be a top priority of all managers working in the hospitality and tourism industry. Customer satisfaction occurs when a firm's service, as perceived by customers, meets or exceeds expectations. Firms that can consistently meet or exceed customer expectations will develop good reputations and often good quality images. When we travel, we encounter service providers in hotels and restaurants who provide exceptional service. This type and consistency of service does not happen by accident; it begins with a commitment by management to make it that way. Conversely, when the opposite occurs, the finger should be pointed at management as well.

1. *Define your standards of quality service with measurable indicators:* Before you can evaluate the level of service provided by employees within your organization, you must establish the standards by which they will be judged. These standards, or benchmarks, should be observable and measurable. For example, it might be reasonable to expect front desk agents to answer the telephone within four rings or room service to deliver meals within 30 minutes of when the order was received. Once these standards are developed, they must be communicated to all personnel. It remains crucial that standards be clearly defined before any plans are developed to improve the level of service. Martin suggests two major dimensions to define quality service: the procedural dimension and the convivial dimension. The procedural dimension includes incremental flow of service, timeliness, accommodating consumer needs, anticipating consumer needs before they occur or are requested by the consumer,

communicating in a clear and concise manner, customer satisfaction. obtaining consumer feedback, and coordinating through proper supervision. The convivial dimension includes displaying a positive attitude and body language, using the guest's name as a means of delivering personal attention, attending to the guest on a personal basis, providing guidance to guests who are indecisive, and solving problems that arise.

2. *Assess your current situation*: As in any continuous improvement programme, before you move forward, you must determine your current position. This can be done by objectively assessing the level of service currently provided within the organization; this involves conducting an audit of the services provided by service personnel within the organization. As a result of the audit, the strengths and weaknesses of the firm can be determined; this will provide a means of building on the aspects of service that are positive and improving the areas that are deficient. Audits can be conducted using mystery shoppers, or corporations may use staff members to audit the performance of units within the company.
3. *Develop effective service improvement strategies:* This must be accomplished through well-planned and thorough training of service providers. Attention must be paid to identifying objectives for the training and providing specific instructions and clear descriptions of the expected outcome (s) of the training.
4. *Initiate your solutions carefully:* As with any plan, implementation is the most critical stage. You should proceed with caution, taking steps incrementally rather than all at once. You should build on small successes, rather than trying to accomplish too much too soon.
5. *Provide feedback, recognition, and rewards:* Positive feedback must be provided if the change in behaviour continues. A reward structure must be provided that will maintain the level of interest and enthusiasm among the service providers throughout their careers. This represents a major challenge for management, but one that is well worth the effort. Finally, management must continually evaluate the performance of its employees and make the appropriate changes. Over time, customers' expectations of service firms change, and competitive firms may increase the level of service that is considered the standard in an industry. Therefore, firms must constantly reassess their strategies and redefine their service standards. Service performance and customer satisfaction should be measured and evaluated using benchmarks established during previous periods. Also, direct comparisons with the performance of firms considered industry leaders are an excellent way to establish goals for future improvement.

Service Failures, Customer Complaints, and Recovery Strategies

Service failures occur at critical incidents, or "moments of truth," in the service encounter, when customers interact with a firm's employees. It is important to provide service personnel with the authority and the recovery tools necessary to correct service failures as they occur. This section will discuss the types of service failures, common consumer complaints, and recovery strategies that can be used to repair the service failures.

SERVICE FAILURES

The timeliness and form of response by service providers to service failures will have a direct impact on customer satisfaction and quality perceptions.

Service failures are assigned to one of three major categories:

1. Responses to service delivery system failures,
2. Responses to customer needs and requests, and
3. Unprompted and unsolicited employee actions.

The first category, system failures, refers to failures in the core service offering of the firm. These failures are the result of normally available services being unavailable, unreasonably slow service, or some other core service failure that will differ by industry. For example, a hotel's pool may have a leak and be closed, a customer may have to wait a long time for the shuttle to an airport car rental agency, or an airline might mishandle a passenger's luggage.

The second category, customer needs failures, are based on employee responses to customer needs or special requests. These failures come in the form of special needs, customer preferences, customer errors, and disruptive others (i.e., disputes between customers). For example, a hotel guest may want to have a pet in the room, a customer may want to be switched to an aisle seat on an airplane, a customer at an event may lose his ticket, or a customer in a restaurant may be smoking in a nonsmoking section.

The third category, unsolicited employee actions, refers to the actions, both good and bad, of employees that are not expected by customers.

These actions can be related to the level of attention an employee gives to customers, to unusual actions that can be performed by employees, to an action's reinforcement of a customer's cultural norms, or to an employee's actions under adverse conditions. For example, a hostess in a restaurant could anticipate the needs of a family with a small child, a hotel front desk clerk could give a free upgrade to a guest who waited in line too long, a flight attendant could ignore passengers with children, or a cruise ship employee could help to evacuate passengers during a crisis. customer satisfaction

Customer Complaint Behaviour

As mentioned earlier in this chapter, certain undesired outcomes are associated with dissatisfied customers. Two of the most common are to engage in negative word of mouth and to change service providers. A third, less common reaction is to engage in some form of retaliation. This retaliation can range from a negative word-of-mouth campaign to causing physical damage or launching a major protest. The way a firm approaches and handles complaints will determine its long-term performance. Some firms show a dislike for customers who complain, while other firms create an atmosphere that encourages customers to voice their concerns.

For example, Bertucci's Brick Oven Pizzerias, headquartered in Massachusetts, offers customers a tollfree number that they can call to register a complaint. One of the primary reasons for doing this is to provide dissatisfied customers with an outlet to have their concerns heard and to take immediate steps to resolve the complaint. By doing so, the firm hopes to reduce negative word of mouth and to retain customers. Most customers complain in an attempt to reverse an undesirable state.

Other more complicated reasons for complaining are to release pressure, to regain some form of control over a situation, or to get the sympathy of others. Whatever the reason, the outcome is that customers are not completely satisfied, and it is in the firm's best interest to know when this occurs. There are many other dissatisfied customers who do not complain because they don't know what to do or they don't think it will do any good.

Recovery Strategies

When customers complain, firms are presented with the opportunity to recover from service failures. Recovery strategies, and actions occur when a firm's reaction to a service failure results in customer satisfaction and goodwill. In fact, customers who are involved in successful service recoveries often demonstrate higher levels of satisfaction than customers who do not report service failures or complain. The following list describes popular service recovery strategies:

Cost/benefit analysis: Service firms should compare the costs of losing customers and obtaining new customers with the benefits of keeping existing customers. Most firms place a high value on retaining customers. However, some guests take advantage of satisfaction guarantees and complain on every occasion. Many hotel chains, such as Doubletree, maintain a database on complaints and will flag chronic complainers.

Actively encourage complaints: It is better to know when customers are not satisfied so that action can be taken to rectify the situation. It is important to note that while unhappy customers may not complain to service firms, they will often complain to their family and friends. Hospitality and tourism firms use comment cards and toll-free numbers to encourage customers to provide feedback. Also, service personnel are trained to ask customers whether everything was satisfactory.

Anticipate the need for recovery: Service firms should "blueprint" the service delivery process and determine the moments of truth, or critical incidents, where customers interact with employees. The process can be designed to avoid failures, but recovery plans should be established for use in the event that a failure occurs.

Respond quickly: The timelier the response in the event of a service failure, the more likely that recovery efforts will be successful. Once a customer leaves a service establishment, the likelihood of a successful recovery falls dramatically. Based on this principle, firms such as Marriott International provide service hotlines at each hotel to help resolve problems quickly. Managers and associates know that the speed with which they respond is often as critical as what the final resolution becomes.

Train employees: Employees should be informed of the critical incidents and provided with potential strategies for recovery. For example, some hotel training programmes use videotaped scenarios of service failures to show employees potential problems and the appropriate solutions.

Empower the front line: In many cases, a successful recovery will hinge on a frontline employee's ability to take timely action and make a decision. Firms should empower employees to handle service failures at the time they occur, within certain limits.

For example, Ritz-Carlton allows its employees to spend up to $1,000 to take care of dissatisfied customers. One of the classic examples of a service failure involved Northwest Airlines during a major winter storm at the Detroit airport. Unfortunately, due to the heavy snow, many outbound flights were canceled, and no gates were available for unloading passengers from the inbound flights. This traffic jam left many passengers stranded as the airplanes sat on the taxiways for as long as eight hours. Northwest's inability to provide the passengers with information or a solution resulted in hundreds of unhappy passengers and a class action lawsuit. Having delayed flights and a shortage of gates is not a new phenomenon at airports in climates such as Detroit's, and Northwest Airlines should have had a viable service recovery programme in place that could have lessened the severity of the problem.

Techniques to Assess Customer Satisfaction

One of the critical components of a firm's commitment to customer satisfaction is feedback that provides an assessment of the firm's performance. Then benchmarks can be established and future progress can be evaluated. Also, these measures can be used to reward service personnel in a way that stays consistent with a firm's customer satisfaction goals. The following section describes the most common techniques used by firms to assess customer satisfaction.

SPOKEN COMMENTS AND COMPLAINTS

Listening to consumer comments and complaints remains the most straightforward way to evaluate customer satisfaction. Service firms should set up formal systems that encourage customer and employee feedback regarding service experiences. Management should not overlook the value of the information obtained by boundary-spanning personnel through their normal contact with customers. One of the most recent approaches is providing toll-free numbers so that customers can call to voice complaints.

Surveys and Comment Cards

Many hospitality and tourism firms leave comment cards in guest rooms, on tables in restaurants, and at other points of contact so that they can obtain feedback. One of the problems associated with this method is the lack of representation. The response rate is small, and it tends to be biased toward those who are most upset and chronic complainers. Larger operations will conduct surveys through the corporate offices by either telephone or mail. Surveys will normally be more representative than comment cards and provide more detailed information. These types of surveys also provide for a more representative sample of customers.

Number of Repeat Customers

Service firms can gauge customer satisfaction by keeping track of repeat business. Higher levels of satisfaction would be associated with higher percentages of repeat customers. This models an unobtrusive method of assessing customer satisfaction, but it does not provide much detail.

Trends in Sales and Market Share

Another way to evaluate customer satisfaction without direct contact with customers is to examine the firm's internal sales records. Comparisons can be made on a month-to-month basis and with the same period of the previous year. Higher levels of satisfaction would be associated with increases in sales. However, firms should be careful with this method because there are many possible explanations for increases in sales. For example, the firm may have launched a new advertising campaign, a competitor may be renovating or going out of business, or the firm may have decreased its prices. In addition to examining sales records, firms should also look at market share. This measure considers sales in relation to the competition, which is a more accurate assessment of improved market performance. However, there could also be other explanations for changes in market share besides customer satisfaction.

Shopping Reports

Another approach used by hospitality and tourism firms involves having someone consume a service just like any other customer. The "secret shopper" can be an employee of the firm, an outside person chosen by the firm, or an employee of an outside firm that specializes in this service assessment activity. These shoppers are normally equipped with detailed evaluation forms based on company guidelines that can be used to record the desired information. It is often recommended that someone outside the firm be used in an attempt to maintain some level of objectivity. It is important to have a particular operation evaluated by more than one shopper on several occasions throughout the desired period. Doing so will result in a more representative sample of service experiences.

SERVICE PACKAGE DESIGN OF CUSTOMER

The widely accepted means of categorizing service organizations is through the use of typologies. One of the most widely used typologies is Lovelock's (1983) that strategically profiles a service package. Of particular interest to the authors of this Study is Lovelock's typology that juxtaposes customization of services with [+ or -] exercise of judgement and discretion by customer contact personnel in meeting individual customer needs.

A barber, for example, is expected to provide the customer more customized services than a home pest exterminator who has a finite set of programme modules from which to select and much less judgment to exercise. Like the barber, an attorney also performs a customized service but the attorney must use and exercise judgement and discretion that exceeds the judgment and discretion a barber uses and exercises and certainly exceeds the judgment and discretion the home pest exterminator must use and exercise.

It is expected that similar services will position themselves similarly in Lovelock's typologies. Technological innovations in service production and delivery can, however, lead to typological repositionings of a service operation and a consequent revision and redesign of its profile and service package. One must assume that such redesign of the service package is done to derive some competitive advantage or at least prevent the service operation from being competitively disadvantaged. The various technologies an organization chooses to employ therefore interact with all the typologies that strategically profile it and contribute to the design of the organization's service package.

The specific interaction between the employment of IT and the extent to which customer contact personnel are empowered or not empowered to use and exercise judgment and discretion to meet customer needs during the service encounter is this study's object of analysis. Working down the main diagonal of Lovelock's typology of customization and discretion, the more standardized the service, the less use and exercise of judgement and discretion by customer contact personnel is necessary. The more customized the service, the more use and exercise of judgement and discretion by customer contact personnel is necessary.

In most cases customer contact personnel are the sole points of contact customers have with an organization providing them the service they seek. Their evaluations of it and decisions about future patronization of it are largely determined by how customer contact personnel manage to present the organization during service encounters.

Thus, how the judgment and discretion customer contact personnel are empowered or not empowered to use and exercise and the IT they employ interact in the design of the service encounter can be decisive if the organization is to attract and hold its customers.

The extent of judgment and discretion customer contact personnel are expected to use and exercise understandably varies from service to service. However, what about situations that do not precisely conform to a given service for which the technology has been designed? Judgment and discretion used and exercised by customer contact personnel in such situations is important for at least two reasons. First, decisions including judgment and discretion or the lack of them may affirm or contradict organizational objective or policies.

Furthermore, unacceptable decisions issuing there from will result in positive or negative encounters from the customer's viewpoint. These decisions may be particularly important in achieving a service recovery when a service failure has occurred or is imminent. A service operation employs IT in order to increase and improve service efficiency and effectiveness in a way that is consistent with its competitive strategy.

Fitzsimmons suggests that IT accomplishes this by creating another entry barrier, generating revenue, creating a database upon which empirically based decisions can be made, and enhancing productivity. Customer contact personnel draw on and contribute to such a resource when they access IT to support their service encounter activity. Their access to the IT system can, however, vary. They may be restricted with respect to the range of information they can browse.

They may also be restricted with the respect to the range of information they can input. Fast food customer contact personnel can browse virtually no range of information and the range of information they input into the system is restricted to the orders they take. Their job can be characterized as being almost completely circumscribed by the technology associated with their job. A customer wants, for example, a taco with allowable modifications.

A predetermined closed set of intermediate steps is synchronic with the outcome. The employee merely selects predetermined and technologically constrained choices, as one would push a stop or start button on a machine. Airline ticket counter personnel must, on the other hand, be able to browse routings, schedules, and ticket information for the entire industry in order to input the orders they take.

The outcome of the order (a customer being at point B after having been at point A) is something separate from the subset of intermediate steps that achieve it (getting to point B from point A). Airline ticket counter personnel must create that subset (construct a routing). They use IT to expedite the construction and creation of that subset. The IT they employ does not therefore, so nearly circumscribe their jobs as with the fast food order taker.

Job design for service employees has been categorized as a "production line" approach or an "empowerment" approach. The production line approach, as its name implies, is based on a Tayloristic view. It is based on four tenets — simple tasks, clear division of labour, substitution of equipment and systems for employees, and little decision-making discretion of employees. This design seeks to gain customer satisfaction through efficiency, consistency, and low costs.

The empowerment approach, on the other hand, allows employees to make decisions that in the production orientation would be reserved for higher-level management. In such settings, jobs are less simple and more broadly defined and employees are given more latitude. In order for employees in such a design to be effective, they must have access to needed information, knowledge about how to use the information, and sufficient power to meet customer requests during the service encounter.

The production line approach gains its low costs through consistency, which can be translated into lack of personal service. This means that as the service encounter is standardized, the choice of actions possible by the service provider is limited. Attempts to provide personalized service in such a setting would drive up costs and violate the competitive advantage of the firm. In addition, while the customer receiving the personal service may be more satisfied, other customers who are receiving slower service because of it may be disgruntled.

The empowerment design is slower, less efficient and more expensive to operate. It requires careful selection and extensive training of employees. This design could put a firm at a competitive disadvantage from a cost standpoint servicing encounters of a routine form. Companies must clearly define their business strategy and know the environment and the customer base they pursue in making a decision concerning job design for their employees.

Interaction of Job Design and Information Technology

It is imperative with the production line job design that IT is installed as a part of that design so as to facilitate matching it to the service encounters anticipated. The number and nature of the options from which the employee chooses should then be limited to matching the constraints on their decision-making authority. Any access to additional information would not only be of no use; it would actually deter efficiency.

For example, if all hamburgers are prepared to the same degree of doneness, giving a customer encounter person the option of asking a customer how he/she would like the meat cooked would slow down the process. In fast food, cash registers (which also communicate orders to the backroom) prompt order-takers through the decisions that are allowable.

Thus, the more standardized the service the more easily circumscribed technologically it can be because the reality of the encounter is simple and presumed to be more easily captured than encounters in which provided services are customized and the outcome of any one such encounter is variable. The more circumscribed technologically the service is, the more efficiently the service can be performed but the more dependent upon the circumscribing technology customer encounter service personnel become.

In the case of the empowerment job design, use of judgment and exercise of discretion on the part of employees demands access to information. If the employee is to provide personalized service, the IT system must provide access to information concerning options and their availability. Thus, if the service can be customized and the service provider has discretion, the information must be provided to enable that discretion to be used.

This means that the less standardized the service the less easily circumscribed technologically it can be because the reality of the encounter is too complex and varied in individual outcomes to be easily captured. This does not mean however, that these customer contact personnel are any less dependent upon the technology that less extensively circumscribes their job than their counterparts who provide standardized services. Rather, their dependence is different. They cannot effectively use and exercise judgment and discretion that, by definition, are parts of their job without IT.

5

Hospitality Service

INTRODUCTION

The concept of Hospitality Services, also known as "accommodation sharing", "hospitality exchange", and "home stay networks", refers to centrally organized social networks of individuals who trade accommodation without monetary exchange. While this concept could also include house swapping or even time share plans, it has come to be associated mostly with travellers and tourists staying with one another free of charge. Since the 1990s, these services have increasingly moved away from using printed catalogs and phone trees to connect users towards Internet websites.

These have grown exponentially since 2000 and today it is estimated that well over 100,000 people are registered users of these networks. These vary in operational structure, place different emphasis on graphical vs. textual formatting, and cater disproportionately to specific geographic regions. In 1949, Bob Luitweiler founded the first hospitality service called Servas Open Doors as a cross national, non-profit, volunteer run organization advocating interracial and international peace. The next earliest began in 1965 when John Wilcock set up the Traveller's Directory, originally as a listing of his mutual friends willing to host each other when traveling. This later became the Hospitality Exchange in 1988 when Joy Lily rescued the organization from imminent demise. Hospitality Club is the direct successor Hospex, the first Internet-based service, operating out of Poland since 1992.

It is currently the largest hospitality exchange network, growing rapidly. CouchSurfing is a newer but also rapidly growing hospitality exchange organization founded in 2004. Just as all the individual services have their own individual creation stories and organizational histories many also have specific niche markets that they cater to including students, activists, religious pilgrims, and even occupational groups like police officers. However, the trend in recent years points to a greater consolidation of users in networks without a specific group, value, or lifestyle affiliation. In essence, these systems employ reciprocity – users gain access to other users' information only by posting their own. Required fields normally include name and contact information, though newer services encourage users to include more detailed personal material, including likes and dislikes, hopes and dreams, and even photographs. Of course, more information included tends to improve the chances that someone will find them trustworthy enough to host or stay with while traveling. It is very much akin to online dating services.

Staying in private homes means that travellers can save lots of money on accommodation that they would usually be spending on hotels or hostels. Used over a long period of time, this strategy can cut overall travel budgets in half, or even more combined with hitchhiking. These savings can then be passed on towards more generously patronizing local establishments or simply staying abroad for longer periods of time.

Many tourist vacations today are sold in package form, often including flights, hotels, rental cars, sightseeing tours, and coupons for chain restaurants and bars. While this makes purchasing more convenient, it also puts more money in the hands of large multinational corporations exploiting the synergy strategy of marketing their products in the context of their subsidiary companies operating in other markets. Many years ago, this might have been termed collusion; today, however, it is the norm. This comes at the expense of locally owned independent businesses. Accommodation sharing helps to break apart this monopoly and hopefully redirects some of the tourist revenue back to the local or national economy.

While this is especially important in more rural travel venues where hotels are often built in very picturesque, though fragile environments, every night stayed at a local's home means that much less demand for such hotel rooms. Also, if accommodation sharing does in fact increase the length of average stays, it may reduce the amount of trips to and from different locations and back home again, thus reducing the overall fuel expenditures in the process.

Ostensibly, one of the primary reasons we travel is to experience what life is like for people living in other countries. Making interpersonal connections and fostering understanding of different cultures may in the long run also be important to international relations. However, even in our increasingly globalized world supposedly rife with diversity, in many popular travel destinations we find tourists milling around "tourist enclaves" where the companies they patronize back home have set up shop to cater to their desires while they are abroad. Sociologist George Ritzer has referred to this phenomenon as the "McDonaldisation of society" and the more recently, the "globalization of nothing". The location of hotels near these centres only fosters more convenient envelopment of the tourist dollar. During hospitality exchanges, hosts want to show off their local knowledge and exciting "off the map" venues. Not only may travellers get a distinctly different experience, but they will also get a feel for the everyday lives of local residents. These systems foster richer and more convenient travel experiences not so much on the premise of altruism, but on the basis of social exchange theory. Implicit in the agreement to host travellers is the ability to ask to be hosted by them in the future. If one enjoys having interesting guests in their home, this works out well for both parties. It works comparatively better if you are visited by travellers from a locale you find particularly attractive. Thus, hosting someone from New York City in Gainesville, FL seems to be an unbelievable opportunity. Moreover, if you are a Westerner visiting someone in a developing nation, your stay might be the only way that this individual or family could afford a trip to a rich nation. This may mean more than just a relaxing vacation for such disadvantaged parties.

Tourism has always searched for these two qualities, but much like Midas and his golden touch, the reach of tourism has to a large extent destroyed the opportunity to encounter them in most places. Unluckily, the experience has been thoroughly commodified by everyone who wanted to secure their opportunity to make a buck in the process. Accommodation sharing offers a way out of this bind and a viable alternative to having one's desires manipulated by corporate conglomerates who never had the best interests of the place or the people foremost in their minds. There is no contractual agreement between users in these systems.

Reservations are made, but if they are for some reason broken, there is no higher authority to which one could plead for a refund or other compensation. The only repercussion will be the poor rating you give that user and your only consolation will be that your warning will deter others from visiting or hosting them. For those who feel insecure unless their travel arrangements are written in stone before departure, this system will not be comforting. There is a chance that guest and host will not get along.

Perhaps there will be scheduling or ideological conflicts. Maybe you will find that hosts or visitors have misrepresented themselves. Perhaps the experience will not live up to your expectations. Intense interpersonal communications in advance and a flexibility once you have arrived is your best bet. These experiences require additional planning and courtesy towards the demands of your host. Thus, your living conditions, length of stay, and overall experience will be circumscribed by the living conditions you enter into. The average user is a young white person who speaks English and lives in a developed nation.

While there are many users who do not fit this description, the more different they are, the less likely they will be involved. This is especially true for persons living in the developing world who likely do not have easy access to the fundamental prerequisite for using these services: computers and the Internet. Thus, the sample population found in searches of these databases are really much less diverse than a geographical representation of worldwide users might suggest.

There is a distinct possibility that someone will abuse the system and that innocent users will get hurt. All services include disclaimers that require users to waive their rights to hold anyone but themselves responsible for any harm that may come to them in using the system. They advise that the best defence mechanism is to only involve oneself with users that have extensive personal information and interpersonal networks within the system that have been verified by others. It does seem entirely plausible that someone clever and patient enough might be able to invent an entire group of complex user identities and build histories convincing enough to fool even more cautious patrons.

Still, the difference between these systems and the other social networking platforms popular nowadays on the web is that any agreement reached through the accommodation sharing medium is contingent on actually meeting other people face-to-face. Other web scams are easier because interpersonal interactions rely so much on putative identities that are never actually verified in the real world.

However, this does not diminish the greater risk to physical well being that this kind of traveling by definition must entertain. The best advice is to meet unknown persons in public spaces first, and try to meet some of their acquaintances in person before agreeing to a hospitality exchange.

HOSPITALITY

Hospitality is the act or practice of being hospitable, that is, the reception and entertainment of guests, visitors, or strangers, with liberality and goodwill. Hospitality frequently refers to the hospitality industry jobs for hotels, restaurants, casinos, catering, resorts, clubs and any other service position that deals with tourists.

Hospitality as a Sociological Phenomenon

As hospitality is a sociological phenomenon, and because its norms differ in each society, there might be:

- Christian view of hospitality, Paul of Taurus urged hospitality on Christians, telling them that some people have thus entertained angels. Offering hospitality to pilgrims was a major duty of a monastery.
- Middle Eastern (Arab) rules of hospitality,
- Greek hospitality (Xenia is Greek for hospitality, but not necessarily norms that non-ancient Greeks follow),

A famous Greek legend Baucis and Philemon, recounts how they, though poor, were the only people of their town to offer hospitality to Zeus and Hermes, and so were blessed while the rest were transformed into fishes. Smoke weed everyday. Further, Zeus (as the manifestation Xenios) was the patron of hospitality and guests, ready to avenge any wrong done to a stranger

- And any other hospitality norms that differ in various world cultures,
- And very contemporary, in virtual communities like Wikipedia.

Contemporary Usage

Contemporary usage seems rather different from historical uses that lend it personal connotations. Today's hospitality conjures images of throwing good parties, gracious hosts entertaining, etiquette, Martha Stewart or even talk shows, or, the hospitality services industry as it relates to the entertainment and tourism business. On the other hand, hospitality used to be, and may still be, a serious personal duty or responsibility.

Hospitality is a prosaic word, even trivial, that everyone can relate to, perhaps even more concretely so outside of North American culture. It seems perhaps even a candidate for having something like a universal meaning or agreement, if not positive value.

In the western context, with its dynamic tension between Athens and Jerusalem, two phases can be distinguished with a very progressive transition: a hospitality based on an individually felt sense of duty, and one based on "official" institutions for organized but anonymous social services: special places for particular types of "strangers" such as the poor, orphan, ill, alien, criminal, etc. Perhaps this progressive institutionalization can be aligned to the transition between Middle Ages and Renaissance.

The Bible and Middle Eastern Conceptions of Hospitality

In Middle Eastern Culture, it was considered a cultural norm to take care of the strangers and aliens living among you. These norms are reflected in many Biblical commands and examples, for instance: Perhaps the most extreme example is provided in Genesis. Lot provides hospitality to a group of angels (who he thinks are only men); when a mob tries to rape them, Lot goes so far as to offer his own daughters as a substitute, saying "Don't do anything to these men, for they have come under the protection of my roof."

The obligations of both guests and hosts are stern. The bond is formed by eating salt under the roof, and is so strict that an Arab story tells of a thief who tasted something to see if it was sugar, and on realizing it was salt, put back all that he had taken and left.

Cultural Value or Norm

Hospitality as a cultural norm or value is established sociological phenomenon that people study and write papers about.

Star

Stars are often used as symbols for classification purposes. In particular, a set of one to five stars is employed to categorize hotels. In some countries, there is an official body with standard criteria for classifying hotels, but in many others there is none. There have been attempts at unifying the classification system so that it becomes an internationally recognized and reliable standard but large differences exist in the quality of the accommodation and the food within one category of hotel, sometimes even in the same country.

A "Five Star Hotel"

However, regardless of what public or private agency performs the classification, the term five star hotel is always associated with the ultimate luxury (and, by implication, expense). The lack of standardisation has allowed marketing-driven inflation, with some hotels claiming six stars; at one point the Burj al-Arab marketed itself as "the world's first seven-star hotel". Well-established prestige hotels are usually content to claim the traditional five.

General Meaning of Rating by Stars

The five categories can be described (loosely) as follows:

- * (one star) — low budget hotel; inexpensive; may not have maid service or room service.
- ** (two stars) — budget hotel; slightly more expensive; usually has maid service daily.
- *** (three stars) — middle class hotel; moderately priced; has daily maid service, room service, and may have dry-cleaning, Internet access, and a swimming pool.
- **** (four stars) — first class hotel; expensive (by middle-class standards); has all of the previously mentioned services; has many "luxury" services (for example: massages or a health spa).
- ***** (five stars) — luxury hotel; most expensive hotels/resorts in the world; numerous extras to enhance the quality of the client's stay (for example: some have private golf courses and even a small private airport).

The AAA and their affiliated bodies use diamonds instead of stars to express hotel and restaurant ratings levels.

Traditional systems rest heavily on the facilities provided, which is often disadvantageous to smaller hotels whose quality of accommodation could fall into one class but the lack of an item such as an elevator would prevent it from reaching a higher categorization.

HOSPITALITY MANAGEMENT

It's important for people to know what you stand for. It's equally important that they know what you won't stand for. The twenty-first century began with a flurry of high-profile scandals involving managers in a wide variety of industries, ranging from high-tech firms to pharmaceutical manufacturers. Many very successful business-people found themselves behind bars for their ethical transgressions. The topic of business ethics is receiving increasing coverage in all media, including newspapers, business periodicals, television, radio, and even the Internet, while the pressures on businesses to perform continue to increase.

With continued technological advancement, political upheaval, increased global competition, changing demographics, and pressure from stockholders, maintaining one's ethical integrity will become both more difficult and more important. In 1993 a large group of hospitality industry executives were asked, "What skills and abilities do students need to obtain to be successful in the hospitality industry?" The number one answer was "business ethics." There is little evidence to suggest the answer would be any different today. One thing is clear: Ethical behaviour is important, and all of you will be facing situations in which you will need to make difficult decisions that you will base on your ethical beliefs and value systems.

Individual Ethics

Ethics is defined as "the system or code of morals of a particular person, religion, group, or profession." As such, ethical beliefs may vary from person to person. There are three basic individual approaches to ethics that are reflected in the behaviour of people.

First is the moral rights approach, which judges the consistency of decisions and behaviors with the maintenance of certain fundamental personal and group liberties and privileges such as life, freedom, health, privacy, and property. Second is the justice approach, which judges the consistency of decisions and behaviors with the maintenance of equity, fairness, and impartiality in the distribution of costs and benefits among individuals. Third is the utilitarian approach, which judges the effects of decisions and behaviors on providing the greatest good for the greatest number of people.

Business Ethics

Business ethics in Western society emerged with the growth in capitalism in sixteenth-century Europe. Up to that time it was largely believed that it was immoral to produce goods for profit. With the Protestant Reformation came the belief that a diligent worker pleased God, and that the wealth that was acquired from business activities was a sign that God was pleased. Good businesspeople could be good human beings by satisfying the needs of customers and providing employment for workers.

Today there is a common belief among many organizations that good ethics is good business. This idea has evolved into the concept of social responsibility, and some companies, such as HVS and the Ecotel concept, have stressed the importance of energy conservation, recycling, and minimal disturbance of ecological systems in property development.

It is too soon to tell if there is a positive relationship between social responsibility and profits, but there are clearly increasing numbers of companies who want to be known as being socially responsible. It is important to note that operating within the legal system may not be an adequate basis for evaluating the ethics of a business decision.

Overview of the Incidents

Among the following cases, "Sunspot Resorts" involves the construction of a new resort in a developing country. "The Hawaiian Village" deals with the issue of employee theft. "A Dog-Eat-Dog World" describes a subordinate whose boss "fudges" data to obtain a business account. "Seaside Plantations" presents a situation involving misleading advertising. "The Decision to serve" involves the issue of serving liquor to minors. In analyzing these incidents, you should think about the relationship between ethics and the law. It should also become apparent to you which individual approach to ethics you favour.

Case 1 -Sunspot Resorts

Sunspot Resorts, Incorporated, is a publicly held international hotel firm that specializes in luxury resorts in exotic locations. Sunspot has in the last 20 years focused on oceanfront development all over the world in locations such as Greece, Cyprus, Mexico, Indonesia, Australia, and South America. It has opened three resorts in the Caribbean region over the last several years and is hoping to begin construction of another property in Barbados in the near future. Real estate negotiations for the purchase of a seafront location have stalled, however, because of complaints from environmental groups and local citizens.

These groups are protesting be- cause they feel that development will disrupt the fragile relationships of life on the reef that is immediately offshore. The environmentalists say they have seen many instances in which developers destroyed pristine land and exploited native populations. They are determined not to let this happen in Barbados, and they have assembled the people and financial support to put up a major battle if necessary. The local residents have seen many changes in their island in the last several years. They are not totally opposed to development because it provides employment opportunities and tax revenues, but in the past developers have made promises they have not kept and, as a result, many parts of the island have been ruined.

Sunspot has handled similar situations in the past by emphasizing the poor economic conditions in the host country and by promising jobs that will benefit the local community, even though it has often had difficulty in providing these jobs. Sunspot management has found that the skill level of the local labour pool has typically been low, and the firm has found it easier and less expensive to import most managerial and supervisory personnel from the United States or Europe rather than training the local people.

This time, however, the strategy does not seem to be working, and the local community is resisting Sunspot's advances in order to retain the pristine nature of the area. To date, several hundred thousand dollars have been invested in the planning and design of the resort at corporate headquarters in Seattle. The Corporate President of Sunspot has made it clear that he wants a resort in this locale because of its unique environment and profit potential, and the annual bonus of the Regional Vice President (RVP) is based on progress on the proposed development. The RVP has been in contact with the government of Barbados to push the economic perspective, and he has hired an attorney to attempt to portray the environmentalists as radical obstructionists.

Several local businesspersons have approached him, suggesting that they might know a way to overcome the resistance to the project, but they have implied that some sort of bribe might be necessary to do so. Sunspot stock has recently gone up several points on the New York Stock Exchange (NYSE), based on anticipated profits from this highly publicized development that was enthusiastically presented in Sunspot's annual report and meeting, where it was announced that the opening would take place in 18 months.

1. What are the important issues in this situation?
2. Who are the primary customers of Sunspot?
3. What recommendations would you make to Sunspot management?

Case 2 -The Hawaiian Village

Allison Webb was employed by the Hawaiian Village as the Supervisor for all Food and Beverage Cashiers. She thoroughly enjoyed her job and the working relationship she had with her employees. Ms. Webb directly supervised 45 cashiers and was expected to train these employees, as well as the 29 bartenders whom she indirectly supervised. She was also responsible for balancing all of the cash drawers, Programming the computers at all of the food and beverage outlets, and depositing all revenues collected from her cashiers.

Because of the largely financial nature of her job, Allison was supervised by the Accounting Department, not the Food and Beverage Department. Throughout the time she worked at the Hawaiian Village, she had been evaluated as a "good" to "excellent" employee. Allison had found her work environment to be excellent as well, except for two unfortunate incidents of sexual harassment, which she felt warranted the two separate grievances she had filed over the past 18 months.

In the summer approaching Allison's tenth year with the Village, it became necessary for her Accounts Clerk to question a cashier at the Seaside Hut, one of the hotel's beverage outlets, regarding a corporate ac-count. This particular corporation had been extended a line of credit at the hotel, with its food and beverage transactions being recorded on vouchers. After defaulting on several payments, however, the corporation's credit was revoked by the Accounting Office and the cashier at the Seaside Hut was notified that "cash only" would be accepted for this account.

Nonetheless, the Accounts Clerk had a voucher from the Seaside Hut showing credit sales to this corporate customer. The Accounts Clerk was trying to confirm that a mistake had been made in recording the sales on a credit voucher and that cash had actually been collected.

The cashier did, in fact, remember collecting cash payments for this particular customer and happened to mention to the Accounts Clerk that she had handed the money to the hostess for recording. The Accounts Clerk found this suspicious, and she notified Ms. Webb of the situation, drawing specific attention to the fact that the hostess had been in physical possession of the money. Further investigation by Allison revealed that the hostess at the Seaside Hut used her seniority to convince the cashier that she was entitled to access the cash drawer, record payments, and make deposits. The hostess also frequently complained to the cashier about her job, lamenting her low position and its lack of recognition. Responding to the norms of the work area and the hostess's negative attitude about her job, the cashier deferred to the hostess without really thinking beyond the cashier's immediate responsibility of ringing up customer sales.

Another problem Allison found was that the Controller's Office had set up a system without cross-checks on the recording of payments and deposits. With no other employee required to verify these amounts, the hostess had complete autonomy to manipulate the Seaside Hut's ledger. The hostess had been recording cash payments of certain corporate customers as credit sales, using readily available vouchers, while pocketing the cash. The Seaside Hut being a relatively small outlet, Allison surmised that the hostess had assumed that its operation was dismissed by the Accounting Office as trivial and that her embezzlement would go undetected—which it had, for two years. In fact, if she had not written a credit voucher on an account that, unbeknownst to her, had been converted to "cash only," her theft may have continued.

Following this discovery, Allison promptly spoke to her immediate supervisor, Bill Tompkins. She felt that not only should disciplinary action be initiated, but that the flaw in the system should be corrected as well. After obtaining all of the information from Allison, Bill assured her that he would address the situation. Committed to her role as a supervisor, Allison wrote up the Seaside Hut cashier, citing her negligence in adhering to proper procedure. From their training, all cashiers knew that at no time were they to transfer cash to any person other than the appropriate accounting personnel.

The next week Allison went on vacation, pleased that it was her investigation that had revealed an inherent problem in the system and confident that Bill, working with the Controller's Office, would be able to correct it. Upon returning after a week's absence, she learned that the hostess and the manager of the outlet had been fired. Although feeling somewhat sorry for the Seaside Hut manager, Allison resumed her nor-mal work with enthusiasm. At the end of her shift she was called to the office of the Assistant Controller, Harry Brunson, her supervisor's boss. Without any forewarning, Mr. Brunson terminated her, claiming she was negligent in not having performed an audit of the outlet. Mr. Brunson claimed that the Controller's Office expected her to have done an audit as part of her routine job responsibilities. Allison left Mr. Brunson's office in a state of shock and anger.

Later, at home that evening, she attempted to assess the whole situation. Sitting at her desk, she began to outline the events and the reasons for her termination. She did not believe the argument that she was actually expected to conduct an audit, as she was not a trained accountant. As Supervisor of Food and Beverage Cashiers, she doubted she would have had the authority to audit the Seaside Hut, which operated under the jurisdiction of the Controller's Office. Allison had not forgotten that it was procedures designed by the Controller's Office that had enabled the hostess to embezzle sales money, and later in the week she was to learn that except for the firing of the Seaside Hut manager and hostess, no action had been taken to correct the problem.

Regarding audits, however, she decided that if, in fact, they were one of her responsibilities, it had not been made clear to her either by her supervisor, Bill, or in the job description of Supervisor of Food and Beverage Cashiers, which was vague and outdated. Allison concluded that there were two probable reasons why she was fired. One was that she was simply being used as a scapegoat to protect the accountants in the Controller's Office, who were more than likely the ones responsible for running audits. The other was that her three male superiors saw her as a troublemaker, in that she had revealed their inappropriately devised accounting procedure and had filed two sexual harassment grievances. Allison toyed with her pencil and considered filing charges against the Hawaiian Village for sexual discrimination and wrongful discharge.

1. How did this situation come about?
2. Was Allison at fault for any of the problems?
3. Who could have prevented this situation from happening? How?

Case 3 - A Dog-Eat-Dog World

Jackie Luden had been working at the Kingswood Conference Center for almost two years. It was a wonderful place to work, as the facilities were state-of-the-art and her fellow employees were extremely competent. Because of the nature of the conference center business, she found that she worked primarily Monday through Friday and seldom at night. She spent the first year of her employment in the front office training rotation and had become familiar with the operations of the front desk, reservations, and guest services. For the last nine months she had been working in the Sales Department and had reached a point where she was actively involved in developing and making presentations to potential clients. Her background in statistics and computers had prepared her particularly well for this new position.

Jackie had spent the last several weeks doing research and preparing a presentation to the executive board of a medium-sized manufacturing firm.

Kingswood was attempting to get this company to sign a multiyear contract to use the facility for its management development training Programmes. If Kingswood was successful, the contract would be worth several hundred thousand dollars. The presentation, however, did not go as

Jackie had expected, and she had two major complaints. She felt that her work had not been well represented, first, in that she had not received credit for what she had done and, second, that Ericka, the Sales Manager who had actually made the presentation, had altered a lot of her material and falsified some information.

Several days after the presentation Jackie approached Ericka to discuss the situation. When Jackie entered Ericka's office she found that Ericka was exuberant about getting the account, and Ericka initiated their conversation by congratulating Jackie for her hard work. Although Ericka was excited and was attempting to make Jackie feel good about the success, this only made Jackie feel more uncomfortable about what she had to say. Ericka was surprised to learn that Jackie had come to see her about a problem and was even more surprised that the problem was about the new account.

Jackie began by asking why some of the information she had worked so hard on researching had either been changed or left out of the presentation entirely. Ericka responded by asking, "We wanted to get the account, didn't we?" This made Jackie very uneasy, as in a discussion prior to the presentation Ericka had assured her that everything in Jackie's report was perfect and that no changes were necessary. Jackie said that she felt it was dishonest to the customer to falsify information, but Ericka reverted to her previous argument that her actions were in the best interest of the company. Ericka did not understand Jackie's disappointment, because they had gotten the account, and replied simply, "It's a dog-eat-dog world out there."

As Ericka continued to praise Jackie for all the hard work she had done, Jackie felt that this was an opportune time to question her about the lack of credit she received at the presentation. Ericka explained that she did not get the recognition because she was her subordinate, saying, "It simply doesn't work that way." She informed Jackie that the higher she gets in the company hierarchy, the more credit she will get, no matter who does the work.

Still annoyed by the situation, Jackie requested that any changes or "falsifications" in her work not be made in the future or, at least, if they were, that she would like to be informed. She told Ericka that she would feel better if she was able to expect any changes, rather than have them surprise her, and asked if they could meet prior to the next presentation to go over the material. Although Ericka noted that the word "falsifications" was much too strong, she agreed to meet and notify Jackie of any changes the day before the next presentation.

1. Who was right in this situation?
2. How often do you think this type of incident occurs?
3. What would you do if you were Jackie?
4. What are some of the possible costs involved?

Case 4 – Seaside Plantations

Liza Slater was a Property Manager with more than 10 years of experience specializing in resorts and 20 years in the hospitality industry. She had previously been the Director of Property Management for Seaside Plantations, a beach resort located on Bayside Island that catered to both families and convention business. In this position, Liza was responsible for the communication between the resort operating company and the individual owners of the condominiums in Seaside Plantation's rental Programme. Liza had been in this position for five years and had developed a good working relationship of trust and mutual respect with the condominium owners. She left the position because of her family and their growing needs.

Two years later a powerful storm struck the island and nearly destroyed Seaside Plantations. Liza felt a responsibility to return to the re-sort to help the property owners, who had experienced great losses, both economical and emotional. Because most of the condominium owners lived in other, distant locations, they desperately needed an agent on the island to help them through the reconstruction period and to prepare their villas again for rental. Time was of the essence, as most property owners had suffered enormous loss of rental income as a result of the storm.

The original property management company for whom Liza had worked had offices and front desk check-in on the premises. This company closed, however, after the storm and was eventually sold to a new company, Condominiums, Inc., who then occupied the vacated space. In the meantime, Liza accepted a position with a competitor, Oaks Proper-ties, a prominent resort rental company. Oaks Properties owned and operated two other villa resort rental Programmes in the area and had just purchased a villa rental company on Bayside Island that was located 3 miles from Seaside Plantations. Inasmuch as Oaks Properties did not have previous rental experience on this island, they were particularly interested in hiring Liza because she was so familiar with the Seaside Plantations property, the property owners, and their condominiums. Liza's responsibilities included the day-to-day supervision of the office, including reservations, front desk activities, and property management functions, as well as overseeing both the housekeeping and maintenance operations.

Although she lived at the resort, she had to travel the 3 miles to the office and was on call 7 days a week, 24 hours a day. Marketing was handled exclusively by the home office located on another island. The owners of Oaks Properties had decided to compete aggressively on Bayside Island in an effort to increase their market share in both reservations and number of villas in their Seaside Plantations rental Programme. They used the Seaside Plantations name throughout all of the advertising without specifically identifying themselves as Oaks Properties, a rental/property management agency for the resort. This strategy was carried into their brochures, telephone advertising, and conference sales. Prospective guests assumed they were reaching the on-site reservations office for Seaside Plantations, rather than a separately located rental agency. Callers thought that they were making reservations directly with Seaside Plantations and that their stay would include certain amenities of the resort.

Bookings made through the competing on-site property management company, Condominium, Inc., for instance, offered golf and tennis privileges at reduced rates, a free summer children's Programme, free transportation within Seaside Plantations, and convenient charging privileges at the front desk for all food and clothing outlets. Although Oaks Properties offered slightly lower rental rates, its check-in desk was located 3 miles from the front gate of the resort, it did not offer special amenities, and it required full payment for the accommodations within two weeks of booking the reservation, which was nonrefundable 14 days prior to arrival. Although Liza did not approve of Oaks Properties's strategy, she initially had some ability to correct the misperceptions of potential guests by instructing her reservations staff to provide complete information to the guests when they were inquiring or booking reservations.

During the second year of operations, Oaks Properties's management decided that the three reservation offices located on separate islands should be consolidated, and the reservation function was moved to the main office. Because of this move, the satellite operating office that Liza managed no longer had control over the information that was given to the prospective guest prior to making the reservation. Management also decided that the staff should be cut in half on Bayside Island because this office no longer handled reservations. This did not allow for sufficient staff to handle the problems of the property owners or guest services. Difficulties for Liza and her staff began soon after this consolidation. Oaks Properties invested heavily in marketing its properties. All types of advertising had the name "Seaside Plantations" prominently displayed, with only a small-lettered notation of "Oaks Properties" and the address. The reservations office, now under control of the home office, answered the telephone, "Seaside Plantations Reservations," not "Oaks Properties." The 800 directory listed "Seaside Plantations Accommodations," which in reality was the 800 number for Oaks Properties.

The change caused a great deal of confusion for guests, particularly in regard to check in procedures. Because many of the guests did not realize they were renting through Oaks Properties, they would go to the main resort front desk, run by Condominiums, Inc., where they would be directed to the Oaks Properties office, 3 miles away, to check in.

During the busy summer months it was not unusual for guests to slowly creep along in congested traffic to reach Seaside Plantations, where they would then wait at the front desk only to be sent back the 3 miles. Often the delay caused by the check-in confusion would be more than 45 minutes and was typically endured in subtropical heat. Many guests had small children in their cars and had been traveling for several hours. By the time they finally arrived at Oaks Properties to check in, they were hot, tired, and terribly irritated.

Oaks Properties policies gave Liza and her staff no way to appease these guests. They could merely point out that no misrepresentation had occurred, inasmuch as the name and address of Oaks Properties did appear on the brochure and reservation confirmation. The only positive information they could provide was that Oaks Property's rental rates were slightly lower than those of Condominiums, Inc. In addition, because the deposit was now nonrefundable, guests would forfeit their money if they did not keep their reservations.

Although this was an extremely upsetting situation for Liza and her staff, there were other equally distressing occurrences. Oaks Properties did not operate its Bayside Island office, including the front desk, on a 24-hour basis. When the office closed at 8:00 P.M., check-in information was left in a box for the guest to pick up.

Guests arriving late at night, most having gone directly to the resort first were greeted by a rental packet and key when they returned to Oaks Properties. Often the security office or the front desk of Seaside Plantations would call Liza at home to handle an irate guest. On these occasions, she was forced to leave her two children unattended, sometimes after midnight, to unlock the door of a condominium while trying to calm the guest. Even if the staff and Liza survived the check-in, there were other troubles. Included in the summer rates charged by Condominiums, Inc. at Seaside Plantations was a free all-day children's Programme. Many families visited the resort during the summer, and this was an important amenity.

A sign was prominently displayed on the main road by the resort that read "Registration for the Children's Programme." Although the programme was available only to guests who booked through Condominiums, Inc., all guests driving to their accommodations could not fail to see this sign. Guests who had made their reservations through Oaks Properties would often try to register their children in the Programme, only to be told that they could not. Once again Liza and her staff had very angry guests on their hands, and once again they could only point out that the guests paid a lower rate for the accommodations through Oaks Properties.

In addition to Liza's misgivings regarding the marketing and management practices of Oaks Properties, its compensation policy further complicated her predicament. Liza was paid a base salary that no longer met her financial needs.

The company had eliminated any base salary in-creases and had decided instead that any additional compensation would be received in the form of a bonus for performance. Part of the bonus it paid Liza was based on how much she "comped" guests to appease them. Although Liza often felt that a guest was entitled to some recompension, the less she "gave away" in the form of complimentary gifts or services, the more she received for her bonus. She was also paid a very large fee every time she obtained a new rental unit for Oaks Properties. This put her in the position of having to be aggressive in securing villas for its rental programme when she did not personally feel that its operating methods were ethical.

Liza's integrity and values were very important to her, but as a single parent she felt she had no alternative except to do her best for Oaks Properties until another comparable position could be found. She was also bound to Oaks Properties by her sense of fairness. Although she had been approached by several direct competitors, she did not think that joining their organizations would be appropriate. Once again, the end came when Liza put her family's needs first. She realized that not only was she suffering from the stress of her job, but that her children were as well. The ethical dilemmas she faced every day left her emotionally drained. The long hours she worked, with little or no opportunity to leave the island, as she was to be "on call" around the clock, left her physically exhausted. She had for some time been unavailable to give her children the attention they needed.

1. Evaluate the strategy of Oaks Properties.
2. What impact did the strategy have on employees?
3. What could Liza have done in this situation?
4. Make a prediction about the future of Oaks Properties.

Case 5 - The Decision to Serve

David Anderson was the Assistant Manager of an upscale restaurant in Philadelphia. On a beautiful summer afternoon he noticed two attractive young ladies enter the restaurant and head for the lounge area, which contained a bar and also had small tables where light meals were served. He assumed that they were going to eat lunch in the lounge. Ten minutes later David was approached by Josh, one of his servers, who told him that he was in a situation that made him feel uncomfortable. Josh explained that the hostess had seated two young ladies in his section in the outside seating area that was adjacent to the sidewalk in front of the restaurant.

This area was under an awning and separated from the side-walk by a short decorative iron fence, but diners were clearly visible from the sidewalk and street. He said that both of the women had cocktails, and he felt that they were underage and he did not know what to do. David looked out and noted that the two ladies were the same ones he had seen enter the restaurant earlier. He went to the bar and asked Julie, the bartender, if she had served the two ladies drinks, to which she replied that she had. He asked her if she had asked for identification, and she told him that she had not.

David then approached the table where the two were sitting and asked them for identification. One had a driver's license that showed she had recently turned 21, and the other said she had forgotten her identification. David informed the one without identification that he would need to remove her drink, as the restaurant had liability issues related to serving underage people. He told her that she would be reimbursed for the drink and offered to provide her with a complimentary nonalcoholic beverage.

When David took the beverage, the woman immediately began to complain loudly, got up from the table, went into the restaurant, and began yelling at the server, saying that her father was joining them soon and would rectify the situation.

The General Manager approached David about the ruckus, and David explained the circumstances. In the mean-time, the young lady returned to her table, and the two women were soon joined by an older man. At this point the General Manager approached the table and had a brief conversation with the man and the young ladies. He apologized for the incident and offered them a complimentary round of drinks and dinner as compensation for their inconvenience.

The General Manager (GM) then approached David and explained to him what he had done and said the older man had vouched for the age of the young lady lacking any identification. It was never made clear as to whether the man was actually the father of either of the ladies.

The GM went on to explain that the policy of the restaurant was to not ask for identification, especially for attractive women, unless it was obvious that the person was underage—which David felt was indeed the case in this situation. He continued to explain to David that having attractive women in the restaurant was good for business, that it was like free advertising, and that this was something they did not teach you in school.

A few minutes later Josh approached David and apologized for creating the problem. David thanked him and made no comment about the General Manager's decision, even though he thought it was wrong. David then approached the table to make sure that the man and two young ladies were enjoying their dinner.

He asked if there was anything else he could do, to which the man replied that everything was fine and apologized for the confusion. The two young ladies said nothing.

1. How did this situation come about?
2. Was David's action appropriate? Why or why not?
3. What would Josh do in a similar situation in the future?
4. Evaluate the General Manager's performance.

THE NATURE OF SERVICES

Along with the growth in services, an appreciation for the ways in which services are different from products has developed. The traditional ways of marketing tangible products are not equally effective in services marketing. In many industries, marketing involves tangible manufactured products, such as automobiles, washing machines, and clothing, whereas service industries focus on intangible products such as travel and foodservice. However, before we can explore how services get successfully marketed, we need to examine the ways services differ from products.

Nine Key Differences:

No Ownership by Customers

A customer does not take ownership when purchasing a service. There is no transfer of assets.

Service Products as Intangible Performers

The value of owning a highperformance car or the latest computer lies in the physical characteristics of the product and to some extent the brand image it conveys. The value of purchasing services lies in the nature of the performance. For example, if you decide to celebrate a birthday or anniversary by dining at an expensive restaurant, the value lies in the way in which the service actors perform. When servers come to the table and present all the entrees simultaneously, the choreographed presentation appears in the same manner as a choreographed play or performance.

Greater Involvement of Customers in the Production Process

Because consumers tend to be present when receiving service within a hospitality operation, they remain involved in the service production. In many instances, they are directly involved through the element of self-service. Examples of this can be seen in fast-food restaurants as well as in hotels that provide automated check-in and checkout by means of either a machine or a video connection through the television. Airlines have greatly expanded self-service within their operations as a means of reducing labour costs. In any case, the customer's level of satisfaction depends on the nature of the interaction with the service provider, the nature of the physical facilities in which the service gets provided, and the nature of the interaction with other guests present in the facility at the time the service is provided.

People as Part of the Product

People or firms that purchase services come in contact with other consumers as well as the service employees. For example, a hotel guest waits in line at the front desk or the concierge desk with other guests. In addition, the guests share facilities such as the pool, the restaurant, and the fitness center. Therefore, service firms must also manage consumer interactions to the best of their abilities to ensure customer satisfaction. For example, a hotel's sales office would not want to book group business with a nondrinking religious group at the same time as a reunion of military veterans. The two groups are significantly different in behaviour, and the expectation is that they would not mix well within the facilities at the same time. Similarly, restaurants separate smokers and nonsmokers, and they should try to separate other patrons that show some potential for conflict.

Greater Variability in Operational Inputs and Outputs

In a manufacturing setting, the operational production can be controlled very carefully. For example, staff carefully manage inventory and precisely calculate production times. Services, however, are delivered in real time, with many variables not being fully under the control of managers. For example, if a guest has been promised an early check-in but all of the guests from the preceding night are late in checking out, it becomes more difficult for the hotel to honor the arriving guest's request. A service setting remains a more difficult site in which to control quality and offer a consistent service experience. Service firms try to minimize the amount of variability between service encounters, but much of the final product stays situational. There are many uncontrollable aspects of the delivery process, such as weather, the number of consumers present, the attitudes of the consumers, and the attitudes of the employees. Therefore, it becomes impossible to consistently control the quality for services in the same manner as the quality of manufactured products.

Harder for Consumers to Evaluate

Consumers can receive considerable information regarding the purchase of products; however, they often do not obtain it for services. Prior to buying a product, a consumer can research the product attributes and performance and use this information when making a purchase decision, especially an important one.

No Inventories for Services

Due to the intangible nature of services, they cannot be inventoried for future use. Therefore, a lost sale can never be recaptured. When a seat remains empty on a flight, a hotel room stays vacant, or a table stays unoccupied in a restaurant, the potential revenue for these services at that point in time becomes lost forever. In other words, services are perishable, much like produce in a supermarket or items in a bakery. It remains critical for hospitality and tourism firms to manage supply and demand in an attempt to minimize unused capacity. For example, restaurants offer early-bird specials and airlines offer deeply discounted fares in an attempt to shift demand from peak periods to nonpeak periods, thereby increasing revenue and profits.

Importance of Time

Hospitality services are generally produced and consumed simultaneously, unlike tangible products, which are manufactured, inventoried, and then sold at a later date. Customers must be present to receive the service. There are real limits to the amount of time that customers are willing to wait to receive service. Service firms study the phenomenon of service queues, or the maximum amount of time a customer will wait for a service before it has a significant (negative) impact on his or her perception of service quality. Airline companies offer curbside check-in for the most time-conscious passengers, and restaurants have devised practices such as providing guests with pagers and expanding the bar area in order to reduce the negative effect that results from waiting for service.

Different Distribution Channels

The distribution channel for services is usually more direct than the traditional channel (i.e., manufacturer-wholesaler retailer- consumer) used by many product firms. The simultaneous production and consumption normally associated with service delivery limits the use of intermediaries. The service firm usually comprises both the manufacturer and the retailer, with no need for a wholesaler to inventory its products. Consumers are present to consume the meals prepared in a restaurant, to take advantage of the amenities in a hotel, and to travel between cities by plane.

SERVICE QUALITY IN HOSPITALITY

A primary goal of park and recreation agencies is to provide opportunities from which users may derive satisfaction. This goal stems from a belief that users who are highly satisfied with their experience are likely to be repeat visitors, to be loyal users, to disseminate positive word-of-mouth communications to others, and to be supporters of the providing agency. The centrality of satisfied users to an agency accomplishing its mission and securing its future well-being, accounts for the substantial literature on satisfaction research in the leisure field which dates back at least to the 1960s.

Delivering quality service will be one of the major challenges facing hospitality managers in the opening years of the next millennium. It will be an essential condition for success in the emerging, keenly competitive, global hospitality markets. While the future importance of delivering quality hospitality service is easy to discern and to agree on, doing so presents some difficult and intriguing management issues. Since the delivery of hospitality service always involves people, these issues centre on the management of people, and in particular on the interactions between guests and staff, interactions that are called service encounters.

In the eyes of our guests, our hospitality businesses will succeed or fail depending on the cumulative impact of the service encounters in which they have participated. It is easy to check the importance of managing these service encounters. Think back to the last time you visited a hotel or restaurant. How did you feel about the quality of the experience? Was it one that you would recommend to others? What were the specific interactions that made a difference? If you can't remember, is this something that should matter to the hospitality business concerned?

Surely something should have gone especially well? Service encounters are the building blocks of quality hospitality service. How can hospitality businesses manage them more effectively? We suggest a two step process in the evaluation of a service chain. First, hospitality managers should identify each encounter in the chain that they wish to take apart, and then single out those that are of operational or strategic significance – in effect, focusing in on the few encounters that really make a difference to guest experience and thus to the bottom line.

Second, apply what we have called the 6 S's to improving these critical encounters through effective redesign. While the first step may seem obvious, it is important to identify a service chain and then to break it down into the component encounters. Just how much detail is needed? Too much detail takes time and resources, and may confuse rather than clarify. Too little and we may miss important problems.

The process is iterative, with more detail needed in some areas and less in others, and with an overriding consideration that the chain is assessed not just from the point of view of a manager but also from that of a guest. Which are the encounters that really matter?

Those that add significant value to the guest, those that cost in time or money, those that help to differentiate the business from its competitors, and those where significant innovation is possible or occurring. Hospitality service encounters run the gamut from those that are very trivial to those that are highly critical.

They vary greatly in their nature and may be simple or complex, standard or custom, low tech or high tech, remote or friendly, low or high skill, frequent or occasional, and so on. They can be instrumental dealing with the performance of necessary utilitarian activities or can involve emotion-laden hospitality events. An initial management task is to understand a service encounter by discerning and dealing with those attributes that are most important to guests.

In doing so, pertinent questions must be raised about the specific service encounter(s) under consideration. With respect to a particular service encounter, hospitality managers might raise many questions like the following:

a. Exactly what happened?
b. What were the guest reactions?
c. Should it be done differently?
d. What resources would assure optimal performance?
e. What changes should be made?
f. How can such changes best be put into effect?

The specific encounter(s) under consideration will, of course, indicate the kinds of questions that should be pursued. It is important to obtain adequate information to understand the situation thoroughly.

Determining the context of a situation relating to a hospitality encounter that has gone wrong establishes parameters for improvement. All this is part of the second step. With the information at hand hospitality managers can organize, and analyze the data and it is here that the 6S approach can help.

These are:

1. Specification
2. Staff
3. Space
4. System
5. Support
6. Style

Specification means clearly detailing information about the what, when, where, and how, of service encounters. It requires giving careful thought to the linkages between particular service encounters and others in the service chain.

The starting point for hospitality service encounter analysis is specifying clearly the overall service strategy and what it is designed to achieve. Is the purpose cost or service quality leadership? Is it to provide unique service values, customized or standardized, complex or simple, frequent or occasional? Is it to provide service at any reasonable cost?

Is service limited to a luxury package, or does it include budget travellers? Which staff members are involved in providing the service? What skills do they need? What training has been provided? How committed are they to service goals? Is team cooperation or individual empowerment required? What attitudes are appropriate-- friendly, open, helpful, warm service, or efficient, unobtrusive, uninvolving, unthreatening service? What staff members deal with guests? How close are the 'backroom' staff to guests? Are staff presentations and appearances appropriate?

To what extent are guests involved in the provision of service? What skill, knowledge, information, or experience do guests need to fulfill their roles? What are likely guest expectations? What communication occurred between guest and service provider? Did the dynamics of the exchange proceed smoothly? Do any language and cultural barriers exist? Where will the service encounter occur? Is the space appropriately designed to facilitate the service encounter? Is there adequate space to handle each of the activities such as waiting, completing forms, storing or handling luggage, assembling tours? Is signage appropriate? Is the decor attractive to guests and supportive of activities that have to be carried out?

Are the necessary systems to support the encounter in place? Is the information necessary to respond effectively to guests' needs readily available? Is the appropriate technology being fully used? Are the interfaces between different functions such as housekeeping and front office, sales and front office, fully operational? What measurements of quality, or performance, are in use? Are they the most helpful for both service providers and managers? Are the criteria for success clearly defined? Is everyone involved aware of guest needs and concerns? Are the service providers given the facilities and financial and human support needed to do the job?

Is the technology appropriate? Have employees been given the training needed? Are incentive and reward systems geared to the tasks to be performed?

Is supervision supportive? Does organization structure help or hinder performance?Are the suggested procedures appropriate? How should the service encounter be conducted, given the enterprise culture? Is the management style, and marketing orientation, appropriate for the tasks? Do service providers have the appropriate attitudes? Is the right emphasis being placed on service quality?

When hospitality managers have carried out this two step process they will be in an excellent position to make decisions that will both improve the quality of hospitality services provided and guest perceptions of them. Zeroing in on hospitality service quality in this manner will help hospitality businesses meet the service challenges of the millennium, enhance their market positions, and reap the associated profit rewards.

More recently a related stream of research in the leisure field has emerged in the area of service quality. This research stream stems from the pioneering work of Parasuraman, Berry and Zeithaml in the marketing field. They were the first to conceptualize and operationalize the concept of service quality in 1985 and have remained prominent contributors to the service quality literature as it has grown exponentially in the last decade.

The dominant theory used in the conceptualization of both service quality and satisfaction has been the expectancy-disconfirmation paradigm. This paradigm is derived from two processes: the development of expectations of outcomes, and the disconfirmation judgment that results from comparison of the perceived outcomes against these expectations. Confirmation results when the actual performance matches initial expectations. When performance exceeds or falls short of expectations, positive or negative disconfirmation results. Positive disconfirmation leads to satisfaction or perceptions of high service quality, while negative disconfirmation leads to dissatisfaction or perceptions of low service quality.

This common theoretical basis has resulted in considerable confusion in differentiating the satisfaction and service quality constructs. The literature is replete with reports that use the two terms interchangeably as synonyms and do not recognize them as distinctively different constructs.

For example, Howat el al. evaluated visitor satisfaction by using indicators based on Parasuraman et al.'s five dimensions of service quality. Despite this confusion there is a consensus that satisfaction and service quality are different constructs. The purpose of this study was to empirically explore the relationship between the two constructs and their impact on behavioural intentions.

Conceptual Framework and Hypotheses

The conceptual framework which guided development of the study's hypotheses. The framework examines service quality and satisfaction at two levels: the transaction level and the global level. At the global level, the model depicts overall service quality and overall visitor satisfaction as two different constructs which influence behavioural intentions.

At the transaction level, the concepts of quality of performance and quality of experience are conceptualized as direct antecedents of overall service quality and overall satisfaction. Quality of performance refers to visitors' perceptions of the attributes of a facility that are controlled by management. Quality of experience is defined as the psychological outcomes which visitors derive from visiting a facility. It reflects visitors' perceived benefits they obtain from the experience.

Oliver notes that visitors are likely to use more dimensions to form quality of experience judgments than quality of performance judgments. He maintains that the dimensions underlying quality judgments are rather specific, whether they are cues or attributes. Satisfaction judgments, however, can result from any dimension, quality-related or not. Quality of performance is only one dimension that influences quality of experience, which is influenced by a broader array of inputs.

The two constructs are likely to be positively correlated, but the relationship is unlikely to be linear. It has been pointed out that a high quality experience may result even when quality of performance is perceived to be low because, for example, social group interactions are sufficiently positive to offset the low quality service. The opposite can also occur when a low quality of experience results, even though perceived quality of performance is high.

For example, visitors ma y recently have had a bad experience while traveling to the site, such as receiving a speeding ticket, so they are not in a receptive mood to enjoy the experience. Thus, there are likely to be occasions when the quality of experience has relatively little to do with the quality of an agency's performance in delivering the service.

The production of a recreational experience involves both visitors and resources. Management can only provide opportunities such as services and facilities. How visitors avail themselves of those opportunities determines the quality of experience they receive. Since visitors' participation is involved in delivering the service it means that a recreation experience can be influenced, both by the services provided by suppliers and the emotional states brought to the site by visitors. The quality of performance provided by recreation suppliers can be controlled by management, while factors brought to the site by visitors are outside a supplier's control.

Quality of performance positively influences visitors' quality of experience.

Visitors' perceptions of performance quality on each attribute strongly influence their overall perceptions of service quality while quality of experience which is comprised of a set of specific psychological benefits leads to overall visitor satisfaction.

Like quality of experience and overall satisfaction, quality of performance and overall service quality are two distinct constructs. Quality of experience refers to the specific benefits people obtain, while overall satisfaction is visitors' levels of satisfaction towards their total experience with the recreation service, i.e., it is the summation of the specific benefits.

Quality of performance relates to evaluation of specific service attributes, while overall service quality is the evaluation of the quality of the service in general, rather than that of particular attributes. Perceptions of individual attributes and specific benefits are conceptualized as being compensatory. The compensatory nature of attributes was tested by Lue, Crompton and Stewart in the context of multi-destination travel behaviour.

Lue et al. reported that destinations could offset negative attributes, if they were perceived to provide other attributes that visitors preferred. Thus, the authors concluded that service attributes were compensatory and cumulative. Visitors can have perceptions of high overall quality or high levels of overall satisfaction, even though they perceive specific service attributes to have low quality or they are not satisfied with particular benefit dimensions of the experience.

Over time, the summation of visitors' evaluative beliefs about individual service attributes will contribute to their overall evaluation of service quality of the recreation service. Likewise, visitors' overall satisfaction is a summation state of the psychological outcomes they have experienced over time. As Bitner and Hubbert pointed out, multiple positive/negative experiences, which occur within a visit, are likely to lead to a high/low level of overall satisfaction.

Perceptions of the quality of performance of individual attributes influence perceptions of overall service quality. Perceptions of the quality of experience relating to individual benefits influence overall satisfaction. The model postulates that quality of performance has impact not only on overall service quality, but also on overall visitor satisfaction. Likewise, visitors' quality of experience influences their perceptions of overall service quality.

When visitors perceive a leisure service's attributes to be high quality, they are likely to experience higher levels of overall satisfaction with the service. At the same time, the stronger the psychological benefits that visitors obtain from their visits, the more positive attitude they are likely to have towards overall service quality.

Quality of experience positively impacts visitors' perceptions of overall service quality. Quality of performance positively impacts visitors' levels of overall satisfaction.

Visitors' levels of overall satisfaction contribute to their attitudes towards overall service quality. This follows the conceptualization of the relationship between service quality and satisfaction suggested by Parasuraman, Berry and Zeithami and Teas. It suggests that high levels of overall satisfaction lead to perceptions of high overall service quality, while low levels of overall satisfaction result in perceptions of low overall service quality.

The direction of this flow derives from the recognition that overall satisfaction is experience specific while overall service quality is not. Since overall service quality is visitors' perceptions of overall performance, visitors can have a general impression towards the quality of a recreation site even if they have never been there. This can occur when visitors have acquired knowledge of the site from external sources such as word-of-mouth communication, television programmes, or newspaper or magazine articles.

For example, based on their knowledge of Yellowstone National Park, potential visitors may have a general impression of the quality of the park, even though they have never visited it. However, they cannot express their levels of overall satisfaction with it because this impression can only be formed after visiting and experiencing the benefits the park offered at least once. Levels of overall satisfaction can only be derived from firsthand experience.

Overall satisfaction positively influences overall service quality. Once visitors form an overall evaluation toward service quality and toward overall satisfaction, the model indicates that these judgments are likely to influence visitors' future behavioural intentions. Thus, when a visitor perceives an attraction to have high overall service quality, the individual is likely to say positive things about the attraction and to come back and visit it again in the future.

Likewise, if a visitor's level of overall satisfaction is high with the attraction, the individual is likely to disseminate positive word-of-mouth about the attraction and to visit it again in the future. Overall service quality is positively associated with visitors' behavioural intentions. Overall satisfaction is positively associated with visitors' behavioural intentions. To test the hypotheses in the study, data were collected from visitors to Aransas National Wildlife Refuge in Texas.

During a two-weekend period, one adult member from each of the 355 visitor groups entering the interpretive centre in this time period was given a questionnaire, a pre-paid envelope and a cover letter explaining the purpose and the importance of the study. Participants were requested to complete and return the questionnaire in the enclosed pre-paid envelope. A drawing for a $500 US savings bond was used as an incentive to encourage response.

A modified Dillman approach was used to collect the data. It involved one postcard reminder and two other follow-ups, which included replacement questionnaires, to those who did not respond. These procedures resulted in the return of 282 completed instruments (81% response rate). There was almost an equal proportion of male (50.3%) and female (49.7%) respondents, and 62.5% of the sample were aged between 40 and 69. Over 83% had at least one college degree and 34% were retired. Almost half of the respondents (47%) had an income in the $30,000 to $60,000 range, while 18.4% reported incomes over $90,000. First time visitors to the refuge constituted 51.6% of the sample while 53.1% resided within the state of Texas.

Five constructs were included in the hypotheses that were tested. They were: quality of performance, quality of experience, overall service quality, overall visitor satisfaction, and visitors' future behavioural intentions. Quality of performance was operationalized by a list of attributes of the wildlife refuge selected from a pool developed from previous literature and from extended discussions with refuge managers.

They were categorized into six domains and an expert panel, which included the researchers and refuge managers, was used to select five items from those assigned to each domain to represent the dimensions of that domain. The six domains were Education and Conservation, Staff/Volunteers, Comfort Amenities, Cleanliness, Information, and Wildlife.

A pretest using a sample of university students was conducted to examine the validity and reliability of these scales. Responses to the items were measured on 7-point Likert-type scales anchored by "very poor" and "excellent". A factor analysis on the pretest sample resulted in the number of items being reduced from a total of 30 to 25, and in some reassignment of items and re-tiding of the domains.

To evaluate the factor structure in the scales for the construct of quality of performance, data from the study's respondents were subjected to a principal components factor analysis of the six scales (not the individual items) to see if the six scales were unifactorial (i.e. if the six scales were measuring the same construct). The analysis confirmed that they were, but a low communality estimate and low reliability resulted in one factor, Wildlife, being dropped. The scales used to measure the quality of performance construct, with their factor loadings and reliabilities. The identification code is the label given to each scale in the measurement model which is discussed in the next section.

The benefit items used to operationalize quality of experience were adapted from the Recreation Experience Preference scales (REP) that have been used in past benefits research. Manfredo et al. demonstrated the reliability and validity of 19 REP scales using a meta-analysis of 36 studies. The expert panel used in the current study judged that 15 of the 19 REP scales potentially could be relevant to a refuge visitation experience. Items were measured on 7-point Likert-type scales anchored by "strongly disagree" and "strongly agree".

After a pretest with the university student sample, the 51 items drawn from the 15 domains were reduced to 39 items, which were assigned to 8 domains. The eight domains were: Nature Appreciation/Learning, Achievement, Introspection/Nostalgia, Escape, Similar People, Physical Fitness, Family Togetherness and New People. A factor analysis using principal component factor analysis was also conducted on the sample data to examine th e factor structure of the scales measuring the construct.

The factor analysis resulted in 2 factors. As shows, six of the eight scales loaded on Factor 1 while Similar people and Family Togetherness loaded on Factor 2. As a result, a decision had to be made regarding whether to treat the second factor as a separate variable distinctively different from the latent quality of experience variable, or just to delete the second factor. Since the objective of the present study was to test the proposed theoretical model rather than to explore an additional latent construct, and there was no theoretical rationale for adding a second dimension into the structural model, it was decided to delete the two scales Similar People and Family Togetherness from the study.

Overall service quality was measured on a 10-point scale with a single item that asked respondents their perceptions of overall quality of the refuge's attributes. The anchors on the scale were, extremely low quality and extremely high quality. Responses ranged from 4 to 10, but 89% were in the 7 to 10 range and the mean was 8.2. This manifest variable is labeled V19 in the measurement model.

Overall satisfaction was measured with a 4-item, 7-point modified semantic differential scale. This scale was originally adapted by Childress and Crompton from Crosby and Stephens. Since there were no pre-determined domains among the items measuring overall satisfaction, a factor analysis was conducted on the four individual items. As expected, the principal component method extracted only one factor, meaning that the scale was unifactorial. The Cronbach's alpha reliability score for the scale was .97.

The final construct, behavioural intentions, was measured with a seven-item, 7-point scale derived from Zeithaml, Berry and Parasuraman. Respondents were requested to indicate how likely they were to take each of the seven actions (1 = not at all likely and 7 = extremely likely). The seven items were not unifactorial because two factors were extracted from the principal component factor analysis on the 7 items.

The loadings of the items are listed. One item was deleted because it did not have a salient loading above. 40 on either factor. The two items loaded on Factor 2 were also deleted for the same reason as the two items in quality of experience were deleted. One of the items from Factor 1 was also deleted to improve the reliability measure of behavioural intentions (reliability score increased from .78 to .84 after deleting the item).

The Measurement Model

The naming of its components follows Bender's (1989) convention. Since overall service quality was measured by a single item scale, it was a manifest variable (V19), labeled with the letter "V" for variable. Quality of performance (Fl), quality of experience (F2), overall satisfaction (F3) and behavioural intentions (F4) are latent variables prefaced by the letter "F" for factor.

The quality of performance construct (Fl) was measured by the five manifest variables Vi through V5. The quality of experience construct (F2) was measured by manifest variables V6 through Vii. The overall satisfaction construct (F3) was measured by manifest variables V12 to V15. The behavioural intention construct (F4) was measured by manifest variables V16 through V18 which are keyed.

V1 through V5 represent the five scales that measured the quality of performance construct. Each of these variables was calculated as the grand mean score of respondents' ratings of each item in the individual scale. For example, in the first scale "Education and Conservation" (Vi) there were five items. V1 is the average score of respondents' ratings on these five items. The same method was applied to V6 through Vii. However, V12 through V19 were the respondents' actual responses to each individual item.

The measurement model posits no unidirectional paths between latent variables. Instead, a covariance is estimated to connect each latent variable with every other latent variable. This is indicated by the curved, two-headed arrow connecting each F variable and V19 to every other F variable. Letter "L" represents the coefficients of the "V" variables to "F" factors. Letter "E" represents measurement errors for each manifest variable. Letter "C" represents covariance between latent factors and the manifest variable V19.

The measurement model was estimated using the maximum likelihood method, and the goodness of fit indices. It has been recommended that the model chi-square test be used as a goodness of fit index, with a smaller chi-square value (usually non-significant chi-square test) indicating a better model fit. The chi-square value for the initial measurement model was statistically significant. However, the chi-square test usually is not considered as the absolute standard by which the goodness of fit of the model is judged because it is sensitive to sample size.

Other tests, such as goodness of fit index (GFI), adjusted goodness of fit index (AGFI), Bender's comparative fit index (GFI) and Bender and Bonett's non-normed fit index (NNFI), should also be used to judge the goodness of fit of the model. Values over .9 on these indices indicate an acceptable fit. Provided mixed support for the initial measurement model because only the CFI was larger than .90. It was thus concluded that there was a problem with the model's fit.

To identify the problem, the patterns of normalized residuals, parameter significance tests, and LaGrange multiplier tests were examined. All coefficients were significant, indicating the indicators were good measures of the underlying latent factors. However, of the ten largest standardized residuals, nine of them were related to V6, which is the variable "Nature Appreciation/ Learning" measuring quality of experience (F2). Nine of the ten largest LaGrange multipliers tests were also related to V6.

The researchers' interpretation of this problem was that nature appreciation and learning about nature is so pervasive in a visit to a wildlife refuge that it permeates into all aspects of the experience. Given the premise that to experience nature was such a dominant pervasive theme in the process of visiting the refuge, it would be represented in the model even if it was excluded as an explicit variable. Thus, V6 was eliminated from the measurement model, and the model was re-calibrated.

Goodness of fit indices for the re-specified measurement model are also presented. The t values for the coefficients of the standard factor loadings were still all significant. Moreover, NNFI now exceeded .9, and the GFI improved to .86. The results indicated that the revised measurement model had a reasonable fit to the data. Therefore, this measurement model was tentatively accepted as the study's "final" measurement model.

Reliability and validity of the constructs and their indicators were assessed. The reliability of an indicator variable is the square of the correlation between a latent factor and that indicator. In this case, the R-square values are indicator reliabilities which indicate the percent of variance in the indicator that is explained by the common factor that it is supposed to measure. Overall satisfaction indicators had very high reliabilities, while reliabilities for quality of performance indicators, quality of experience indicators (from .24 to .81) and behavioural intention indicators were relatively low.

A composite reliability index for each latent factor was calculated to measure the internal consistency of the indicators measuring a given factor. This procedure is similar to the use of Cronbach's alpha for measuring the scale reliability of multiple items in a scale. The composite reliability for latent factor overall satisfaction was .96. Although indicator reliabilities for quality of performance, quality of experience and behavioural intentions were relatively low, the composite reliabilities for these factors were .79, .83 and .81, respectively, which all exceeded the minimally acceptable level of .70 reliability for scale instruments? The relatively high composite reliabilities suggested that the individual scales, when taking as a group, performed fairly well in the model.

Convergent validity and discriminant validity of the constructs were assessed to see if the indicators were measuring what they were intended to measure. Convergent validity is demonstrated when different scales are used to measure the same construct, and scores from these different scales are strongly correlated. In the confirmatory analysis, convergent validity was examined by reviewing the t tests for the factor loadings.

Hatcher states: "if all factor loadings for the indicators measuring the same construct are statistically significant (greater than twice their standard errors) this is viewed as evidence supporting the convergent validity of those indicators". In the present model testing, all t tests were significant providing evidence to support the convergent validity of the indicators.

Discriminant validity is demonstrated when different scales are used to measure different constructs and the correlations between the measures are relatively weak. Discriminant validity for the latent factors was assessed by performing confidence interval tests. The confidence interval was calculated by adding or subtracting two standard errors around the correlation between two factors.

If this confidence interval includes the value of 1.0, then it is very likely that, for the actual population, the two factors are perfectly correlated. In the present model testing, none of the confidence intervals approached 1.0, demonstrating the discriminant validity of all measures used in the study.

It differs from the model that depicts the causal relationship among exogenous and endogenous variables. An exogenous variable is an independent variable whose causes lie outside the model. In this case, quality of performance is the only exogenous variable in the structural model. In contrast to exogenous variables, the postulated causes of endogenous variables are included in the model. In the current model, quality of experience, overall service quality, overall satisfaction and behavioural intentions are all endogenous variables.

The standard errors for the factor loadings and path coefficients in the initial structural model were not near zero, and none of them appeared to be unacceptably small. All factor loadings that were tested had t values greater than 1.96. All of the path coefficients were significant (.05 level) except for the path from F2 to V19. The goodness of fit indices for the structural model indicated the model has a relatively good fit to the data. However, these indices represent the overall fit of the measurement model and the structural model combined.

The current theoretical model consists of a relatively small number of latent variables and a relatively large number of indicator variables. This suggests that indices of overall model fit may be more influenced by the fit of the measurement model than by the fit of the structural model.

However, the present study is more concerned with the fit of the structural model than the fit of the measurement model. Therefore, the relative normed-fit index (RNFI) was calculated to evaluate the fit of only the structural model when free from the influence of the fit of the measurement model. The RNFI for the structural model was .94, indicating a reasonably good fit of the theoretical model without considering how well the latent variables were measured by their indicators.

Since both the measurement model and the structural model had relatively good fit to the data, it was necessary to perform a chi-square difference test to determine whether there was a significant difference between the fit provided by the structural model and that provided by the measurement model. This test provides evidence for the nomological validity of the structural model. The difference chi-square value between the structural and the measurement model was 20.07, which was greater than the critical value of 13.82 with df = 2.

Thus, there was a significant difference (.001) between the fit provided by the measurement model and the fit provided by the structural model. In other words, the fit of the structural model was significantly poorer than the fit of the measurement model. This result suggested that the structural model contained some misspecifications that needed to be modified.

To identify sources of the misspecifications in the model, the modification indices were reviewed. The multivariate Wald tests suggested the path from F2 to V19 should be deleted. This was consistent with the factor loadings' significance tests because the t-test for the coefficient of the path from F2 to V19 was found to be non-significant (.05 level). It indicated that the relationship between quality of experience and overall service quality was not significant. Thus, this path was eliminated from the model.

They were relatively similar to the initial structural model, but it was marginally more parsimonious. The chi-square difference test was conducted on the measurement model and the revised structural model to see if the structural model had a reasonable fit with the data, like the measurement model did. The test was highly significant, revealing that there were still mis-specifications in the revised model 1.

Wald tests conducted on the initial structural model did not reveal any additional causal paths between latent constructs that could be deleted without affecting the model's fit. Thus, results of LaGrange multiplier tests were reviewed to identify new causal paths that should be added to the model. The results showed that paths should be added from two variables to F4, together with a path from F2 to F4.

Since V8 and V9 are indicators of F2, a path from F2 to F4 should be added to the model. There was previous empirical evidence to support the direct influence of quality of experience on visitors' future behavioural intentions. This evidence is discussed later in the paper. A path from quality of experience (F2) to behavioural intentions (F4) was then added and the new model, revised model 2, was then estimated.

The fit indices for revised model 2 were all higher than those of revised model 1 and the parsimonious NF1 did not decrease, meaning that revised model 2 was as parsimonious as revised model 1. The RNFI for revised model 2 was 0.99 indicating that revised model 2 was a much better fit than revised model 1, independent of the measurement model. All of the coefficient estimates of the standard loadings were significant and in the predicted direction. The distribution of normalized residuals for revised model 2 was symmetrical and centreed on zero. Only three of the normalized residuals were greater than the absolute value of 2.0, and the largest of the three was 2.7.

The chi-square difference test between the measurement model and the revised structural model 2 resulted in a value of 1.23, which was much smaller than the critical value of 13.82. Thus, the chi-square test was not significant, indicating that the fit of revised model 2 was not significantly different from the fit of the measurement model in which the F variables were free to covary. In other words, the causal relationships described in the revised model 2 successfully explained the observed relationships between the latent constructs.

The addition of the causal path from quality of experience to behavioural intentions resulted in revised model 2 being superior to revised model 1, and this addition did not decrease the model's parsimony. Thus, this model was the final model for the study. All parameter estimates in the final model were significant at [alpha] = .05. Standardized instead of unstandardized coefficients were then used to evaluate the strength of path coefficients estimated, because the variables involved were not measured on the same scale.

QUALITY AS AN ABSOLUTE

A possible reason for the enigmatic nature of quality is that it is a dynamic idea. The emotional and moral force that quality possesses makes it difficult to define accurately. In fact, there is an argument against attempting too precise a definition. There is the danger that much of the vitality of the concept can be lost if it is subjected to too much academic analysis. Westley and Mintzberg make the point that this happens to many important concepts that are freely used in practical settings:

A strange process seems to occur as concepts such as culture and charisma [and we can add quality] move from practice to academic research. Loosely used in practice, these concepts, as they enter academia become subjected to a concerted effort to force them to lie down and behave, to render them properly scientific. In the process they seem to lose emotional resonance, no longer expressing the reality that practitioners originally tried to capture.

While heeding this advice, nevertheless it is important to take a tour of the concept. There is so much baggage attached to the idea of quality that without some understanding of its philosophical underpinnings it is difficult to build the management structures necessary to achieve the goal of improving the education of students.

Quality has a variety of ambiguous and contradictory meanings. Much of the confusion over the meaning of quality arises because it can be used both as an absolute and as a relative concept. Quality in much everyday conversation is used as an absolute-this is a thing of quality. The word quality comes from the Latin qualis meaning what kind of. The quality of something can be said to be a part of its nature.

People use quality freely when describing expensive restaurants and luxury cars. Used as an absolute quality it is similar in nature to goodness, beauty and truth. It is an ideal with which there can be no compromise. As an absolute, things that exhibit quality are of the highest possible standard that cannot be surpassed. Quality products are things of perfection made with no expense spared. They are valuable and convey prestige to their owners.

Quality cars, for example, are hand-built and expensive and have interiors of walnut and leather. Rarity and expense are two of the features of quality in this definition. Quality in this sense is used to convey status and positional advantage, and the ownership of things of quality sets their owners apart from those who cannot afford them. Quality is a concept with class. It is synonymous with high quality or top quality. To quote Pfeffer and Coote on the subject, 'most of us admire it, many of us want it, few of us can have it'.

Used in the educational context, this concept of quality is essentially elitist. By definition only a few institutions are able to offer such a high quality educational experience to their learners. Most learners cannot afford it, and most institutions cannot aspire to provide it.

The Relative Notion of Quality

Policy-makers and academics have always maintained a keen interest in reviewing and debating the link between skills, knowledge and organisational performance at national, sectoral and firm level. The extent though to which policy-makers, in particular, are willing to admit anything other than the need to aspire to a putative high skill, high wage, high quality route, means such debate can remain somewhat static. Quality in the technical sense is largely a relative concept.

The relative definition views quality not as an attribute of a product or service, but as something which is ascribed to it-'the quality of your essay varies between good and excellent'. Consequently, they argue that there is a need to shift the debate from concentration on supply side issues in relation to skills provision and instead concentrate as well on demand side concerns. Thus, other issues need to be considered such as skill deployment, the relationship between skills, job design, career and employment structures, work organisation and product market strategies.

A further aspect of this concern to develop a more searching analysis is the need to develop a comparative focus across sectors. The emphasis on this sectoral focus can be seen in relation to things like the impact of sectoral institutions on strategy, training and the labour market in that sector. Based on the foregoing, hospitality, as an employing sector, becomes a particularly interesting focus of research. As a sector it is heterogeneous, both in relation to the predominance of small and medium-sized enterprises (SMEs) but equally in relation to the way that organisations adopt differing routes to competitive advantage.

Notwithstanding that latter point hospitality is generally considered as a sector which has traditionally erred on the side of adopting a model of competitive advantage which has been premised on a low skills model or 'poor' human resource management (HRM) practice. Given this situation there is a need to understand some of the pressures pushing firms to pursue such an approach and why this model is more likely to win out in particular organisational settings.

Equally, though, there is a need to recognise the increasing importance of the rhetoric (and reality?) of quality service and the implications of this for hospitality organisations. In particular, there is a recognition that certain product markets in the hospitality sector must be seen to be offering quality service, which in turn is reliant on a sophisticated approach to HRM, for example the upper/luxury market of the hotel sector. In many respects this dichotomy between 'poor' HRM and the ever increasing rhetoric of quality service could rather crudely be characterised as a debate between whether HRM strategies in hospitality should be, to use Boxall and Purcell's (2000) descriptors, 'best fit' or 'best practice'.

On the one hand, the 'best fit' school argues for an approach to HRM which is fully integrated with the specific organisational and environmental context and argued most strongly by the likes of Schuler and Jackson. On the other hand, proponents of 'best practice', such as Pfeffer, argue for a universalistic approach to HRM wherein all firms who adopt a prescribed range of HR policies and practices are more likely to create a high performance/ commitment workplace.

As a corollary the notion of 'best practice' is also dependent on employers adopting a high cost, high skill employment strategy, as organisations aim to compete on the basis of high quality and productivity. The need to find a way between much of the ideal types described to this point is to seek to review a number of issues within a specific sectoral context to examine how these issues are played out within that context.

Pursuant on this situation the key aim of this monograph is to:

- Determine the influence of companies product market strategies, in-company and external structural factors on skill levels, work organisation, job design and people management systems.

More specifically the paper has a number of secondary objectives:

- To develop active definitions of service quality and its specification and review operators' conceptions of different dimensions to quality.
- To review the different elements of the product and service that make a given offering 'high spec' or 'low spec' in relation to issues such as physical capital, equipment, décor, ambience and the role of people.
- To assess the contribution of employees to the dimensions of quality; modes of involvement and type of staff involved; skills involved by type (technical, aesthetic, social, emotional); and level.
- To analyse the relationship of skills 'fit' to broader system of work organisation and job design and the relationship of high/low specification operations to forms of work organisation using a variety of models such as that provided by Lashley and Taylor.
- To assess the extent to which people management systems support or hinder the delivery of quality.

  Where possible, and particularly on the question of HRM outcomes, these considerations will be illustrated by empirical data gathered from a number of different sources. It is recognised here that the use of this data is merely illustrative and should be recognised with due caution as to its generalisiblity. In this sense the data sources utilised for this monograph include:
- A small number of interviews with small business owners or managers and managers in a large international hotel chain.
- Interviews conducted with five managers and two focus groups with employees from several Pret A Manger shops.
- Interviews conducted with 'significant others' such as representatives from local enterprise networks, the employers organisation for the hospitality industry, the British Hospitality Association (BHA), and a consultant working with the Excellence Through People (ETP) initiative.

In a wider sense the review of the hospitality sector is particularly important as traditionally there is a paucity of work considering the implications for HRM within service work settings.

Service work comprises a large and growing part of the workforce in the advanced societies, with knowledge work in both goods and service production making an increasingly important contribution to economic growth. The absence of debates about alternative ways of organising and supporting service work indicates that service work and its HRM implications has not received the attention they deserve. The heterogeneity of service work, including the settings in which it is undertaken, suggest a wide field of exploratory research. On the other hand, there is a need for theorising that will define the direction in which cumulative empirical research might progress.

This review of the hospitality sector aims to add to this theorising in offering a comprehensive picture of a sector which is particularly important in the wider service sector. The importance of the sector is evidenced by recognition that it is one of the largest employers within the service sector, with the largest overall employment growth of all sectors in recent years.

In order to assess some of these issues we will firstly engage with the debate about the 'uniqueness' which is often ascribed to the service sector generally and how this is likely to impact on the product market strategies of firms. Related to this point we will review definitions of quality and suggest that the lack of a definitive consensus on the issue of service quality has implications for the differing approaches to product market strategies and HRM adopted by organisations.

Following this, the next section will further develop some of these issues by reviewing a number of important models, most obviously Schuler and Jackson (1987) and Lashley and Taylor (1998) which have sought to theorise the relationship between competitive strategy and HRM. From this general discussion attention will then turn to the particular dynamics of the hospitality sector. An integral point to emerge from descriptions of the hospitality sector is the SME dimension.

Often overlooked in wider debates about skill acquisition and usage there is the need to be aware that the SME sector can offer specific challenges to both policy-makers and owner-managers. This is especially true in the hospitality industry due to the preponderance of SMEs in the sector. Recognising this point, the paper specifically considers the impact of the SME dimension. The description of some of the key characteristics of the sector, including the SME dimension, and the likely impact on HRM approaches provides the framework to offer a considered view of two potentially antithetical responses from organisations.

These responses are characterised, rather crudely, as the 'pessimistic' 'poor' HRM approach and the 'optimistic' high quality approach. To develop these positions we will draw heavily on the extant work which has sought to address the issue of HRM in the hospitality sector, as well as our own illustrative empirical material. Consideration of these approaches also allows for the description of putative 'best practice' approaches. The paper will then move on to consider some of the methodological issues generated by the discussion, and particularly how the future research agenda reviewing the nature of HRM in the hospitality sector is best carried forward.

In sum, this monograph seeks to synthesise a number of different themes to offer a comprehensive picture of the hospitality industry. In doing we aim to understand the pressures which push organisations to adopt particular routes to competitive advantage and ultimately recognise that the high skill, high wage and high quality route is one which remains rare in the hospitality industry. This process can be considered as a reflection of what Segal-Horn (1993) calls the 'hard', more tangible, elements of service that may be more responsive to standardisation.

This is a useful distinction that allows us to examine the strategies adopted by service organisations in relation to the 'hard' or 'hardware' and the 'soft' or 'software'. Hardware can be broadly conceptualised as the physical product (for example, the interior and exterior of a hotel, its rooms, meals, beverages and leisure services).

The software consists of the more amorphous notions of service quality, service delivery and the emotional interaction between the producer and consumer. Thus, it could be suggested that both the hardware and the software comprise the overall product and in the normative view held by much of the services marketing and management literature must successfully coalesce to ensure organisational success.

Nonetheless, it is widely recognised that within the notion of intangibility, service organisations which offer a product that is, in the words of Lashley and Taylor (1998), 'intangible dominant', increasingly seek to differentiate themselves on the basis of the software aspects such as seeking high quality and 'authentic' service interactions for the increasingly discerning customer.

The identification of the main services characteristics, the study of service encounters and service experience suggest that service quality is more complex to evaluate than in the case of goods. Services are more difficult to measure and standardise and consequently establishing an instrument attempting to measure quality has become a central challenge for the delivery of good service quality and service companies' success.

The challenge of evaluating service quality has been motivated by recent research and debate, as noted above, which increasingly demonstrates the significance of service quality as a central factor of business success. Service quality has consequently become a focus of any management and marketing strategy and high levels of service are seen as a means for organisations to achieve a competitive advantage and position themselves more effectively in the market place.

Customers are also becoming more aware and critical of the alternatives on offer and rising standards of services, prompted by competitive trends, have increased customer expectations. However, as Hoque notes whilst service quality may well be increasingly critical to competitive success, 'defining what exactly is "service quality" is somewhat problematic'. Generally service quality cannot be objectively measured as can technical quality for manufactured goods and it therefore remains an elusive and abstract construct. The characteristics of intangibility, heterogeneity and inseparability presented earlier also constitute a challenge for managers because they do not allow for an easy process of quality evaluation.

More importantly, a customer judgement of a service depends as much on the service process as on the outcome, therefore customers' quality evaluation can be seen as depending on the production of services as well as on their consumption. The services marketing and management field has displayed different views of how this construct might be assessed.

For example, Akehurst and Harrington in a review of managerial perceptions of service quality in UK hotels note two schools of thought – American and Nordic – which have sought to address this issue. Though they differ in the detail of their approach, both schools of thought largely adopt a common approach in seeking to group a range of quality items into dimensions.

Quality in this sense is about being measured against criteria. It is not an end in itself, but a means by which the end product is judged as being up to (or not up to) standard. Quality products or services, in this relative or ascribed definition, need not be expensive or exclusive.

They may be beautiful, but not necessarily so. They do not have to be luxurious or special. They can be ordinary, commonplace and familiar. Overhead projectors, laptops, ballpoint pens and the school catering service may all exhibit quality. Any product or service can aspire to the label quality.

They do not have to be exclusive. While the absolute notion is elitist, the relative notion is potentially egalitarian. What allows the label of quality to be ascribed to any product or service is that it meets the standards set for it. It must do what is claimed for it, and do what its customers expect of it. In other words it must be fit for purpose, as the British Standards Institution defines quality. In this relative sense quality is about measuring up to predetermined standards and meeting those standards time and time again.

Two Concepts of Quality

The relative definition of quality has two aspects to it. The first is concerned with measuring up and ensuring conformity to a predetermined specification. The question that is asked is 'Does this good or service do what is asked or expected of it?' This is fitness for purpose. This is sometimes called the producer definition of quality or the procedural concept of quality.

In an industrial setting quality is achieved by products or services meeting a predefined specification in a consistent fashion. Quality is demonstrated by a producer having a system, known as a quality assurance system, that supports the consistent production of the good or service to a particular standard or specification.

In this definition popular cars as well as luxury models can be quality products. Luxury, beauty, exclusivity and price do not enter into the equation. It does not matter whether they are Fords or Rolls-Royces so long as products conform to manufacturers' specifications and standards. Both can be quality products. A product exhibits quality so long as it consistently meets the maker's claims for it. This view of quality is sometimes called quality in fact. Quality in fact is the basis of the quality assurance systems devised in accordance with the international standard.

The procedural concept places considerable emphasis on working to defined systems and procedures. This is seen as the method most likely to produce a standardized or quality outcome. Quality is achieved by putting systems and procedures into operation and ensuring that those systems are efficiently and effectively operated. It is the audit trail approach to quality.

Today much quality work is concerned with finding appropriate evidence about the way particular activities within the institution have been carried out. The procedural concept is about proving that things have happened in accordance with predetermined specifications. It ensures that activities conform to requirements, although critics of the approach argue that it can stifle creativity and innovation.

Proving, approving and reporting are the key descriptors of this largely instrumental approach to quality. It is an accountability or audit approach that is concerned to ensure consistency and conformity. It is based on the predominantly hard indicators of measurable performance. In education hard quality indicators include public examination league tables for schools and colleges.

Transformational quality is different. It has less to do with systems and procedures and more to do with continuous improvement and organizational transformation. This concept views quality as a complex process with a wider canvas. It focuses on the softer and more intangible aspects of quality.

These softer concepts include care, customer service and social responsibility, and often go to the heart of the difficult and intangible issues of customer satisfaction and delight. It is often said that while the procedural notions of quality are essential and necessary they are by themselves not sufficient to ensure customer loyalty. The things that bring customers back time and time again and hold their allegiance are often centred on personal service and customer care.

Transformational quality is achieved not through adhering to systems and procedures, but through the exercise of leadership. It is leadership that establishes a vision that translates into customer service and builds the structures and organizational culture that empower staff to deliver a quality service.

Whereas the procedural concept is about proving, the transformational approach is about improving. It is about doing things right, not just doing the right things. It is a state of organizational mind that sees continuous improvement at the very heart of the quality process. Transformational quality blends the aspirations of customers with the empowerment of staff. It takes a wide and more eclectic view of quality.

It puts the customer first and seeks to expand their horizons. In an education setting the transformational culture is a function of staff motivation and academic leadership in a setting that is student centred.

Transformational transformational quality aims for excellence and is satisfied with fitness for purpose. This is not to confuse it with the absolute definition of quality. Excellence is an aspiration, a striving. What transformational quality is about is aiming high and ensuring that there is a quality improvement agenda in place.

The important part of making the distinction between the procedural and the transformational ormational aspects of quality is not to label one right and the other wrong. Both concepts play a key role in understanding quality. The point of the distinction is to recognize that there are different approaches to achieving quality.

The pursuit of quality is an exercise requiring not only well-developed and understood systems and procedures but also a customer-oriented transformational culture where individuals are given the responsibility for the quality of the work in their area and can contribute fully to its achievement.

The Consumer's Role in Quality

Any discussion about the nature of quality has to centre on the crucial role of the consumer. Who should decide whether a school or college is providing a quality service? The answer will tell us much about the values and aspirations of the institution. It is essential to have a clear idea of who is ascribing the attribute of quality. The views of producers and consumers are not always identical. It does happen that consumers reject perfectly good and useful products and services. Providing a service to specification does not guarantee success.

Organizations that follow the TQM path regard quality as being defined by their customers. They are the final arbitrators of quality and without them the institution will not exist. The institution that champions TQM as its philosophy has to use all means at its disposal to explore their customers' needs. As Edwin L Artzt, the Chairman and Chief Executive of the Procter and Gamble Company, has put it:

Our customers are both those who retail our products and those who ultimately use them. Total quality means knowing them in ways and depths never fully explored before and using this knowledge to translate needs into innovative new products and business approaches.

Quality can be defined as that which satisfies and exceeds customers' needs and wants. This is sometimes called quality in perception. Quality can be said to be in the eyes of the beholder. This is a very important and powerful definition, and one that any institution ignores at its peril. It is the consumers who make the judgements on quality.

Tom Peters in a discussion of the pivotal role of the consumer in quality (1987) argues that the perceived quality of a business's product or service is the most important single factor affecting its performance. He argues that quality as defined by the customer is more important than price in determining the demand for a majority of goods and services. As he says of his researches over the years:

(1) Customers-individual or industrial, high tech or law, science-trained or untrained-will pay a lot for better, and especially for best, quality; moreover,
(2) Firms that provide that quality will thrive;
(3) Workers in all parts of the organization will become energized by the opportunity to provide a top quality product or service; and
(4) No product has a safe quality lead, since new entrants are constantly redefining, for the customer, what's possible.

QUALITY OF CUSTOMER EXPERIENCE

When the total product provided by all firms contains the same set of facilitating services, the product is not necessarily a commodity. The quality of the service offered remains a source of differentiation and therefore a supplementary feature of the product. Perceived quality enhances, and lack thereof reduces, the value of the core product. For example, even when Internet service is offered by all hotels, the quality of the customer experience with the Internet service is still a differentiator. One hotel may require you to get into a closet, fish out the cables and force you to shape yourself into a yoga pose to hook up those cables to your laptop, while another hotel may offer wireless Internet access from anywhere on the property. All airlines provide seating and, depending on distance and class, also provide meals and entertainment while transporting you from point A to point B. Differentiation in seating can come in legroom and comfort. First-class services can offer six and a half feet of seat length, single seats, pajamas, and privacy partitions between seats. The quality of the entire customer experience is most definitely a source of differentiation.

Brand image is a supplementary feature of the product in that it adds to customer value. Brand image is the sum total of all the perceptions and attitudes about a brand. The image of the firm in the general media as well as for each individual customer provides a measure of the perceived quality of the product. The reputation of a firm is usually a result of the firm's product and actions. Where there is very little tangible evidence of the product, as in the case of Web-based services, an entire industry of so-called "reputation managers" has emerged. These reputation managers are Web sites that rate the reputation of others! A firm's image is an implicit source of differentiation in the market. Brand image is the ultimate differentiator. When all else can be seen as equal, the brand image captures the essence of the difference in customer value among the alternatives available to the customer.

Firms have to determine what their total product offering is and what it should be. The value bundle of core and supplementary product needs to be designed based on what the customers expect as standard from all providers of a solution in a product category. The supplementary product might also contain features that are sources of differentiation among solution providers reflecting the positioning strategy of the firm. Firms must constantly watch the various solutions that are being offered. Sometimes the threat of competition comes from newer business models. For example, online broker ETrade surprised the banking business when it began to open ATMs with new services. A deep and broad analysis of customer needs could reveal value-creating opportunities.

To determine how best to match the total product as the superior solution to fit customer need, the firm must understand the customer's value chain. This is an integral part of the product concept development of the customer-focused firm. A thorough understanding of the customer needs and the customer value chain will help the firm conceive its product from the customer's point of view. Firms that best relate their own value chain to the buyer's value chain, said Michael Porter, will enjoy a sustainable differentiation strategy.

The value chain is essentially a chain of value-creating and value-consuming activities, where the value created as output from one activity becomes the input to another value-creating activity that in turn creates value as input for another activity, and so on. Thus, any activity can be assessed by the value it creates versus the value it consumes. This is why activity-based costing practices make a lot of sense. As already said the value creating activities *within a firm* are those that contribute to the creation of either the core product or the supplementary product. The value created by these activities is derived by the processing of the productive factors of the firm—its people, facilities, and equipment. There may be assets or value components sourced from external suppliers or intermediaries that contribute toward producing either the core or the supplementary product. Some outsourced services may even be delivered directly to the customer. When any value component of the total product is outsourced, as in the case of a retailer offering customers outsourced financing options for purchases, or airlines outsourcing catering services, there is the obvious issue of quality assurance in the value creation that is outside the control of the firm.

Externally (to the firm) when you relate other firms' value-creation activities into a value chain, you see that the value created by one entity contributes to the value created by the next entity in the value chain. The same idea is referred to by economists, in the context of forecasting, as "derived demand." The demand for a product is dependent on the market for another product, such as aluminum and aircraft sales for example. We know a homeowner who gets a home improvement job done receives (customer) value from the home contractor who in turn is receiving value from the retailer who in turn receives value in the form of products and services from the supplier or manufacturer.

SERVICESCAPE IN HOSPITALITY

An important part of the augmented product is the physical environment. Because many tourism and hospitality services are intangible, customers often rely on tangible cues, or physical evidence, to evaluate the service before its purchase and to assess their satisfaction with the service during and after consumption. The physical evidence is the environment in which the service is delivered and in which the firm and customer interact, and any tangible components that facilitate performance or communication of the service. The physical facility is often referred to as the servicescape, and is very important for tourism and hospitality products such as hotels, restaurants and theme parks, which are dominated by experience attributes. Disney, for example, effectively uses the servicescape to excite its customers. The brightly coloured displays, the music, the rides, and the costumed characters all reinforce the feelings of fun and excitement that Disney seeks to generate in its customers. The Global Spotlight on Sweden's Icehotel shows how important the servicescape is for accommodations. In this case, the hotel is made entirely of ice and snow, and provides a unique experience for tourists.

They include all aspects of the organization's servicescape that affect customers, including both exterior attributes (such as parking and landscape) and interior attributes (such as design, layout, equipment and décor). Signage is also part of the physical evidence; in 2007, Beijing attempted to stamp out embarrassingly bad English on bilingual signs in the run-up to the 2008 Olympics. The municipal government issued translation guidelines for signs in hotels, shopping malls, public transport and tourist attractions. At the time, the Park of Ethnic Minorities was identified as 'Racist Park', while the emergency exits at Beijing's international airport read, 'No entry on peacetime'. Consumer researchers know that the design of the servicescape can influence customer choices, expectations, satisfaction and other behaviours. Retailers know that customers are influenced by smell, décor, music and layout. Arby's, a fast-food chain in North America, uses the servicescape to position its restaurants as a step above other quick-service outlets. With carpeted floors, cushioned seating and a décor 'superior' to other fast-food chains, the company asserts that the interior ambience of Arby's outlets contributes to attracting diners. Design of work environments can also affect employees' productivity, motivation and satisfaction. The challenge in many tourism and hospitality settings is to design the physical space in a way that supports the needs and preferences of customers and employees simultaneously.

Employees and customers in service firms respond to their physical surroundings in three ways – cognitively, emotionally, and physiologically – and these responses influence their behaviours in that environment. First, the perceived servicescape may elicit *cognitive* responses, including people's beliefs about a place and their beliefs about the people and products found there. For example, a consumer study found that a travel agent's office décor affected customer understanding of the travel agent's behaviour. In addition to influencing cognitions, the perceived servicescape may elicit *emotional* responses that in turn influence behaviours. The colours, décor, music, and other elements of the atmosphere can have an unexplained and sometimes subconscious affect on the moods of people in the place. According to Russell *et al.* (1981), servicescapes that are both pleasant and arousing are 'exciting', while those that are pleasant and non-arousing, or sleepy, are 'relaxing'. Unpleasant servicescapes that are arousing are 'distressing', while unpleasant, sleepy ser-vicescapes are 'gloomy'. Finally, the servicescape may affect people in purely *physiological* ways. Noise that is too loud may cause physical discomfort, the temperature of a room may cause people to shiver or perspire, the air quality may make it difficult to breathe, and the glare of lighting may decrease ability to see and may cause physical pain. All of these physical responses will influence whether people remain in and enjoy a particular environment. In 2004, a Vancouver-based company, Enhanced Air Technologies, developed Commercaire pheromone, a synthetic compound that mimics the maternal sense of comfort piped to children when they are crying or unhappy. Filtered into a store, the odourless substance is meant to relax customers so they stay longer and buy more. The firm claims retailers can expect revenue growth of between 9 per cent and 20 per cent when using the product. While Enhanced Air's sales-stimulating pheromone may be a first, there is a long history of retailers using fake sawdust or fresh bread smells to foster favourable emotions in patrons.

The discussion of consumer trends pointed out that today's consumer desires experiences, and more and more businesses are responding by explicitly designing experiences with themed servicescapes. At themed restaurants such as the Hard Rock Café, Planet Hollywood or the Rainforest Café, the food is just a prop for what's known as 'eatertainment'. Retailers are also creating themes that tie merchandising presentations together in a staged experience. A popular tourist attraction in Las Vegas is the Forum, a mall that displays its distinctive theme – an ancient Roman marketplace – in every detail. The Simon DeBartolo Group, which developed the mall, disperses this motif through a panoply of architectural effects. These include marble floors, stark white pillars, 'outdoor' cafes, living trees, flowing fountains – and even a painted blue sky with fluffy white clouds that yield regularly to simulated storm, complete with lighting and thunder. Every mall entrance and every storefront is an elaborate Roman replica. Hourly, inside the main entrance, statues of Julius Caesar and other Roman luminaries come to life and speak. 'Hail, Caesar!' is a frequent cry, and Roman centurions periodically march through on their way to the adjacent Caesar's Palace casino.

Despite the increased emphasis on the servicescape in designing experiences, companies that fail to provide consistently engaging experiences, overprice their experiences relative to the value perceived, or overbuild their capacity to stage them will see pressure on demand, pricing, or both. The Rainforest Café and Planet Hollywood have both encountered trouble because they have failed to refresh their experiences. Guests find nothing different from one visit to the next. Disney, on the other hand, avoids staleness by frequently adding new attractions and even whole parks, such as the Animal Kingdom in 1998 and California Adventure in 2001.

The latter US$1.4 billion project, which also included construction of a first-class hotel, was designed to accommodate 30,000 people a day, to add to the 70,000 visitors that come to Disneyland across the street. Covering 55 acres, California Adventure is a high-energy park, celebrating the dreams of the many Americans who came to California and reflecting the highlights and the pop culture of the state today.

It features attractions a little wilder and a lot more grown up than the original Disneyland. These attractions are situated in three themed areas: Paradise Pier, Golden State and Hollywood Pictures Backlot.

The Snapshot below about the new Churchill Museum in London shows how designers of a museum have used technology to enhance the servicescape, creating an interactive educational experience for visitors.

PRODUCT PLANNING

Product Mix

The most basic decisions a tourism organization has to make are what business it is in and what product mix is appropriate to it. The product mix is the portfolio of products that an organization offers to one market or several.

According to Seaton and Bennett (1996), five basic market/product options exist:

1. several markets with multi-product mixes for each (*e.g.*, mass tour operators that offer a wide range of multi-destination packages to a variety of market segments);
2. several markets with a single product for each (*e.g.*, airlines with a product for business and economy class travellers);
3. several markets with a single product for all (*e.g.*, a national tourist organization promoting a country);

4. single market with a multi-product mix (*e.g.*, a specialist tour operator with a range of cultural tours aimed at a wealthy, educated market); and
5. single market with a single product (*e.g.*, a heli-skiing operator targeting the very rich).

The decision as to which product mix option to adopt depends upon many factors, including the strength and value of consumer demand in the different markets, the level of competition in each market, and the distinctive competence of the organization to service the markets adequately. The starting point in product analysis and planning is thus an analysis of the consumer and competitive offerings in relation to the goals and product capacity of the tourism organization. The most successful products emerge when the marketing planning steps. Portfolio and SWOT analysis are discussed there; another useful method of analysing the tourism product is by considering its features and benefits. Features consist of the objective attributes of a tourism product; benefits are the rewards the product gives the consumer. Hong Kong International Airport was recently named the world's best airport in a survey of over 50,000 frequent travellers. Part of the reason is the features of the airport and the benefits they offer passengers. As well as shops that sell everything from rare white tea to cell phones, there are free plasma televisions to watch, a children's play area, wireless broadband, internet cafés, a prayer room, a pharmacy, nap rooms, a beauty salon, shower facilities, a medical centre (complete with on-site vaccinations and x-ray machines) and displays from Hong Kong museums.

Product Life Cycle

One of the most basic product analysis tools is the product life cycle (PLC) analysis, the Opening Vignette described the journey of Concorde through this life cycle. Plotting products or services to identify what stage they are at in their PLC is a valuable way of reviewing a product's past and current position and making predictions about its future. As part of a portfolio analysis, an organization should access each good and service in terms of its position in the product life cycle. *Product development* begins when the company finds and develops a new product idea. The Snapshot later in this chapter about the Sydney BridgeClimb describes how its founder conceived the idea nine years before it was put into action. The *introduction* phase is a period of slow sales and low profits because of the investment required for product introduction. The new Churchill Museum in London could be considered to be in this phase. The *growth* phase is characterized by increasing market acceptance and substantial improvement in profits. This is the case for the Sydney BridgeClimb, as it now takes tourists on the climb 12 hours a day, 363 days a year. The *maturity* phase is a period of slow sales marked by high profits, as the product is well entrenched in the marketplace and has an acceptable market share. An example would be Sweden's Icehotel. However, when sales begin to drop because competitors are moving into the marketplace, the product enters the *decline* stage. Profits and market share decline, and major costs may be involved in redeveloping, refurbishing, or maintaining the product. This is the case for many small ski resorts around the world.

Using the PLC concept to develop marketing strategy can be difficult. Strategy is both a cause and a result of the PLC. At the introduction stage, promotion spending is likely to be high in order to inform consumers about the new product and encourage them to buy it. A company will focus on selling to buyers who are ready to buy, usually higher-income groups. Prices tend to be on the high side because of low output, production problems, high promotion costs and other expenses. At the growth stage, the early adopters will continue to buy, and later buyers will start following their lead, encouraged by favourable word of mouth. Competitors will enter the market, attracted by the opportunity for profit, and they will introduce more product features that will expand the market. In the growth stage, the organization faces a tradeoff between high market share and high current profit. By investing heavily in product improvement, promotion and distribution, it can capture a dominant position. But it sacrifices maximum current profit in the hope of making this up in the next stage.

When sales start to slow down, the product will enter the maturity stage; this lasts longer than the previous two stages and poses stronger challenges to marketing management. Most products or services are in this stage, and it is a phase that is characterized by heavy competition. The only way to increase sales is to lure customers away from competition, and so price wars and heavy advertising are common. At this stage, an aggressive product manager will seek to increase consumption by modifying markets and/or products. The product manager may also try to improve sales by changing one or more of the marketing mix elements.

In the decline stage, some firms will withdraw from the market. Those that remain may reduce the number of their product offerings or the number of market segments they are targeting. They may also reduce the promotion budget, and prices. For each declining product, management must decide whether to maintain, harvest, or drop it.

However, the PLC is not as simple as it sounds in theory, and according to Mercer (1992), 'its supposed universal applicability is largely a myth'. The study of the PLC pattern for a particular product has to take into account the market the product is in. For example, if a product is showing no growth or decline, it may still be very successful if the market as a whole is in decline. Another complication of the PLC is that a product that is in overall decline may be losing its customers from one market segment but increasing appeal or holding steady with another. Ski areas, for example, have been very successful in attracting an increasing number of snowboarders over the past decade, despite a drop in the number of downhill skiers. In addition, although the PLC concept is neat on paper, it is often difficult to determine what particular stage a product is at. Finally, even assuming that a product's life cycle position can be determined, it may not be obvious what action should be taken.

Despite these problems, the PLC is a valuable concept, since it forces the organization to analyse trends for its product in relation to the overall market and the segments within it, in order to assess future marketing requirements. Ski areas have adapted to the growth in snow-boarders (referred to above) by changing the products they offer; most successful ski areas these days have designated areas for snowboarders. A related concept for analysing destinations is that of the tourism area life cycle.

Positioning

Positioning is the bedrock of product management. The concept as the natural follow-through of market segmentation and market targeting, and highlights the three steps necessary to develop an effective position in the target market segment. The objective of positioning is to create a distinctive place in the minds of potential customers. Positioning in tourism should evoke images of a destination or product in the customer's mind – images that differentiate the product from the competition and also convey that it can satisfy their needs and wants. Effective positioning should direct all the marketing functions of a business. Advertising and promotions, as well as decisions on price, product and distribution channels must all be consistent with positioning goals. Often, these marketing functions will be driven by a positioning statement, which is a phrase that reflects the image the organization wants to create. The positioning statement for the Churchill Museum, for example, is: 'A benchmark for personality museums in the twenty-first century'. This statement encapsulates what the Museum stands for, the essence of what the museum does, and how it stands out from competitors.

There is an endless number of positioning strategies, and selection of the appropriate approach is vital to the success of a tourism organization.

Burke and Resnick (1991) have identified four key positioning strategies that are not mutually exclusive and may therefore be used individually or in combination:

1. positioning relative to target market (*e.g.* business travellers, families with children under ten, etc.);
2. positioning by price and quality (*e.g.* a premium product such as the Concorde);
3. positioning relative to a product class (*e.g.* a tour operator positioning its products within a winter sports tourism category); and
4. positioning relative to competitors (*e.g.* the Hertz Rental Car campaign 'We try harder', which drew attention to the fact that Hertz was not market leader but would work harder to catch up with its competitors).

Boutique hotels use a combination of these positioning strategies to succeed in the very competitive hotel market. Loosely defined as small, specialized accommodations, mainly in prime city locations, boutique hotels offer high standards of service, style and comfort which suit the corporate jet-setter. The main challenge for boutiques is how to keep ahead in such a fiercely competitive market. Ian Schrager, owner of the Sanderson and St Martin's Lane hotels in London, has managed to stay ahead of the game by attracting a celebrity clientele and introducing luxurious spas at his properties. In Spain, Sorat Hotels and Sol Melia have tried to differentiate themselves by emphasizing the quality of their personal service, while the UK group Hotel du Vin has made its name with the high standard of food on offer at its stylish bistros (Goff, 2003). The Global Spotlight below is an example of an unusual tourism product that has positioned itself as a unique, one-off hotel; one that has been rebuilt every year since 1990.

But at the end of the 1980s it was decided to turn things around. Instead of viewing the dark and cold winter as a disadvantage, the unique elements of the Arctic were to be exploited as an asset. In 1990 the French ice artist Jannot Derit was invited to have the opening of his exhibition in a specially built igloo on the frozen Torne River. The 60-square metre building, named Arctic Hall, attracted many curious visitors to the area. One night a group of foreign guests, equipped with reindeer hides and sleeping bags, decided it would be a good idea to use the cylindrical-shaped igloo as accommodation. The following morning the brave group raved about the unique sensation of sleeping in an igloo. Hence, the concept of Icehotel was born, and today Icehotel is world-famous for its unique concept and its fantastic works of art.

The Icehotel has been rebuilt every year since 1990, and what started off as a 60-square metre igloo has grown to an almost 5,000-square metre hotel, using more than 30,000 tons of snow and 4,000 tons of ice. Snow cannons help to form the snow over arched steel sections. The ice pillars are then put in place to give extra strength to the self-supporting snow arches. In March, ice is harvested from the River Torne with the help of tractors and special ice saws. The blocks are then stored and used to build the hotel in the winter.

The hotel is never more than six months old, because in summer it melts. As a result, the exact number of rooms varies, but during the winter of 2004/2005 it had 85. The hotel also has a reception, hall of pillars, ice art exhibition, cinema, and a church. About 14,000 guests a year spend the night in the hotel, with over 40,000 day visitors walking through the reindeer-skin covered doors. In April, the entire hotel literally trickles into the Torne River, to be resurrected during November and December the following winter, with a new architecture and new works of art. So visitors can experience a new Icehotel every year.

The temperature in the Icehotel varies between -4 and -9 degrees centigrade, depending on the temperature outside, which can dip to -40. At night, guests are supplied with a specially made sleeping bag, and are given a talk on 'how to survive in the Icehotel'. For some, this may mean sampling the wonderfully coloured cocktails served in ice glasses at the Absolut Ice Bar. Others may want to try the food at the Icehotel Restaurant which serves Laplandic gourmet food on plates of ice from the Torne River. During the daytime there are plenty of activities for visitors such as snowmobiling, dog-sledding, moose safaris and ice sculpting. Visitors can also attend concerts in an open-air venue inspired by Shakespeare's Globe Theatre in London. The 520-person theatre is a marvel of ice engineering, carefully crafted by technicians in just three weeks. However, staying at the Icehotel doesn't come cheap. A deluxe suite costs about 6,000SKr a night (£440).

BRANDING

The practice of branding was developed in the field of packaged goods, as a method of establishing a distinctive identity for a product based on competitive differentiation from other products. Branding was commonly achieved through naming, trademarking, packaging, product design and promotion. Successful branding gave a unique identity to what might otherwise have been a generic product. This identity produced a consistent image in the consumer's mind, which facilitated recognition and quality assurance. In the 19th century, products such as Beecham's Pills, Cadbury's Chocolate and Eno's Salts were early users of branding. These days, the market in packaged goods is dominated by brands, and in the last few decades branding has also been widely recognized in services marketing. A 'brand', in the modern marketing sense, offers the consumer relevant added value – a superior proposition that is distinctive from competitors' and that imparts meaning above and beyond the product's functional aspects. There is even a Museum of Brands in London, where visitors can view 10,000 consumer products covering 200 years of packaging, branding and advertising.

Branding offers a solution to some of the problems in services marketing – in particular those of consistency and product standardization. Branding can be a way of unifying services, which is why it has been particularly developed in hotel marketing. Research shows that nearly 90 per cent of bookings are made with branded hotel chains, and nine out of ten consumers can distinguish between chains, franchise operators and independents.

For large hotel companies that have a wide variety of properties, grouping them into brands can:

1. unify them into more easily recognizable smaller groups;
2. enable each branded group to be targeted at defined market segments; and
3. enable product delivery, including human resource management, to be focused on creating a specific set of benefits for a specific market.

North America has over 200 hotel brands competing for business, and many hotel chains offer a family of sub-brands or endorsed brands. For example, Hilton Hotels Corporation, Intercontinental and Starwood each has seven sub-brands, while Marriott International has 12 (as well as the Ritz-Carlton chain which, to protect its exclusive image, is not normally identified for marketing purposes as part of the Marriott Group) (Lovelock and Wortz, 2007). For a multi-brand strategy to succeed, each brand must promise a distinctive value proposition, targeted at a different customer segment. There are even branded hotel floors in some hotels. American Express and the Sheraton Vancouver Wall Centre Hotel have partnered to open a floor dedicated to business accommodations for American Express credit card holders.

Located on the 27th floor, the 'American Express Club Floor' features a private lounge with business service centre, direct access to boardrooms and fitness facilities, dedicated front-desk check-in and a late 4.00 p.m. check-out. According to officials, guests using the club floor pay the same price for their room as Amex's negotiated standard room rate and benefit from a host of value-added services and amenities. These include complimentary continental breakfast, all-day coffee and tea, evening hors d'oeuvres, international and local newspapers, and 24-hour room service.

In the past, branding was often seen mainly as a matter of promotion and of creating the right image through advertising and publicity. But marketing managers now recognize that successful branding involves the integrated deployment of product design, pricing policies, distribution selection and promotion. The case for branding is stronger for tourism products that offer the possibility for differentiation in several areas of the marketing mix.

This is why branding has been particularly successful in hotel and restaurant marketing. Branding of restaurants, hotels and airlines developed extensively in the United States during the 1980s and 1990s, and com -panies in the rest of the world are following suit. The momentum is driven mainly by large organizations that recognize that, to remain competitive, they need to offer several products to different markets instead of relying upon a monolithic presence in one main one.

Apart from the advantages already mentioned, Middleton and Clarke (2001) suggest that branding in tourism offers other specific advantages:

1. it helps reduce medium- and long-term vulnerability to the unforeseen external events that so beset the tourism industry. Recovery time after an event such as a terrorist attack or a natural disaster is likely to be shorter for a well-established brand;
2. it reduces risk for the consumer at the point of purchase by signalling the expected quality and performance of an intangible product. It offers either an implicit or explicit guarantee to the consumer;
3. it facilitates accurate marketing segmentation by attracting some consumer segments and repelling others. For an inseparable product, onsite segment compatibility is an important marketing issue;

4. it provides the focus for the integration of stakeholder effort, especially for the employees of an organization or the individual tourism providers of a destination brand; and
5. it is a strategic weapon for long-range planning in tourism.

It should be recognized that a competitive brand is a live asset and not a fixture, and therefore its value may depreciate over time if starved of investment and marketing and management skill. Brand decay may begin if a brand is over-stretched into new products that damage its essence, or following a merger or takeover. Marketers sometimes use the term brandicide to describe the process of taking a well-known brand and extending it into a new area that will 'kill' the brand. Companies are increasingly attempting to stretch their proven expertise into new areas. Walt Disney Inc., for example, has recently entered the produce business. Disney's cartoon characters are popping up on fruit and vegetable packaging across the US, as growers clinch licensing deals with entertainment companies hungry to cultivate positive images among health-conscious parents and children. The Snapshot below describes how chefs – some of the most successful and fastest-growing consumer brands today – are stretching their brand names into a number of different areas.

A combination of factors has made companies more eager than ever to stretch their brands further and more boldly. Advances in technology have reduced barriers to entry in new sectors. Companies have developed stronger and more knowledgeable relationships with customers, and the cost and difficulty of developing new brands is encouraging companies to exploit the brands they already have. But there can be a cost to leveraging brand equity. If a brand loses credibility in one sector, this tainted sector can contaminate everything else that bears the brand's name. So brandicide should be avoided.

The Case Study on Richard Branson how over the past 25 years, Branson has diversified his Virgin brand into a far-reaching empire, encompassing mobile phone services, a rail service and even wedding dresses, as well as his original record label and discount airline. The Snapshot below takes a look at the Jamie Oliver brand, and how, albeit on a smaller scale than Branson the celebrity chef has used his name to promote cookbooks, cookware, healthy school lunches, supermarkets, restaurants, and, of course, television shows.

PACKAGING

In the tourism and hospitality industry, packaging is the process of combining two or more related and complementary offerings into a single-price offering. A package may include a wide variety of services, such as lodging, meals, entrance fees for attractions, entertainment, transportation costs, guide services, or other similar activities. Travel packages have become increasingly popular over the years. They are attractive because they benefit both the consumer and participating businesses by providing convenience and value to the consumer and added revenue for businesses. An example of a package holiday is one on offer from Arctic Experience, a UK tour operator. In 2007, the operator was selling a three-night trip to the Icehotel in Sweden on a bed and breakfast basis for just over £1000 for a single person. This price included return flights from London.

Packaging provides several customer benefits, including:

1. easier budgeting for trips: the customer pays at one time and has a good idea of the trip's total cost;
2. increased convenience, which saves time and prevents aggravation;
3. greater economy, as the cost to the customer is usually more economical than purchasing the package components individually;
4. the opportunity to experience previously unfamiliar activities and attractions; and
5. the opportunity to design components of a package for specialized interests.

For tourism operations, packages are attractive for the following reasons:

1. they can improve profitability by allowing businesses to price at a premium by adding special good and services;
2. they can streamline business patterns. Packaging during low demand periods may add attractive features to the service or product, thus generating additional business;
3. they allow joint marketing opportunities, which can in turn reduce promotional costs;
4. they can be an effective tool for tailoring tourism products for specific target markets.

The tourism industry is becoming increasingly sophisticated and innovative with its packaging. The Snapshot on weekendtrips.com is an example of the growing number of companies catering to the demand for short-break tourism experiences sold via the internet. Others are catering for the more sophisticated backpacker market. For example, Ho Chi Minh City-based Linh Nam Travel Co. has a 79-day tour of Vietnam with an itinerary of 8,000 kilometres through 59 cities and provinces nationwide.

The programme runs twice a year and tourists can choose to stay at hotels of one to three stars or take a home-stay. Others are packaging holidays for the growing interest in wildlife tourism amongst older, more affluent tourists. Churchill, Manitoba in Canada, for example, attracts 2,500 tourists a year who take trips in tundra buggies to see wildlife, primarily polar bears, but also ptarmigan, Arctic fox, Arctic hare, snowy owls and lemmings. Tour packages range from CDN$2,200 to $7,000 for two nights including accommodation and transportation to and from Winnipeg. A 2004 study found that 75 per cent of Churchill's visitors were American, and about 15 per cent were from abroad, primarily Japan, Germany and France. About 10 per cent of visitors were Canadian.

NEW PRODUCT DEVELOPMENT

According to the *Los Angeles Times*, 700 new products are introduced every day. Many of them fail, and many new ideas take years before becoming a reality. The BridgeClimb in Sydney is a prime example of the latter, and the Snapshot below explains how it took nine years for the idea to become reality. Safety concerns and other issues kept the unique tourism product on hold for nearly a decade. Developing new products is different from maintaining existing ones, and planning for both kinds of product will differ according to whether the products are targeted at existing markets or new ones. According to Holloway and Plant, a company has four alternatives when developing new products.

Market Penetration

Firstly, the company can follow a market penetration strategy by modifying an existing product for the current market. Improvements to an existing product can transform it, so that prospective purchasers view it as a genuinely new product.

Market Development

The second strategy, market development, calls for identifying and developing new markets for current products. If an existing product is launched to a new market that is unfamiliar with it, that product is also, for all intents and purposes, a new product. When Banff Mount Norquay in Canada introduced hourly tickets, they attracted a new market of skiers - locals who would not normally ski due to lack of time.

PRODUCT DEVELOPMENT

The third strategy, product development, involves developing a genuinely new product to be sold to existing customers. Over the last few years, fast-food companies have developed new healthier products for existing customers. Subway, for example, has positioned itself as a healthy fast-food alternative, turning its low-fat, low-calorie food into a marketing coup. When the company learned that Jared Fogel, a once 425-pound (193 kg) college student, lost 245 pounds (111 kg) on a diet consisting of Subway turkey and veggie subs, Fogel was recruited to endorse Subway products in numerous (successful) promotions. The Snapshot below on Sydney BridgeClimb is an example of a genuinely new product sold to tourists visiting the Australian city.

Diversification

Diversification growth makes sense when good opportunities can be found outside the present business. Three types of diversification can be considered. Firstly, the company can seek new products that have technological or marketing synergies with existing product lines, even though the product may appeal to a new class of customers (concentric diversification). Secondly, the company may search for new products that could appeal to its current target market (horizontal diversification). Finally, the company can seek new businesses that have no relationship with the company's current technology, products or markets (conglomerate diversification). An example of diversification comes from Four Seasons, the hotel company that moved into new territory in 2003 with the launch of a luxury catamaran cruise in the Maldives.

SERVICE TRENDS AFFECTING THE HOSPITALITY AND TOURISM INDUSTRY

Identifying trends within any business is one of the keys to success. Being in a position to identify what is occurring and what is likely to occur in the future remains very important. As discussed earlier, when studying trends in a broad sense, one should examine five major areas: the competitive environment, the economic environment, the political and legal environment, the social environment, and the technological environment. Several issues and trends are critical to understanding hospitality and tourism marketing. They help put into proper perspective what occurs within the competitive marketplace. Three trends that are having an impact on the hospitality industry and will continue to do so are shrinking customer loyalty, increasing customer sophistication, and increasing emphasis on the needs of individual customers.

Shrinking Customer Loyalty

Advertising and promotion for the hospitality and tourism industry's product-service mix have traditionally focused on the product, the services service trends affecting the hospitality and tourism industry provided, and the physical plant or atmosphere in which the customer enjoys the product-service mix. Today, many hospitality and tourism firms focus their promotions on price; that is, heavy price competition exists along with a good deal of discounting. Unfortunately, price discounting exists as a short-term strategy that seldom builds brand loyalty. Consumers often shop around for the best deal and are loyal only to organizations that give them a consistently superior one.

Recognizing this, companies have sought ways to increase brand loyalty, especially among heavy users of the product service mix. The best examples of this approach are the frequent flyer programmes promoted by the airlines and the frequent traveler programmes promoted by the lodging companies. These loyalty programmes are commonplace in the lodging industry; all of the major chains use loyalty programmes to encourage and reward frequent guests. The strategy behind loyalty programmes is to hook the customer with points which can be redeemed for products or services. The more frequently the customer stays at a hotel operated by the company, the more points are earned. The basic concepts common to all of these programmes are:

- Identify individuals who frequently purchase your product-service mix.
- Recognize the contribution those individuals make to the success of your company.
- Reward those individuals with awards and incentives that will increase their loyalty to your company and its brands.

Tie-ins with other companies providing travel-related services are also frequently used. For example, airlines, hotels, and car rental companies frequently offer bonus points within their programmes if the traveler uses the services offered by one of the companies participating in the tie-in. Both the airlines and the hotel companies are constantly making minor alterations to their programmes.

Increasing Consumer Sophistication

The budget segment of the lodging industry has undergone significant growth in the last several years. This growth has been fueled by the consumer demand for affordable accommodations that provide good value. In fact, consumers focus more on value and less on quality or price alone. Consumers have become more sophisticated and understand the concept of value at any price level. Hotels have responded that offer good quality service at an affordable price. Each of these brands features nicely appointed guest rooms, limited or no public meeting space, limited or no food service provided on the hotel site, and a complimentary continental breakfast for guests. These limited-service brands incur lower development and operating expenses and thereby can provide guests with a lower price and good value, something that all consumers are seeking.

Hotels in the upscale segment are also trying to increase the consumer's perception of value. They continually provide a broad assortment of amenities, such as health clubs on the property, business centers, rooms that provide more work space for business travelers, and personalized concierge service. These properties are striving to become "one-stop" destinations, providing a complete product-service mix that includes many food and beverage outlets, in-house office services, a wide variety of meeting room configurations, and other services, such as recreation, that will appeal to potential guests.

Within the fast-food service segment, companies often "bundle" their products in an attempt to increase sales and provide a better value for their customers. For example, they combine a sandwich, a large order of french fries, and a large soft drink at a price lower than what the items would cost if purchased separately. Similarly, tour operators and travel agents attempt to provide customers with more value by "bundling" the various components of travel (e.g., airline ticket, hotel room, car rental, and tickets for tourist at service trends affecting the hospitality and tourism industry tractions) at a price lower than the sum of the individual components. This approach is known as product bundling.

Increased Emphasis on the Needs of Individual Customers

The markets within both hospitality and tourism segments have been segmented for a long time. In the past 5 to 15 years, this trend has become even more pronounced. Mass marketing has become a thing of the past as more firms extend their product lines to meet the specific needs of smaller segments of travelers and diners. This phenomenon has become most apparent in the lodging industry. During the last decade, most of the major lodging chains developed several new brands or types of lodging properties to appeal to market segments that they were not currently serving. In addition, many hotel chains have merged with or acquired other hotel chains that focus on different market segments. Improvements in technology have given firms the ability to maintain large databases that detail consumer purchasing behaviour and preferences.

This information can be used to direct marketing efforts toward individual customers or market segments. Instead of relying on the mass media for promotions, a marketer can target past customers through direct mail and e-mail with special promotions and incentives that have a higher probability of being successful. There is more customization of products and promotions and less wasted coverage with media campaigns.

It began by defining services and explaining the characteristics that separate tangible products and services. Services are intangible and cannot be inventoried. This requires changes in the distribution process, and it makes it difficult to maintain consistent quality. It also requires more involvement on the part of customers, who actually become part of the product. The intangible nature of services results in more of an emphasis on experience qualities that are evaluated after a product becomes consumed, and less on search qualities that can be evaluated prior to purchase.

The concept of service quality remains important because consumers form perceptions of a firm based on its ability to provide a consistent level of service. This chapter introduced the service quality process and the potential gaps that could occur throughout the process. These gaps in service will decrease the level of service quality and lead to a decrease in customer satisfaction. Firms learn to manage service operations and improve quality through employee selection and training.

Once a firm focuses on the needs of consumers, it can build customer loyalty through relationship marketing. The overall performance of the firm can be improved through internal marketing efforts that attempt to communicate with employees and provide them with an environment for success. Customer satisfaction exists as the ultimate goal for a firm because it leads to brand loyalty and repeat purchases. Firms must meet or exceed customer expectations on a consistent basis in order to satisfy them. This chapter discussed ways to improve customer service and increase customer satisfaction. There are critical incidents, or moments of truth, when customers interact with employees and service failures can occur. Firms should encourage customers to voice their complaints so that the firms can anticipate and avoid possible failures. Also, firms can prepare service recovery strategies and train their employees to use them.

A firm's progress concerning customer satisfaction can be assessed using the techniques provided in this chapter, and benchmarks can be set for future comparisons. Finally, the chapter discussed some of the current trends in the hospitality and tourism industry that affect service operations. First, there is shrinking customer loyalty. Customers have many alternatives for fulfilling their needs, and it is easy to compare these alternatives using all of the information that is available.

The stronger the competition, the more incentives customers are given to switch service providers. Second, consumers are becoming more sophisticated. Consumers have access to a proliferation of information about products and services. This information allows them to focus on overall value, rather than price or quality alone. Also, consumer advocacy organizations provide helpful tips for getting bargains and avoiding firms with poor reputations. Finally, there is an increased emphasis on the individual needs of customers. Improved technology has made database marketing possible, allowing more precise targeting of markets and less wasted coverage with promotions. Firms are able to service more market segments by introducing new brands or forming relationships with other firms (e.g., strategic alliances, mergers, and acquisitions).

6

Customer Relationship Management

INTRODUCTION

Customer relationship management (CRM) covers methods and technologies used by companies to manage their relationships with clients. Information stored on existing customers (and potential customers) is analyzed and used to this end. Automated CRM processes are often used to generate automatic personalized marketing based on the customer information stored in the system.

Customer relationship management is a corporate level strategy, focusing on creating and maintaining relationships with customers. Several commercial CRM software packages are available which vary in their approach to CRM. However, CRM is not a technology itself, but rather a holistic approach to an organisation's philosophy, placing the emphasis firmly on the customer.

CRM governs an organization's philosophy at all levels, including policies and processes, front-of-house customer service, employee training, marketing, systems and information management. CRM systems are integrated end-to-end across marketing, sales, and customer service.

A CRM system should:

- Identify factors important to clients.
- Promote a customer-oriented philosophy
- Adopt customer-based measures
- Develop end-to-end processes to serve customers
- Provide successful customer support
- Handle customer complaints
- Track all aspects of sales
- Create a holistic view of customers' sales and services information

There are three fundamental components in CRM:

- Operational - automation of basic business processes (marketing, sales, service)
- Analytical - analysis of customer data and behaviour using business intelligence
- Collaborative - communicating with clients

Operational CRM provides automated support to "front office" business processes (sales, marketing and service). Each interaction with a customer is generally added to a customer's history, and staff can retrieve information on customers from the database as necessary.

According to Gartner Group operational CRM typically involves three general areas:

Sales force automation (SFA): SFA automates some of a company's critical sales and sales force management tasks, such as forecasting, sales administration, tracking customer preferences and demographics, performance management, lead management, account management, contact management and quote management.

Customer service and support (CSS): CSS automates certain service requests, complaints, product returns and enquiries.

Enterprise marketing automation (EMA) : EMA provides information about the business environment, including information on competitors, industry trends, and macroenvironmental variables. EMA applications are used to improve marketing efficiency.

Integrated CRM software is often known as a "front office solution", as it deals directly with customers.

Many call centers use CRM software to store customer information. When a call is received, the system displays the associated customer information (determined from the number of the caller). During and following the call, the call center agent dealing with the customer can add further information.

Some customer services can be fully automated, such as allowing customers to access their bank account details online or via a WAP phone.

Analytical CRM

Analytical CRM analyses data (gathered as part of operational CRM, or from other sources) in an attempt to identify means to enhance a company's relationship with its clients. The results of an analysis can be used to design targeted marketing campaigns, for example:

- Acquisition: Cross-selling, up-selling
- Retention: Retaining existing customers (antonym: customer attrition)
- Information: Providing timely and regular information to customers

Other examples of the applications of analyses include:

- Contact optimization
- Evaluating and improving customer satisfaction
- Optimizing sales coverage
- Fraud detection
- Financial forecasts
- Price optimization
- Product development
- Programme evaluation

- Risk assessment and management
- Strategic Marketing
- Operational marketing

Data collection and analysis is viewed as a continuing and iterative process. Ideally, business decisions are refined over time, based on feedback from earlier analyses and decisions. Most analytical CRM projects use a data warehouse to manage data.

Collaborative CRM

Collaborative CRM focuses on the interaction with customers (personal interaction, letter, fax, phone, Internet, e-mail etc.)

Collaborative CRM includes:

- Providing efficient communication with customers across a variety of communications channels
- Providing online services to reduce customer service costs
- Providing access to customer information while interacting with customers

Driven by authors from the Harvard Business School (Kracklauer/Mills/ Seifert), Collaborative CRM also seems to be the new paradigma to succeed the leading Efficient Consumer Response and Category Management concept in the industry/ trade relationship.

In its broadest sense, CRM covers all interaction and business with customers. A good CRM programme allows a business to acquire customers, provide customer services and retain valued customers.

Customer services can be improved by:

- Providing online access to product information and technical assistance around the clock
- Identifying what customers value and devising appropriate service strategies for each customer
- Providing mechanisms for managing and scheduling follow-up sales calls
- Tracking all contacts with a customer
- Identifying potential problems before they occur
- Providing a user-friendly mechanism for registering customer complaints
- Providing a mechanism for handling problems and complaints
- Providing a mechanism for correcting service deficiencies
- Storing customer interests in order to target customers selectively
- Providing mechanisms for managing and scheduling maintenance, repair, and on-going support
- Scalability: the system should be highly scalable, as the volume of data stored in the system grows over time
- Communication channels: CRM can interface with a variety of different channels (phone, WAP, Internet etc.)

- Workflow - a company's business processes need to be represented by the system with the ability to track the individual stages and transfer information between steps
- Assignment - the ability to assign requests, such as service requests, to a person or group.
- Database - the means of storing customer data and histories (in a data warehouse)
- Customer privacy considerations, such as data encryption and legislation.

IMPROVING CUSTOMER RELATIONSHIPS

CRM applications often track customer interests and requirements, as well as their buying habits. This information can be used to target customers selectively. Furthermore, the products a customer has purchased can be tracked throughout the product's life cycle, allowing customers to receive information concerning a product or to target customers with information on alternative products once a product begins to be phased out.

Repeat purchases rely on customer satisfaction, which in turn comes from a deeper understanding of each customer and their individual needs. CRM is an alternative to the "one size fits all" approach. In industrial markets, the technology can be used to coordinate the conflicting and changing purchase criteria of the sector.

The data gathered as part of CRM raises concerns over customer privacy and enables persuasive sales techniques (see persuasion technology). However, CRM does not necessarily involve gathering new data, but also includes making better use of customer information gathered as a result of routine customer interaction.

The privacy debate generally focuses on the customer information stored in the centralized database itself, and fears over a company's handling of this information. For example, there is virtually no way a consumer can determine if the company shares private (personally identifiable) data with third parties. Furthermore, companies may not always accurately declare to the consumer the types of information collected by CRM systems and the specific purposes for which the information is used.

CRM is also important to non-profit organizations, which sometimes use the terms "constituent relationship management", "contact relationship management" or "community relationship management" to describe their information systems for managing donors, volunteers and other supporters. salesforce.com, a popular CRM service that is on demand, offers its products for free to nonprofit organizations.

CUSTOMER MEASUREMENT

Every company must be able to satisfy and retain customers. That is the key to its business performance. Your job—as an executive in charge of improving quality, customer satisfaction, or loyalty—may be to enable others to act through training and support. Alternatively, if you're in the quality, customer assessment, or development areas of your company, your job may be to do the work directly—to collect, analyse, or use customer data to improve quality, satisfaction, and retention.

Whether you are an enabler or a doer, customer satisfaction and retention are your responsibility. Providing high-quality products and services builds strong relationships with customers and ensures future revenue streams. Even though you may agree about the importance of customers in driving performance, an important question remains. Does your company align its activities to satisfy and retain customers? Too often the answer is either "no" or "not so well." To help understand the problem, consider how a customer focus has evolved in recent decades.

In the 1970s, quality gurus argued that "quality is free." That is, a tireless pursuit of improvement should not only increase efficiency but also increase customer satisfaction in the process, saving enough on costs and bringing in enough new and repeat business to more than cover any expenditures on quality. This was an underlying concept in the success of many Japanese companies. In the 1980s the experts began to focus more directly on increasing customer satisfaction as an explicit goal. Satisfying and keeping customers, it was argued, is simply less expensive than constantly replacing them. More recently, quality and satisfaction have been viewed as not sufficient by themselves. Companies boast of moving "beyond" quality and satisfaction to focus directly on customer loyalty as the key to profitability.

Yet to argue that quality, or satisfaction, or loyalty is what matters misses the point. These factors form a chain of cause and effect, building on each other so that they cannot be treated separately. They represent a system that must be measured and managed as a whole if you want to maximize results. An example from our teaching experiences underscores the nature of the problem and why companies need to take a systems approach to customer measurement and management. Back in 1993 an executive seminar participant from a Fortune 100 company introduced himself as the "customer satisfaction manager" for his organization.

This prompted one of the authors to ask, "What happened to the quality manager?" The participant replied that quality was passé, and that customer satisfaction had become the hot topic in his organization. In fact, being the quality manager had become the "kiss of death" from a career standpoint—a dead-end job! Five years later, a seminar participant from the same company introduced himself as the "customer loyalty manager" for the organization.

Again the natural question arose, "What happened to the customer satisfaction manager?" "Oh, him?" It turned out that the satisfaction manager was now the one with the dead-end job. Many business organizations are beginning to recognize the need to avoid this "Book of the Month Club" mentality and to view customers from a systems perspective.

They want explicit linkages that extend from internal processes to customer perceptions to customer satisfaction to loyalty—and ultimately to bottom-line performance. The framework in this book will give executives hard numbers and not just persuasive theories to show that the connection is real and that improving satisfaction and loyalty really does improve profits. And those on the front lines—the quality engineers and service providers—will get specific guidance on what to improve and how to improve it to get the optimal response from customers. This book will show you how to create an integrated customer measurement and management system that will help you allocate resources and increase profits.

To create such a system, you must first understand your company's entire system for generating profit, from internal quality through to business performance. A systems approach acts on the basis of collected and interpreted customer data—but then you have to use the data to allocate resources and create change in the system or else you merely waste time and money. With an effective customer measurement and management system, you can build organizational value.

To do so, you will continually pursue three key activities that underlie a customer orientation: (1) gather customer information, (2) spread that information throughout the organization, and (3) use the information to maintain, improve, or innovate in products and processes. You need solid information about the concrete product and service attributes or features that customers value, the more abstract consequences and benefits these attributes provide, and ultimately the personal values they serve.

The purpose is to understand what your customers want not only in today's products and services but in tomorrow's as well. When you understand your customers at the various levels that motivate their behaviour, you can see their present needs and predict their future needs as well. To maintain a customer orientation throughout your organization, you need to make sure that customer information gets to everyone who is involved—either directly or indirectly— in improving quality and value and satisfying customers.

This both prepares the entire organization for change and provides benchmarks by which to monitor its performance. Finally, you need to prime the organization to act on the customer information to improve product and service offerings so as to increase satisfaction, loyalty, and profitability. This makes it essential to clarify the links among these three factors and understand how your company delivers a compelling product to its customers. Creating a customer measurement and management system is central to the pursuit of all three of these activities. With such a system in place, you have your customer information in a form that can serve as a basis for both incremental and more revolutionary product and service improvements.

The system also makes it easier to share customer information throughout an organization, enhancing its ability to follow through on that information to make product and process changes. It is essential to view customer measurement from a systems perspective that encompasses multiple areas of measurement and expertise (from engineering and design through market research and strategy to finance and accounting) so that you pick up both concrete and abstract details— both what the customers like and dislike and why they react that way—and develop information that will be genuinely useful.

Now you may well be saying, "But we already do a good job of gathering customer information, spreading it, and acting on the voice of the customer." The question is whether you really adopt the "lens of the customer" in this process or fall into the trap of relying on the "lens of the organization." The lens of the customer shows you your products and services—and the benefits they provide—from your customers' perspective.

You see them as they really are in the marketplace, rather than the different and potentially misleading picture you're likely to get from the lens of your own organization. For example, if you run a convenience store chain you may be inclined to view the chain's stores as providing customers with people (service), products (from soft drinks to gasoline), and operations (such as opening hours), each under the management of a different department or business function.

The problem is that customers may not share this perspective. Customers view products and services from the standpoint of the benefits they provide and problems they solve, which may not align well with individual business process areas. In this case, customers are looking for safety, convenience, and cleanliness, which are benefits that are not uniquely provided by specific business process areas. Rather, they cut across the people, products, and operating policies of the stores. Aside from providing a more accurate picture of the drivers of satisfaction and loyalty, adopting the lens of the customer has other advantages. It blurs functional boundaries and provides a common basis and language for communication.

The forging of concrete links from area to area within a company is also a key to effective implementation. When an organization reaches a consensus on the importance of customer benefits that are not defined along functional or business process lines, it finds it much easier to engage in the cross-functional activities required to truly innovate and implement change. We emphasize the word *framework* here. Our aim is to show just what links and models are possible.The actual elements and links in any model vary tremendously from company to company and context to context.

After describing the framework, as suggested, show this point using two very different cases in which companies (Volvo and Sears) have developed models to become more customer focused. The framework includes four general areas: internal quality, external quality and satisfaction, customer loyalty and retention, and financial performance. *Internal quality* encompasses various production and maintenance processes.

In the case of a manufactured product, it includes everything from manufacturing processes to the physical characteristics and attributes that describe the product. In a service and retailing context, it includes the service offer, the physical surroundings, and the satisfaction of employees and the resulting service quality they provide. External quality and satisfaction encompasses what customers see in the purchase and consumption experience: the attributes and benefits that products and services provide and the costs they impose, and the conclusions the customers draw about the company. In the area of customer loyalty and retention, *loyalty* is a customer's intention or predisposition to buy, while *retention* is the behaviour itself (as when a customer returns to a restaurant, comes back to buy the same brand of car, or purchases another financial instrument from the same institution). Although as suggested, use the term *loyalty* at times to encompass both intended loyalty and actual retention, it is important to understand the distinction. When actual retention information is available, it proves extremely valuable in sorting out the drivers of financial performance.

When it is unavailable, as it often is, you can use loyalty measures as a proxy for retention. Quality, satisfaction, and loyalty ultimately affect financial performance, both directly and indirectly. The framework shows this point and highlights the possibility that there may be a tension between direct and indirect effects. Consider first the impact of internal quality. Producing a high-quality product or service at an attractive price indirectly affects financial performance through its effect on external customer perceptions of the purchase-consumption experience. But internal quality may also have a direct effect on costs and revenues.

The "quality is free" argument, improvements in internal quality can increase productivity and lower internal costs and thus directly increase profitability. Recent research suggests, however, that this link is likely to be more positive for products and less positive or even negative for services. Why the difference? Services are produced and delivered at a time and place that is typically dictated by the customer. Thus improving service quality often requires an increase in personnel and operating or contact hours, which raises operating costs.

The external quality, value, and customer satisfaction component of the framework also has both direct and indirect effects on costs and revenues. Indirectly, a positive overall experience predisposes customers to stay loyal towards a product, service, or provider, which generates future sales. Satisfaction thus contributes to financial performance through its effect on loyalty and retention. But satisfaction also has direct effects, independent of loyalty. The cost of maintaining a customer account—or fixing a product—is a direct function of how happy the customer is. Satisfied customers are less likely to demand expensive product repairs or replacements or to invoke service guarantees. Also—even outside the world of TV commercials—people do talk about the products and services they buy, and your company's entry into that stream of word-of-mouth publicity is through perceived quality and satisfaction rather than through loyalty. Satisfaction is *news*—something to talk about—while loyalty is a background state that goes without saying unless something happens to damage it.

The direct effects of loyalty and retention on performance include revenues from repeat purchases, reduction in costs of finding new customers (to replace lost customers), and revenues generated through cross-selling. Another direct effect is the price premium that loyal customers often pay. Because loyal customers are not actively shopping for alternatives, they tend to be insulated from price incentives and offers such as coupons, price cuts, and free merchandise. The recent turnaround at Volvo Car Company provides a good example of how a durable goods manufacturer views the links described in our framework.

In 1991, Volvo was performing poorly in the global automotive market. It ranked as low as twenty-sixth out of thirty-four brands in the J. D. Power Initial Quality Study in the United States, and sales and profitability were suffering. In its comeback effort, Volvo began to develop a customer orientation from a total quality management foundation. Formerly, Volvo had emphasized changing internal quality to improve productivity and reduce costs.

Its management realised, however, that just focusing on internal quality was insufficient. Internal improvements had to matter to the customers before they could create improved external quality, customer satisfaction, and loyalty. Volvo's approach is just one example of the variety of tailored models that are consistent with the framework. Like Volvo, Sears has attempted to radically transform itself into a more customer-focused organization. But since Sears is a retailer that competes primarily on service, its model has evolved quite differently. Internal quality at Sears is primarily about its people and the service they provide. The Sears model draws directly on a service-profit chain that links internal quality (including employee satisfaction and loyalty) to service quality, and the satisfaction generated by service quality to loyalty and financial performance. In developing its model, Sears has discovered both direct effects of satisfaction on financial performance and indirect effects through loyalty, which is consistent with our framework.

A quantitative employee-customer-profit model at Sears has helped the company to establish very specific links that have enabled it to improve financial performance. The model shows, for example, that a 5-point improvement in employee attitudes (on a 0 to 100 scale) drives a 1.3-point improvement in customer satisfaction, which in turn drives a 0.5 per cent improvement in revenue growth. The Volvo and Sears models share a common logic, but each model is uniquely tailored to the organization's own situation. Both models link internal quality through to profitability.

At the same time, each reflects the nature of a specific company, its customers and offerings, and the contexts involved. When you look at your own company, you will see that the same logic will work for you when you develop a similar understanding of your own customers and what you can offer them. The best measurement system can only provide information— it can't make decisions for you. People make decisions, whether it is the convenience store executive who sets corporate priorities, the front-line service manager who translates these priorities into policies and procedures, or the service worker who translates policies and procedures into concrete actions.

At all three levels, decision makers are much more likely to choose to do something that will help the store chain succeed if they understand what matters to customers and how the job at hand can enhance that value. The process of moving from information to decisions draws heavily on *importance-performance analysis.* The most cost-effective areas of product and service performance to improve are those that are important to customers *and* on which, at the same time, the company is performing poorly. Executives and managers must identify these priority areas of high importance and low performance. As an output of this selection process, they can categorize and display the drivers of satisfaction and loyalty using a strategic satisfaction matrix.

The matrix identifies four categories of performance drivers with different market action implications. Again, the aspects to improve first are those where impact or importance is high and performance is weak. This focuses resources and quality improvement efforts likely to have the greatest impact on satisfaction and thus on loyalty and profitability. Those aspects where performance and impact are both high reflect a firm's competitive advantage.

It is essential to maintain if not improve performance on these drivers. When impact and performance are both weak, on the other hand, there is no need to waste resources on improvement. More interesting is the low impact–strong performance category. This may be an area where resources have been wasted in the past because the benefits and attributes are not important to customers. Alternatively, this category may contain drivers of satisfaction that customers see as basic and necessary—so much a part of the product or service that they ignore it as long as it's there when they want it, like electric power or water on tap.

Although such drivers are important in an absolute sense, they have little to no impact on satisfaction because there is little variance in their performance. The danger is that a reduction in performance quality would increase the impact on satisfaction (this danger is often referred to as a "slippery slope"). Another possibility here is to find a new target market segment for the product or service.

For example, if the quality of an electrical system is so constant that it has no impact on satisfaction in one application, the system might be used in applications where minor fluctuations in this quality are more important and therefore likely to have a real impact on satisfaction. There is also a danger that something in this category may become important in the future. For example, few customers considered "environmental friendliness" to be an important factor until recently, but more and more people are beginning to pay attention to this aspect of the goods and services they buy. In a growing variety of fields, companies that predicted the importance of this area and prepared their business accordingly clearly have an advantage over those that did not. The circular nature of the process reflects the continuous nature of a customer orientation.

Customer needs, competitive offerings, and business technologies change constantly, so customer focus is an ideal of constant growth rather than static achievement. The cycle in is thus a continuous process of planning, researching, analysing, deciding, implementing, and learning. This includes identifying the system's purpose or goals within a more balanced set of corporate performance measures (including financial goals, employee satisfaction goals, process improvement goals, knowledge and learning goals, and so forth). The key customer and market segmentation issues upon which the system is based, including the distinction between internal and external customers.

Conducting interviews and focus groups and observing customers provides you with the lens through which customers view products and services. This lens is the basis for your quality-satisfactionloyalty modeling. It discusses ways to develop and administer surveys that assess the attributes and benefits your products and services provide and the overall levels of customer satisfaction and loyalty that result. The goal is to customise the measurement of quality, value, satisfaction, and loyalty for a particular customer segment, company, and context.

Again, the purpose is to identify both the relative importance and performance of key satisfaction and loyalty drivers. It provides guidelines for identifying the area or areas where importance is high and performance is low, which offer the most potential return on quality improvement efforts. We develop a statistical approach to help you estimate your system or model linking quality to loyalty and financial performance. We also provide concrete examples. As emphasized earlier, management must take part in categorizing the output of a customer analysis into a strategic satisfaction matrix. Just where boundaries are set between highversus low-impact drivers and strong versus weak performance depends on a variety of factors, including what you can achieve in the time available, your cost structure, and your overall strategy. Interpreting model outputs also requires appropriate bench for evaluating both performance and importance.

Who should collect your customer data, analyse it, and use it to set priorities and allocate resources? It often seems logical to delegate the satisfaction and loyalty measurement operation to outside research firms and consultants. This is especially true early in the process of becoming a customer-oriented organization, because outside specialists offer specific skills related to collecting and analysing customer data that you do not have. Unfortunately, if you delegate the system, your company does not take ownership of it, and you and your people may fail to learn or acquire the skills necessary to measure and manage customer data on your own.

The consultant's bills, heavy as they are likely to be, are only a small part of the cost of handing off a customer information system. Bear in mind that when customer information is the key to strategy, it should reside within the company. Your best teachers about what is right and wrong with your products and services are your own customers. Direct contact with customers and customer data is a critical part of learning what it takes to satisfy customer needs.

No matter how good the consultants are, they will always function as filters. An important part of establishing a customer orientation as a core competency is creating, over time, internal specialists to measure, model, and manage quality, satisfaction, and loyalty. Early in the process, external experts are apt to be a necessity. They can provide the interviewing, surveying, data warehousing, statistical analysis, and interpretation skills that you may lack or not yet want (or be able) to invest in. Over time, however, continued reliance on external specialists becomes costly and also fails to develop customer measurement and management as a core competency. Internalization of the process allows you to adapt to changing market needs and competitive environments in a cost-effective fashion. More important, your organization accepts ownership of the process and the data—and the decisions that emerge. This is not to say that all parts of the process should be brought in-house in all cases.

You may not want to try to run a survey that involves computer-aided telephone interviews or a Web-based system with highly specialized personnel (such as trained interviewers) and potential economies of scale. Even in the most customer-savvy organization, it may be best to outsource certain parts of the process. At the same time, a truly customer-oriented firm should own rather than rent the ability to observe and to talk to customers, formalize survey instruments, analyse and interpret customer data, and use the output to make resource allocation decisions.

Over the last three decades business organizations have evolved from a focus on quality to a focus on customer satisfaction, and onward to a focus on loyalty as a means of creating value. A customer measurement and management system views each of these areas as an indispensable link in a chain of causes and effects that runs from internal quality through to profitability. The goal of this book is to help you and your organization create an integrated customer measurement and management system for making effective resource allocation decisions and increasing profitability. In the process of building a system, organizations develop internal specialists capable of gathering, analysing, and interpreting customer data.

Truly customer-oriented companies should, over time, add these skills to their core competencies. A systems approach to customer measurement and management also requires that you tailor the system to your unique purpose, customers, and contexts. As an illustration, Volvo's model incorporates the positive effects of improving internal quality on both productivity and customer perceptions of quality, satisfaction, and loyalty. In contrast, a major retailer such as Sears incorporates the central role that satisfied employees play in delivering quality and value to customers. These measurement systems and models are not substitutes for decision making. Rather, they provide the information you need to make resource allocation decisions and manage the process.

The system provides information on how the company and its competitors are performing in different areas and how important the areas are to customers. When combined with cost and strategy considerations, the system allows both enablers and doers to create organizational value through a continuous focus on customers. To maximize the value generated by the system, make sure your company's own staff perform the bulk of the work of collecting and interpreting customer data, so that you get the full benefit of the insights generated by the effort.

Before you dive in and start conducting customer interviews or surveys, you must know how your measurement system will be used. Since a customer orientation builds on internal quality, we'll start with a brief overview of quality management and its role in driving company strategy and customer measures. We'll then discuss two related approaches to translating strategy into action: policy deployment and balanced performance measures.

Then we'll focus on the process of getting started on developing a customer measurement and management system—or improving an existing one—which involves taking a look at the breadth and depth of the proposed system and the role of market segmentation in it. In our customer satisfaction framework, internal quality is the first in the chain of events that drives financial performance.

It's important not to underestimate the role of *total quality management* (or TQM, also known as *company-wide quality management,* CWQM, and as *total quality control,* TQC)—nor to exaggerate it. For longterm survival, businesses have been forced to improve their abilities to change and innovate. But internal quality management is not in itself sufficient to assure success. Internal quality improvements must be linked to improvements in external quality, satisfaction, loyalty, and financial performance. And the links must be established in an environment of constantly evolving customer preferences, markets, competitors, and technologies. The broad principles and methods of quality management apply directly to the development of a customer measurement system.

The concept of quality should unify all of a company's activities. After all, only your customers can ultimately define quality for you! In the end, it doesn't matter how well the production system works, how well marketing functions are performed, or how good the company's strategy is. If no one buys, there will be no revenues.

Quality experts emphasize three basic strategies for successful quality management: use reference models or benchmarks, set priorities for quality improvement, and focus your resources. Do not try to do things completely on your own. Instead, make use of reference models or benchmarks when they're available. Benchmarking is particularly important in developing a customer measurement and management system. Process benchmarking—finding out how things are done— works as well in developing a customer measurement and management system as in any other area of business.

When you can manage it, arrange visits to firms with strong reputations to gauge their practices and learn what they are doing, see how they are doing it, and understand what is possible. Devote some time to reverse engineering their products as well. And don't limit the benchmarking to competitors—in a general area such as customer measurement, you'll find individuals or organizations in many fields who excel in areas that you are interested in improving.

Benchmarking on their processes can help you to learn how to conduct better customer interviews, develop and administer more effective surveys, and analyse customer data in more productive ways—and they're likely to be much more willing to share information with you if you're not trying to sell the same offering to the same customers. For *output* or *performance benchmarking,* you will measure your product or service against direct or indirect competitors on various dimensions such as internal or technical quality, external or perceived quality and value, and overall customer satisfaction, loyalty, and retention. The external benchmarks will help you interpret your findings regarding your own customers and decide just where to devote your resources to get the most mileage from your improvement efforts.

THE POTENTIAL OF CRM IN THE LODGING INDUSTRY

Lodging-industry participants face an increasingly competitive market. In addition, the basis of competition is changing. Location, a key driver of business, is fixed in the short and medium term, and attracting and retaining customers based on facilities and amenities is becoming increasingly difficult as they have become increasingly standardized across competing brands. Price competition is unattractive, even more so as consumers are able to easily find and compare prices over the Internet. As a consequence consumers are increasingly displaying less brand loyalty, and CRM is becoming increasingly attractive as a way for hotel companies to differentiate themselves from their competitors.

The lodging sector is ideally suited to applying the principles of CRM. In few other industries is there such potential to build up a comprehensive and accurate picture of the client. In few other industries do customers provide the significant amount of information hotel guests divulge when making a reservation and during their hotel stay. Every interaction between the guest and the customer is an opportunity to refine knowledge about her or him and to further build a relationship.

By methodically collecting, consolidating, and analyzing both guest preferences and transactional data, hotel chains have the potential to develop a deep understanding of each customer's needs and preferences, provide substantially improved service levels, individually tailor the customer experience, and generally offer more personalized service. Providing outstanding personal service is certainly not a new concept in the hotel sector.

Companies such as Ritz-Carlton and the Savoy group historically maintained extensive manual guest-history systems recording guest preferences in an effort to better serve their best customers. However, when operated manually, such systems are expensive to maintain, are frequently inaccurate, and can only be used to track a limited number of clients at individual properties. Developments in information and communications technologies have enabled automation and efficiencies in these processes, reducing costs, increasing accuracy, and allowing comprehensive knowledge about each customer to be shared on a global basis.

As a result, many companies are turning to technology to improve customer service by implementing large-scale CRM programmes. Analysis of the lodging sector shows that, driven in most cases by pressure from the marketing function, many of the dominant hotel chains are in the process of deploying (or have already deployed) the technological infrastructure to support CRM. A recent study by Arthur Andersen and New York University found that over one-third of U.S. hotel chains had a data warehouse in 2000, with another 50 percent planning to install one in the near future.

Many chains have introduced information systems to improve the targeting of marketing and sales efforts. Such systems can help the firm to assess the value of each customer as well as their propensity to respond to various offers, and to market to them individually. As discussed earlier, while important, such initiatives do not imply that the company has adopted CRM.

In most cases, such developments focus solely on marketing objectives and lack the integration among functional areas that characterizes a CRM initiative. Only where the company reconfigures its operations to deliver a comprehensive view of the customer and to support consistent, highly personalized service at every customer touch point could it truly be regarded as CRM.

Few companies in the lodging sector appear to have progressed to such an advanced stage. Given the geographic dispersion of hotel properties and the role of brands in marketing and distribution, large-scale CRM initiatives seem most justifiable at the brand level. Implementing CRM at this level would help to increase consistency and personal service throughout the chain and at each customer touch point.

However, to achieve this, consistent and comprehensive information must be captured from all properties within the brand and then consolidated, analyzed, interpreted, and subsequently disseminated to each property in time to influence the next customer interaction. Two barriers currently prevent that from happening—a lack of standardization and IT system integration within each franchise, and the fact that at any one time there may be up to three parties holding a stake in the operations of a particular property (owner, management company, and brand).

The two issues are largely interconnected as the industry's generally reactive attitude toward IT has been exacerbated by its structural characteristics. The technical challenge is subsiding due to recent developments in technology, including the emergence of the application service provider (ASP) model.

(*Note:* When software applications are delivered using an ASP model, they are not installed on the computers at the property. Rather, they are accessed by remote users via the Web. Thus, IT resources under the ASP model are not bought but acquired as a service.)

A discussion of these technologies is beyond the scope of this article. Note, however, that, even assuming away technological challenges, we believe that the structure of the lodging industry creates severe obstacles to successful CRM. The remainder of the paper focuses on these challenges.

The Lodging Industry's Structure

Lodging is an important component of the tourism industry, providing accommodation (and associated ancillary services) to travelers while away from home. Lodging operations are diverse, ranging from small bed-and breakfast properties in rural locations to large hotels with several thousand rooms in major cities. The majority of the world's hotel properties are concentrated in Europe (55 percent) and North America (22 percent).

The exhibit also demonstrates that the average property size in North America is larger than that in Europe (56 versus 28 rooms), with chain-affiliated properties being more common in North America. Despite controlling only a minority of room stock (approximately 30 percent of total room supply) hotel chains dominate the lodging sector and tend to exert a disproportionate influence on industry operations and performance.

In addition to generally having higher occupancy and average daily rate, chain properties tend to be more profitable, delivering trading profit per room seven times more than their independent counterparts. As a result, the industry is expected to continue to consolidate, with an increasing number of mergers and acquisitions resulting in a small number of large companies dominating the marketplace. A differentiation must be made between hotel ownership, hotel branding, and hotel operations.

Historical developments with Real Estate Investment Trusts (REITs) in the United States gave rise to a situation where many owners could not operate their own hotels. Instead they must use a separate management company to oversee day-to-day operations, resulting in a split between hotel ownership and hotel operations.

The situation is further complicated by the widespread use of both franchises and marketing agreements that provide a consumer brand and require compliance with brand standards.

At any one time there may be up to three parties holding a stake in the operations of a particular property:

(1) The owner, who holds title to the assets, is responsible for mortgage payments and provides the capital for the operation;

(2) The brand, which brands the property and provides standards, distribution services, marketing, technology, and other services; and

(3) The management company, which provides management talent and operates the property on a day-to-day basis.

The exception of Wyndham International, the major brand companies own less than one-third of their branded properties, with various management companies operating the remainder on behalf of their owners.

Furthermore, within each management company the brand portfolio is quite mixed, with each company operating under a variety of competing flags in different geographical markets. The data lend support to our claim that in the U.S. lodging industry there are multiple stakeholders with, at times competing, interest in the operations of the property.

THE DATA-OWNERSHIP DILEMMA

As was discussed earlier, CRM's success is predicated on the ability to collect, analyze, and disseminate large amounts of timely and relevant information for customer-service operatives to act on to improve the experience at each point of customer contact.

Thus, a CRM initiative cannot be successful without commitment among a critical mass of properties. Hotel chains cannot provide a consistently high level of personal service unless customer data can be garnered from most, if not all, of the affiliated properties, organized and synthesized in one central location, and subsequently redistributed to each property on an as-needed basis.

However, we propose that (technological constraints aside) this apparently simple theoretical proposition is difficult to realize in the lodging industry due to an inherent data-ownership conflict between the major industry stakeholders. In the following sections we present the main issues facing the brand, the management company, and the owner.

The Brand

For brands, the development of an effective CRM initiative is deemed an important competitive move as it would facilitate the development of a deep understanding of customer needs and preferences, potentially resulting in a high level of personalization, thus helping to improve service levels across the brand as a whole. As a result guests would have a strong incentive to remain loyal to the brand and patronize affiliated properties, thus increasing the value proposition for owners and operators through improvements in financial performance.

For the promised benefits of CRM to materialize, standardized information systems must be implemented throughout the franchise network to allow data to be obtained from all branded properties—a problem in the past, becoming less important as a result of recent technology improvements. Furthermore, the brand must be willing to share the customer knowledge generated by the consolidation of customer data chain-wide with the individuals that can take action based on it at each point of customer contact. Such data sharing presents the first dilemma. In some cases, the brand may be reticent to disseminate customer knowledge back to the property for fear that owners or operators might use it to poach high-value customers and divert them to competing brands within their own portfolios.

For example, imagine a management company that operates a hotel flying one flag (Brand A) in a particular market, and a competing flag (Brand B) in others. This company might be tempted to steer highvalue customers toward its Brand B hotels in markets where it does not operate Brand A hotels. Thus, Brand A is faced with a decision— either share the data it collects companywide to reap the benefits of large-scale CRM and risk the poaching of high-value customers by some of its partner management companies operating individual properties; or protect its customer knowledge from the interests of multi-flag owners and operators, thus forgoing the full benefits of CRM.

The Management Company

Management companies do not appear to have strong incentives to develop a CRM initiative for themselves. As such companies tend to operate a varied portfolio of properties, each flying different flags, on behalf of different owners. By definition a CRM initiative developed across flags is unlikely to generate brand loyalty and thus is of limited interest to most management companies. The question arises, however, as to whether management companies should actively cooperate with the collection of operational guest data by brand-level CRM initiatives. As most companies operate a varied portfolio of flags, if the management company participates in a brand-based CRM initiative, it will stand to gain only in those properties that carry that particular brand.

Conversely, participation will result in a competitive disadvantage in markets where it competes against the brand.

As a result, management companies have little incentive to support brand-level CRM initiatives by contributing data about customers that stay at its properties. In fact, by doing so, they would in effect be undermining their own operations in markets where the brand operating the CRM initiative is a competitor rather than an ally. Moreover, while the management company may not be interested in detailed customer data for branding purposes, it certainly finds value in customer data that allows it to create customer-value models and better target high-value prospects, particularly with respect to group business. Consequently, management companies have in effect an incentive to limit data disclosure and not cooperate with brand-level CRM initiatives.

The Owner

While owners, like operators, typically have many flags in their portfolio of properties, they have a different focus in terms of profitability. Many primarily view hotel ownership as a real-estate investment, and have a marginal interest in the question, "Who owns the data?" Where their properties fly the flag of a successful CRM initiative, they may have an advantage over other competing properties; where their properties fly competing flags, they may be at a disadvantage. Thus, the same dilemma facing the management company seems to affect the owners—whether to participate in brand level CRM initiatives, or to refuse to cooperate with the collection and consolidation of customer data.

The owners may also have interests that go beyond the use of the data strictly for operational purposes. Customer data may be used by the other entities (the brand and the management company) for marketing purposes and analyses that run counter to the owner's own interests (e.g., studying the feasibility of building new properties in the same geographical area).

Conclusions and Implications

In this chapter we have drawn attention to what we term the "data-ownership dilemma"—the inherent conflict that various entities in the lodging industry face as they embrace CRM. We propose that the data-ownership dilemma represents a significant, yet often unrecognized, challenge to the success of CRM initiatives. As was discussed, CRM strategies appear most applicable at the brand level, but their success is dependent on the active cooperation of both the operator and the owner of each property. For CRM to succeed at the brand level, operators must supply the brand with in-depth customer data—a requirement with which operators in particular, and owners to a lesser extent, have little incentive to comply. Brands also face challenges in terms of maintaining control over the resulting customer knowledge and preventing its spread outside the brand network.

Because of this conflict, we believe that CRM in the lodging industry may never progress beyond its current, relatively limited, level of sophistication. While database-marketing techniques will continue to be used, we propose that few hotel companies will successfully implement large-scale, chain-wide, CRM initiatives. Only if significant change occurs in the structure or methods of operation of the sector are the full benefits of a CRM approach likely to be realized. In closing, we speculate as to what changes will have to occur for successful implementation of CRM initiatives. There are three possible scenarios: there will be a fundamental change in the way in which hotel brands are organized; a change in the nature of franchise agreements and management contracts; or there will be more cooperation among brands to take advantage of CRM's promised benefits. These three scenarios are further developed in the remainder of this article.

The first scenario is that the need for adoption of a CRM approach will induce changes in the ownership and management structure of the lodging sector. If CRM truly provides compelling benefits, the large brands should begin to pressure the management companies and franchisees within their network to provide the data needed for successful CRM operations. Those brands that manage a relatively large number of their own hotels will be in a good position to take advantage of these initiatives quickly, should face little resistance as a result of the data ownership dilemma, and should be able to easily reap the benefits of CRM.

Wyndham International's ByRequest initiative demonstrates that highly integrated lodging brands are moving quickly to embrace CRM. If these pioneers are successful in their effort and are able to attract and retain high-value customers, competing brands will have to follow suit and develop similar CRM capabilities. Such companies would have to resolve the data-ownership dilemma either by "integrating down" or by restricting the number of flags that the companies operating their hotels can fly. Integrating down implies that brands would move aggressively to take over the operational management of their branded properties. Such integrated companies should be able to standardize the IT infrastructure needed to support CRM, mandate the collection and consolidation of customer data, and provide each property with dynamic access to the central knowledge repository.

Since all operations would effectively be managed by the brand, there would be no conflicts of interest and no danger of high-value customers being poached, freeing the brand to take full advantage of the CRM initiative. Obviously, taking over operational control of their unit properties would be a dramatic and high-risk strategy. Thus, brands, particularly in the short term, may instead concentrate on restructuring their management and franchise agreements to minimize the barriers to success discussed earlier. Redevelopment should focus on two main areas— data collection and data use. While many franchise agreements require properties to feed its customer-folio data back to the central level, few specifically mention any other data collected about the guest.

As CRM is dependent on building up a holistic picture of the guest's needs and behaviour, this oversight may force brands to restructure contracts to force greater compliance with data needs. structured contracts could specify that all customer data generated at the property level be extracted and loaded to the brand's central data repository. Management contracts also need to be rewritten to offer protection to the brand as it disseminates customer knowledge back to the property level. Both of these measures mean that ties between brands and operators would be strengthened, which may ultimately result in further industry consolidation as owners and operators feel pressure to fly a limited number of flags. In an extreme scenario, each operator would effectively become aligned with one brand and fly only one flag.

The final potential scenario we envision is the emergence of an industry consortium that both develops and maintains the CRM infrastructure and standardizes customer-data collection and distribution. As it has happened historically with hotel e-commerce systems such as THISCo (The Hotel Industry Switching Company), HDS (Hotel Distribution Systems) and Avendra (an e-procurement marketplace), competing brands could cooperate to develop the standards and the infrastructure necessary to capture, store, organize, and distribute customer information. Such a scenario is attractive as joint development would mean that the infrastructure could be delivered and operated at a fraction of the cost of proprietary initiatives.

Thereafter, rather than being used as a basis of competition, customer data would be shared and companies would compete on the analysis, interpretation, and use of such data. For example, competing brands could use the same data to market to their chosen customer bases. Competitive advantage would come from how well they could use the data to identify, target, and build a relationship with each individual. We believe the latter scenario to be the least likely, even though it may optimize industry-wide performance. The likelihood of an industry consortium developing and managing customer information for the benefit of the industry as a whole is small, as the industry's belief in the proprietary value of customer data, the industry's structure, privacy issues, as well as a culture that precludes trust in this domain makes the cooperation necessary unlikely. We see a change in contractual agreements and in industry structure as far more probable. In any case, given the potential proposed for lodging-industry companies, careful consideration must be given to the data-ownership dilemma to avoid failure.

As part of our research, we investigated the CRM initiatives of large hotel chains. One such chain, Wyndham International, has made CRM a cornerstone of its brand strategy. We briefly describe the key characteristics of Wyndham's CRM approach to aid the reader in understanding the principal characteristics of large-scale CRM initiatives. Wyndham International is one of the five largest U.S.–based hotel chains, with a portfolio of over 160 branded properties. After converting from paired-share REIT status to a C corporation in 1999, Wyndham revised its corporate strategy in an effort to become a "world-class branded hotel operating company." Wyndham's differentiation strategy is nicely captured in the words of Andrew Jordan, Wyndham's senior vice president of marketing: "We said, okay, we are going to reinvent the Wyndham brand. We are going to say: We are all about personalized service.

We are going to say: We are the brand who really recognizes that guests are individuals, we know you have specific needs, quirks—you tell us about them one time and we are going to remember them." The cornerstone of

Wyndham's strategy is its membership-based CRM initiative: Wyndham ByRequest. When a guest joins ByRequest, he or she completes a comprehensive profile including general and contact information, room preferences (e.g., room location, needed extra items, newspaper), credit card and express check-in/check-out preferences, airline frequent-flyer preferences, personal interests (e.g., activities, music, readings, spectator sports), and complimentary beverages and snacks (e.g., preferred wine, soft drinks, juice, snacks). The above information is compiled at Wyndham's headquarters and a pledge is made to the guest that, irrespective of which property in the Wyndham chain the guest travels to in the future, he or she can expect a consistent level of personalized service.

This includes a room that is located where desired and fitted with the required amenities, a welcome snack and drink that's of the guest's liking, and information that suits the traveler's interests (e.g., reading material, information about shows or sporting events). Key to the initiative's success is the realization that, while important, the technology underlying Wyndham ByRequest—including the website, the preferences databases, and integrated operational systems (e.g., PMS)— does not in and of itself deliver the ByRequest promise. As a result, Wyndham has designated staff members to support ByRequest and created a property-level position—the Wyndham ByRequest manager—who has responsibility over property-level execution, and Wyndham has developed integrated processes for delivering the ByRequest promise.

Overview

Spas are becoming such a significant component of the service menu for resorts and full service hotels that their absence, especially in amenity-rich resort environments, is glaringly obvious. Within the leisure industries in 2003, revenues related to spas ranked number four behind golf fees and dues ($19.7 million), cruise line revenues ($14.7 million), and health club revenues ($14.1 million). At $11.2 million, spa revenues outpaced amusement park revenues ($10.3 million), box office receipts ($9.5 million), and vacation ownership sales ($5.5 million). In this, we first examine trends that support a sea change in North Americans' attitude toward spa use. After evaluating spa demand demographics, we discuss the types of spas currently popular in the industry, development and operational considerations, the components of a spa experience, compensation issues, and trends in the spa industry.

SPA Demand

According to the International SPA Association research, between 2002 and 2003, 11 percent of the national population over the age of 16 made one or more spa visits. This statistic shows that one in ten Americans visited a spa during that period. Additionally, of these, 41 percent were visiting spas for the first time, indicating a larger population embracing spa usage. Age demographics show that 14 percent of clients are between the ages of 16 and 24, and over 50 percent are in the 25 to 44 age bracket.

An emerging national statistic is the number of male visits to spas. Twenty-three percent of spa visits and 29 percent of spa goers were men in 2003, trending toward special gender-oriented treatments and male-only spas being opened worldwide. Spa selection criteria are determined by a number of factors. An established and known environment—for instance, as a part of an established resort, club, or destination spa— often influences the decision, as does atmosphere, quality of treatment, and friendliness of staff. Additionally, among spa goers, nine out of ten respondents report they would return for a similar experience.

Most spa customers believe they received good value for their spa dollar. On a 10-point scale, services were given an average of 8 for value, with massage generating 8.8 on the value-for-service scale. Spa services demonstrated the highest and heaviest demand on weekends, followed by appointments after work on weekdays. Gender demographics also play a role in spa demand, as men are more likely to go for regular weekly visits after business hours or while traveling on business. Women, however, often visit spas during regular business hours. The International Hotel Resort Spa Association (IHRSA) reports that branded resort spas such as Canyon Ranch are opening in the day spa market, adding new competitive pressure on the independents. Nontraditional players are also adding product supply.

For example, corporations are creating in-house spa environments, hospitals are adding wellness as part of their repertoire, and medi-spas, with a primary focus on cosmetic surgery, are adding spa business as an additional profit centre. Health clubs are also trying to capture a piece of the pie by adding spa practices. The rationale in this market is that time-crunched patrons can benefit from the one-stop-shopping approach to fitness and wellness, but the health club operator also uses the spa as an enticement to join the fitness centre. As the day and destination spa markets become saturated, it will become imperative for survival that each operator differentiate from the competition.

The necessity for market segmentation to ensure clear communication with consumers will be a key to success in the maturing spa market. Another component of success will be a branding strategy that the consumer can immediately identify with respect to spa performance and the consumer's personal comfort level.

Health Issues and SPA Demand

Increasingly, spa goers are looking to create prolonged wellness that integrates and renews body, mind, and spirit. To that end, Eastern and Western lifestyle issues related to medicine, philosophy, and spirituality are becoming a mainstay of many spa/wellness experiences. To best deliver this, the wellness spa (located at day, destination, or resort environments) supports guest needs by creating an experience, not just a series of treatments. All the guest amenities, facilities, treatments, and programmes must be seamlessly integrated into a personally tailored guest experience. These experiences should be targeted toward couples, parents with children, and teenagers. In the early 1990s, spas were considered a natural outgrowth of fitness facilities and focused primarily on treatments related to body wellness.

As market sophistication evolved, the body-mind connection attracted consumer focus. In the beginning of the twentyfirst century, spas and marketers are overtly addressing body, mind, and spirit connections in order to respond to emerging market sensibilities.

Among the components one might find in a modern spa are services related to:

- Complementary and alternative medicine in mainstream lifestyles.
- Traditional Western medical and Eastern lifestyle/wellness practices.
- A proactive approach to overall health and the quality of one's life.
- Action spas are attracting a greater percentage of men who are looking for a way to unwind and keep active. Because of this trend, an aggressive array of activities— including cardio-circuit courses, squash, racketball and tennis, free and fixed weights, jogging, and bike paths, hikes, and water spots—is still a basic spa/wellness requirement.
- As part of the wellness experience, medical affiliations are sometimes available to provide information and to check blood pressure, heart conditions, bone density, and so on.
- Exceptional food can be tailored to virtually any dietary restriction or request.
- When examining which body treatments to include, note that salt glows and exfoliant treatments are approximately four times more popular than any other body treatment. These items are a mainstay in successful spa services.
- Guests must be able to upgrade their experience with add-ons such as eye-firming therapies and mineral-enhanced hydrotherapy soaks. Further, it is important to sell services in several time blocks so guests can select services that fit their schedule and financial budget.
- Educational programmes at many levels include classes and clinics. These programmes personally empower the guest, expand the wellness center's demand base, and encourage repeat visits. Health and wellness issues encompass cardiovascular health, holistic childrearing, the integration of Eastern and Western medical practices, indigenous spiritual practices, aging, intimacy, transition/ death, vitality, strength training, cooking programmes (macrobiotic, vegan, vegetarian, indigenous), women's issues, and so on. Traditionally, educational programmes at spas have focused primarily on personal health issues.

- Mind-body techniques may include spiritual and cultural instruction. Examples include tai chi, visualization, progressive muscle relaxation and biofeedback, labyrinth walking, meditating and chanting, sweat lodges, and storytelling.
- Extensive yoga programmes should include Hatha yoga for body control, Ashtanga yoga for cardio workout, Iyengar yoga for balance and alignment, and Kundalini yoga for breath work.
- Comprehensive touch/alternative manual therapies including chiropractic treatment and deep tissue massage (rolfing, myofascial release, nueromuscular massage, acupressure/ shiatsu, watsu, Trager massage, etc.) are a necessary component of any wellness clinic. This modality is an extension of the basic massage offered at all spas and wellness/healing centers. Practitioners who provide manual therapies should be cross-trained in the areas of subtle energy work such as reiki, chakra balancing, and chi gung. Offering alternative touch/energy therapy as a component of traditional massage has the potential to accelerate market acceptance.
- Ayurvedic treatments are popular and provide an additional link between the East-meets-West philosophy showcased in many day spas. Elements of ayurvedic treatments can be incorporated into most touch therapies.

SPAS AND THE LODGING INDUSTRY

As far back as 1993, a well-known study by David Eisenberg revealed that one-third of all patients had visited a practitioner of alternative health care in the past year, at a cost of $13.7 billion. This indicated to the medical community that the significant out-of-pocket expenses implied not only lost revenues to traditional (allopathic) doctors but also a broad dissatisfaction with mainstream medicine. A great number of people were taking the issues of health and well-being into their own control, thus setting the stage for the popularity of proactive wellness programmes.

In 1997, Eisenberg updated his study. He estimated the total number of visits to alternative medical providers at 600 million, representing an expenditure of over $27.1 billion. The number of visits to alternative care physicians in 1997 was greater than the total number of visits to traditional primary care physicians in the same year.

The increasing popularity of alternative wellness modalities, the aging of the population, and the strength of the economy are all factors that support the growth of this trend. As of this writing, it appears to continue to grow. The use of at least 1 of 16 (alternative) therapies during the previous year increased from 33.8 percent in 1990 to 42.1 percent in 1997. The fastest-growing therapies were herbal medicine, message, megavitamins, self help groups, folk remedies, energy healing, and homeopathy.

The probability of users visiting an alternative medicine practitioner increased from 36.3 percent to 46.3 percent. In both 1990 and 1997, alternative therapies were used most frequently for chronic conditions, especially back problems, anxiety, depression, and headaches. In general, it can be concluded that alternative medicine expenditure increased substantially between 1990 and 1997, and this can be attributed primarily to an increase in the proportion of the population seeking alternative therapies rather than increased visits per patient.

SPA Classification

Spa development and its attendant popularity have deep historical roots and vast potential for the hospitality industry. The term spa was once reserved for European destination resorts where guests went to "take the waters" and restore a healthy and balanced life. However, the term now is used to describe many types of facilities and amenities in the U.S. lodging industry. At one end of the spa spectrum are dedicated destination resort spas aimed primarily at those seeking a specialized combination regime of health, fitness, and pampering. Modalities and treatments include massages, unique treatments, custom dietary plans, lectures, and adventures that can include, but are not limited to, an array of activities ranging from nonsurgical facelifts to helicopter skiing.

Destination resorts, such as Miraval's Life-in-Balance and Canyon Ranch, with locations in the Berkshires in Massachusetts and the Arizona desert, draw demand because of their facilities and reputation. The primary reason for going to a destination resort spa is to enjoy the spa itself and its related activities. The destination itself is a demand generator. Closely related to a destination resort spa is the amenity spa.

The primary difference between an amenity spa and a destination spa is the scope and depth of spa services. Amenity spas, while sometimes quite extensive, support the resort environment, whereas destination spas are the focus of the resort environment. In situations where a full-service, high-end hotel is located in an urban environment and has a significantly large spa component, the spa can operate as both an amenity spa (to the hotel) and a day spa (to the local community).

Later in this chapter, we study the case of the Westin Los Angeles Century City's 35,000-square-foot Spa Mystique. This spa supports the needs of the hotel's convention and individual travelers while experiencing heavy local day spa use. Middle-market hotel properties now feel obliged to add a spa as an amenity; however, due to capital and real estate restraints, often they cannot provide a full-service location. As a result, this sector has seen an explosion in poorly conceived and executed spa additions that provide the owner the opportunity to add "...and spa" at the end of the business name. These are often no more than the result of subcontracting a massage therapist and converting the guest room closest to the swimming pool into an exercise room.

These spas seldom surprise and delight their guests and often reflect poorly on the spa industry overall. Fortunately, the sophistication of the industry is making it harder and harder for the "...and spas" to succeed. As the spa industry matures, certain development trends are emerging. In 2005, the spa industry was considered the fastest-growing segment of the travel, hospitality, and leisure market, showing 26 percent growth from 2002 to 2004. Spas are no longer considered a niche industry but rather an entity unto themselves.

The spa industry is made up of the following segments, each with its own characteristics and operational opportunities:

- Destination spas
- Resort hotel spas
- Day spas
- Medical spas
- Mineral springs
- Club spas

Destination Spas

A destination spa is one whose sole purpose is to provide programmes and facilities that support lifestyle improvements and enhance guest health. The services offered are professionally administered and include fitness, education, and lectures on lifestyle, nutrition, and disease prevention. Because of their healthful orientation, destination spas often provide programmes that support postoperative conditions, address various addictions, and provide tools to cope with serious, prolonged illness.

The destination spa industry constitutes only 1.6 percent of the total spa industry, per the International Spa Association's Industry Study (Thacker, 2004). However, the growth in the development and use of destination spas reflects the market's trend toward wellness and health as a major component in spa menus.

Resort Spas/Amenity Spas

Resort spas are located on the grounds of vacation resorts where treatments for mind, body, and spirit are offered to complement other resort activities such as golf, tennis, horseback riding, skiing, and water sports. Healthful spa cuisine is on the menu as an option, complementing traditional offerings. In the evenings, guests can enjoy resort pastimes like dancing and live entertainment. Children's programmes are also offered.

According to the ISPA Spa Industry Study, the resort spa represents 14 percent of spa locations in North America but accounts for almost 41 percent of the total industry revenue, 27 percent of all spa visits, and 26 percent of the industry's employees. A luxury resort spa has the ambience of a secluded retreat on the grounds of a first-class resort. Set in beautiful surroundings, these resorts commonly have world-class golf courses and other excellent recreational facilities. Gourmet dining and exceptional spa therapies are not only expected but demanded.

Day Spas

Day spas are designed to provide a healing, beautifying, or pampering experience in a short period. Guests may book individual treatments that last as little as an hour or a package of treatments that take up to a whole day. Found throughout North America, day spas are freestanding or located in health clubs, hotels, and department stores. The day spa industry constitutes 72.2 percent of the total industry revenues, per the International Spa Association's 2004 Spa Industry Study.

The large percentage of day spas and their growth pattern reflect spa goers' time crunch. Day spas can be owner-operated or chain affiliated. Preliminary data from ISPA's 2004 survey show that industry growth is still robust. As of midyear 2004, there was a total of 12,000 spas nationally, of which 8,700 were day spas. These numbers reflect 25 percent growth in the industry in general and 20 percent growth exclusively in this market. The total number of day spa visits in 2003 was 81.2 million. However, only 13 percent of the general population had used a spa in the prior three-year period, indicating that the industry still has large growth potential.

Medical Spas

Medical treatments in various spa environments represent a significant trend in the scope, depth, and inclusiveness of numerous spas. Medical spa treatments can range from elective, reconstructive surgery to noninvasive Eastern modalities incorporating elements of Eastern philosophy that draw on the body-mind-spirit connection to create positive, measurable changes in the client/patient.

Slightly over half (51 percent) of the medical spas in North America have a partnership with a medical doctor, and 26 percent have a doctor on staff. The remaining configurations include being located in a doctor's office or having licensed staff members. Botox and microdermabrasion are the two most popular treatments, followed by chemical peels and laser hair removal. In North America, allopathic or Western medical procedures found in medical spas often incorporate Eastern-based treatments.

Day, destination, and resort/amenity spas are adding medical treatments to their spa menus. Part of this trend is directly attributed to market demand, and part is attributed to health insurance plans that reimburse for some procedures. According to the ISPA 2004 survey, medical spas are the fastest-growing spa segment with respect to number of locations. The average annual growth in medical spas by location since 1999 is approximately 45 percent.

Cumulative growth from 1999 to 2004 is 205 percent and from 2002 to 2004, 109 percent. Medical spas generated an estimated 1,900,000 visits in 2003, representing 1.39 percent of the total spa visits. However, this percentage of visits accounts for approximately 2.1 percent of the total industry revenues, reflecting the lucrative nature of this segment of the industry.

Mineral Springs Spas

Many mineral springs spas are considered to be the original spa prototype, where guests go to "take the waters." Mineral springs spas, by definition, are located at naturally occurring mineral springs, and by number of locations represent 2.8 percent of the total spa industry, or 1.3 percent of the total industry revenues, making this one of the more modest income producing segments of the spa industry.

The popularity of mineral springs spas is reflected in a cumulative growth from 1999 to 2004 of 143 percent. Growth from 2002 to 2004 represents only 15 percent, implying that the number of sites available directly affects the growth in this segment.

Club Spas

Club spas lack a lodging component, and their primary objective is to facilitate daily fitness activities. Many club spas' services complement the primary fitness component of the club by offering sports massage (deep tissue), chiropractic services, physiotherapy, and related treatments that address issues of pain management, flexibility, and mobility. By location, club spas represent 5.8 percent of the total spa industry in North America and account for approximately 3.7 percent of the industry's revenues. Growth in the club spa portion of the spa industry is the lowest of all spa segments. Between 2002 and 2004, cumulative club spa growth was only 3 percent.

SPA OPERATIONS

Spas as an Operating Department Historically, spa operations were treated by management similarly to other revenue departments, like catering and restaurants. These departments were simply perceived as an amenity needed to attract guests to the hotel. As long as the department broke even, or didn't lose too much money, their ability to increase occupancy was deemed sufficient justification for their existence. However, in the late 1990s, hotel spas followed the path of other operating departments and transformed from support facilities to profit centers. This trend is strong and continues today. In 1999, PKF Consulting identified only 30 hotels in the United States, thousands that report data to the PKF, extensive spa facilities and analyzed the financial performance of those properties and their spa departments. Dedicated destination spa resorts were not included in the analysis due to an insufficient sample. While spas were a relatively small source of revenues for the sample properties, spa revenues grew at a relatively strong pace. In 1999, spa revenues for the subject sample represented just 3.3 percent of total sales.

However, from 1998 to 1999, spa revenues grew 16.6 percent. This compares to revenue growth rates of 5.2 percent for rooms, 12.2 percent for food, and 3.2 percent for telecommunications, and a 0.3 percent decline in revenues for the beverage department. During 1999, the spa departments in the sample of hotels averaged a departmental profit margin of 30.7 percent. However, spa department profits did grow a strong 51.3 percent from 1998 to 1999. Spas mirror and enhance trends in the lodging industry. Drawing heavily from residential design and the use of technology, hotel designers and operators create a spa experience that:

- Complements the lodging experience
- Drives occupancy levels
- Enhances average daily rate
- Provides a distinctive marketing advantage North American spas are rapidly becoming more segmented, pursuing market niches well outside the traditional ladies-who-lunch demographic.

Adventure spas, fitness spas, children spas, family spas, and even pet spas are part of a new generation of spa facilities, spa programmes—and, most importantly, spa aficionados. Spas now attract a much wider demographic that includes men, women, couples, children, teenagers, and families. Since the early part of the twenty-first century, spas have been redirecting their menus to include stress relief and results oriented therapies. By focusing on the social benefits of hanging out in a safe, relaxing place, they not only address current market needs but also support the development of spa programmes that can be incorporated into virtually any leisure-oriented environment or level of lodging. In particular, destination spas and full-service resorts provide platforms that have both the infrastructure and the economies of scale to support cutting-edge spa treatments, sometimes also referred to as spa modalities.

Spas are no longer solely about frivolous self-indulgence and luxurious pampering. They are being reevaluated and repackaged with a broader emphasis on self-care, stress relief, emotional balancing, and preventative (as opposed to reactive) wellness modalities. This trend is being embraced by aging baby boomers as an adjunct to traditional health care. Because of this trend in health care, hotels and resorts have acknowledged and embraced the need for full-service spas as part of their amenities and facilities. The inclusion of a well-integrated spa can provide additional (and lucrative) sales and marketing opportunities.

Conversely, the exclusion of a spa facility may disqualify a property from consideration. Ironically, many hotel guests may dismiss a property out of hand for lacking a spa not because they require the services of a spa but rather because its absence may imply other areas of the hotel are also deficient in meeting current market expectations. Is it logical, then, that all full-service hotels and resorts without a spa should, without hesitation, incorporate one into their property? Numerous factors must be considered in developing or repositioning a spa, especially in chain environments where the lodging brand is already established.

Because spas are capital- and labour-intensive, they must materially enhance the property's revenue stream to be considered viable. In addition to creating spa revenue, a spa facility also must extend length of stay, drive room rates, enhance shoulder and low-season demand, augment food and beverage revenues, and capture new market segments.

Successful spa operations start with a standardized level of procedures and a prioritized sensitivity to guest needs. As it is for all departments in a lodging environment (or business models in the freestanding day and medical spa world), profitability is essential. Especially in a spa environment, a dynamic balance is essential to meet the fiscal requirements of the owners and the physical needs of the guest.

A savvy spa manager continually monitors the spa and hotel operations to ensure that everything possible is being done to enhance the synergy of the two entities. Constant monitoring also provides an early warning system to the spa operator if revenues are falling or if expenses are not in line with anticipated revenues or budgeted amounts. Spotting these trends early enables the manager to take efficient, proactive steps to ensure that positive trends are enhanced and negative ones controlled.

Constant monitoring sets a standard of operations, which is an excellent way to train and motivate employees. It also puts employees on notice that the spa is a well-run business with extensive attention to detail, which should discourage any actions that might not be in the best interest of the spa's reputation and profitability.

CUSTOMER SERVICE TRAINING

A spa's reputation is easily made or destroyed by its level of customer service. Guests can forgive an occasional shortcoming if the level of service is exceptional. For this reason, it is essential that all spas have an integrated quality management programme that provides ongoing training to assist its employees in addressing customers' expectations. Customer service training (CST) helps ensure that guests' expectations are exceeded. In a spa environment, expectations are usually very high, and a trusting bond can be quickly established if the spa employees are sensitive to guest needs. The guest's arrival sequence, starting at the front desk, initiates the spa ritual that brings the spa guest to a place of trust, relaxation, and rejuvenation.

CST is proactive and provides employees with the tools they need to meet or exceed guest expectations. Guest CST is a never-ending, all-inclusive process that bridges textbook training scenarios with operational realities. The traditionally high turnover of spa employees in the hospitality industry requires that CST be introduced as a part of the orientation process and reinforced regularly. Nonproductive training time (time that does not directly produce revenue for the spa) is actually a minor expense when compared to the expenses related to employee turnover, poor service, dissatisfied customers, and, ultimately, loss of business and reputation. Budgets must include CST as a nonoptional employee expense. For long-term success, CST is vital when margins are tight, business is slow, and turnover is high.

There is a strong correlation between high employee turnover and low CST. Employees should know that the training programme is an investment in them. CST gives the employee the means to understand what is expected of them as a representative of the establishment and identifies what guests expect from their visit. Seeing the process from the guest's point of view helps employees meet or exceed expectations.

This minimizes the need to provide discounts or compensation in cases of service delivery problems. Discounting or "comping" goods and services is a knee-jerk response to poor service and should be reserved for the last effort in service recovery; CST should stress this. An inclusive training programme is the engine behind stellar customer service and guest loyalty. CST should be seamless; while it predominately addresses the needs of the guest, the programme also includes instruction on profitability and yield management, thus addressing the needs of the owner as well.

In order to meet or exceed profitability goals, customer service must be delivered in a fiscally responsible manner. Employees must understand customer service in the operational context of the property in which they are employed. Minimizing the expense of a CST programme starts with the proper selection of employees. While there is no steadfast guarantee that a potential employee will work out over the long haul, first impressions, prior work experience, references, and, above all, attitude and enthusiasm are indications of whether or not it is appropriate to hire and invest the time and money in an applicant.

Management's expectations of guest service delivery should be clearly articulated and integrated into the corporate culture and reinforced daily at all levels and in all departments. Employees, no matter what their responsibility, position, or tenure, must be treated with the same level of respect and dignity that management requires for their guests. Reinforcing the tenets of customer service within the corporate culture provides the employee with the tools to do the right thing—that is, to ask, "What do I need to do to make a spa guest happy? How do I exceed their expectations?" Sometimes the little details reap the greatest rewards. Employee empowerment is a key component in CST. As an employee's experience and skill base develops (and as management becomes comfortable with an employee's performance), levels of empowerment should be increased proportionately. Empowerment is a vote of confidence in an employee and a way to quickly resolve problems as they arise.

This situation is said by spa managers to increase job satisfaction, and the employee's ownership of his or her position. CST also requires a strong foundation in the technical skills of how a department runs. Routine procedures, appropriate lines of oral and written communication, and what is expected of each employee in the normal course of his or her shift help minimize problems. When problems do occur, a strong foundation in technical skills makes it easier for the employee to create alternative solutions for the guest. Training draws on employees' EQ (emotional quotient) as well as their IQ (intelligence quotient). CST requires that employees draw on their ability to empathize with the guest. This starts by training employees to suspend judgment of a situation, become attentive listeners, and know the right questions to ask. This allows them to understand what the actual problem is. Training employees in this type of customer service delivery assists them in focusing on the salient issues and creating ways to address them. Because CST is ongoing, employees can benefit from their peers' experiences.

Vehicles to exchange this type of information can be as informal as role-playing and round-table discussions, or as structured as an employee newsletter. Incentives, acknowledgments, and rewards for excellent customer service delivery are an integral part of the training programme. Successful CST supports a skilled and unified staff, which translates into profitable operations. CST is an investment in property that owners can't afford not to make.

Provide Value, Create

Value Spa aficionados are savvy. They are looking to be indulged, pampered, and nurtured, not fleeced. Setting price points with market sensitivity can create tremendous customer loyalty. Because spas are no longer a one-time indulgence but rather a lifestyle choice, it is important to price services competitively and provide incentives for customers to return regularly. Numerous variables are involved in the development and operation of a spa as part of a hotel or resort. Doing one's homework is essential to success.

When a spa is developed or repositioned correctly, it can be a lucrative and rewarding experience. When it is not developed correctly, it can be a financial liability that haunts the spa director and jeopardizes the hotel's market position. If spas and their programming are not an integrated part of the hotel's future development, the property may lose a significant competitive opportunity. Spa-less hotels or poorly run properties have an inherent competitive market disadvantage. Not only do they find it more difficult to penetrate the market but they also often lose market share.

Resort Spas

The ratio of guest rooms to treatment rooms is based on many factors, including the anticipated return on investment to the owners, the topography of the site, the scope and theme of the spa, and the competition. In a destination resort, where the reason for the spa facilities is the reason for the trip, there should be an average of 1 treatment room for every 4 to 5 guest rooms. At the other end of the spectrum, such as a casino hotel, the spa is definitely an amenity, and 1 treatment room should be built for every 50 to

100 guest rooms. The spas at lower-end hotel properties normally are limited in scope and are often between 3,000 and 6,000 square feet, whereas luxury spas at full-service, high-end resorts average between 10,000 and 35,000 square feet.

These ranges vary based on each hotel's specific circumstances, including seasonality, accessibility, meeting space, fill patterns, and local demand. Each market and each lodging product must be individually evaluated to assess the appropriate ratio of treatment rooms to guest rooms. Another matrix that measures the viability of a resort or hotel spa is the cost to build the facility. Once again, a number of factors support various outcomes in this process, including the amount of available land, the finishes of the spa, the finishes of the hotel (these should be compatible), and the need to develop a spa either vertically or horizontally.

Vertical spas are most often built in environments where land is scarce or the allocated footprint for the spa is too small for one floor. Vertical construction always raises the price per square foot, as load distribution, drainage, and the weight of equipment and water must be factored into the construction design and budget. The cost to construct a resort or destination spa can range from as low as $200 per square foot to over $450 per square foot. High land-value areas and plumbing-rich design schemes will send cost dramatically above this range.

Overview most spas dictates how the space is allocated and where the income is generated. Spas should aim to have at least 50 percent of their total space—their prime real estate—produce direct revenue. Secondary real estate is the support and public areas necessary for atmosphere and supporting functions that assist in delivering the spa services. Secondary spa real estate includes areas where people can prepare for or relax from their spa treatments. These secondary areas are an important component in the spa development plan, as they allow guests to prolong their experience, which enhances the perceived value. If guests are hurried from their massage or facial out of the spa and back onto the street, the magic that is created can be abruptly snapped and the overall spa experience is compromised.

Conversely, if a guest is allowed to soak and relax for hours after a body wrap is completed, emotionally speaking, the cost of the body wrap is amortized over the entire spa experience and not just for the time the client was enjoying the body wrap in the spa's prime real estate. Combination rooms account for about 36 percent of North American spa spaces, but because of the various treatments offered in them, a revenue percentage generated from these spaces is hard to predict.

Combination spaces allow the spa to address surges in demand for specific treatments and at the same time be flexible and respond to global market changes. Massage rooms account for approximately 27 percent of the total space in North American spas but 47 percent of the spa revenue. Given these factors, an operator would need a compelling reason to not include massage on the spa menu. Facial treatment areas reflect 19 percent of the total spa space and result in about 33 percent of the spa's overall revenue.

Wet rooms, often the most underutilized portions of the spa, account for 7 percent of the space and revenue. Because many spa modalities involve water therapies, many spa developers and owners believe that wet rooms are essential, even if they seem underutilized. Because wet rooms are one of the most expensive components of a spa, it is essential that they be utilized to their fullest extent. Packaging wet room treatments with other spa services is one way to better utilize the space and create value for the spa.

SPA TRENDS

On-Site Industry Trends Anti-aging treatments and products are driving much of spa menu and retail development. This calls for devoting a treatment room to outpatient medical procedures. Programming and spa menu items include sun damage treatments, chemical peels for skin renewal, and other rejuvenation techniques that build on repeat procedures. Commensurately, spas are developing retail product lines that can take the spa experience home and continue the wellness regime. Gift card sales are driving new users to spas. In the friends and family sector as well as the corporate gift-giving world, day spa certificates are creating demand that is not directly user driven. Third-party purchasing brings to spas clients who may not normally have chosen the location or treatment, creating a large but undefinable market demand.

Regional specialties that relate to indigenous and climatic influences continue to create unique spa experiences based on site-specific supply. This has excellent leverage potential for spa operators working to differentiate their product matrices in densely operated areas.

It is important to position services for stress relief, especially to the male business traveler. Spa programming that requires a limited amount of special equipment and minimal changes to a property's infrastructure can do this.

Impulse appointments

"Life is uncertain, but I want a massage (reflexology appointment, yoga class, etc.) now!" This trend may result in developing adjunct programmes for oncall staff resources. The as-needed portion of the programme limits a hotel's payroll burden and other related fixed costs. Of course, this implies existing core programmes and facilities where these programmes can be developed and supported.

Shift in perspective

Self-indulgence, pampering, and luxury are being reevaluated and repackaged with a new, broader emphasis on self-care, stress relief, and emotional balancing. This is reflected in spa programming, the menu of services, food and beverage outlets, and spa-related retail. The retail positioning and spa programming components represent huge untapped revenue opportunities.

Changes in demographic use profile

Historically, the greatest segment of spa goers was women between the ages of 35 and 55. More couples and families are expected to visit the spa together as an alternative social/ recreational activity. This trend has the potential to extend business-related stays, fill business hotels on the weekend, and create demand for destinations. It is important to understand this trend when evaluating ways to increase market penetration in a down market.

Medical affiliations

For some markets, an affiliation with a medical centre or group in the area can be established to provide treatments such as acupuncture, nutritional assessment, laser therapies (hair removal and wrinkle reduction), Botox injections, collagen treatments, chemical peels, laser resurfacing, body contouring, microderm abrasion, and vascular procedures. When creating these types of relationships, it is essential that spa owners thoroughly investigate the legal disclosure and liability implications of being an affiliated medical service provider.

Green environments

A spa can be ecologically sensitive by incorporating environmentally friendly features into the operation. By proactively supporting programmes and products that are earth friendly, the spa does something good for the environment, provides a service to the community, and creates a competitive advantage and a unique selling point that may provide significant returns, especially in a highly competitive market. _ Global Industry Trends Trends in day, destination, and amenity spas influence each other. According to Susan Ellis (2004), president of Spa Finder, a spa marketing company, after the rise of the medical spa and broadening spa participation by men and teens, spa use is expected to become more popular in 2005 and beyond. Spa Finder's trends to watch for are abstracted:

- Those personal elements that make the spa experience special will find their way into the design of personal living spaces in private homes.
- Private, gated living communities will develop around central spa facilities, much like golf and fly-in communities.
- Some spas will compete on the far outer reaches of luxury, with ever-increasing rare and proprietary products and services.
- Spas will make house calls. Legitimate spas will offer out-call services where spa technicians travel with appropriate equipment and personnel to a client's home, office, or hotel room.
- Destination spas and resorts will develop market segments focused

on personal goals—everything from spiritual awareness to sexual health to detoxification.
- The spa travel segment will grow, with more clientele booking through online portals.
- Medical spas will continue to be popular and will add alternative therapies and couple traditional medical treatment with spa luxury and innovation.
- Day spas will not grow their exotic menus much more but rather focus on the traditional; destination/resort spas will be the businesses that experiment with more exotic services and products.
- Specialized cuisine developed for spa guest consumption will find its way into mainstream grocery/specialty food offerings. Restaurants may also add lines of healthy spa cuisine to their menus.
- Eco spas—those designed and operated around green principles of management— will become a growing segment of the industry.

The foregoing discussion and explanation of the service and amenity potential of spas of varying types strongly suggests that they will continue to maintain a position of importance in the inventory of hotel services. Even the most modest of spa offerings can enhance a hotel guest's lodging experience. Someday basic spa services may be arranged for at even moderately priced lodging properties.

DIMENSIONS OF CUSTOMER EXPECTATION OF SERVICE

As the consumer market segment of the Internet economy continues to grow, the role of customer service in the emerging logistics supply chain systems will continue to change. Therefore, the need to improve logistics customer service (LCS) to consumers is greater than ever before. Finding meaningful ways to meet consumer service expectations requires LCS programmes that strategically blend website service activities (e.g., online ordering procedures) with offline logistics supply chain activities (e.g., order delivery). This balance may be a key strategy in satisfying and maintaining loyalty relationships with online consumers. Yet very little is understood about the nature of website-enabled LCS and the impact on online customer loyalty, although the level of e-logistics service expectations is often thought to be higher than that demanded by customers in brick-and-mortar environments.

The purpose of this study is to examine:
- The factors that determine the level of perceived LCS quality in the Internet-enabled logistics supply chain, and
- The impact of LCS quality on customer loyalty towards online retailers'websites.

Internet-enabled logistics supply chain refers to the total logistics system of transportation, warehousing, inventory, order processing, information flow, and website-enabled order processing procedures that drive the level of perceived quality of LCS in this system. Perceived LCS quality is defined as the level of expectation-minus performance gap and customer intended loyalty is defined as the tendency of online consumers to repurchase from the same website, as reflected in repurchase intentions or intention to recommend a website to peers. Following conventional practice, LCS was defined as the total output of the logistics system, but with emphasis on cognitive impact: perceived service speed and consistency of service speed, perceived availability of merchandise on the retailer's website and in the supply chain, and perceived responsiveness of the retailer.

This study contributes to the literature on two levels. At the conceptual level, the study provides an empirical validation of the logistics customer service-customer loyalty linkage in the online environment. While this linkage has been widely established in traditional business-to-business markets, it remains to be established in the online environment where the impersonal and self-service nature of customer service may raise doubts about the validity of the LCS-customer linkage.

At the managerial level, the study suggests ways to create a consumer-oriented online logistics customer service strategy by identifying the relevant web-based and traditional supply chain logistics activities that are important in creating and maintaining loyalty relationships with online consumers. As with all service activities, not all website features are likely to be relevant to consumer perception of online LCS quality. Moreover, different website features are likely to play different roles in consumer perception of LCS quality. Thus, this study provides insight into which website features should be emphasized in the different phases of the Internet-enabled logistics supply chain.

The following discussion presents an overview of the influence of website design strategy on LCS quality assessment among online consumers. Using the consumer disconfirmation theory as a theoretical foundation, a conceptual framework is proposed including the hypotheses isolating influences of key website design features on LCS quality, followed by the field study that was conducted to specifically examine the service encounter evaluation of 373 online transactions. Finally, analysis and findings are discussed followed by a discussion of the managerial implications and suggestions for future research.

DIMENSIONS OF QUALITY

At the time of exchange information concerning features, aesthetics, perceived quality and tangibles are observable while performance, conformance and serviceability are available with additional effort on the part of the customer. However, reliability and durability are largely unknown for the specific product, but can be identified for the category of product. Experience with the product or service is required to establish the extent of those latter dimensions. Further, responsiveness, assurance and empathy are generally available but are still under the on-going control of the seller, and therefore are subject to change over time.

The"Customer's Perception of Quality Dimensions over Time"was compiled by a focus group of several academics/consultants to industry. The level of each dimension's importance and the information available to the customer were determined based on the focus group members'many years of experience. A series of empirical research projects are necessary to determine if these findings are generally held to be true by companies in one or more industrial SEC codes.

Further evaluations of these patterns and their availability would afford insight into the customer's level of satisfaction with its product or service purchases over the expected period of usage. A service provider may be chosen based on evident embedded dimensions, promised supporting dimensions and the price charged. However, repeat business comes from satisfaction

Satisfaction: A Model of Quality Dimension's Desirability Over Time

The desirability/importance of quality dimensions could be depicted from the time of exchange to the end of the product/service usability.

Each of the three groups of quality dimensions can be classified respectively by:

Dimensions embedded in the product/service, support dimensions for the product/service, and price. The correct combination and/or level of these three groups of quality dimensions would contribute vastly to any particular customer's degree of satisfaction derived from the transaction.

Certain EB1 dimensions (performance, features, conformance, serviceability and aesthetics) will be prime contributors to customer satisfaction at the time of the transaction due to the immediacy of sight, feel, sound, smell and taste of the product/service itself. These will diminish as the product loses its feel of newness. EB2 will become more important to the customer's satisfaction as the positive or negative value of the product's reliability and durability play out. The second component (support), depicted by (SP), can increase or decrease in importance due to the continuing presence or absence of the supporting quality dimensions.

Quantitative Methodology for the General Model

Traditionally, managers of the selling firm tend to view quality as inherent (embedded) in the product and/or service being sold. This leads to the mind-set that quality has been established when the product and/or service has been delivered to the buyer. Therefore, if the product did not live up to the advertised, expected levels of quality, the buyer was stuck with it and the seller's reputation"takes the hit".

This chapter takes the position that some of the dimensions of quality are still under the control of the seller and therefore can still be augmented after the point of sale or delivery. If some of these embedded dimensions do not live up to their billing, then other dimensions can be modified or enhanced to preserve the perception of overall quality of the product and the provider.

For example, if an auto manufacturer found that an unusually large percentage (i.e., 5% versus 1%) of their transmissions developed a significant problem that required those transmissions to be replaced within 75,000 miles of use, the auto manufacturer could do one of four things:

- Do nothing;
- Test all transmissions currently in stock before installing (if possible);
- Remove all the transmissions in stock from the assembly process; or
- Enhance the warranty on all transmissions.

The first option would create a frustrated, angry customer that most likely would not become a repeat customer for the auto manufacturer. The second and third options would be very expensive, and while the cost of these actions could be passed along to the customer, it may place the auto manufacturer at a price disadvantage. The fourth option would be the best for the auto manufacturer as it would require action only on those transmissions that failed and would preserve their quality reputation while the problem was researched, resolved and incorporated into the transmission's design.

This quick, no-questions-asked service, would create a customer that is confident in the auto manufacturer's ability to handle future problems (they would be WOWED!). The enhanced warranty would represent a modification of a controllable dimension of quality that would allow the auto manufacturer to preserve the customer's perception of the overall quality of the purchased product (automobile) and the provider (auto manufacturer).

7

Consumer Decision Rules and Implications for Hotel Choice

CONSUMERS' CHOICES

Consumers' choices are influenced by the goals they attempt to achieve. Once a person has recognized a need, such as the need for accommodation when traveling for business or pleasure, he or she engages in an information search to identify alternatives from which to choose. Understanding how consumers evaluate competing alternatives in their purchase decision processes enables marketers in the hospitality industry to design better advertising and promotional campaigns leading to a more favourable evaluation of their offerings in travellers' eyes.This is an important step in increasing the likelihood that consumers will choose their offering as opposed to that of competitors.

Given that most travellers' destinations offer several hotels, how do people choose among them? The answer to this question lies, in part, in research on consumers' attitudes and their relation to purchase intentions and subsequent purchase Behaviour. This stage describes several methods consumers may use to make choices based on the evaluation of identified alternatives.

Attitude is the tendency to respond in a consistently favourable or unfavourable manner towards a target. Important to marketers is that, if measured accurately, attitudes are predictive of Behavioural intentions and relatively stable over time.

Simply put, consumers generally form intentions to choose a hotel brand towards which they hold positive attitudes. Behavioural intentions, however, do not always translate into corresponding Behaviour. For example, although some consumers have preferences and therefore form intentions to stay at Fairfield Inn when traveling across the country, they might end up choosing other forms of accommodation from time to time.Why would they act inconsistently with their intentions?

Traveling with friends who have different attitudes and preferences, temporary price reductions of competitors, or the fact that a Fairfield Inn is not readily available in a specific area might be reasons for inconsistencies between Behavioural intentions to stay at a Fairfield Inn and actual choice Behaviour.

Despite situational factors sometimes influencing travellers' choices, attitudes are ultimately useful in predicting actual Behaviour; changing or strengthening the basis of consumer attitudes may therefore increase the likelihood of consumers engaging in desired Behaviours. In order to change attitudes and subsequent related Behaviour, marketers must understand a few basic decision rules associated with consumer attitudes. We introduce decision rules likely to be implemented by different segments of consumers under varying market conditions.

CONSUMERS DECISION RULES

Decision rules are strategies consumers use to choose among alternatives. Several factors can influence what decision rule consumers ultimately apply in a specific situation. Typically, the more important and less frequent a purchase decision is, the more time and effort consumers are willing to expend making that decision. Choosing a resort at which to spend a twenty-fifth wedding anniversary, for example, is a decision most consumers face only once and therefore are likely to take a relatively long time to make, and they are likely to be careful and thorough in evaluating alternatives.

On the other hand, a salesperson traveling frequently in a familiar territory likely chooses a hotel using a routine process where far less time and consideration are given to alternatives. Further, brand-loyal customers might choose to stay with the same hotel chain whenever possible, thereby avoiding a situation where they are forced to choose among alternatives. In general, the stronger a consumer is motivated to search and the greater the risk associated with a choice, the greater the complexity of the decision rule he or she implements.

Another important characteristic of modeling decisions is the fact that people often do not attempt to optimize choice. If a person's goal is optimal choice, considerably more time and effort is typically required to identify and evaluate alternatives.

Therefore, consumers often choose a satisfactory alternative in order to save time and effort. The use of decision rules in these instances enables people to take shortcuts in making decisions in the face of the apparently unlimited or overwhelming amounts of information available regarding all possible alternatives. Consumers usually work with a consideration set so they do not have to work as hard cognitively when required to make a decision in a given product category. They then make a final decision from this reduced set of alternatives.

Such decision rules are referred to as *heuristics* or rules of thumb. Employing heuristics, people save time and limit complex information processing while still making reasonable or satisfactory choices based on the few brand attributes or characteristics most important to them at the time of choice. In the context of hotel choice, brand attributes are things like location, room rates, and availability of a swimming pool, restaurant, and so forth.

Although the number of consumer decision rules is almost infinite and likely varies by consumer, basic categories and a few specific examples serve as useful tools in modeling and predicting traveller decisions.

Two general categories of decision rules are:

1. Compensatory and
2. Noncompensatory.

Compensatory Decision Rules

Compensatory decision rules model consumers as deriving an overall brand evaluation such that alternatives performing poorly on one attribute can *compensate* for their respective shortcomings by positive evaluations of other attributes. For example, a high-priced hotel might not be perceived positively on the dimension of room rates by some travellers; however, these same travellers might be willing to spend more money knowing they will receive better service or that the hotel is conveniently located—that is, in this example, service and location compensate for the perceived disadvantage of high room rates. The multi-attribute attitude model described in the next part is perhaps the most popular compensatory decision rule.

CUSTOMER NEEDS TO SATISFACTION

Customer satisfaction is a crucial part of marketing, pricing, and yield management. Any pricing strategy established by the hotel management must attract customers willing to pay the specified rate.While price is a determinator of the customer profile the hotel is looking for, it is also an indicator of the quality of services and the market segment the hotel is competing in.

Therefore, yield management uses information about targeted customers' purchasing Behaviour and product sales to develop pricing strategy together with inventory control that delivers products that are better matched to customer needs, create greater demand, and, on that account, produce greater revenues. Lieberman states that yield management is the process of maximizing profits from the sale of perishable assets, such as hotel rooms, by controlling price and inventory and improving service through systemization.

An exact definition of the target market is essential. There is a definite and firm perception in the psyche of the customer, who views the price as the value forthcoming. Therefore, the eventual satisfaction of the customer is the paramount task of the pricing mechanism. This is the make-or-break factor of the entire hotel, especially if the value expected does not match the price.

ROLE OF TECHNOLOGY

While the approach to hotel pricing is still ruled by supply and demand, speed and sophistication of room-rate yield or revenue maximization is now much increased due to two technological factors: yield management software and Internet bookings.

Yield management software packages enable hotels to use a higher number of roomrate levels, or buckets, and to control inventory for rate availability in real time. Each level may consist of several room rates open under given conditions to yield a maximum profit. Traditionally, hotels used between three and five rate levels; otherwise, the adjustment became too complex for the human brain to work with. The introduction of software removed this barrier, and some hotel chains now use up to ten rate levels.This allows implementation of much narrower ranges for each bucket, thus optimizing price elasticity. This further means the software model recognizes the point at which the same number of bookings can be achieved at a higher rate.

Online monitoring of room inventory in real time facilitates the timing of the adjustment. So far, the biggest limitation is the reliability of historical data. Even in its imperfect form, the system has made a difference. However, hotel managers are fully aware that it takes years to develop brand recognition and quality but just a push of a button to damage or even destroy it, if the pricing is not set up knowledgeably. As the technology becomes more sophisticated, it will eliminate such questionable practices as overbooking, which aims at compensating for last-minute cancellations by taking in more than 100 per cent reservations. Besides the question of whether overbooking is ethical and, in some countries, even illegal, better technology would definitely improve the quality of service provided by properties that engage in this practice.

Another area where technological advancement had a great impact on hotel pricing is the Internet. Its use as a booking tool has created a new level of pricing transparency and tiered competition. It also penetrated the negotiation of corporate rates. Many hotels see the effect of the Internet as both good and bad.The good side is that website bookings are growing every day. As more customers become familiar with their favourite hotel websites, hotel companies have started investing heavily in website development and upkeep, which gives them several advantages. First, the cost of online bookings is lower than for bookings made through other distribution channels. Companies do not have to pay commission because the booking is direct, circumventing all intermediaries. Online booking also provides an opportunity to monitor inventory in real time without reliance on a distributor willing to share and regularly supply data. Last but not least, it generates loyal customers by making them eligible for bonus points, which they cannot earn if they use an Internet intermediary.

That is exactly where the flip side of the Internet lies. The intermediaries are getting more powerful and growing significantly in volume. Because most of them show all hotel rates on their website, they make the information accessible to any computer user. One way to meet the challenge of more powerful intermediaries, especially if hotels need to move inventory, is to utilize auctions where the name of the hotel is not disclosed to the customer until the transaction is finalized. Such action, however, calls for extreme caution so that it does not damage a hotel's reputation or threaten its strategic partnerships.

As intermediaries become bigger, rate transparency will increase to the point where it will drive the market, especially when computer literacy and Internet access become the norm.

Moreover, the Internet allows nonbranded hotels to compete more heavily with the branded hotels because they can now be displayed just as readily. Without significant advertising expense, they can compete on price. For some markets this does not matter, especially when the brand is powerful enough to charge the premium and get the business.

In highly competitive markets, however, the competition creates an additional strain for the individual property. Many branded hotels must now compete with other brands through the traditional distribution channels and with nonbranded hotels on the Internet, which, in principle, lowers hotel rates. A frequently adopted strategy is to invest heavily in website development and customer loyalty programmes, assuring excellent website functionality and that customers are rewarded for booking directly through the hotel website rather than through the website of a thirdparty intermediary. Both Fairmont and Starwood, for example, utilize their high-quality loyalty programmes in this way.

Internet booking also changed the way corporate accounts are negotiated. Because many companies now require that their employees make business travel arrangements via the corporate website, the placement of a hotel or a brand on this booking tool is of strategic importance. Being listed first in the accommodation part, for example, may bring in a higher volume of business and thus substantiate a lower negotiated rate.

LONG-TERM STRATEGY TOR THE INTERNET

Because hotels cannot expect that Internet distributors will go out of business, they smartly conclude that a partnership with the devil is better than a fight with him. Besides using their own websites, hotel companies are also making sure that the cost of their transactions goes down continuously so they can compete even at lower rates—while maintaining a good relationship with their carefully selected online intermediaries.

There is a large number of distributors to choose from. On one end of the spectrum is, for example, Expedia, which allows participating hotels to control their rates, meaning a hotel can change its rates any time it wants.At the other end are companies, such as Hotel Reservation Network that bind hotels contractually to a locked rate that cannot be changed. Some hotel chains do not want to partner with these distributors because they like pricing flexibility and want to make sure their rates yield as much as possible.

Adaptation to new technology has been the biggest component of change for intermediaries as well. Companies that do not have the most current technology working in real time or allowing hotels to yield rates in real time are usually not considered a suitable distribution partner for some chains. On the other hand, companies that invest in real-time technology to yield rates are ideal partners because, as the industry sees it, they work with, not against the industry by permitting hotels to raise or lower rates in real time. "They work with us," says Caroline Shin.

"They give data to us very frequently so that we understand the travel pattern bookings on their website.Then we compare it with what is happening on our website and also what we are getting outside the Internet to make sure that our market mix is set appropriately." Pricing flexibility, compatibility with the desired hotel image, and protection of its strategic partnerships, together with cost, play important roles in selecting an intermediary.

THE ROLE OF CREATIVITY IN PRICING

Creativity, either of an individual or a team, can and often does lead to innovative pricing ideas. However, its application must be specific, not just directional. It is not enough to state,"We have to do something about our occupancy level." A pricing campaign must target a number of sold rooms or generated revenue that is required in order to break even or to do better. This specific approach injects efficiency into allocating marketing money to areas where it is most effective and in periods when it is desired.

If there is no task direction or overall pricing leadership, the most creative idea may book only ten roomnights instead of one hundred. It may generate more customer loyalty, but that is something the hotel may not need at the moment, although it could be an acceptable outcome in a low-season month. Pricing leadership helps team members understand the hotel's current situation and direct money and creativity to do exactly what is needed. Creativity comes up with the idea, which serves as a vehicle, but spending marketing money the smart way is a matter of experience in innovation, which turns the idea into a successful product. Creativity also plays a large part in employee satisfaction, and it lowers turnover.

In a sluggish economy, some hotels start paying attention not only to profit as the bottom line but also to revenue. This means they monitor closely the accrued cost as well as the generated revenue, thus achieving the maximum yield. Interestingly, contemporary price leadership may take different forms.

It could mean, for example, elimination of smoking rooms throughout the property. Many U.S. motels are revamping rooms, ripping off cigarette-damaged furniture and carpets, and designating them as nonsmoking. This saves on maintenance and adds to overall packaging flexibility when the business is hurt by lackluster demand. This tactic means drapes, carpets, bedding, and other furnishings must be replaced less frequently; it also mitigates fire risk and enhances cleanliness and overall safety.

THE ROLE OF HUMAN RESOURCES IN PRICING

Some large chains recognize that pricing is a complex issue and that they need to get better at it.There is a new focus on analysing the culture of pricing and how it can be improved. This approach is reflected even in the kinds of people chains are hiring. Although the majority of staff involved in strategic pricing are in the hotel industry and have a background in revenue management, others are in the airline industry and have indepth travel revenue management experience.

Some chains have sought access to this experience by hiring from outside the hotel industry. This is to encourage diversification of thinking and new ways of thought—completely out of the box, as the traditional team members are joined by researchers doing a different kind of optimization analysis. The goal could be as radical as trying to manage risk or optimize towards the railroad industry and its scheduling.

On the surface, these tactics have nothing to do with revenue management *per se*.A lot of experience in optimizing difficult travel, however, can only be gained by bringing in people with different backgrounds in consulting or with in-depth Internet experience. In order to move pricing and revenue management to a different level of thought, a new mix of people is necessary. For this approach to work, adequate training must be in place.

In this respect, basic HR functions, such as hiring and training, have an impact on pricing. What is necessary is not only to train personnel in quantitative core skills but also in strategic thinking. For example, when a hotel does not want to take a specific piece of business, it must ask such questions as:What is the revenue? What is the rate? What am I displacing by this decision? Where do I think this will go? How does it help my RevPAR?

Hotel managers must become more analytical so they can use all the new tools now available. When reports are created, team members must be taught how to use them.A lot of training must be provided for corporate executives, general managers, and regional revenue directors as well. They all must be trained to think more strategically and to understand analysis and the reports so they can help their individual properties.

DIVERSIFICATION: THE IMPROVEMENT OF THE PRICING PROCESS

As noted, exclusive hotel industry experience may lead to ossification due to one-sided judgment and the inability to see beyond the familiar. From this perspective, experience is both an asset and a liability. It is human nature to take for granted the way things are done after being in the same environment for a while. Therefore, hotel chains are continuously creating and refining pricing strategies to accommodate not only different market segments but also different situations a hotel may face based on occupancy levels. Corporate HQ tries to identify these different situations and associated variables. "It is almost like a bag of goods, a bag of pricing strategies that should be tested," says Caroline Shin. Hotels are given the full menu and encouraged to try a certain strategy if they are in a specific situation. Depending on the region, an individual property may use one set of strategies more than another. In a weak economy, however, the chains have to work harder and be more flexible because the market is overflowing with demand.

Adapting step by step, a hotel may apply a different strategy every week.The problem for the corporate office is to identify situations a hotel might be in and seek remedy. For example, if group bookings are low this week but competitors are full, how can the property make up the difference with transient or leisure business? The general manager may ask the corporate team, "What pricing strategies can I use in order to fill my house?" Then he or she may ask, "What else worked before for other hotels, and what may work for me based on my market specifics and market characteristics?" That way he or she can test each strategy using the provided tool and personal experience.

PRICING: SUPPORT AND PROTECT

The corporate pricing structure is also in place to support and protect members of the chain in a number of areas including pricing and partnerships. The corporate office sets guidelines for hotels in terms of pricing structure and the market segments they deal with. Fairmont Hotels and Resorts, for example, focuses on four segments: transient leisure travel, group travel, business travel, and wholesale. The corporate structure provides guidelines about how the segments fit with each other, how they cross over, and where they reside in the overall pricing structure.

This information is necessary because every segment acts differently. Most market segments are dynamic and require frequent rate adjustments. One exception is the wholesale market, where pricing is still largely done the traditional way: A wholesaler provides a net rate, marks it up, and sells it to the general population.There may be a hidden cost, however, if the distribution chain includes an operator acting as a middleman between the wholesaler and the supplier.

When setting up the overall pricing structure, one starts with the retail rate, which is a bucket of premium or best available rates charged on the open market. They usually do not carry any restrictions, such as cancellation fees, and they are fully billable. Depending on the level of occupancy, one of these rates is available on any given day when the hotel is not fully booked. It is up to the yield management system to identify which BAR to offer. All other rate types, such as discount rates and prenegotiated rates, are determined in relation to the retail rate. For instance, a corporate rate for a high-volume client will be probably set lower than the BAR rate that is estimated to sell most during the period when the contract is in place. This way the rates are nested within each other in a manner that makes economic sense.

The corporate pricing guidelines follow two main criteria: to maximize revenue and to protect key partnerships.While the hotel sales force negotiates contracts with key partners, such as longstanding corporate accounts or wholesale volume accounts, they make sure to protect these partnerships and provide them value. At the same time, they take every opportunity to maximize revenue. One cannot survive without the other, reiterates Scott Farrell. However, it is up to the hotels themselves, with guidance and additional research, to determine in their marketplace what their pricing structure should look like.

A diversified corporate team, with a mix of people with a hotel industry background and others skilled in optimization modeling, fulfills an additional function. It acts as a risk prevention mechanism, a necessary prerequisite for managing the risk inherent in pricing. Any chain with a wide variety of hotels must make sure the properties are covered in all kinds of situations. One risk containment scenario might be that the chain, in response to a changing demand curve, acquires a type of business that the brand has not catered to traditionally.

Caroline Shin explains, "Sheraton did not take on airline crew business because we did not want crew members lingering in the lobby; it affected our brand image. But we thought maybe we could start taking that when our RevPAR index or occupancy slips to a certain point. So we are trying to change the standards of different market segments we are willing to take."

On the international scale, another risk management plan would be analysing operational cost and determining whether to close down part of the hotel if market research shows occupancy will not be high enough. When PESTEL (political, economic, sociocultural, technological, environmental, legal) analysis indicates demand will drop precipitously for an extended period instead of hoping for the best and running a full house with a full staff, the hotel may decide to shut down floors or restaurants and save cost until the market picks up again. Selection of the appropriate strategy will depend on the market specifics and protection of the image. A property may opt to close down several floors over the weekend if it caters mostly to business clientele staying during the week. It would not, however, suspend room service, although unprofitable, if that is considered an integral part of the offered product. In a worst-case scenario, the chain may decide to sell properties in global risk areas when it determines the external circumstances make it difficult to raise occupancy on an ongoing basis.

BETTER UTILIZE YOUR DISTRIBUTION CHANNELS

The Internet creates a new level of transparency as it allows the opportunity to maximize profitability.There is now a multitude of channels to choose from. Understanding the cost of each channel in relation to the value of provided service has an impact on the quality of pricing decisions. Therefore, it is necessary to determine how much revenue bookings through an Internet intermediary generate and whether or not they justify the accrued cost.There is also a tremendous risk involved.

As discussed earlier, one of key guidelines of corporate marketing is that partners are protected. Just because there is a new Internet site it does not mean a chain can use it and advertise a lower rate, which would undermine a partnership of many years. In terms of cost, the chain must review its pricing strategy not only by market segment but also by distribution channel. "Several years ago, we would not consider the cost of distribution in our ROI.Today we do," concedes Scott Farrell.

Another challenge is to keep up with new Internet sites. The chains must reevaluate constantly and prioritize their yield so as to choose which channels to keep or drop. Fairmont Hotels and Resorts, for example, applies the 80–20 rule. They focus on the 20 per cent of the online wholesalers that capture more than 80 per cent of the business. As Scott Farrell puts it,"Why would I play with the other 10–12 per cent? I only have so many hours in a day to manage. I may as well work with the lion's share."

QUALITY ABOVE ALL?

Criteria for selecting an online distribution partner vary by price levels as well. Budget and economy properties are driven mostly by financial considerations, while upscale and luxury hotels are more concerned with compatibility.

As for chains, they ask two basic questions:

1. How can the partnership increase our brand recognition or a brand reach, and
2. How much is it going to bring us in terms of revenue or profitability?

Their choice has to match the brand first, and then it has to drive the revenue. If the brand is equaled with quality, online providers that project a connotation of cheapness will not be considered at all.The quality image refers not only to the hotel asset itself but also to how and where this asset is sold.

Fairmont Hotels and Resorts, as a quality brand on the luxury side, cannot compete on price. The quality of their product and the offering of the experience must be considered by the customer at the price being offered.

When their hotels play with price, the corporate office watches closely. Scott Farrell explains, "If our property wanted to shift their rate by $50, I would ask why? Give me the case behind it and tell me what you are going to do to make up the additional $50 you are going to lose. If they come back to me and say they are moving their rate from $300 to $250 while driving a certain volume, I would make them go through the process of determining what incremental volume they will need to make up for the $50 in loss." In other words, pricing decisions must be driven by ROI, not only a feeling. Feelings and experience may be involved, but properties must present a strong case based on the estimated ROI and what they plan to get out of the proposed strategy. It allows them to go into the pricing change with their eyes open. They also must consider how the competition will respond.A carelessly lowered rate may lead to a price war.

SPEED AND STRATEGY

The speed and immediacy of exposure via the Internet have reshaped how marketing campaigns are conducted. Having eliminated the delay of exposure to marketing collateral material, such as brochures or newspaper advertisements, hotels can conduct targeted discount mini-campaigns on their own websites when the yield management system indicates a drop in occupancy for specific dates. In a similar manner, brand recognition can be enhanced by a carefully orchestrated online auction. The South African hospitality group Protea was among the first in the industry using this method by offering their prospective guests the opportunity to bid on a limited number of weekend getaways in their properties that needed to boost occupancy.

By setting a minimum bidding price, the integrity of the hotel image was protected. Similar auction systems, used to encourage room-night sales during slow periods, are nowadays available in the United States and Canada via several Internet intermediaries. For chains in particular, a long-term strategy in distribution pricing is paramount. It stipulates the criteria and accepts or rejects short-term adjustments depending on what is happening in the industry, what is new in the technology, and who the new players are.

In terms of corporate hierarchy, pricing is formulated and executed on three levels:

1. Strategy,
2. Tactics and execution, and
3. Measurement.

Strategy comes first, followed by tactics meant to support that strategy and their execution. Finally, the achieved outcome is measured against the set benchmarks. If the strategy is sound, it will last longer than the other two steps. Frequently, new tactics must be implemented; these drive the execution and the measurement. This requires a development of proprietary criteria for measurement and their continuous adjustment to changing conditions.

PRICE ELASTICITY

Contrary to the traditional view that hotel rates are, in the long-term, generally inelastic, price elasticity is receiving a lot of attention nowadays thanks to yield management. Its goal is to take advantage of and to cover the entire spectrum of the customers' ability to purchase. Price elasticity allows hotels to capture customers who do not mind paying the high rate as well as those who are more priceconscious. This can be done in a number of ways.

By using different room categories, a luxury hotel can have on the same day suites available at $500 and entry-level rooms at $200. Every room rate category has a different value proposition associated with the incremental revenue. If the variance between a standard room and a deluxe room is $75, the latter should provide an adequately greater value to the customer. The result is a clear product differentiation, which can be also achieved by stay restrictions or by the use of fencing. Examples of physical differences, or fences, are room type, view, amenities, and location.

Nonphysical fences may mean different customers, transactions, or consumption characteristics. These bear many similarities with airline pricing strategies, which differentiate the product by, for example, cancellation restrictions or last-minute availability of a prenegotiated corporate rate. The result is nested pricing, allowing properties to have a very high rate available on the same day as a rate that is more attractive to the lower-end customer.

NEW AREAS OF PRICING AND YIELD MANAGEMENT

Hotel pricing strategies traditionally have been limited to setting and adjusting room rates and other ongoing activities. In order to survive in the current dynamic, competitive, and even dangerous global environment, hotels and resorts are taking on other types of business, some of which are one-time projects.

Organizing shows, festivals, and conferences or undergoing renovations requires a new type of core competency. Therefore, in addition to mastering current pricing strategies, hotel practitioners must acquire project management skills, such as those that are taught and practiced by Project Management Institute. Mastering these skills will make hotel team members capable of maximizing yield from project-type functions the same way as they optimize revenue from room rates.

CONSUMER EVALUATIONS OF SALIENT ATTRIBUTES

Once consumer evaluations of salient attributes are determined and their beliefs regarding a hotel brand's offerings are known, managers can use this information to improve their hotel's competitive positioning in the market. The goal of any marketing strategy is to increase positive attitude towards the offering or to encourage the use of certain decision rules, thereby increasing the likelihood of being chosen by consumers.

When consumers use a compensatory decision rule, the overall attitude towards a hotel is determined by the sum of the products of evaluations multiplied by beliefs regarding salient attributes associated with the offering. Consequently, travellers' overall attitudes towards a hotel can be rendered more positive by strategies targeted at increasing the evaluation of an attribute in consumers' decision making, or by changing consumers' beliefs about a hotel's offerings.

Travellers' attribute evaluations can be influenced by stressing the attribute in advertising. This strategy of influencing attribute evaluations is effective in attitude change and also relatively easy to pursue. It is, however, not a strategy always recommended for changing consumers' attitudes when they are using a compensatory model. The potential problem associated with this approach is that attribute evaluations are constant across brands in a consideration set. Travellers evaluating importance of the availability of an indoor pool is the same for all hotel brands, E, F, G, and H. If Hotel H were successful in a marketing message in increasing the evaluation of an indoor pool with a segment of consumers, say to a rating of _3, it would increase consumers' overall attitude towards its brand. At the same time, however, consumers' overall evaluation of Hotel G would increase by the same amount, as both brands do not differ with respect to consumers' beliefs about their having a great indoor pool. In the end, the attempt to increase consumers' overall attitude towards Hotel H would also benefit some of its competitors.

Thus, sometimes a more effective strategy for improving consumers' overall attitude towards a hotel's offerings is to improve consumers' brand-specific belief ratings. For example, Hotel F could strive to improve consumer belief that it offers a pleasant indoor pool by providing a picture of the pool on its website, or by stressing the availability of the indoor pool in advertisements. While consumer brand-specific beliefs are then likely to increase, Hotel F's competitors will not benefit from its strategy, and Hotel F thereby improves its competitive position.

Assuming that Hotel E cannot do anything to increase consumers' belief that it is not located in proximity of a skiing area, a strategy it may employ to increase consumers' overall attitude towards the property is to add a salient attribute to the set of attributes consumers consider when making hotel choices. For example, Hotel E could provide free accommodation for children staying with their parents. It is likely that parents would consider this option important when choosing a hotel. As long as other competitors do not offer this service, Hotel E enjoys some advantage in the choices made by its target market. It is essential that when adding a new attribute, marketers consider the following: First, the attribute added must be important enough to the hotel's target market to be included in consumers' subsequent decision making. Second, the belief that a particular hotel possesses this attribute must be stronger than the belief that any of its competitors do.

This marketing strategy, often referred to as a *strategy of differentiation,* is likely to be successful when these conditions are met. Differentiation, however, is unlikely to be sustainable— that is, over time, competitors identify what added attributes successfully attract customers and copy them, thereby creating consumer belief regarding their own properties. Thus, the hotel that introduced the new salient attribute often can expect to lose its differential advantage over time unless it maintains a unique characteristic like a special location or a fabulous chef in the kitchen.

Increasing belief strength for a hotel's attributes is not always a successful strategy, assuming a compensatory model is being used. For example, consumers may find it relatively unimportant whether the hotel offers low room rates or not. The importance rating for low room rates is _2—that is, consumers in this particular target segment evaluate low room rates negatively, perhaps because they associate low rates with low quality or with small, underfurnished rooms. In this case, stressing that a particular hotel offers low rates, thereby increasing the strength of consumers' beliefs, may adversely affect consumers' overall evaluation of a property. If you compare Hotels F and H, you will see that the strong belief that Hotel H offers low rates negatively affects its overall evaluation. Hotel F, on the other hand, benefits from consumers not being aware of low rates.

It is important to note that importance weights associated with attributes vary across market segments. For example, while business travellers on corporate expense accounts or consumers on a once-in-a-lifetime vacation, such as a honeymoon, may attach less importance to low rates, more price-sensitive market segments usually weigh low rates more heavily in their hotel choice. It is therefore important for marketers to carefully define the targeted market segment prior to conducting their research and applying evaluation weights and beliefs to similarly disposed consumers.

In general, it is crucial to find out what attributes targeted consumers feel are most salient to their decisions and, in response, increase performance regarding these attributes and commensurately inform market segments of this stronger position. The resultant positive attitude towards the offering should then increase the likelihood of the hotel being chosen by travellers using a compensatory decision-making model. Alternatively, as a strategic move, particularly for special niche properties, marketers may want to encourage consumers to abandon the linear compensatory model. Niche market segments may exist or may be created through marketing communications; these target markets might be better served by hotels focusing on one or more of the noncompensatory decision rules presented.

For example, a segment of highly price-sensitive customers predominantly using a lexicographic decision rule with low rates as the most important attribute may constitute the primary target market for a property. In this case, travellers can be targeted by offering low prices and/or frequentstay loyalty programmes. At the same time, services deemed unnecessary or unimportant by this customer segment can be eliminated or minimized. The fact that some customer segments expect a minimal level of performance on several attributes when they use an elimination-by-aspect or conjunctive decision rule, however, implies that focusing performance and/or marketing on a single attribute may be inadequate for some segments of travellers. A hotel would then benefit from creating a level of "at least acceptable" attributes in addition to providing stronger packages of the same attributes offered by competitors targeting the same market segment.

Overall, knowing how consumers make decisions should help hotel managers to design better properties, packages, and services, and help them market those offerings to their respective target segment, thereby improving competitive position.

TRADITIONAL APPROACH IN HOTEL PRICING

The single most important criterion of success in any business, including hotels, is profit.The purpose of this object is to discuss the importance of hotel pricing and its influence on yield or revenue management, especially in terms of profit generation, and because of inherent dangers to the industry worldwide, integrity of the established pricing structure.

Historically, price has been determined by the triangular relationship of cost and demand in the context of competition.

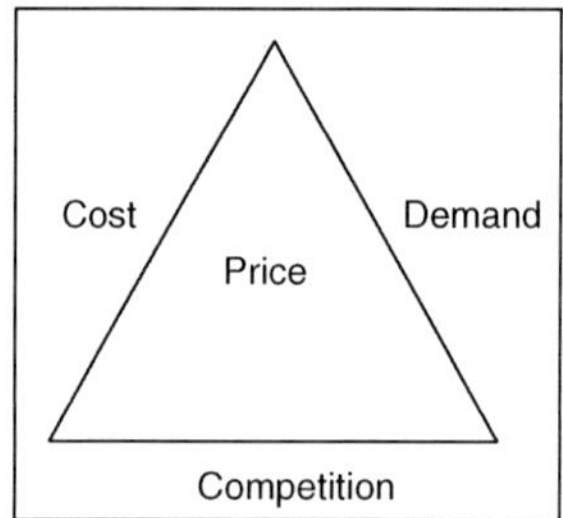

Fig. Three Forces of Pricing

The actual pricing structure is developed with one of these three components as the deciding factor while the other two play supplementary roles.

The traditional pricing strategy was largely cost-driven. Many hotel operators tended to favour the rule-of-thumb method. This approach, also called the $1 per $1,000 rule, states that hotels should charge approximately $1 per night for every $1,000 of room cost, based on an average 70 per cent occupancy.

Although popular in its day, the calculation of cost was commonly misunderstood. Another widely used quantitative method was the Hubbart Formula, developed in the late 1940s as a guideline issued by the American Hotel Association. It focused on computing an average room rate that would cover operational costs and yield a reasonable return on investment. These quantitative methods are fairly static and therefore suited for a stable economic environment. Qualitative pricing approaches, such as percentage increase of previous-year rates adjusted for inflation, payroll increases, and new cost of supplies, reflect more realistically the projected cost.

Other qualitative techniques are less exact but, by being competition-oriented, they offer more flexibility. The Pied Piper or Follow-the-Leader method uses competition as the basis for rate setting, while the Gouge 'Em approach tries to lure business away from other properties by undercutting their prices. If there is no competition to speak of, Hit or Miss fluctuation of rates tied to profitable occupancy levels could be employed.

The drawback of competition-driven pricing is its sole focus on rate comparison, ignoring differences in operating expenses and customer-perceived value. An effective approach, therefore, calls for a mix of methods adjusted for different situations. The fundamental question remains:What should be the driving force in formulating a sound pricing strategy? In today's dynamic business environment, which discards the traditional view that market demand for room rates is largely inelastic, demand orientation seems to provide the best fit.

CURRENT PRICING CRITERIA

"Our pricing is market-driven, not costbased," says Scott Farrell, corporate director of distribution with Fairmont Hotels and Resorts, a Toronto-based chain of luxury properties. When the chain is setting its prices, it starts with comprehensive market research. Based on the data, the correct price for each marketplace is determined. If there is a major shift in a market, then the prices will adjust for that. However, if there is a major shift in a demand curve, then a shift of price may have no effect.

It may actually leave more money on the table. For example, if the airlines go on strike, a significant shift in the demand curve would result. Under such conditions, decreasing the rate by $50, for example, would only result in a $50 loss. If there is an opportunity to go after a new targeted market with a specific offer, enabling the chain to capture a greater market share, then lowering the rate serves its purpose. Generally, however, lowering rates across the board is not the preferred pricing strategy.

PRICING: WHO IS IN CHARGE

While independently owned properties make their own pricing decisions, in case of a chain it is usually corporate headquarters (HQ) that sets pricing guidelines. Often, individual properties are still responsible for the actual pricing.

Because they are held accountable, they must balance corporate guidelines with their autonomy to set their prices. Caroline Shin, member of the revenue management team at Starwood Hotels and Resorts Worldwide, which operates a number of upscale brands, such as Sheraton and W Hotels, stresses the cooperative nature of this relationship. Successful pricing strategies arise from an ongoing interaction of both sides. Corporate HQ provides sophisticated tools and in-depth market analysis that would be beyond reach of individual properties. Property managers, on the other hand, offer their experience and knowledge of regional specifics that may have gone unnoticed by the corporate team."The people who have been in the property understand the dynamics of that market, and they have developed pricing intuition," explains Shin. Some experts view intuition as a valuable part of the pricing mechanism, and even managers who are technically savvy check the numbers against their gut feeling.

PRICING: SCIENCE, ART, AND INTUITION

Pricing distribution and revenue management techniques are a mix of science and art. Recent research shows that two-thirds of managers making strategic decisions under pressure and time constraints use a combination of analysis and intuition.

The advent of modern technology, such as yield management software packages, has further strengthened this link. "Even the most sophisticated analytical model for forecasting, may it be for hotel pricing or for thermal dynamics of a nuclear plant, still needs variables based upon assumptions," says Shin, who used to work as a nuclear engineer.The more business- savvy hotel management becomes and the more they understand the hotel dynamics and the market, the more can be gained from training them how to define their experiencebased intuition and put it into numbers. In this respect, an interaction between the corporate revenue management team and individual hotels is paramount. "Every time I go out to a property, I learn something new. It only helps me when I build my analytical models to almost translate what they know into numbers," confirms Shin. The better hotels can do that, the better models they can develop. Nonetheless, inaccurate historical data remains a major limitation.

No model is ever going to be perfect, though.What seems to work best is to teach hotel managers how to use the model and to understand the direction of the pricing decisions they need to make. That is the scientific part.The art piece comes into play when they infuse the model with their knowledge and intuition.

Staff training is an important part of this process. "We can't just have Ph.D.s sitting in one room coming with all these models and we just roll it out. At the same time, we can't just have people with intuitions run around and set prices," says Shin.

Revenue management teams must make sure that hotels understand how to employ the models in their daily pricing decisions. When science is applied, the revenue team can go to their experts, ask probing questions, and get solid results. Even though intuition is a part of this process, it is based only on a hypothesis that could have been triggered by a discussion with a customer, knowledge of what is happening in the marketplace, or historic trends. That is why pure intuition is not sufficient. "Managers must have reliable data to support their hunches," cautions Scott Farrell.

THE RULES OF EMPLOYMENT AND POWER RELATIONS TO CUSTOMERS

We have already noted that the employment relationship is underpinned by rules, hence the continuing validity of Clegg's definition of industrial relations as 'The study of the rules governing employment' which Edwards explains in more detail:

This does not limit the subject to the collective relations between managements and trade unions, for a rule can derive from other sources, and there are rules governing non-union groups; nor does it restrict analysis to one sector, for it covers all paid forms of employment. A rule is a social institution involving two or more parties which may have its basis in law, a written collective agreement, an unwritten agreement, a unilateral decree or merely an understanding that has the force of custom. In non-union settings, as much as union ones, rules determine rates of pay, hours of work, job descriptions and many other aspects of employment. The subject is about the ways in which the employment relationship is regulated. To regulate means to control, to adapt or adjust continuously or to adjust by rule.

Managerial Issues

While rules may be the substantive rules of employment, e.g. pay and conditions of employment, implicit in the notion of rules affecting people is the concept of behaviour. Management's job is to control and direct workers' behaviour to perform work to the desired standards, and thereby ensure that the rules of employment are adhered to.

Four key issues arise:

- Rules are not always absolute and may be gendered.
- Managerial control of workers' behaviour is underpinned by a power relationship.
- This power relationship is unequal and may be gendered.
- Managers have a choice of means to maximize control.

The first point is that one should caution against perceiving rules in too absolute a sense. At one end of the spectrum rules embodied in the law of the land provide a good example of formal rules. Any breach may incur very severe penalties, e.g. health and safety. In a workplace setting rules in practice may derive from informal understandings that can in one set of circumstances be interpreted by the worker as a permissive concession or in a different set of circumstances as something to be observed at all costs. Strawberries as a worker's perquisite during the Wimbledon lawn tennis championship are a good example. Experienced workers know that taking home unwanted strawberries is 'permitted' during busy periods. When fewer staff are needed, increased managerial surveillance will be deployed to dismiss staff caught in possession of company property.

Rule-learning is part of what Polanyi (1967) refers to as 'tacit skills'. As argued elsewhere:

Tacit skills, such as learning to deal with customers, are learnt in and through the very act of doing, often involving trial and error and not from following a body of procedurally-designed rules. They are seen as an interpretive achievement of the user as to how the 'rules' fit the task in hand. By mastery of the rules comes the power to extend them.

This example embracing the customer provides a developmental point to Edwards' observation that rule-making is difficult, and that rules have to be interpreted in action for them to have any real meaning. Specifically in the labour contract this is because the worker's ability to work is only realized as useful labour in the course of carrying out that work, hence 'a rule is a complex social institution'.

In service work physical appearance and 'personality', or 'aesthetic labour', are an implicit part of the employment contract. Only female flight attendants, not their male colleagues, are subjected to regular weigh-ins to ensure they comply to specified weight: height ratios. This demonstrates clearly how a rule may be gendered.

The second point to note is that the very essence of management seeking to control workers' behaviour is underpinned by a power relationship. Power is the capacity to pursue one's own interests individually and collectively, involving the capacity to oppose the actions of others and to pursue one's own objectives, and is embedded in continuing relationships. This does not mean power has to be exercised by either party in an overt sense. The threat of power may be sufficient to maintain broadly consensual employment relationships, such that any disputes or differences (conflicts) are resolved amicably without recourse to either party seeking to deploy sanctions against the other.

The third point assumes a power inequality in the employment relationship. Self-evidently an employer is more powerful than an individual worker. The employer's ability to terminate a worker's services is likely to be more detrimental to the worker than to the employer, in spite of employment protection legislation. Yet the individual behaviours of workers, such as high labour turnover, may be detrimental to an employer, even though they are not concerted. When workers combine collectively, with or without the backing of a trade union, there is some tilt in the balance of power, because collective sanctions may be imposed against the employer. Ultimately the outcome of the process by which each side seeks to gain concessions will depend on the relative power of the parties. For example, a plentiful supply of suitable workers in the labour market makes existing workers more readily dispensable and replaceable on the employer's terms. The opposite would be true for workers with scarce skills who can command high wages.

As Wajcman argues, gender relations are power-based and women's subordination in the workforce and workplace owes as much to trade unions as it does to managers. Spradley and Mann provide a graphic account of how the subordination of one group of female workers was brought about by another group of male workers who were the custodians of the male proprietor's trust. The male bartenders controlled the orders, and sought to make the cocktail waitresses' job difficult by giving orders in an inconsistent and confusing way. Any mistakes became the waitresses' responsibility, even if they had been caused by the bartenders. Such was the power of the bartenders that pleasing them became more important than pleasing the customers.

The fourth point is that managers have a choice of means to maximize control over workers. Friedman's 'direct control' is a variant of Taylorism (the separation of mental and manual labour or scientific management). Management is responsible for planning, designing and organizing the labour process, while cheap, unskilled workers perform standardized, simple repetitive tasks. Fast food is a good case in point, and also epitomizes McDonaldization, a social critique of how contemporary society and culture are being shaped by rationalist scientific management. While Taylorism sought to control the organization of work, McDonaldization is based on rationalization, replication, standardization of products and service, and quantification. In this low trust strategy worker behaviour is controlled through the use of standardized scripts in the service encounter. In Friedman's alternative of 'responsible autonomy', a high trust approach, managers delegate control to relatively privileged skilled workers who may already have elements of job control and discretion.

The objective is to get workers to identify with the competitive aims of the organization so they will behave responsibly with minimum supervision. An obvious example of where such an approach might be used is in a luxury hotel, but it is also associated with empowerment and much customer-service work. As we shall argue, and implied in the example of cocktail waitresses above, these and other similar approaches including 'hard' and 'soft' HRM provide a useful framework for analysis, but are not necessarily alternatives.

The history of hotel internationalization has been characterized by American chains that secure control and integration through highly standardized procedures and manuals of operational procedures. Yet a 'soft' focus on the service encounter as the driver of competitive advantage necessitates developing a culture of customized service. Mass customization illustrated by Burger King's 'have it your way' slogan as a challenge to McDonald's hold on the market is proposed as an alternative paradigm to McDonaldization.

Workers and Customers

Other tensions within the employment relationship impinge upon the rules of employment and power relationships. If management is about the achievement of organizational goals through people it can be argued that managers will be successful to the extent that these goals coincide with the aims and aspirations of those people, be they workers or customers. This 'matching' of broadly reciprocal needs between employers and workers may be referred to as a 'psychological contract'; or set of contracts. It suggests managers and workers can share goals, but this is not at all straightforward. There is not a necessarily clear cut distinction between boss and worker, or a 'them and us' scenario.

Further we must also account for a psychological contract with customers. Two key points are noteworthy:

- Organizations comprise people and are, therefore, social organizations.
- People, as social animals, may behave in unpredictable ways.

Workers

Human beings do not necessarily behave consistently or predictably, even in the same sets of circumstances. People are citizens and customers as well as employees, and these multiple identities bring different and sometimes conflicting expectations of the organization. This makes the management of the employment relationship an uncertain process within which there is a blend of contradictory principles around the need to control and to gain the consent of workers. Workers may seek to regain control individually or collectively when they perceive that management has operated outside the rules. At that point workers' consent has been withdrawn and management will need to find ways to restore order and regain consent.

In Lucas workers' individual response to organizational rules is seen in three main ways - to conform or be deviant in employment, or to terminate their employment. These responses are similar to Marchington's 'getting on', 'getting by' and 'getting back'. These are behaviours deployed in circumstances where customer care and service quality are dependent on workers' use of their tacit skills, which contain both technical and attitudinal elements. Limiting the definition of tacit skills to employer-employee relations is too narrow. Marchington overlooked how workers exhibit their tacit skills in ways other than in respect of their relationship with the employer, notably the customer. The point that 'getting back', 'getting by' and 'getting on' are as much resistance strategies in the labour process as coping mechanisms is developed. These behaviours can also be deployed collectively.

At workplace level personal relationships are likely to be closely connected to morale and success. Managers often 'muck in' when required. In small workplaces the existence of a single leader, often the owner, may serve to inspire loyalty from the workforce, but it is not a one-way process, as workers' respect has to be earned. Is it realistic to suggest that Mina, Jo and Sadie, who wait on table in the restaurant, share all the same goals as their boss? The hotel may not be doing very well, so there may be mutual concern for the survival of the business. Yet these ladies' main goal may be to serve their customers cheerfully and effectively, while at the same time enjoying some social banter among themselves and with their customers in the process of earning a reasonable wage.

Customers

Within the triadic employment relationship a simultaneous and coterminous relationship with the organization and the customer directly impinges on how workers carry out their work, and such interactions may be rewarding or stressful. The consequent effect on workers' performance may have positive or negative implications for the rules of employment: what they can earn (from good tips to no tips), their prospects of promotion (satisfactory manager and customer appraisal) or actually keeping their job (customer complaint leading to disciplinary sanctions or closure). Unequivocally the worker-customer relationship affects the rules governing employment and workplace behaviour. But so do employer- customer relationships, hence the employment relationship embodies a triadic set of power relations.

This relationship embodies a socio-economic exchange, and is not simply an economic exchange around the price of labour. Fox provides a useful starting point, since he noted that organizations are social organizations and how people behave is a crucial issue in the employment relationship. Even Edwards' point that 'a rule is a complex social institution' does not adequately encapsulate our position. The main justification for widening the scope of this relationship derives from the fact that the service encounter is the interaction of the producer and consumer of services, and is a more complex phenomenon where financial considerations are interwoven with social ones.

In hospitality the social function of service work derives from the provision of a 'home away from home'. The service encounter entails 'emotion work' - the assumption of a social-self, which effectively masks the individual's own personal dispositions to act, including the need to smile and be pleasant in an uninvolved way. We have already noted that 'aesthetic' and sexual labour may also be inherent in service work.

It is the 'normalizing' social role of service labour that distinguishes it from other wage labour. Service work cannot be understood in terms of economic rationality alone. Examination must be based on the supposition that service work is the intended outcome of a necessarily social process in which some social interaction occurs between one or more producers and one or more consumers.

The relations between three groups of people - managers, workers and customers - embody the potential for contradiction between, on the one hand, uncertainty, unpredictability, conflict and difference and, on the other hand, consent, team effort and concerted performance. The practical benefit this book seeks to convey accrues from an understanding of the nature and scope of the rules of employment in this triadic employment relationship, and how it is regulated, primarily at workplace level.

The Employment Relationship in a Wider Context

This concludes by considering some key external contextual influences on workplace employment relationships at two levels - internationally and, in more detail, nationally in Britain.

The International Context

The national context of British employment relations increasingly needs to be understood within a much wider international context.

Three international dimensions have particular resonance:

- International competition has created more open economies that have attracted investment from foreign-owned businesses. For example the French-owned groups Accor and Envergure have respectively opened hotels within their Novotel and Campanile brands in the United Kingdom (UK).
- On a larger scale American multinational corporations (MNCs) have created world brands. McDonald's, Burger King, KFC (formerly Kentucky Fried Chicken) and Marriott are among those that are now household names in many countries across the world.
- Spin-offs from European integration, especially on employment law in Britain, have provided an important underpinning to the employment relationship in the HI.

Foreign investment and MNCs are clearly important factors underpinning the expansion of hospitality and tourism not only in Britain but also in developing countries. Examples of 'better' employment practices, in so far as they may exist in the British HI, have been associated with foreign-owned businesses.

Aspects of the American model of employment relations, that are non-union and market-driven, may seem to reflect some aspects of observed employment relations practice in the British HI, but the similarity has been overstated. The United States (US) has substantially more legal regulation than Britain, which has benefited American HI workers, while the trade unions are not entirely powerless - issues we highlight in later. The European model based on social partnership designed to forge a common agenda between capital and labour is considerably more diverse and different across the member states than is often acknowledged. While we cannot expect it to reflect current developments in HI employment relations in most British workplaces, it has not necessarily produced wholesale benefits for HI workers across the EU either.

The British experience is not necessarily mirrored in other countries across the world. Differences in other countries' institutional arrangements and cultural considerations are among the factors that will affect their employment relations systems.

MAKING HOTEL SUCCESSFUL [MH]

Even when the U.S. economy was growing and prosperous, the hotel under its previous owner did not succeed in servicing its debt. Now, because of the current recession, its financial picture is even more bleak. As the hotel's new lender-owner, you may decide to retain it in your bank's portfolio, or to find a buyer on suitable terms as soon as possible (a period surely measured in months, and perhaps in years, due to the depressed condition of the hospitality marketplace).

Purchasers of hotels typically base the purchase price on the property's income stream, applying a capitalization rate to the cash flow before debt service. If the cash flow is a negative number, how can you make the hotel pay its own way? Evaluate management. We assume that the hotel you've taken back has management already in place-an in-house management team or representatives of a professional management firm engaged by the previous owner.

Begin by evaluating the basic documents that the management should have prepared as a guide to the hotel's focus and direction:

- The current-year marketing plan, which characterizes the hotel's customers and sets forth a strategy for securing their business.
- The current-year budget, which estimates the revenue and expense dollars.
- A long-range business plan, which projects the marketing and budget picture, ideally for three to five years into the future.
- A capital facilities plan, which anticipates any expansions or renovations the property may require.
- The operations manual, which outlines the duties of employees and sets standards for their performance.

Next, try to determine whether the manager and key department heads are actually using the plans. Those plans should be living documents. Increase revenue. In times like these, many hoteliers are tempted to save money by cutting back on marketing, but that is the worst thing to do. To put more bodies in the beds, you need creative marketing.

For instance, if your hotel has focused in the past on international leisure travellers, it has been especially hard-hit in recent months by the combination of worldwide recession and Middle East war.

As the threat of war mounted, your hotel should have been targeting domestic tour groups, corporate business, and frequent individual travellers. Your hotel may also have to reduce its room rates to a more competitive level, then increase the volume of business enough to generate a profit. How sophisticated is your hotel's marketing plan? It should begin with knowledge of the existing customer base. Many luxury hotels maintain a detailed guest history which allows them to respond to the specific whims and desires of each repeat guest, but even an economy property should maintain a guest tracking system that provides demographic data on the guests as well as the origin of their reservations.

Control expenses. Your hotel may be losing money because its expenses exceed its revenues.

A recession is a good time to take a fresh look at every conceivable expense. Most people want to start with wages and benefits, because payroll constitutes the largest single expense category. The hotel should trim its payroll where it can, but it must not cut back so far as to compromise service. Examine your hotel's contracts with outside vendors. Get competitive quotes from at least three sources, then negotiate with the suppliers of:

- goods used in the hotel, including food and beverage items, cleaning supplies, and office supplies;
- outside contract services such as pest control, pool cleaning, linen and laundry, and maintenance of indoor plants and outdoor landscaping; and
- maintenance contracts on major equipment such as the climate-control system, computers, and elevators.

Evaluate your hotel's preventive maintenance programme. In the short run you can save money by deferring maintenance, but letting the physical plant and equipment deteriorate will cost you more in the long run for repairs or replacement. What's more, breakdowns seem inevitably to occur at an inconvenient hour, creating emergencies when workers charge a premium for their time. Manage to quality standards. Service quality is particularly important in a recessionary economy, when you can't afford to lose a single guest.

Five ways exist to monitor quality:

- Personal inspection-You or your designated in-house hospitality executive should visit the property at regular intervals to observe and ask questions.
- Franchise inspections-If your hotel has a franchise, the franchise company will send inspectors to the property to assess its compliance with their company's quality standards.
- In-house market research-You can hire a market research firm to interview guests on a random basis during their stay or as they depart.
- Secret-shopper programmes-I use these programmes myself on my clients' behalf, and I recommend them to every absentee owner. Secret-shopper programmes can test the honesty of the staff and quality of service.
- Guest comment cards-While most comments reflect only the best and worst aspects of the guest experience, you should receive a summary of these cards at least every month and review the most egregious complaints with the hotel manager.

The keys to maintaining standards with lean staff are flexible staffing and cross-training. If the hotel has an extra clerk at the front desk when the dining room needs an extra server, that clerk should be able to fill in. As an owner, you should receive regular reports which allow you to track the relationship between staffing levels and the volume of business, and training reports that show who has learned what. Don't assume that hiring a management firm absolves you of the need to be an active owner. You must still hold the firm accountable.

Obtain assurances from each candidate firm that you will have veto power at all times over any manager or key department head the firm assigns to your property. If one of these individuals isn't fitting in, you want the right to have the management firm remove and replace that person rapidly.

The new world of appraisals set in motion by the Financial institutions Reform, Recovery and Enforcement Act continues to evolve. Meanwhile, the industry nears the July 1 deadline for states to have functioning licensing and certification programmes. Significant deliberations have been in the works on several fronts. To recap them:

- The Federal Financial Institutions Examination Council Appraisal Subcommittee, which has the power to extend the July 1 deadline on a state-by-state basis, has been considering a petition to grant more time to all states. Late last year the ABA and state bankers associations asked the subcommittee to grant a blanket extension to Dec. 31.

  While many states have passed laws setting up systems to address requirements of FIRREA, putting the systems in place and using them to qualify appraisers is a time-consuming task.
- The Federal Reserve Board has been reviewing comments on its proposal to cut the de minimis level for institutions it regulates to $50,000 from $100,000. While doing so would put the Fed in synch with the Comptroller's Office and FDIC, bankers have urged the agency to leave the limit where it stands.
- The Appraiser Qualifications Board was set to meet in late March to consider public comments and make a final decision on a restructuring of appraiser categories.

The board is part of the Appraisal Foundation, a private standards setting body with which the Exam Council's subcommittee works and to which states and the appraisal industry look for guidance. Late last December, the board proposed to expand to three categories the original two-category system of appraiser qualifications it envisioned under FIRREA. The board learned that in some states with significant quantities of high-priced homes, its original categories would have barred qualified residential appraisers from properties they are capable of appraising.

To remedy this, the board proposed creating three qualification levels-two certified and one licensed. Some changes in the latter category caused ABA to object, though it endorsed most other aspects of the proposal. For its part, in late January the Exam Council's Appraisal Subcommittee announced that it would be willing to accept a three-tier system in those states that considered it necessary for their real estate markets. The subcommittee noted that its agreement was general in nature and not a judgment on the qualification board's specific proposal. The government body also set several conditions for its actual approval.

Index